Everyday
Mathematics®

Student Reference Book

The University of Chicago
School Mathematics Project

Everyday
Mathematics®

Student Reference Book

The University of Chicago
School Mathematics Project

EVERYDAY
LEARNING

Chicago, Illinois

UCSMP Elementary Materials Component

Max Bell, Director

Authors

Max Bell, Jean Bell, John Bretzlauf, Amy Dillard, Robert Hartfield, Andy Isaacs, Deborah Arron Leslie, James McBride (Director), Kathleen Pitvorec, Peter Saecker

Technical Art

Diana Barrie

Everyday Learning Development Staff

Editorial: Anna Belluomini, Mary Cooney, Christine Fraser, Elizabeth Glosniak, Janet Kapche Razionale
Design: Fran Brown
Production: Annette Davis, Tina Dunlap, Elizabeth Gabbard

Additional Credits

Black Dot Group, Loretta Becker, Kathleen Burke, Phil Ciciora, Lindaanne Donohoe, Lauren Harper, Herman Adler Design Group, Lucy Lesiak, Precision Graphics, Regina Thoeming

Photo Credits

Phil Martin/Photography
Secretary of State/State of Illinois, p. 2
M. Ferguson/PhotoEdit, p. 110
Mark Gibson/Visuals Unlimited, p. 126 (second right)
Mark Gibson/Visuals Unlimited, p. 126 (third right)
John Edwards/Tony Stone Images, p. 130
©The British Museum, p. 200
Loren Santow/Tony Stone Images, p. 223
Gene Peach/Tony Stone Images, p. 314
Jack Demuth, p. 327

 The *Student Reference Book* is based upon work supported by the National Science Foundation under Grant No. ESI-9252984. Any opinions, findings, conclusions, or recommendations expressed in this material are those of the authors and do not necessarily reflect the views of the National Science Foundation.

ISBN 1-57039-919-0

Any questions regarding this policy should be addressed to:

Everyday Learning Corporation

P.O. Box 812960
Chicago, IL 60681
www.everydaylearning.com

2 3 4 5 6 7 8 9 QW 05 04 03 02 01

Contents

About the *Student Reference Book*

A reference book is organized to help people find information quickly and easily. Dictionaries, encyclopedias, atlases, cookbooks, even telephone books are examples of reference books. Unlike novels and biographies, which are usually read in sequence from beginning to end, reference books are read in small segments to find specific information at the time it is needed.

You can use this *Student Reference Book* to look up and review information on topics in mathematics. It consists of the following sections:

- A **table of contents** that lists the topics covered and shows how the book is organized.

- Essays on **mathematical topics,** such as whole numbers, fractions, decimals, percents, geometry, measurement, data analysis, and problem solving.

- Descriptions of how to use a **calculator** to perform various mathematical operations and functions.

- Directions on how to play some of the **mathematical games** you may have played before.

- A **glossary** of mathematical terms consisting of brief definitions of important words.

- A set of **tables and charts** that summarize information, such as a place-value chart, prefixes for names of large and small numbers, tables of equivalent measures and of equivalent fractions, decimals, and percents.

- An **answer key** for every Check Your Understanding problem in the book.

- An **index** to help you locate information quickly.

This reference book also contains an **American Tour.** It is a collection of numerical information about the history, people, and environment of the United States.

How to Use the
Student Reference Book

Suppose you are asked to solve a problem and you know that you have solved problems like it before. But at the moment, you are having difficulty remembering how to do it. This is a perfect time to use the *Student Reference Book.* You can look in the **table of contents** or the **index** to find the page that gives a brief explanation of the topic. The explanation will often show a step-by-step sample solution.

In some essays you will see a small book symbol. The symbol gives page number references to essays that are related to the topic under discussion. For example, simplifying fractions involves finding equivalent fractions, so in the side-column, next to the paragraphs that discuss simplifying fractions, there is a reference to the page which contains a description of how to find equivalent fractions.

There is also a set of problems at the end of most essays, titled **Check Your Understanding**. It is a good idea to solve these problems and then turn to the answer key at the back of the book to check your answers to make sure that you understand the information presented on the page.

Always read mathematical text with paper and pencil in hand. Take notes; draw pictures and diagrams to help you understand what you are reading. Work the examples. If you get a wrong answer in the **Check Your Understanding** problems, try to find your mistake by working back from the correct answer given in the answer key.

It is not always easy to read text about mathematics, but the more you use the *Student Reference Book,* the better you will become at understanding this kind of material. You may find that your skills as an independent problem-solver are improving. We are confident that these skills will serve you well as you undertake more advanced mathematics courses.

Whole Numbers

Uses of Numbers

Try to imagine living even one day without using or thinking about numbers. Numbers are used on clocks, calendars, car license plates, rulers, scales, and so on. The major ways that numbers are used are listed below.

- Numbers are used for **counting.**

> **EXAMPLES** Students sold 158 tickets to the school play.
>
> The first U.S. Census counted 3,929,326 people.

- Numbers are used for **measuring.**

> **EXAMPLES** He swam the length of the pool in 33.4 seconds.
>
> The package is 28 inches long and weighs $3\frac{1}{8}$ pounds.

- Numbers are used to show where something is in a **reference system.**

> **EXAMPLES**
>
> | Situation | Type of Reference System |
> |---|---|
> | Normal room temperature is 21°C. | Celsius temperature scale |
> | Harry was born on June 22, 1992. | Calendar |
> | The time is 10:08 A.M. | Clock time |
> | Detroit is located at 42°N and 83°W. | Earth's latitude and longitude system |

- Numbers can be used to **compare amounts** or **measures.**

> **EXAMPLES** The cat weighs $\frac{1}{2}$ as much as the dog.
>
> There were 2 times as many boys as girls at the game.

- Numbers can be used for **identification** and as **codes.**

> **EXAMPLES** phone number: (709) 555–1212
>
> ZIP code: 60637   driver's license number: M286-423-2061

Kinds of Numbers

The **counting numbers** are the numbers used to count things. The set of counting numbers is 1, 2, 3, 4, and so on.

The **whole numbers** are any of the numbers 0, 1, 2, 3, 4, and so on. The whole numbers include all of the counting numbers and the number zero (0).

Counting numbers are useful for counting, but they do not always work for measures. Most measures fall between two consecutive whole numbers. **Fractions** and **decimals** were invented to keep track of such measures. For example, fractions are often used in recipes for cooking and for measures in carpentry and other building trades. Decimals are used for almost all measures in science and industry.

> **EXAMPLES** The turkey weighed 15.6 pounds.
>
> The recipe called for $2\frac{1}{2}$ cups of flour.
>
> The window sill is 2 feet $7\frac{3}{4}$ inches above the floor.

Negative numbers were invented to express quantities with reference to a zero point.

> **EXAMPLES** A temperature of 10 degrees below zero is written as $-10°F$, or $-10°C$.
>
> A depth of 235 feet below sea level is written as -235 feet.

Negative numbers are also used to indicate changes in quantities.

> **EXAMPLES** A weight loss of $7\frac{1}{2}$ pounds is recorded as $-7\frac{1}{2}$ pounds.
>
> A decrease in income of $1,500 is recorded as $-$1,500$.

Place Value for Whole Numbers

Any number, no matter how large or small, can be written using one or more of the **digits** 0, 1, 2, 3, 4, 5, 6, 7, 8, and 9. A **place-value chart** is used to show how much each digit in a number is worth. The **place** for a digit is its position in the number. The **value** of a digit is how much it is worth according to its place in the number.

Study the place-value chart below. As you move from right to left in the chart, the value of each place becomes 10 times greater.

10,000s	1,000s	100s	10s	1s
ten thousands	thousands	hundreds	tens	ones
8	3	9	0	4

EXAMPLE   The number 83,904 is shown in the place-value chart above. It is read "eighty-three thousand, nine hundred four."

The value of the 8 is 80,000 (8 * 10,000).
The value of the 3 is 3,000 (3 * 1,000).
The value of the 9 is 900 (9 * 100).
The value of the 0 is 0 (0 * 10).
The value of the 4 is 4 (4 * 1).

In larger numbers, groups of 3 digits are separated by commas. Commas help identify the thousands, millions, billions, and trillions, as shown in the following place-value chart:

trillions			billions			millions			thousands			ones		
100	10	1	100	10	1	100	10	1	100	10	1	100	10	1
1	3	5	2	4	6	0	1	5	8	0	8	2	9	7

EXAMPLE   The number 135,246,015,808,297 is shown in the place-value chart above.

This number is read as 135 **trillion**, 246 **billion**, 15 **million**, 808 **thousand**, 297.

CHECK YOUR UNDERSTANDING

Read each number to yourself. What is the value of the 9 in each number?

1. 39,207   **2.** 85,937,001   **3.** 456,096   **4.** 6,390,405

Check your answers on page 385.

Powers of 10

Numbers like 10, 100, and 1,000 are called **powers of 10.**
They are numbers that can be written as products of 10s.

100 can be written as 10 * 10 or 10^2. 1,000 can be written as 10 * 10 * 10 or 10^3.

The raised digit is called the **exponent.** The exponent tells how many times 10 is multiplied by itself.

A number that is written with an exponent, like 10^3, is in **exponential notation.** The number 1,275 is written in **standard notation.**

NOTE

10^2 is read "10 to the second power" or "10 squared." 10^3 is read "10 to the third power."

The chart below shows powers of 10 from ten through one billion.

Powers of 10

Standard Notation	Product of 10s	Exponential Notation
10	10	10^1
100	10*10	10^2
1,000 (1 thousand)	10*10*10	10^3
10;000	10*10*10*10	10^4
100,000	10*10*10*10*10	10^5
1,000,000 (1 million)	10*10*10*10*10*10	10^6
10,000,000	10*10*10*10*10*10*10	10^7
100,000,000	10*10*10*10*10*10*10*10	10^8
1,000,000,000 (1 billion)	10*10*10*10*10*10*10*10*10	10^9

EXAMPLE   1,000 * 1,000 = ?

Use the table above to write 1,000 as 10*10*10.
1,000 * 1,000 = (10 * 10 * 10) * (10 * 10 * 10)
$\qquad\qquad$ = 10^6
$\qquad\qquad$ = 1 million

So, 1,000 * 1,000 = 1 million.

EXAMPLE   1,000 millions = ?

Write 1,000 * 1,000,000 as (10*10*10) * (10*10*10*10*10*10).
This is a product of nine 10s, or 10^9.

1,000 millions = 1 billion

Exponential Notation

A **square array** consists of the same number of rows and columns. A whole number that can be represented by a square array is called a **square number.** Any square number can be written as the product of a number multiplied by itself.

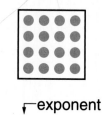

EXAMPLE   16 is a square number. It can be represented by an array consisting of 4 rows and 4 columns. $16 = 4 * 4$.

Here is a shorthand way to write square numbers: $16 = 4 * 4 = 4^2$. 4^2 is read as "4 times 4," "4 squared," or "4 to the second power." The raised 2 is called the **exponent.** It tells that 4 is used as a factor two times. The 4 is called the **base.** Numbers written with an exponent are said to be in **exponential notation.**

$$4^2 \begin{array}{l} \text{—exponent} \\ \text{—base} \end{array}$$

Exponents are also used to show that a factor is used more than twice.

EXAMPLES

$2^3 = 2 * 2 * 2$

The number 2 is used as a factor 3 times. 2^3 is read "2 cubed" or "2 to the third power."

$9^5 = 9 * 9 * 9 * 9 * 9$

The number 9 is used as a factor 5 times. 9^5 is read "9 to the fifth power."

Any number raised to the first power is equal to itself. For example, $5^1 = 5$.

Some calculators have special keys for renaming numbers written in exponential notation as standard numerals.

244

EXAMPLES   Use a calculator. Find 15^2 and 2^4.

To rename 15^2, press 15 ⌃ 2 (Enter) . Answer: 225

To rename 2^4, press 2 ⌃ 4 (Enter) . Answer: 16
$2^4 = 16$ You can verify this by keying in 2 ⊗ 2 ⊗ 2 ⊗ 2 (Enter) .

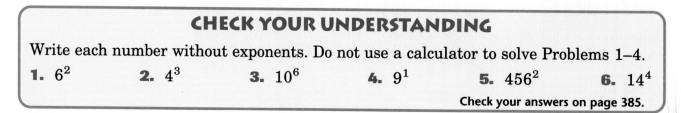

CHECK YOUR UNDERSTANDING

Write each number without exponents. Do not use a calculator to solve Problems 1–4.

1. 6^2 **2.** 4^3 **3.** 10^6 **4.** 9^1 **5.** 456^2 **6.** 14^4

Check your answers on page 385.

Positive and Negative Exponents

Positive exponents tell how many times to use the base as a factor.

2^6	64
2^5	32
2^4	16
2^3	8
2^2	4
2^1	2

2^0	1
2^{-1}	$\frac{1}{2}$
2^{-2}	$\frac{1}{4}$
2^{-3}	$\frac{1}{8}$
2^{-4}	$\frac{1}{16}$
2^{-5}	$\frac{1}{32}$

EXAMPLES
$$5^3 = 5 * 5 * 5 \qquad 10^4 = 10 * 10 * 10 * 10$$
$$25^2 = 25 * 25 \qquad 2^6 = 2 * 2 * 2 * 2 * 2 * 2$$

Exponents are helpful for writing large numbers. People have been using them for a long time. As people used positive exponents, however, they noticed patterns like those in the table at the right. These patterns suggest what expressions like 2^0 or 2^{-3} might mean.

Note that as the exponents in the left-hand column become 1 less, the numbers in the right-hand column are divided in half.

Many people have trouble understanding how 2^0 equals 1. After all, it's hard to see how you multiply 2 by itself 0 times. But mathematicians like patterns, and so they have decided that 2^0 equals 1, because that fits the pattern in the table.

Similar patterns hold for powers of other numbers. This is why we say that any number (except 0) raised to the 0 power equals 1.

EXAMPLES $\quad 4^0 = 1 \qquad 8^0 = 1 \qquad 12.893^0 = 1 \qquad 1^0 = 1$

NOTE

For all numbers n (except 0), $n^0 = 1$.

Most people have less trouble with negative exponents. A number raised to a negative power is equal to the fraction 1 over the number raised to the positive power.

EXAMPLES

$$2^{-3} = \frac{1}{2^3} = \frac{1}{2 * 2 * 2} = \frac{1}{8}$$
$$2^{-5} = \frac{1}{2^5} = \frac{1}{2 * 2 * 2 * 2 * 2} = \frac{1}{32}$$

$$10^{-2} = \frac{1}{10^2} = \frac{1}{10 * 10} = \frac{1}{100}$$
$$5^{-3} = \frac{1}{5^3} = \frac{1}{5 * 5 * 5} = \frac{1}{125}$$

CHECK YOUR UNDERSTANDING

Solve.

1. 4^{-2} **2.** 10^{-3} **3.** 5^0 **4.** 3^{-1} **5.** 2^5 **6.** 10^0

Check your answers on page 385.

Scientific Notation

The population of the world is about 6 billion people. The number 6 billion can be written as 6,000,000,000 or as $6 * 10^9$.

The number 6,000,000,000 is written in **standard notation.** The number $6 * 10^9$ is written in **scientific notation.** $6 * 10^9$ is read "six times ten to the ninth power."

Look at 10^9. 10^9 is the product of 10 used as a factor 9 times:

$$10^9 = 10 * 10 * 10 * 10 * 10 * 10 * 10 * 10 * 10$$
$$= 1,000,000,000$$
$$= 1\ billion$$

So $6 * 10^9 = 6 * 1,000,000,000$
$$= 6,000,000,000$$
$$= 6\ billion$$

Numbers in scientific notation are written as the product of a number that is at least 1 and less than 10 and a power of 10. We often change numbers from standard notation to scientific notation so that they are easier to write and to work with.

EXAMPLES Write in scientific notation.

7,000,000 = ?	240,000 = ?
7,000,000 = 7 * 1,000,000	240,000 = 2.4 * 100,000
1,000,000 = 10*10*10*10*10*10 = 10^6	100,000 = 10*10*10*10*10 = 10^5
So, 7,000,000 = 7 * 10^6.	So, 240,000 = 2.4 * 10^5.

EXAMPLES Write in standard notation.

$4 * 10^3$ = ?	$56 * 10^7$ = ?
10^3 = 10*10*10 = 1,000	10^7 = 10*10*10*10*10*10*10 = 10,000,000
So, $4 * 10^3$ = 4 * 1,000 = 4,000.	So, $56 * 10^7$ = 56 * 10,000,000 = 560,000,000.

CHECK YOUR UNDERSTANDING

Write each number in standard notation.

1. 5^2 **2.** 3^3 **3.** 8^1 **4.** $5 * 10^6$ **5.** $84 * 10^4$

Write each number in scientific notation.

6. 600   **7.** 55,000   **8.** 800,000,000

Check your answers on page 385.

Comparing Numbers and Amounts

When two numbers or amounts are compared, there are two possible results: They are equal, or they are not equal because one is larger than the other.

Different symbols are used to show that numbers and amounts are equal or not equal.

- Use an **equal sign** (=) to show that the numbers or amounts *are equal.*
- Use a **not-equal sign** (≠) to show that they are *not equal.*
- Use a **greater-than symbol** (>) or a **less-than symbol** (<) to show that they are *not equal* and to show which is larger.

EXAMPLES

Symbol	=	≠	>	<
Meaning	"equals" or "is the same as"	"is not equal"	"is greater than"	"is less than"
	$\frac{1}{2} = 0.5$	$2 \neq 3$	$9 > 5$	$3 < 5$
	$40 = 8 * 5$	$3^2 \neq 6$	$1.42 > 1.4$	$989 < 1{,}001$
	$3^3 = 27$	$1 \text{ m} \neq 100 \text{ mm}$	16 ft 9 in. > 15 ft 11 in.	98 minutes < 3 hours
	4 cm = 40 mm		$9 + 8 > 10 + 6$	$3 * (3 + 4) < 5 * 6$
	$6 + 6 = 7 + 7 - 2$		$4 * 7 > \frac{26}{2}$	$100 - 2 < 99 + 2$
	$2 * 5 = 9 + 1$		$10^3 > 100$	$\frac{1}{10^3} < 1$

When you compare amounts that include units, use the same unit for both amounts.

EXAMPLE   Compare 30 yards and 60 feet.

The units are different—yards and feet.
Change yards to feet, then compare.
1 yd = 3 ft
So, 30 yd = 30 * 3 ft, or 90 ft.
90 ft > 60 ft

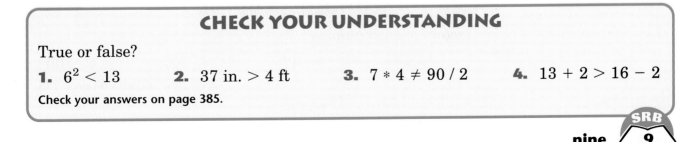

Therefore, 30 yd > 60 ft.

CHECK YOUR UNDERSTANDING

True or false?

1. $6^2 < 13$ **2.** 37 in. > 4 ft   **3.** $7 * 4 \neq 90 / 2$ **4.** $13 + 2 > 16 - 2$

Check your answers on page 385.

Factors

A **rectangular array** is an arrangement of objects in rows and columns. Each row has the same number of objects, and each column has the same number of objects. A rectangular array can be represented by a multiplication **number model.**

> **EXAMPLE** This rectangular array has 15 red dots.
>
> It has 3 rows with 5 dots in each row.
> 3 * 5 = 15 is a number model for this array.
> 3 and 5 are whole-number **factors** of 15.
> 15 is the **product** of 3 and 5.
> 3 and 5 are a **factor pair** for 15.
>
>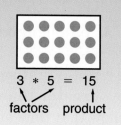
>
> 3 * 5 = 15
> factors   product

Numbers can have more than one factor pair. 1 and 15 are another factor pair for 15 because 1 * 15 = 15.

To test whether a number is a factor of another number, divide the larger number by the smaller number. If the result is a whole number and the remainder is 0, then the smaller number is a factor of the larger number.

> **EXAMPLES** 4 is a factor of 12 because 12 / 4 gives 3 with a remainder of 0.
>
> 6 is *not* a factor of 14 because 14 / 6 gives 2 with a remainder of 2.

One way to find all the **factors of a whole number** is to find all the factor pairs for that number.

> **EXAMPLE** Find all the factors of the number 24.
>
> **Number Models**   **Factor Pairs**
> 24 = 1 * 24   1, 24
> 24 = 2 * 12   2, 12
> 24 = 3 * 8   3, 8
> 24 = 4 * 6   4, 6
>
> The factors of 24 are 1, 2, 3, 4, 6, 8, 12, and 24.

CHECK YOUR UNDERSTANDING

List all the whole-number factors of each number.

1. 8   **2.** 27   **3.** 49   **4.** 36   **5.** 13   **6.** 100

Check your answers on page 385.

Divisibility

When a counting number is divided by a counting number and the quotient is a counting number with a remainder of 0, then the first number is **divisible by** the second number.

> **EXAMPLE** 124 / 4 → 31 R0 The remainder is 0, so 124 is divisible by 4.

When a counting number is divided by a counting number and the quotient is a whole number with a non-zero remainder, then the first number is *not divisible by* the second number.

> **EXAMPLE** 88 / 5 → 17 R3 The remainder is not 0, so 88 is *not divisible by* 5.

For some counting numbers, even large ones, it is possible to test for divisibility without dividing.

Here are **divisibility tests** that make it unnecessary to divide:
- All numbers are **divisible by 1.**
- All numbers with a 0, 2, 4, 6, or 8 in the ones place are **divisible by 2.** They are the even numbers.
- Any whole number with 0 in the ones place is **divisible by 10.**
- Any whole number with 0 or 5 in the ones place is **divisible by 5.**
- If the sum of the digits in a whole number is divisible by 3, then the number is **divisible by 3.**
- If the sum of the digits in a whole number is divisible by 9, then the number is **divisible by 9.**
- If a whole number is divisible by both 2 and 3, it is **divisible by 6.**

> **EXAMPLES** Tell which numbers 216 is divisible by.
>
> 216 is divisible by
> >   2 because 6 in the ones place is an even number
> >   3 because the sum of its digits is 9, which is divisible by 3
> >   9 because the sum of its digits is divisible by 9
> >   6 because it is divisible both by 2 and by 3.
>
> 216 is not divisible by 10 or by 5 because it does not have a 0 or 5 in the ones place.

CHECK YOUR UNDERSTANDING

Which numbers are divisible by 2? By 3? By 5? By 6? By 9? By 10?

1. 105   **2.** 6,270   **3.** 526   **4.** 711   **5.** 13,680

Check your answers on page 385.

Prime and Composite Numbers

A **prime number** is a counting number greater than 1 that has exactly two factors: 1 and the number itself. A prime number is divisible only by 1 and itself.

A **composite number** is a counting number that has more than two factors.

NOTE
The number 1 is neither prime nor composite.

EXAMPLES   11 is a prime number because its only factors are 1 and 11.

20 is a composite number because it has more than two factors. Its factors are 1, 2, 4, 5, 10, and 20.

Every composite number can be renamed as a product of prime numbers. This is called the **prime factorization** of that number.

EXAMPLE   Find the prime factorization of 48.

The number 48 can be renamed as the product 2 * 2 * 2 * 2 * 3.

The prime factorization of 48 can be written as $2^4 * 3$.

One way to find the prime factorization of a number is to make a **factor tree.** First, write the number. Then, underneath, write any two factors whose product is that number. Repeat the process for these two factors. Continue until all the factors are prime numbers.

EXAMPLE   Find the prime factorization of 24.

No matter which two factors are used to start the tree, the tree will always end with the same prime factors.

24 = 2 * 2 * 2 * 3

The prime factorization of 24 is 2 * 2 * 2 * 3.

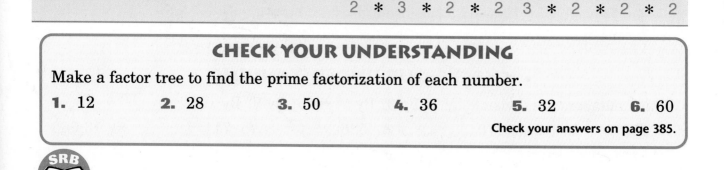

CHECK YOUR UNDERSTANDING

Make a factor tree to find the prime factorization of each number.

1. 12   **2.** 28   **3.** 50   **4.** 36   **5.** 32   **6.** 60

Check your answers on page 385.

Addition Algorithms

Partial-Sums Method

The **partial-sums method** is used to find sums mentally or with paper and pencil.

To use the partial-sums method, add from left to right, one column at a time. Then add the partial sums.

EXAMPLE   348 + 177 = ?

		100s	10s	1s
		3	4	8
	+	1	7	7
Add the 100s.	300 + 100 →	4	0	0
Add the 10s.	40 + 70 →	1	1	0
Add the 1s.	8 + 7 →		1	5
Add the partial sums.	400 + 110 + 15 →	**5**	**2**	**5**

348 + 177 = 525

Column-Addition Method

The **column-addition method** can be used to find sums with paper and pencil, but it is not a good method for finding sums mentally.

To add numbers using the column-addition method:

- Draw lines to separate the 1s, 10s, 100s, or any other places.
- Add the numbers in each column. Write each sum in its column.
- If the sum of any column is a 2-digit number, adjust that column sum. Trade part of the sum into the column to the left.

EXAMPLE   359 + 298 = ?

	100s	10s	1s
	3	5	9
+	2	9	8
Add the numbers in each column.	5	14	17
Adjust the 1s and 10s:	5	15	7

Adjust the 1s and 10s:
17 ones = 1 ten and 7 ones
Trade the 1 ten into the tens column.

	100s	10s	1s
Adjust the 10s and 100s:	6	5	7

Adjust the 10s and 100s:
15 tens = 1 hundred and 5 tens
Trade the 1 hundred into the hundreds column.

359 + 298 = 657

A Short Method

This is the method for adding that most adults in the United States were taught.

Add one column at a time from right to left, without displaying the partial sums.

> **EXAMPLE** 248 + 187 = ?
>
> | **Step 1:** | **Step 2:** | **Step 3:** |
> |---|---|---|
> | Add the ones. | Add the tens. | Add the hundreds. |
> | 1

  2 4 8
+   1 8 7
———
       5 | 1 1

  2 4 8
+   1 8 7
———
     3 5 | 1 1

  2 4 8
+   1 8 7
———
   4 3 5 |
> | 8 ones + 7 ones =
15 ones = 1 ten + 5 ones | 1 ten + 4 tens + 8 tens =
13 tens = 1 hundred + 3 tens | 1 hundred + 2 hundreds + 1 hundred =
4 hundreds |

The Opposite-Change Rule

Addends are numbers that are added. In 8 + 4 = 12, the numbers 8 and 4 are addends.

Here is the **opposite-change rule:** If you subtract a number from one addend, and add the same number to the other addend, the sum is the same.

Use this rule to make a problem easier by changing either of the addends to a number that has zero in the ones place.

> **EXAMPLE** 59 + 26 = ?
>
> **One way:** Add and subtract 1.
>
> | 59 | (add 1) | 60 |
> |---|---|---|
> | + 26 | (subtract 1) | + 25 |
> | | | 85 |
>
> **Another way:** Subtract and add 4.
>
> | 59 | (subtract 4) | 55 |
> |---|---|---|
> | + 26 | (add 4) | + 30 |
> | | | 85 |

> ## CHECK YOUR UNDERSTANDING
>
> Add.
>
> 1.   263   2.   75   3.   188   4.   769   5. 538 + 427   6. 941 + 89
>   + 425   + 38   + 33   + 348
>
> Check your answers on page 385.

Subtraction Algorithms
Trade-First Subtraction Method

The **trade-first method** is similar to the method for subtracting that most adults in the United States were taught.

- If each digit in the top number is greater than or equal to the digit below it, subtract separately in each column.

- If any digit in the top number is less than the digit below it, adjust the top number before doing any subtracting. Adjust the top number by "trading."

EXAMPLE Subtract 275 from 463 using the trade-first method.

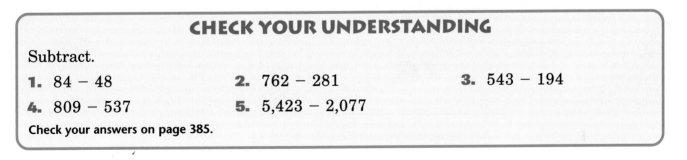

100s	10s	1s
4	6	3
− 2	7	5

Look at the 1s place.
You cannot remove 5 ones from 3 ones.

100s	10s	1s
	5	13
4	6̸	3̸
− 2	7	5

So trade 1 ten for 10 ones.
Look at the 10s place.
You cannot remove 7 tens from 5 tens.

100s	10s	1s
	15	
3	5̸	13
4̸	6̸	3̸
− 2	7	5
1	8	8

So trade 1 hundred for 10 tens.
Now subtract in each column.

463 − 275 = 188

Larger numbers with 4 or more digits are subtracted in the same way.

CHECK YOUR UNDERSTANDING

Subtract.

1. 84 − 48   **2.** 762 − 281   **3.** 543 − 194

4. 809 − 537   **5.** 5,423 − 2,077

Check your answers on page 385.

Counting-Up Method

You can subtract two numbers by counting up from the smaller number to the larger number. The first step is to count up to the nearest multiple of 10. Then count up by 10s and 100s.

EXAMPLE 425 − 48 = ?

Write the smaller number, 48.

As you count from 48 up to 425, circle each number that you count up.

Add the numbers you circled:
2 + 50 + 300 + 25 = 377

You counted up by 377.

425 − 48 = 377

$$
\begin{array}{r}
4\,8 \\
+\quad \textcircled{2} \quad \text{Count up to the nearest 10.} \\
\hline
5\,0 \\
+\textcircled{5\,0} \quad \text{Count up to the nearest 100.} \\
\hline
1\,0\,0 \\
+\textcircled{3\,0\,0} \quad \text{Count up to the largest possible hundred.} \\
\hline
4\,0\,0 \\
+\quad \textcircled{2\,5} \quad \text{Count up to the larger number.} \\
\hline
4\,2\,5
\end{array}
$$

Left-to-Right Subtraction Method

Starting at the left, subtract column-by-column.

EXAMPLES 932 − 356 = ?   782 − 294 = ?

Subtract the 100s.

Subtract the 10s.

Subtract the 1s.

$$
\begin{array}{r}
9\,3\,2 \\
-\ 3\,0\,0 \\
\hline
6\,3\,2 \\
-\quad 5\,0 \\
\hline
5\,8\,2 \\
-\qquad 6 \\
\hline
5\,7\,6
\end{array}
\qquad
\begin{array}{r}
7\,8\,2 \\
-\ 2\,0\,0 \\
\hline
5\,8\,2 \\
-\quad 9\,0 \\
\hline
4\,9\,2 \\
-\qquad 4 \\
\hline
4\,8\,8
\end{array}
$$

932 − 356 = 576   782 − 294 = 488

CHECK YOUR UNDERSTANDING

Subtract.

1. 315 − 72   **2.** 824 − 578   **3.** 375 − 249   **4.** 604 − 381

Check your answers on page 385.

Partial-Differences Method

1. Subtract from left to right, one column at a time.

2. Always subtract the smaller number from the larger number.

   - If the smaller number is on the bottom, the difference is **added** to the answer.
   - If the smaller number is on the top, the difference is **subtracted** from the answer.

EXAMPLE $846 - 363 = ?$

$$
\begin{array}{r}
8\ 4\ 6 \\
-\ 3\ 6\ 3 \\
\hline
+\ 5\ 0\ 0 \\
-\ \ \ \ 2\ 0 \\
+\ \ \ \ \ \ 3 \\
\hline
4\ 8\ 3
\end{array}
$$

Subtract the 100s.	$800 - 300 \rightarrow +\ 5\ 0\ 0$
Subtract the 10s.	$60 - 40 \rightarrow -\ \ \ \ 2\ 0$
Subtract the 1s.	$6 - 3 \rightarrow +\ \ \ \ \ \ 3$
Find the total.	$500 - 20 + 3 \rightarrow 4\ 8\ 3$

(The smaller number is on top, so include a minus sign.)

$846 - 363 = 483$

Same-Change Rule

Here is the **same-change rule** for subtraction problems:

- If you add the same number to both numbers in the problem, the answer is the same.
- If you subtract the same number from both numbers in the problem, the answer is the same.

Use this rule to change the second number in the problem to a number that has zero in the ones place.

EXAMPLE $92 - 36 = ?$

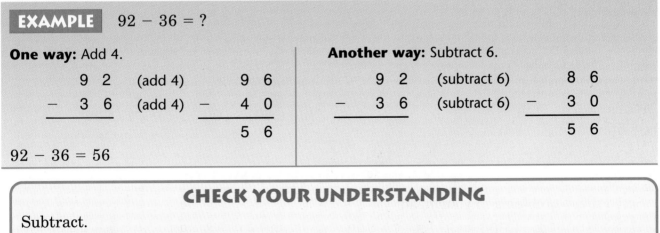

One way: Add 4.

$$
\begin{array}{rcr}
9\ 2 & \text{(add 4)} & 9\ 6 \\
-\ 3\ 6 & \text{(add 4)} & -\ 4\ 0 \\
\hline
& & 5\ 6
\end{array}
$$

$92 - 36 = 56$

Another way: Subtract 6.

$$
\begin{array}{rcr}
9\ 2 & \text{(subtract 6)} & 8\ 6 \\
-\ 3\ 6 & \text{(subtract 6)} & -\ 3\ 0 \\
\hline
& & 5\ 6
\end{array}
$$

CHECK YOUR UNDERSTANDING

Subtract.

1. $429 - 53$
2. $683 - 219$
3. $524 - 362$
4. $4,226 - 2,419$

Check your answers on page 385.

Extended Multiplication Facts

Numbers such as 10, 100, and 1,000 are called **powers of 10.**

It is easy to multiply a whole number, *n*, by a power of 10. To the right of the number *n*, write as many zeros as there are zeros in the power of 10.

EXAMPLES

$10 * 74 = 740$	$10 * 40 = 400$	$100 * 380 = 38{,}000$
$100 * 74 = 7{,}400$	$100 * 40 = 4{,}000$	$10{,}000 * 71 = 710{,}000$
$1{,}000 * 74 = 74{,}000$	$1{,}000 * 40 = 40{,}000$	$1{,}000{,}000 * 9 = 9{,}000{,}000$

If you have memorized the basic multiplication facts, you can solve problems such as $8 * 70$ and $5{,}000 * 3$ mentally.

EXAMPLES

$8 * 70 = ?$
Think: 8 [7s] = 56
8 [70s] is 10 times as much.

$8 * 70 = 10 * 56 = 560$

$5{,}000 * 3 = ?$
Think: 5 [3s] = 15
5,000 [3s] is 1,000 times as much.

$5{,}000 * 3 = 1{,}000 * 15 = 15{,}000$

You can use a similar method to solve problems such as $40 * 50$ and $300 * 90$ mentally.

EXAMPLES

$40 * 50 = ?$
Think: 4 [50s] = 200
40 [50s] is 10 times as much.

$40 * 50 = 10 * 200 = 2{,}000$

$300 * 90 = ?$
Think: 3 [90s] = 270
300 [90s] is 100 times as much.

$300 * 90 = 100 * 270 = 27{,}000$

CHECK YOUR UNDERSTANDING

Solve these problems in your head.

1. $8 * 100$ **2.** $1{,}000 * 49$ **3.** $7 * 700$ **4.** $5{,}000 * 9$ **5.** $90 * 40$ **6.** $800 * 60$

Check your answers on page 385.

Multiplication Algorithms

The symbols × and * are both used to indicate multiplication.
In this book, the symbol * is used more often.

Partial-Products Method

In the **partial-products method,** you must keep track of the
place value of each digit. It may help to write 1s, 10s, and 100s
above the columns. Each partial product is either a basic
multiplication fact or an extended multiplication fact.

EXAMPLE 4 * 236 = ?

	100s	10s	1s
	2	3	6
*			4
4 * 200 →	8	0	0
4 * 30 →	1	2	0
4 * 6 →		2	4
	9	4	4

Think of 236 as 200 + 30 + 6.

Multiply each part of 236 by 4.

Add these three partial products.

4 * 236 = 944

EXAMPLE 43 * 26 = ?

	100s	10s	1s
		2	6
*		4	3
40 * 20 →	8	0	0
40 * 6 →	2	4	0
3 * 20 →		6	0
3 * 6 →		1	8
	1, 1	1	8

Think of 26 as 20 + 6.

Think of 43 as 40 + 3.

Multiply each part of 26 by 43.

Add these four partial products.

43 * 26 = 1,118

CHECK YOUR UNDERSTANDING

Multiply. Write each partial product. Then add the partial products.

1. 284 * 3   **2.** 37 * 75   **3.** 60 * 67   **4.** 78 * 43   **5.** 237 * 50

Check your answers on page 385.

Lattice Method

The **lattice method** for multiplying has been used for hundreds of years. It is very easy to use if you know the basic multiplication facts.

EXAMPLE $6 * 815 = ?$

The box with cells and diagonals is called a **lattice.**
Write 815 above the lattice.
Write 6 on the right side of the lattice.

Multiply $6 * 5$. Then multiply $6 * 1$.
Then multiply $6 * 8$.
Write the answers as shown.

Add the numbers along each diagonal.

Read the answer. $6 * 815 = 4,890$

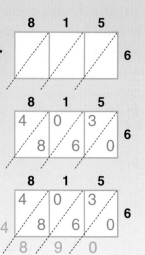

EXAMPLE $42 * 37 = ?$

Write 37 above the lattice.
Write 42 on the right side.

Multiply $4 * 7$. Then multiply $4 * 3$.
Multiply $2 * 7$. Then multiply $2 * 3$.
Write the answers as shown.

Add the numbers along each diagonal.

When the numbers along a diagonal
add up to 10 or more:
• record the ones digit in the sum
• add the tens digit to the sum
  in the next diagonal above

Read the answer. $42 * 37 = 1,554$

CHECK YOUR UNDERSTANDING

Draw a lattice for each problem. Then multiply.

1. $7 * 89$ **2.** $44 * 25$ **3.** $88 * 97$ **4.** $7 * 335$ **5.** $487 * 8$

Check your answers on pages 385 and 386.

Extended Division Facts

Numbers such as 10, 100, and 1,000 are called **powers of 10.**

In the examples below, use the following method to divide a whole number, *n*, by a power of 10:

- Cross out zeros in the number *n*, starting in the ones place.
- Cross out as many zeros as there are zeros in the power of 10.

EXAMPLES

70,000 / **10** = 7000~~0~~	46,000 / **10** = 4600~~0~~	830,000 / **10,000** = 83~~0000~~
70,000 / **100** = 700~~00~~	46,000 / **100** = 460~~00~~	3,000,000 / **100,000** = 30~~00000~~
70,000 / **1,000** = 70~~000~~	46,000 / **1,000** = 46~~000~~	

If you know the basic division facts, you can solve problems such as 240 / 4 and 15,000 / 3 mentally.

EXAMPLES

240 / 4 = ?
Think: 24 / 4 = 6
240 / 4 is 10 times as much.

240 / 4 = 10 * 6 = 60

15,000 / 3 = ?
Think: 15 / 3 = 5
15,000 / 3 is 1,000 times as much.

15,000 / 3 = 1,000 * 5 = 5,000

You can use a similar method to solve problems such as 18,000 / 30 mentally.

EXAMPLE   18,000 / 30 = ?

Think: 18 / 3 = 6
Try 6 as the answer: 6 * 30 = 180
You want 18,000, or 100 times 180.
Try 100 * 6 = 600 as the answer: 600 * 30 = 18,000

So, 18,000 / 30 = 600.

CHECK YOUR UNDERSTANDING

Solve these problems mentally.

1. 53,000 / 1,000
2. 36,000 / 4
3. 24,000 / 8
4. 4,200 / 10
5. 4,200 / 70
6. 42,000 / 70

Check your answers on page 386.

Division Algorithms

Different symbols may be used to indicate division. For example, "94 divided by 6" may be written as $94 \div 6$, $6\overline{)94}$, $94 / 6$, or $\frac{94}{6}$.

- The number that is being divided is called the **dividend.**

- The number by which the dividend is divided is called the **divisor.**

- The answer to a division problem is called the **quotient.**

- Some numbers cannot be divided evenly. When this happens, the answer includes a quotient and a **remainder.**

Partial-Quotients Method

In the partial-quotients method, it takes several steps to find the quotient. At each step, you find a partial answer (called a **partial quotient**). These partial answers are then added to find the quotient.

Study the example below. To find the number of 6s in 1,010 first find partial quotients and add them. Record the partial quotients in a column to the right of the original problem.

EXAMPLE $1,010 / 6 = ?$

Write partial quotients in this column.

$6\overline{)1,010}$	↓ *Think:* How many [6s] are in 1,010? At least 100.	
$-\ 600$	100	The first partial quotient is 100. 100 * 6 = 600
410		Subtract 600 from 1,010. At least 50 [6s] are left.
$-\ 300$	50	The second partial quotient is 50. 50 * 6 = 300
110		Subtract. At least 10 [6s] are left.
$-\ 60$	10	The third partial quotient is 10. 10 * 6 = 60
50		Subtract. At least 8 [6s] are left.
$-\ 48$	8	The fourth partial quotient is 8. 8 * 6 = 48
2	168	Subtract. Add the partial quotients.
↑	↑	
Remainder	Quotient	

The answer is 168 R2. Record the answer as $6\overline{)1,010}^{\,168\ R2}$ or write $1,010 / 6 \rightarrow 168\ R2$.

The partial-quotients method works the same whether you divide by a 2-digit or a 1-digit divisor. It often helps to write down some easy facts for the divisor.

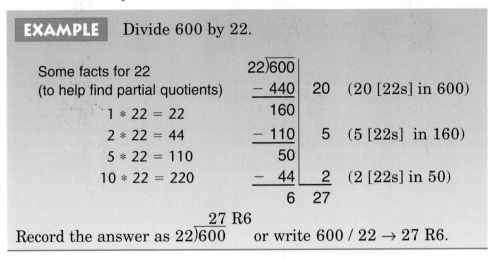

EXAMPLE   Divide 600 by 22.

Some facts for 22
(to help find partial quotients)

1 * 22 = 22
2 * 22 = 44
5 * 22 = 110
10 * 22 = 220

$$22)\overline{600}$$
$$-\ 440 \quad 20 \quad (20\ [22s]\ in\ 600)$$
$$160$$
$$-\ 110 \quad 5 \quad (5\ [22s]\ in\ 160)$$
$$50$$
$$-\ 44 \quad 2 \quad (2\ [22s]\ in\ 50)$$
$$6 \quad 27$$

Record the answer as $22)\overline{600}^{\ 27\ R6}$ or write 600 / 22 → 27 R6.

There are different ways to find partial quotients when you use the partial-quotients method. Study the example below. The answer is the same for each way.

EXAMPLE   381 / 4 = ?

One way:

$$4)\overline{381}$$
$$-\ 200 \quad | \ 50$$
$$181$$
$$-\ 120 \quad | \ 30$$
$$61$$
$$-\ 40 \quad | \ 10$$
$$21$$
$$-\ 20 \quad | \ 5$$
$$1 \quad 95$$

Another way:

$$4)\overline{381}$$
$$-\ 200 \quad | \ 50$$
$$181$$
$$-\ 160 \quad | \ 40$$
$$21$$
$$-\ 20 \quad | \ 5$$
$$1 \quad 95$$

Another way:

$$4)\overline{381}$$
$$-\ 360 \quad | \ 90$$
$$21$$
$$-\ 20 \quad | \ 5$$
$$1 \quad 95$$

The answer, 95 R1, is the same for each way.

CHECK YOUR UNDERSTANDING

Divide.

1. $4)\overline{63}$ **2.** 655 / 5   **3.** 386 ÷ 4   **4.** $3)\overline{704}$

Check your answers on page 386.

Column-Division Method

In the example below, think of sharing $763 among 5 people.

EXAMPLE $5\overline{)763} = ?$

1. Draw lines to separate the digits in the dividend (the number being divided).
   Work left to right. Begin in the left column.

$$5\overline{)7 \mid 6 \mid 3}$$

2. Think of the 7 in the hundreds column as 7 $100 bills to be shared by 5 people.
   Each person gets 1 $100 bill. There are 2 $100 bills remaining.

$$5\overline{)\begin{array}{c} 1 \\ 7 \\ -5 \\ \hline 2 \end{array} \mid 6 \mid 3}$$

3. Trade the 2 $100 bills for 20 $10 bills.
   Think of the 6 in the tens column as 6 $10 bills. That makes 20 + 6 $10 bills in all.

$$5\overline{)\begin{array}{c} 1 \\ 7 \\ -5 \\ \hline 2 \end{array} \mid \begin{array}{c} \cancel{6} \\ 26 \end{array} \mid 3}$$

4. If 5 people share 26 $10 bills, each person gets 5 $10 bills. There is 1 $10 bill remaining.

$$5\overline{)\begin{array}{c} 1 \\ 7 \\ -5 \\ \hline 2 \end{array} \mid \begin{array}{c} 5 \\ \cancel{6} \\ 26 \\ -25 \\ \hline 1 \end{array} \mid 3}$$

5. Trade the 1 $10 bill for 10 $1 bills.
   Think of the 3 in the ones column as 3 $1 bills. That makes 10 + 3 = 13 $1 bills.

$$5\overline{)\begin{array}{c} 1 \\ 7 \\ -5 \\ \hline 2 \end{array} \mid \begin{array}{c} 5 \\ \cancel{6} \\ 26 \\ -25 \\ \hline \cancel{1} \end{array} \mid \begin{array}{c} \cancel{3} \\ 13 \end{array}}$$

6. If 5 people share 13 $1 bills, each person gets 2 $1 bills. There are 3 $1 bills remaining.

$$5\overline{)\begin{array}{c} 1 \\ 7 \\ -5 \\ \hline 2 \end{array} \mid \begin{array}{c} 5 \\ \cancel{6} \\ 26 \\ -25 \\ \hline \cancel{1} \end{array} \mid \begin{array}{c} 2 \\ \cancel{3} \\ 13 \\ -10 \\ \hline 3 \end{array}}$$

Record the answer as 152 R3.
Each person receives $152 and $3 are left over.

Decimals & Percents

THIS SALE $ 10.00

6.854 GALLONS

1.459

Decimals

Both decimals and fractions are used to write numbers that are between consecutive whole numbers. Decimals use the same base-ten place-value system as whole numbers. You can compute with decimals in the same way as you compute with whole numbers.

Decimals are another way to write fractions that have denominators of 10, 100, 1,000, and so on.

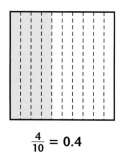

$\frac{4}{10} = 0.4$

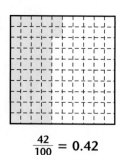

$\frac{42}{100} = 0.42$

This square is divided into 10 equal parts. Each part is $\frac{1}{10}$ of the square. The decimal name for $\frac{1}{10}$ is 0.1.

$\frac{4}{10}$ of the square is shaded. The decimal name for $\frac{4}{10}$ is 0.4.

This square is divided into 100 equal parts. Each part is $\frac{1}{100}$ of the square. The decimal name for $\frac{1}{100}$ is 0.01.

$\frac{42}{100}$ of the square is shaded. The decimal name for $\frac{42}{100}$ is 0.42.

Like mixed numbers, decimals are used to name numbers that are greater than one.

EXAMPLE

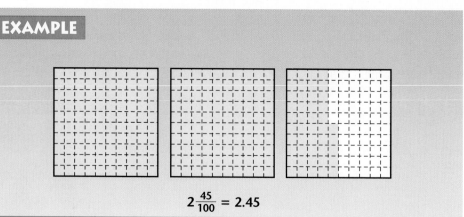

$2\frac{45}{100} = 2.45$

In a decimal, the dot is called the **decimal point.** It separates the whole-number part from the decimal part. A decimal with one place after the decimal point names *tenths;* a decimal with two places after the decimal point names *hundredths;* a decimal with three places after the decimal point names *thousandths.*

> **NOTE**
>
> Decimals were invented by the Dutch scientist Simon Stevin in 1585. But today, even after hundreds of years of use, there is still no single worldwide form for writing decimals. For 3.25 (American notation), the British write 3·25, and the Germans and French write 3,25.

EXAMPLES

tenths	hundredths	thousandths
$0.4 = \frac{4}{10}$	$0.34 = \frac{34}{100}$	$0.162 = \frac{162}{1,000}$
$0.8 = \frac{8}{10}$	$0.75 = \frac{75}{100}$	$0.003 = \frac{3}{1,000}$
$0.9 = \frac{9}{10}$	$0.03 = \frac{3}{100}$	$0.098 = \frac{98}{1,000}$

Reading Decimals

One way to read the decimal part is to say it as you would a fraction. For example, $7.9 = 7\frac{9}{10}$, so 7.9 can be read as "seven and nine-tenths." $0.001 = \frac{1}{1,000}$ and is read as "one-thousandth."

You can read decimals by first saying the whole number part, then saying "point," and then saying the digits in the decimal part. For example, 6.8 can be read as "six point eight"; 0.15 can be read as "zero point one five." This way of reading decimals is often useful when there are many digits in the decimal.

EXAMPLES

0.18 is read as "18 hundredths" or "0 point 18."
24.5 is read as "24 and 5 tenths" or "24 point 5."
0.008 is read as "8 thousandths" or "0 point 008."

CHECK YOUR UNDERSTANDING

Write a decimal for each picture.

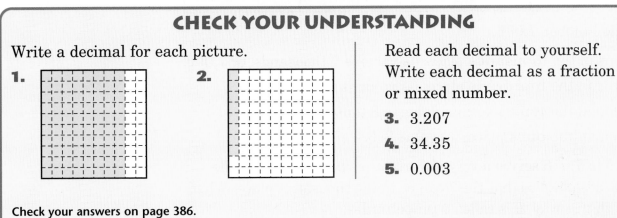

1.

2.

Read each decimal to yourself. Write each decimal as a fraction or mixed number.

3. 3.207

4. 34.35

5. 0.003

Check your answers on page 386.

Extending Place Value to Decimals

The first systems for writing numbers were primitive. Ancient Egyptians used a stroke to record the number 1, a picture of an oxbow for 10, a coil of rope for 100, a lotus plant for 1,000, and a picture of a god supporting the sky for 1,000,000.

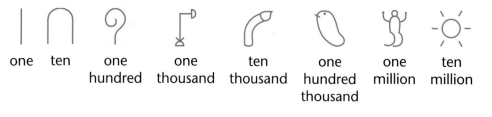

| one | ten | one hundred | one thousand | ten thousand | one hundred thousand | one million | ten million |

This is how an ancient Egyptian would write the number 54:

10 + 10 + 10 + 10 + 10 + 1 + 1 + 1 + 1

Our system for writing numbers is a **base-ten** system. This should come as no surprise. People probably counted on their fingers when they first started using numbers.

Our base-ten system was invented in India and later improved in Arabia. It uses only 10 symbols, which are called **digits:** 0, 1, 2, 3, 4, 5, 6, 7, 8, and 9. In this system, you can write any number using only these 10 digits.

For a number written in the base-ten system, each digit has a value that depends on its **place** in the number. That is why it is called a **place-value** system.

1,000s	100s	10s	1s
thousands	hundreds	tens	ones
7	0	8	6

In the number 7,086,

> 7 is in the **thousands** place; its value is 7 thousands, or 7,000.
>
> 0 is in the **hundreds** place; its value is 0.
>
> 8 is in the **tens** place; its value is 8 tens, or 80.
>
> 6 is in the **ones** place; its value is 6.

The 0 in 7,086 serves a very important purpose: It "holds" the hundreds place so that the 7 can be in the thousands place. When used in this way, 0 is called a **placeholder.**

As you move from right to left in the decimal place-value chart, the value of each place is **ten times** the value of the place to its right.

EXAMPLE

$*10 \quad *10 \quad *10$

1,000s	100s	10s	1s	.	0.1s	0.01s	0.001s
thousands	hundreds	tens	ones	.	tenths	hundredths	thousandths

- The value of the tens place is $10 * 1 = 10$.
- The value of the hundreds place is $10 * 10 = 100$.
- The value of the thousands place is $10 * 100 = 1,000$.

As you move from left to right in the decimal place-value chart, the value of each place is **one-tenth** of the value of the place to its left.

EXAMPLE

$*\frac{1}{10} \quad *\frac{1}{10} \quad *\frac{1}{10}$

1,000s	100s	10s	1s	.	0.1s	0.01s	0.001s
thousands	hundreds	tens	ones	.	tenths	hundredths	thousandths

- The value of the hundreds place is $\frac{1}{10}$ of $1,000 = 100$.
- The value of the tens place is $\frac{1}{10}$ of $100 = 10$.
- The value of the ones place is $\frac{1}{10}$ of $10 = 1$.

- The value of the place to the right of the ones place is one-tenth of the value of the ones place: $\frac{1}{10}$ of $1 = \frac{1}{10}$. This place is called the **tenths** place and is written 0.1.
- The value of the place to the right of the tenths place is $\frac{1}{10}$ of $\frac{1}{10} = \frac{1}{100}$. This place is called the **hundredths** place and is written 0.01.
- The value of the place to the right of the hundredths place is $\frac{1}{10}$ of $\frac{1}{100} = \frac{1}{1,000}$. This place is called the **thousandths** place and is written 0.001.

The base-ten system works the same way for decimals as it does for whole numbers.

EXAMPLES

1,000s thousands	100s hundreds	10s tens	1s ones	.	0.1s tenths	0.01s hundredths	0.001s thousandths
		4	7	.	8	0	5
			4	.	3	6	7

In the number 47.805,

> 8 is in the **tenths** place; its value is 8 tenths, or $\frac{8}{10}$, or 0.8.

> 0 is in the **hundredths** place; its value is 0.

> 5 is in the **thousandths** place; its value is 5 thousandths, or $\frac{5}{1,000}$, or 0.005.

In the number 4.367,

> 3 is in the **tenths** place; its value is 3 tenths, or $\frac{3}{10}$, or 0.3.

> 6 is in the **hundredths** place; its value is 6 hundredths, or $\frac{6}{100}$, or 0.06.

> 7 is in the **thousandths** place; its value is 7 thousandths, or $\frac{7}{1,000}$, or 0.007.

CHECK YOUR UNDERSTANDING

1. What is the value of the digit 2 in each of these numbers?
   a. 20,005.3   **b.** 0.02   **c.** 15.702

2. Using the digits 9, 3, and 5, what is
   a. the smallest decimal you can write?
   b. the largest decimal less than 1 you can write?
   c. the decimal closest to 0.5 you can write?

Check your answers on page 386.

Powers of 10 for Decimals

Study the decimal place-value chart.

1,000s thousands	100s hundreds	10s tens	1s ones	.	0.1s tenths	0.01s hundredths	0.001s thousandths
5	2	4	6	.	0	8	1
five thousand, two hundred forty-six				and	eighty-one thousandths		

Notice that the value of each place is $\frac{1}{10}$ of the value of the place to its left. This is true both for whole-number places and decimal places.

Whole Numbers	Decimals
$100 = \frac{1}{10}$ of 1,000	$0.1 = \frac{1}{10}$ of 1
$10 = \frac{1}{10}$ of 100	$0.01 = \frac{1}{10}$ of 0.1
$1 = \frac{1}{10}$ of 10	$0.001 = \frac{1}{10}$ of 0.01

A whole number that can be written using only 10s as factors is called a **power of 10.** A power of 10 can be written in exponential notation.

Powers of 10

100	$10 * 10$	10^2
1,000	$10 * 10 * 10$	10^3
10,000	$10 * 10 * 10 * 10$	10^4
100,000	$10 * 10 * 10 * 10 * 10$	10^5

Decimals that can be written using only 0.1s as factors are also powers of 10. They can be written in exponential notation with negative exponents.

Powers of 10 (less than 1)

0.01	$0.1 * 0.1$	10^{-2}
0.001	$0.1 * 0.1 * 0.1$	10^{-3}
0.0001	$0.1 * 0.1 * 0.1 * 0.1$	10^{-4}
0.00001	$0.1 * 0.1 * 0.1 * 0.1 * 0.1$	10^{-5}

The value of each place in a decimal place-value chart is a power of 10.

100,000s 10^5	10,000s 10^4	1,000s 10^3	100s 10^2	10s 10^1	1s 10^0	.	0.1s 10^{-1}	0.01s 10^{-2}	0.001s 10^{-3}	0.0001s 10^{-4}	0.00001s 10^{-5}

Note the pattern in the exponents: Each exponent is 1 less than the exponent in the place to its left. According to this pattern:

$$10^1 = 10 \qquad 10^0 = 1 \qquad 10^{-1} = 0.1$$

Comparing Decimals

One way to compare decimals is to model them with base-10 blocks. If you don't have the blocks, you can draw shorthand pictures of them.

Base-10 Block	Name	Shorthand Picture
	cube	
	long	
	flat	
	big cube	

EXAMPLE Compare 2.3 and 2.16.

2.3

2.16

For this example:

A flat ☐ is worth 1.

A long │ is worth 0.1.

A cube ▫ is worth 0.01.

2 flats and 3 longs are more than 2 flats, 1 long, and 6 cubes.

So, 2.3 is more than 2.16.

2.3 > 2.16

A decimal place-value chart can also be used to compare decimals.

EXAMPLE Compare 4.825 and 4.862.

1s ones place	.	0.1s tenths place	0.01s hundredths place	0.001s thousandths place
4	.	8	2	5
4	.	8	6	2

The ones digits *are the same*. They are both worth 4.

The tenths digits *are the same*. They are both worth 8 tenths, or $\frac{8}{10}$, or 0.8.

The hundredths digits are *not* the same.

The 2 is worth 2 hundredths, or 0.02. The 6 is worth 6 hundredths, or 0.06.

So, 4.862 is more than 4.825.

You can write a 0 at the end of a decimal without changing the value of the decimal: 0.7 = 0.70. Adding 0s is sometimes called "padding with 0s." Think of it as trading for smaller pieces.

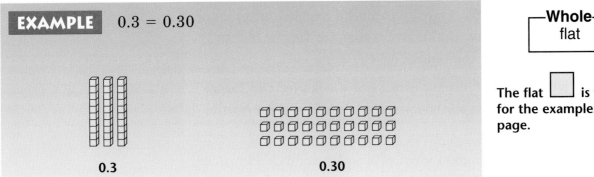

┌─Whole─┐
│ flat │
└────────┘

The flat ☐ is worth 1 for the examples on this page.

EXAMPLE 0.3 = 0.30

0.3   0.30

Padding with 0s makes comparing decimals easier.

EXAMPLE Compare 0.3 and 0.06.

0.3 = 0.30 (Think about trading 3 longs for 30 cubes as above.)
30 cubes is more than 6 cubes.
30 hundredths is more than 6 hundredths.

0.30 > 0.06, so 0.3 > 0.06.

EXAMPLE Compare 0.97 and 1.

1 = 1.00 (Think about trading 1 flat for 100 cubes.)
97 cubes is less than 100 cubes.
97 hundredths is less than 100 hundredths.

0.97 < 1.00, so 0.97 < 1.

CHECK YOUR UNDERSTANDING

Compare the numbers in each pair.

1. 0.39, 0.039   **2.** 0.099, 0.2   **3.** $\frac{1}{4}$, 0.35   **4.** 0.99, 0.100

Check your answers on page 386.

Addition and Subtraction of Decimals

There are many ways to add and subtract decimals. One way is to use base-10 blocks. When working with decimals, we usually use a flat as the ONE.

ONE

To add with base-10 blocks, count out blocks for each number, put all the blocks together, make any trades for larger blocks that you can, then count the blocks for the sum.

To subtract with base-10 blocks, count out blocks for the larger number, take away blocks for the smaller number, then count the remaining blocks.

Using base-10 blocks is a good idea, especially at first. However, drawing shorthand pictures is usually easier and quicker.

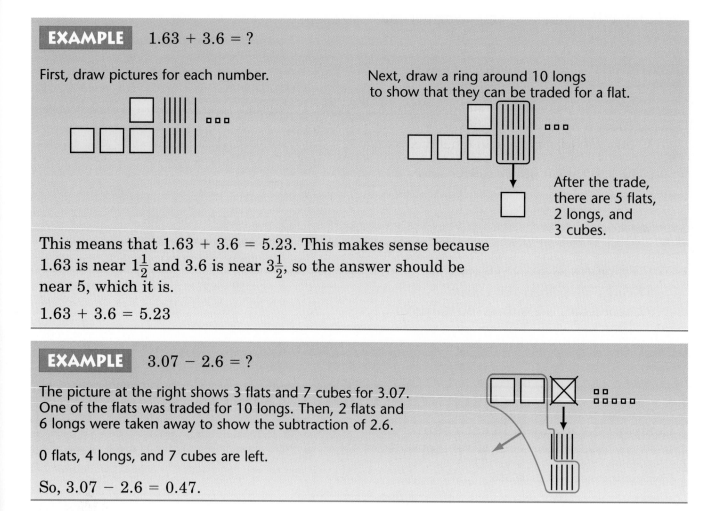

EXAMPLE   1.63 + 3.6 = ?

First, draw pictures for each number.

Next, draw a ring around 10 longs to show that they can be traded for a flat.

After the trade, there are 5 flats, 2 longs, and 3 cubes.

This means that 1.63 + 3.6 = 5.23. This makes sense because 1.63 is near $1\frac{1}{2}$ and 3.6 is near $3\frac{1}{2}$, so the answer should be near 5, which it is.

1.63 + 3.6 = 5.23

EXAMPLE   3.07 − 2.6 = ?

The picture at the right shows 3 flats and 7 cubes for 3.07. One of the flats was traded for 10 longs. Then, 2 flats and 6 longs were taken away to show the subtraction of 2.6.

0 flats, 4 longs, and 7 cubes are left.

So, 3.07 − 2.6 = 0.47.

Most paper-and-pencil strategies for adding and subtracting whole numbers also work for decimals. The main difference is that you have to line up the places correctly, either by adding 0s to the end of the numbers or by lining up the ones place.

EXAMPLES $4.56 + 7.9 = ?$

Partial-Sums Method:

	1s	0.1s	0.01s
	4 .	5	6
+	7 .	9	0

Add the ones.	$4 + 7 \rightarrow$	11 . 0	0
Add the tenths.	$0.5 + 0.9 \rightarrow$	1 . 4	0
Add the hundredths.	$0.06 + 0.00 \rightarrow$	0 . 0	6
Add the partial sums.	$11.00 + 1.40 + 0.06 \rightarrow$	**12** . **4**	**6**

Column-Addition Method:

	1s	0.1s	0.01s
	4 .	5	6
+	7 .	9	0
	11 .	14	6
	12 .	**4**	**6**

Move 10 tenths to the ones column:
14 tenths = 1 one and 4 tenths.
Trade the 1 one into the ones column.

$4.56 + 7.9 = 12.46$, using either method.

EXAMPLE $9.4 - 4.85 = ?$

Trade-First Method:

First, write the problem in vertical format, being sure to line up the places correctly. Also, since 4.85 has two decimal places, write 9.4 as 9.40.

1s	0.1s	0.01s
9 .	4	0
− 4 .	8	5

1s	0.1s	0.01s
	3	10
9 .	̶4̶	̶0̶
− 4 .	8	5

1s	0.1s	0.01s
	13	
8	̶3̶	10
̶9̶ .	̶4̶	̶0̶
− 4 .	8	5
4 .	5	5

Look at the 0.01s place. You cannot remove 5 hundredths from 0 hundredths.

So trade 1 tenth for 10 hundredths. Look at the 0.1s place. You cannot remove 8 tenths from 3 tenths.

So trade 1 one for 10 tenths. Now subtract in each column.

$9.4 - 4.85 = 4.55$

EXAMPLE   9.4 − 4.85 = ?

Left-to-Right Subtraction Method:

Again, since 4.85 has two decimal places, write 9.4 as 9.40.

$$
\begin{array}{r}
9.40 \\
\text{Subtract the ones.} \quad - 4.00 \\
\hline
5.40 \\
\text{Subtract the tenths.} \quad - 0.80 \\
\hline
4.60 \\
\text{Subtract the hundredths.} \quad - 0.05 \\
\hline
4.55 \\
\end{array}
$$

9.4 − 4.85 = 4.55

EXAMPLE   9.4 − 4.85 = ?

Counting-Up Method:

There are many ways to count up from 4.85 to 9.4. Here is one.

$$
\begin{array}{r}
4.85 \\
\boxed{+ 0.15} \\
\hline
5.00 \\
\boxed{+ 4.00} \\
\hline
9.00 \\
\boxed{+ 0.40} \\
\hline
9.40 \\
\end{array}
$$

Add the amounts you circled and counted up by:

$$
\begin{array}{r}
0.15 \\
4.00 \\
+ 0.40 \\
\hline
4.55 \\
\end{array}
$$

You counted up by 4.55, so 9.4 − 4.85 = 4.55.

Calculator:

If you use a calculator, it's important to check your answer by estimating because it's easy to accidentally press a wrong key.

CHECK YOUR UNDERSTANDING

Add or subtract.

1. 2.53 + 10.7

2. 2.08 − 0.39

3. 1.3 − 1.288

Check your answers on page 386.

Multiplying by Positive Powers of 10

Multiplying decimals by a positive power of 10 is easy. One way is to use **partial-products multiplication.**

N O T E

Some positive powers of 10 are

$10^1 = 10$

$10^2 = 10 * 10 = 100$

$10^3 = 10 * 10 * 10$
$\quad = 1,000$

$10^4 = 10 * 10 * 10 * 10$
$\quad = 10,000$

EXAMPLE Solve 1,000 * 45.6 by partial-products multiplication.

Step 1: Solve the problem as if there were no decimal point.

$$
\begin{array}{r}
1000 \\
*\quad 456 \\
\hline
\end{array}
$$

$$
\begin{array}{rr}
400 * 1000 \rightarrow & 400000 \\
50 * 1000 \rightarrow & 50000 \\
6 * 1000 \rightarrow & 6000 \\
\hline
& 456000
\end{array}
$$

Step 2: Estimate the answer to 1,000 * 45.6 and place the decimal point where it belongs.

1,000 * 45 = 45,000, so 1,000 * 45.6 must be near 45,000.

So, the answer to 1,000 * 45.6 is 45,600.

Another way to multiply a number by a positive power of 10 is just to move the decimal point. Think of this as a *shortcut*.

EXAMPLE 1,000 * 45.6 = ?

Locate the decimal point in the power of 10.

1,000 = 1000.

Move the decimal point LEFT until you get the number 1.

1.0 0 0.

Count the number of places you moved the decimal point.

3 places

Move the decimal point in the other factor the same number of places, but to the RIGHT. Insert 0s as needed. That's the answer.

4 5.6 0 0.

So, 1,000 * 45.6 = 45,600

CHECK YOUR UNDERSTANDING

Multiply.

1. 100 * 3.45   **2.** 0.16 * 10,000   **3.** 1,000 * $5.50   **4.** 1.08 * 10

Check your answers on page 386.

Multiplication of Decimals

You can use the same procedures for multiplying decimals as you use for whole numbers. The main difference is that with decimals you have to decide where to place the decimal point in the product.

One way to solve multiplication problems with decimals is to multiply as if both factors were whole numbers, then adjust the product:

Step 1. Make a magnitude estimate of the product.

Step 2. Multiply as if the factors were whole numbers.

Step 3. Use the magnitude estimate to place the decimal point in the answer.

> **N O T E**
>
> A *magnitude estimate* is a very rough estimate that answers questions like: *Is the solution in the ones? Tens? Hundreds? Thousands?* A magnitude estimate helps you judge whether the solution to a problem is "in the ballpark."

EXAMPLE $15.2 * 3.6 = ?$

Step 1: Make a magnitude estimate.
- Round 15.2 to 20 and 3.6 to 4.
- Since $20 * 4 = 80$, the product will be in the tens. (*In the tens* means between 10 and 100.)

Step 2: Multiply as you would with whole numbers using the partial-products method. Work from left to right. Ignore the decimal points.

$$
\begin{array}{r}
152 \\
* \ 36 \\
\hline
\end{array}
$$

30 * 100	→	3000
30 * 50	→	1500
30 * 2	→	60
6 * 100	→	600
6 * 50	→	300
6 * 2	→	12
		5472

Step 3: Place the decimal point correctly in the answer.
Since the magnitude estimate is in the tens, the product must be in the tens. Place the decimal point between the 4 and the 7 in 5472.

So, $15.2 * 3.6 = 54.72$.

EXAMPLE   3.27 * 0.8 = ?

Step 1: Make a magnitude estimate.
- Round 3.27 to 3 and 0.8 to 1.
- Since 3 * 1 = 3, the product will be in the ones.
  (*In the ones* means between 1 and 10.)

Step 2: Multiply as you would with whole numbers. Ignore the decimal points.

$$
\begin{array}{rcr}
 & & \mathbf{327} \\
 & & *\quad\mathbf{8} \\
 & & \overline{} \\
8 * 300 & \rightarrow & 2400 \\
8 * 20 & \rightarrow & 160 \\
8 * 7 & \rightarrow & 56 \\
2400 + 160 + 56 & \rightarrow & \mathbf{2616}
\end{array}
$$

Step 3: Place the decimal point correctly in the answer.
Since the magnitude estimate is in the ones, the product must be in the ones. Place the decimal point between the 2 and the 6 in 2616.

So, 3.27 * 0.8 = 2.616.

There is another way to find where to place the decimal point in the product. This method is especially useful when the factors are less than 1 and have many decimal places.

EXAMPLE   3.27 * 0.8 = ?

Count the decimal places in each factor.	2 decimal places in 3.27 1 decimal place in 0.8
Add the number of decimal places. This is how many decimal places there will be in the product.	2 + 1 = 3
Multiply the factors as if they were whole numbers.	327 * 8 = 2616
Start at the right of the product. Move left the necessary number of decimal places.	2.6 1 6.

So, 3.27 * 0.8 = 2.616.

CHECK YOUR UNDERSTANDING

Multiply.

1. 2.8 * 4.6   **2.** 1.44 * 9.3   **3.** 0.52 * 3.03   **4.** 0.2 * 0.016

Check your answers on page 386.

Lattice Multiplication with Decimals

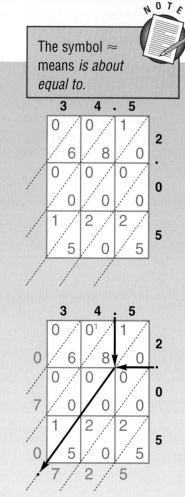

NOTE

The symbol ≈ means *is about equal to.*

EXAMPLE Find 34.5 * 2.05 using lattice multiplication.

Step 1: Make a magnitude estimate. 34.5 * 2.05 ≈ 35 * 2 = 70
The product will be in the tens.

Step 2: Draw the lattice and write the factors, including the decimal points, at the top and right side. In the factor above the grid, the decimal point should be above a column line. In the factor on the right side of the grid, the decimal point should be to the right of a row line.

Step 3: Find the products inside the lattice.

Step 4: Add along the diagonals moving from right to left.

Step 5: Locate the decimal point in the answer as follows. Slide the decimal point in the factor above the grid down along the column line. Slide the decimal point in the factor on the right side of the grid across the row line. When the decimal points meet, slide the decimal point down along the diagonal line. Write a decimal point at the end of the diagonal line.

Step 6: Compare the result with the estimate.

The product, 70.725, is very close to the estimate of 70.

EXAMPLE Find 73.4 * 10.5 using lattice multiplication.

A good magnitude estimate is 73.4 * 10.5 ≈ 73 * 10 = 730.

The product, 770.70, is close to the estimate of 730.

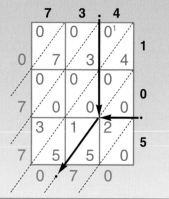

CHECK YOUR UNDERSTANDING

Draw a lattice for each problem and multiply.

1. 24.5 * 3.5   **2.** 3.02 * 19   **3.** 6.7 * 25.2

Check your answers on page 386.

Dividing by Positive Powers of 10

Here is one method for dividing by a positive power of 10.

Some powers of 10:

$10^1 = 10$
$10^2 = 100$
$10^3 = 1,000$
$10^4 = 10,000$
$10^5 = 100,000$
$10^6 = 1,000,000$

EXAMPLE   45.6 / 1,000 = ?

Step 1: Locate the decimal point in the power of 10.

1,000 = 1000.

Step 2: Move the decimal point LEFT until you get the number 1.

1,0 0 0.

Step 3: Count the number of places you moved the decimal point.

3 places

Step 4: Move the decimal point in the other number the same number of places to the LEFT. Insert 0s as needed.

0.0 4 5.6

45.6 / 1,000 = 0.0456

EXAMPLES

350 / 100 = ?

100 = 100.

1.0 0.

2 places

3.5 0.

350 / 100 = 3.50

350 / 10,000 = ?

10,000 = 10000.

1.0 0 0 0.

4 places

0.0 3 5 0.

350 / 10,000 = 0.0350

$290.50 / 1,000 = ?

1,000 = 1000.

1.0 0 0.

3 places

0.2 9 0.5 0

$290.50 / 1,000 = $0.29

Note: When the dividend (the number you are dividing) does not have a decimal point, you must locate the decimal point before moving it. For example, 350 = 350.

CHECK YOUR UNDERSTANDING

Divide.

1. 67.8 / 10   **2.** 0.54 / 100   **3.** $290 / 1,000   **4.** 40 / 10,000

Check your answers on page 386.

Division of Decimals

Here is one way to divide decimals:

Step 1: Make a magnitude estimate of the quotient.

Step 2: Divide as if the divisor and dividend were whole numbers.

Step 3: Use the magnitude estimate to place the decimal point in the answer.

> **NOTE**
>
> A **magnitude estimate** is a rough estimate of the size of an answer. A magnitude estimate tells whether an answer is in the ones, tens, hundreds, and so on.

EXAMPLE   97.24 / 26 = ?

Step 1: Make a magnitude estimate.

• Since 26 is close to 25 and 97.24 is close to 100, the answer to 97.24 / 26 will be close to the answer to 100 / 25.

• Since 100 / 25 = 4, the answer to 97.24 / 26 should be in the ones. (*In the ones* means between 1 and 10.)

Step 2: Divide, ignoring the decimal point.

```
26)9724
 − 7800  | 300
   1924
 − 1040  |  40
    884
 −  780  |  30
    104
 −  104  |   4
      0  | 374
```

9724 / 26 = 374

Step 3: Decide where to place the decimal point. According to the magnitude estimate, the answer should be in the ones.

So, 97.24 / 26 = 3.74.

CHECK YOUR UNDERSTANDING

Divide.

1. 208.8 / 6   **2.** 31.32 / 12   **3.** 4.90 / 3.5

Check your answers on page 386.

The answers to decimal divisions do not always come out even.

> The symbol $\approx$ means *is about equal to.*

EXAMPLE 80.27 / 4 = ?

Make a magnitude estimate.

- Since 80.27 is close to 80, 80.27 / 4 $\approx$ 80 / 4.
- Since 80 / 4 = 20, the answer to 80.27 / 4 should be in the tens. (*In the tens* means between 10 and 100.)

Divide, ignoring the decimal point.

```
4)8027
 − 8000    2000
    27
  − 24        6
     3     2006
```

8027 / 4 → 2006 R3. The quotient is 2006, and the remainder is 3.
Write the remainder as a fraction: 8027 / 4 = $2006\frac{3}{4}$.
Round this answer to the nearest whole number, 2007.

Decide where to put the decimal point. According to the magnitude estimate, the answer should be in the tens.

So, 80.27 / 4 = 20.07.

CHECK YOUR UNDERSTANDING

Divide.

1. 9.4 / 3

2. 76.8 / 24

3. 56.9 / 3

Check your answers on page 386.

Column Division with Decimal Quotients

Column division can be used to find quotients that have a decimal part. In the example below, think of sharing $15 among 4 people.

EXAMPLE 4)‾15‾ = ?

1. Draw a line to separate the digits in the number being divided. Work left to right. Think of the 1 in the tens column as 1 $10 bill.

```
       |
4)  1  | 5
```

2. The 1 $10 bill cannot be shared by 4 people. So trade it for 10 $1 bills. Think of the 5 in the ones column as 5 $1 bills. That makes 10 + 5, or 15 $1 bills in all.

```
       |
4)  1̶  | 5̶
       |
       | 15
```

3. If 4 people share 15 $1 bills, each person gets 3 $1 bills. There are 3 $1 bills left over.

```
        3  |
4)  1̶   | 5̶
        |
        | 15
        |
        | −12
        |‾‾‾‾
        |  3
```

4. Trade the 3 $1 bills for 30 dimes. Use decimal points to show that the amounts are now smaller than $1.

```
             3.  |
4)   1̶   |  5̶.  | 30
             |
             | 15
             |
             | −12
             |‾‾‾‾
             |  3̶
```

5. If 4 people share 30 dimes, each person gets 7 dimes. There are 2 dimes left over.

```
            3.  |  7
4)   1̶  |  5̶.  | 30
            |
            | 15  | −28
            |     |‾‾‾‾
            | −12 |  2
            |‾‾‾‾
            |  3̶
```

6. Trade the 2 dimes for 20 pennies.

```
            3.  |  7
4)   1̶  |  5̶.  | 30 | 20
            |
            | 15  | −28
            |     |‾‾‾‾
            | −12 |  2̶
            |‾‾‾‾
            |  3̶
```

7. If 4 people share 20 pennies, each person gets 5 pennies.

```
            3.  |  7  |  5
4)   1̶  |  5̶.  | 30 | 20
            |
            | 15  | −28 | −20
            |     |‾‾‾‾ |‾‾‾‾
            | −12 |  2̶  |  0
            |‾‾‾‾
            |  3̶
```

The column division shows that
15 / 4 = 3.75.
This means that $15 shared among 4 people is $3.75 each.

Rounding Decimals

Sometimes numbers have more digits than we need to use. This is especially true of decimals. When a calculator is used for a calculation, the display may show eight or more decimal places, even when only one or two places are needed to make sense.

Rounding is a way to get rid of unnecessary digits. There are three basic ways to round numbers: a number may be rounded down, rounded up, or rounded to a nearest place. (The examples here involve rounding to hundredths, but rounding to tenths, thousandths, or any other place is done in a similar way.)

Rounding Down

To round down to a given place, just drop all the digits to the right of the desired place.

When a bank computes the interest on a savings account, the interest is calculated to the nearest tenth of a cent. But the bank cannot pay a fraction of one cent. So the interest is **rounded down,** and any fraction of one cent is ignored.

> **EXAMPLE** The bank calculates the interest earned as $17.218. Round down to the next cent.
>
> First, find the place you are rounding to: $17.2**1**8.
> Then, drop all the digits to the right of that place: $17.21.
>
> The bank pays $17.21 in interest.

Rounding Up

To round up, look at all the digits to the right of the desired place. If any digit to the right of the desired place is not 0, then add 1 to the digit in the place you are rounding to. (You will have to do some trading if there is a 9 in that place.) If all the digits to the right of the desired place are 0, then leave the digit unchanged. Finally, drop all the digits to the right of the desired place.

Running events at the Olympic Games are timed with automatic electric timers. The electric timer records a time to the nearest thousandth of a second and automatically **rounds up** to the *next* hundredth of a second. The rounded time becomes the official time.

EXAMPLES   The winning time was 11.437 seconds.

Round up 11.437 seconds to the next hundredth of a second.

First, find the place you are rounding to: 11.4**3**7.
The digit to the right is not 0, so add 1 to the digit you're rounding to: 11.4**4**7.
Finally, drop all digits to the right of hundredths: 11.44.

The official winning time is 11.44 seconds.

11.431 seconds is rounded up to 11.44 seconds.

11.430 seconds is rounded up to 11.43 seconds because every digit to right of the hundredths place is a 0. In this problem, rounding up does not change the number at all:
11.43 equals 11.430.

Rounding to the Nearest Place

Rounding to the nearest place is sometimes like rounding up and sometimes like rounding down. To round to the nearest place, follow these steps:

Step 1: Find the digit to the right of the place you are rounding to.

Step 2: If that digit is 5 or more, round up. If that digit is less than 5, round down.

EXAMPLES   Mr. Wilson is labeling the grocery shelves with unit prices so customers can compare the cost of items. To find a unit price, he divides the quantity by the price. Often, the quotient has more decimal places than are needed, so he **rounds to the nearest** cent (the nearest hundredth).

$1.23422 is rounded down to $1.23.

$3.89822 is rounded up to $3.90.

$1.865 is rounded up to $1.87.

CHECK YOUR UNDERSTANDING

1. Round *down* to tenths.   **a.** 2.53   **b.** 45.891   **c.** 0.96

2. Round *up* to tenths.   **a.** 2.53   **b.** 45.891   **c.** 0.96

3. Round to the *nearest* tenth.   **a.** 2.53   **b.** 45.89   **c.** 10.96

Check your answers on page 386.

Percents

A percent is another way to name a fraction or decimal. **Percent** means *per hundred,* or *out of a hundred.* The word *percent* comes from the Latin *per centum: per* means *for* and *centum* means *one hundred.*

The statement "60% of students were absent" means that 60 out of 100 students were absent. This does *not* mean that there were exactly 100 students and that 60 of them were absent. It does mean that for *every* 100 students, 60 students were absent.

A percent usually represents a percent of something. The "something" is the whole (or ONE, or 100%). In the statement, "60% of the students were absent," the whole is the total number of students in the school.

Percents are used in many ways in everyday life:

- *Business*: "50% off" means that the price of an item will be reduced by 50 cents for every 100 cents the item usually costs.

Sale—50% Off
Everything Must Go

- *Statistics*: "55% voter turnout" means that 55 out of every 100 registered voters will actually vote.

Voter Turnout Pegged at 55% of Registered Voters

- *School*: An 80% score on a spelling test means that a student scored 80 out of 100 possible points for that test. One way to score 80% is to spell 80 words correctly out of 100. Another way to score 80% is to spell 8 words correctly out of 10.

- *Probability*: A "30% chance of showers" means that for every 100 days that have similar weather conditions, you would expect it to rain on 30 of the days.

For Wednesday, there is a 30% chance of showers.

Percents that Name Part of a Whole

Fractions, decimals, and percents are simply different ways to write numbers. Any number can be written in any of these three ways.

EXAMPLE

The amounts shown in the pictures below can be written as $\frac{1}{4}$, or 25%, or 0.25.

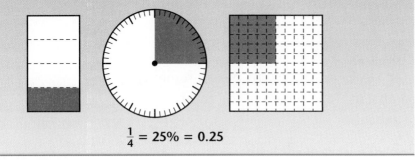

$$\frac{1}{4} = 25\% = 0.25$$

Percents are another way of naming fractions with a denominator of 100.

> You can think of the fraction $\frac{25}{100}$ as 25 parts per hundred, or 25 out of every 100, and write 25%.

> You can rename the fraction $\frac{1}{5}$ as $\frac{1 * 20}{5 * 20}$, or $\frac{20}{100}$, or 20%.

> 75% can be written as $\frac{75}{100}$, or $\frac{3}{4}$.

Percents are another way of naming decimals in terms of hundredths.

> Since 0.01 can be written as $\frac{1}{100}$, you could think of 0.39 as $\frac{39}{100}$, or 39%.

> 58% means 58 hundredths, or 0.58.

Percents can also be used to name the whole.

> 100 out of 100 can be written as the fraction $\frac{100}{100}$, or 100 hundredths. This is the same as 1 whole, or 100%.

Finding a Percent of a Number

Finding a percent of a number is a basic problem that comes up over and over again.

A backpack that regularly sells for $40 is on sale for 20% off. What is the sale price?

The sales tax on food is 5%. What is the tax on $60 worth of groceries?

A borrower pays 10% interest on a car loan. If the loan is $5,000, how much is the interest?

There are many different ways of finding the percent of a number.

Use a Fraction

Some percents are equivalent to "easy" fractions. For example, 25% is the same as $\frac{1}{4}$. It is usually easier to find 25% of a number by thinking of 25% as $\frac{1}{4}$.

EXAMPLE What is 25% of 48?

Think: $25\% = \frac{25}{100} = \frac{1}{4}$, so 25% of 48 is the same as $\frac{1}{4}$ of 48. If you divide 48 into 4 equal groups, each group has 12.

So, 25% of 48 is 12.

EXAMPLE What is 20% of 60?

Think: $20\% = \frac{20}{100} = \frac{1}{5}$, so 20% of 60 is the same as $\frac{1}{5}$ of 60. If you divide 60 into 5 groups, there are 12 in each group.

So, 20% of 60 is 12.

Decimals and Percents

If a percent does not equal an "easy" fraction, you might find
1% first.

EXAMPLE   What is 7% of 300?

$1\% = \frac{1}{100}$, so 1% of 300 is the same as $\frac{1}{100}$ of 300.

If you divide 300 into 100 equal groups, there are 3 in each group.
1% of 300 is 3. Then 7% of 300 is 7 * 3.

So, 7% of 300 = 21.

Sometimes it is helpful to find 10% first.

EXAMPLE   What is 30% of 60?

$10\% = \frac{10}{100} = \frac{1}{10}$. 10% of 60 is $\frac{1}{10}$ of 60. If you divide 60 into 10 equal
groups, each group has 6. 10% of 60 is 6. Then 30% of 60 is 3 * 6.

So, 30% of 60 = 18.

Use Decimal Multiplication

Finding a percent of a number is the same as multiplying the
number by the percent. Usually, it's easiest to change the
percent to a decimal and use a calculator.

EXAMPLE   What is 35% of 55?

$35\% = \frac{35}{100} = 0.35$

First, change the percent to a decimal, then multiply using a calculator.

Key in: 0.35 ⊗ 55 Ⓔⁿᵗᵉʳ   Answer: 19.25

If your calculator has a Ⓟ key, you don't need to rename the percent
as a decimal. To find 35% of 55, key in 35 Ⓟ ⊗ 55 Ⓔⁿᵗᵉʳ.

35% of 55 is 19.25.

CHECK YOUR UNDERSTANDING

Solve.

1. A backpack that regularly sells for $40 is on sale for 20% off.
   What is the sale price?

2. The sales tax on food is 5%. What is the tax on $60 worth of groceries?

3. A borrower pays 10% interest on a car loan.
   If the loan is $5,000, how much is the interest?

Check your answers on page 386.

Calculating a Discount

A **discount** is an amount taken off a regular price; it's the amount you save. Sometimes stores display the regular price and the percent of discount and the customer has to figure out the sale price.

If the percent discount is equivalent to an "easy" fraction, then a good way to solve this kind of problem is by using the fraction.

> **EXAMPLE**   The list price for a computer joystick is $50, but it is on sale at a 20% discount (20% less than the list price). What are the savings?
>
> Change 20% to a fraction: $20\% = \frac{20}{100} = \frac{1}{5}$
>
> Since $20\% = \frac{1}{5}$, the discount is $\frac{1}{5}$ of $50.
>
> $\frac{1}{5} * \$50 = \frac{1}{5} * \frac{\$50}{1} = \frac{1 * \$50}{5 * 1} = \frac{\$50}{5} = \$10$
>
> The discount is $10.

If the percent discount is not equivalent to an "easy" fraction, it's usually best to change the percent to a decimal first, then to multiply with paper and pencil or a calculator.

> **EXAMPLES**   The list price for a lamp is $45. The lamp is sold at a 12% discount (12% off the list price). What are the savings? (*Reminder*: $12\% = \frac{12}{100} = 0.12$)
>
> **Paper and pencil:** $12\% \text{ of } \$45 = \frac{12}{100} * 45 = \frac{12}{100} * \frac{45}{1}$
> $$= \frac{540}{100}$$
> $$= \$5.40$$
>
> **Calculator:**
>
> Key in: 0.12 ⓧ 45 ⏎. Interpret the answer, 5.4, as $5.40.
> The discount is $5.40.

CHECK YOUR UNDERSTANDING

Solve.

1. The list price of a pair of jeans is $20. The jeans are being sold at a 10% discount. What are the savings?

2. Movie tickets regularly cost $8.00, but for shows starting before 4 P.M. there is a 25% discount. How much cheaper are the early shows?

Check your answers on page 387.

Finding the Whole in Percent Problems

Sometimes you know a percent and how much it's worth, but you don't know what the ONE is.

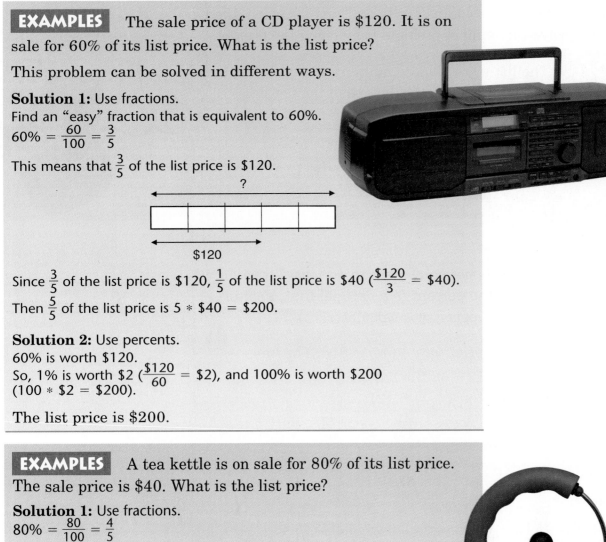

EXAMPLES The sale price of a CD player is $120. It is on sale for 60% of its list price. What is the list price?

This problem can be solved in different ways.

Solution 1: Use fractions.
Find an "easy" fraction that is equivalent to 60%.

$60\% = \frac{60}{100} = \frac{3}{5}$

This means that $\frac{3}{5}$ of the list price is $120.

Since $\frac{3}{5}$ of the list price is $120, $\frac{1}{5}$ of the list price is $40 ($\frac{\$120}{3} = \$40$).

Then $\frac{5}{5}$ of the list price is 5 ∗ $40 = $200.

Solution 2: Use percents.
60% is worth $120.
So, 1% is worth $2 ($\frac{\$120}{60} = \$2$), and 100% is worth $200
(100 ∗ $2 = $200).

The list price is $200.

EXAMPLES A tea kettle is on sale for 80% of its list price. The sale price is $40. What is the list price?

Solution 1: Use fractions.
$80\% = \frac{80}{100} = \frac{4}{5}$

This means that $\frac{4}{5}$ of the list price is $40.

Since $\frac{4}{5}$ of the list price is $40, $\frac{1}{5}$ of the list price is $10 ($\frac{\$40}{4} = \$10$).

Then $\frac{5}{5}$ of the list price is 5 ∗ $10 = $50.

Solution 2: Use percents.
80% is worth $40.
So, 1% is worth $0.50 ($\frac{\$40}{80} = \$0.50$), and 100% is worth $50
(100 ∗ $0.50 = $50).

The list price is $50.

EXAMPLE In the United States, there are about 60 million children aged 14 and younger. These children make up about 22% of the U.S. population. What is the U.S. population?

Use a 1% strategy. First find 1%. Then multiply by 100 to get 100%.

• Use your calculator to divide 60 million by 22:

Key in: 60,000,000 ➗ 22 ⎡Enter⎤   Answer: 2727272.727

• Multiply by 100:

Key in: 100 ✖ 2727272.727 ⎡Enter⎤   Answer: 272727272.7

The total U.S. population is 272,727,272.7, or about 273 million.

CHECK YOUR UNDERSTANDING

Solve.

1. A bicycle is on sale for 50% of the list price. The sale price is $80. What is the list price?

2. A cellular telephone is on sale for 20% of the list price. The sale price is $30. What is the list price?

3. In Canada, there are about 6 million children aged 14 and younger. These children make up about 19% of Canada's population. What is the population of Canada?

Check your answers on page 387.

The Whole Circle

One full turn of a circle can be divided in various ways. One way is to divide it into four parts: a quarter turn, a half turn, three-fourths (or three-quarters) of a turn, and a full turn. A full turn can also be broken into 360 or 100 parts.

A Circle Protractor

There are 360 equally spaced marks around the edge of the Circle Protractor. Each mark measures **one degree (1°)** of angle measure. That means there are 360 degrees (360°) in the whole circle.

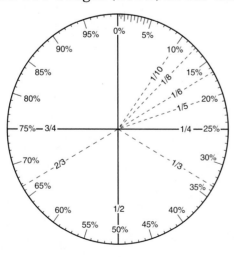

The Percent Circle

There are 100 equally spaced marks around the edge of the Percent Circle. The marks define 100 thin, pie-shaped wedges. Each wedge contains **one percent (1%)** of the total area of the circle. There are 100 wedges (100%) in the whole circle.

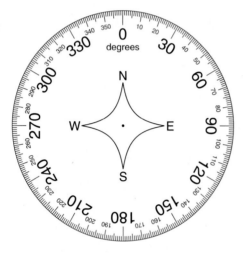

Fractions &
Rational Numbers

Fractions

Fractions were invented thousands of years ago to name numbers between whole numbers. People probably first used these in-between numbers for making more exact measurements.

The stone must be exactly five and two-thirds cubits high.

Today most rulers and other measuring tools have marks to name numbers that are in-between whole measures. Learning how to read these in-between marks is an important part of learning to use these tools.

Fractions are used not only in measurement. Many fractions are used to name parts of wholes. The whole might be one single thing, like a cake, or it might be a collection, like a carton of eggs. In *Everyday Mathematics,* the whole is sometimes called the ONE. In measurements, the whole is called the *unit.*

Whole
24 Cookies

The "whole" box names the ONE being considered.

To understand fractions like these you need to know what the ONE is. Half a package of cookies might be many cookies or a few cookies depending on the size of the package. Half an inch is much less than half a mile.

COOKIES

Fractions are also used to show division, in rates and ratios, and in many other ways.

Naming Fractions

Fractions are written as $\frac{a}{b}$, where a can be any number at all and b can be any number except 0. The number below the fraction bar is called the **denominator.** In fractions that name parts of wholes, the denominator names the number of equal parts into which the whole is divided. The number above the fraction bar is called the **numerator.** The numerator names the number of parts under consideration.

$$\frac{a}{b} \begin{array}{l} \leftarrow \text{numerator} \\ \leftarrow \text{denominator} \end{array}$$
$$b \neq 0$$

A number can be written as a fraction in many ways. Fractions that name the same number are called **equivalent.** Multiplying or dividing a fraction's numerator and denominator by the same number (except 0) results in an equivalent fraction. Numbers also have decimal and percent names, which can be found from any of its fraction names by dividing the numerator by the denominator.

$$\frac{1}{2} = \frac{2}{4} = \frac{3}{6} = 0.5 = 50\%$$
$$\frac{1}{3} = \frac{2}{6} = \frac{3}{9} = 0.\overline{3} = 33\frac{1}{3}\%$$

Two fractions can be compared, added, or subtracted by using equivalent fractions with the same denominator.

Fraction Uses

Fractions can be used in many ways.

Parts of Wholes

Fractions are used to name a part of a whole object or a part of a collection of objects.

$\frac{5}{6}$ of the hexagon is shaded.

$\frac{6}{10}$ of the dimes are circled.

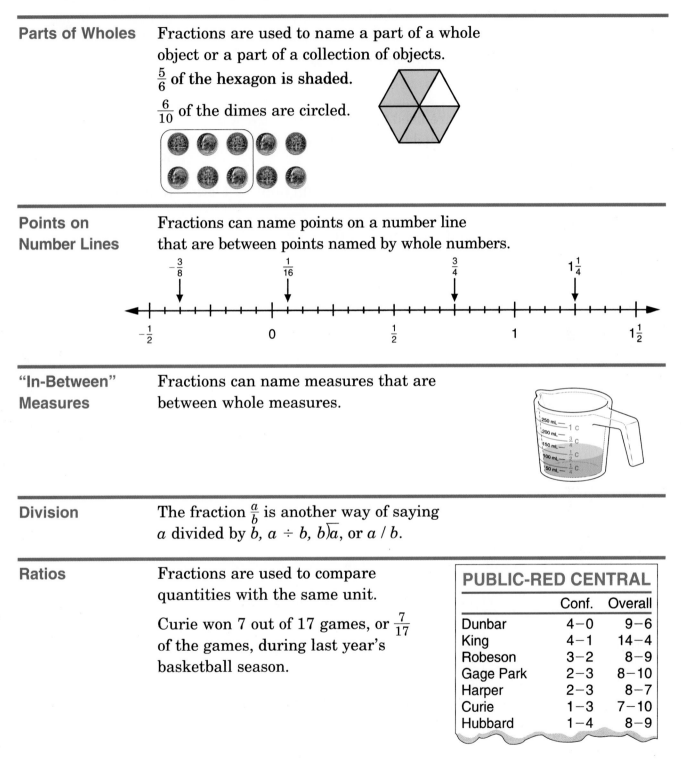

Points on Number Lines

Fractions can name points on a number line that are between points named by whole numbers.

"In-Between" Measures

Fractions can name measures that are between whole measures.

Division

The fraction $\frac{a}{b}$ is another way of saying a divided by b, $a \div b$, $b\overline{)a}$, or $a\,/\,b$.

Ratios

Fractions are used to compare quantities with the same unit.

Curie won 7 out of 17 games, or $\frac{7}{17}$ of the games, during last year's basketball season.

PUBLIC-RED CENTRAL		
	Conf.	Overall
Dunbar	4−0	9−6
King	4−1	14−4
Robeson	3−2	8−9
Gage Park	2−3	8−10
Harper	2−3	8−7
Curie	1−3	7−10
Hubbard	1−4	8−9

Rates

Fractions are used to compare quantities with different units.

Bill's car can travel about 35 miles on 1 gallon of gasoline. At this rate, it can travel about 245 miles on 7 gallons of gasoline.

$$\frac{35 \text{ miles}}{1 \text{ gallon}} = \frac{245 \text{ miles}}{7 \text{ gallons}}$$

Scale Drawings, Scale Models, and Map Scales

Fractions are used to compare the size of a drawing or model to the size of the actual object.

A scale on a map given as 1:100,000 (another way of expressing $\frac{1}{100,000}$) means that each inch on the map represents 100,000 inches, or about $1\frac{1}{2}$ miles.

SCALE 1:100,000

1 inch = 100,000 inches = $1\frac{1}{2}$ miles

Probabilities

Fractions are a way to describe the chance that an event will happen.

In a well-shuffled deck of 52 playing cards, the chance of selecting the ace of spades on a given draw is $\frac{1}{52}$, or about 2%. The chance of drawing any ace is $\frac{4}{52}$, or about 8%.

Miscellaneous

People use fractions in a variety of ways every day.

A film critic gave the new movie $3\frac{1}{2}$ stars.

The stock closed at $14\frac{5}{8}$ — down $1\frac{1}{2}$ dollars from yesterday.

Your half-birthday is 6 months after your birthday.

It was a half-baked idea — I'm not surprised that it didn't work.

Equivalent Fractions

Fractions are called **equivalent** if they represent the same amount. The fractions $\frac{1}{2}$, $\frac{2}{4}$, and $\frac{3}{6}$ are equivalent. When you solve problems with fractions, it can often be easier to work with equivalent fractions instead of the given fractions.

Using the Fraction-Stick Chart

To use the Fraction-Stick Chart to find equivalent fractions, first locate the fraction. Then use a vertical straightedge to find equivalent fractions. You can find a large Fraction-Stick Chart on page 357.

EXAMPLE   Find equivalent fractions for $\frac{3}{4}$.

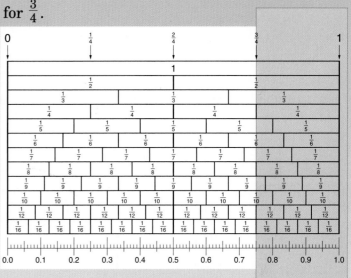

- Locate $\frac{3}{4}$ on the "fourths" stick.
- Place one edge of a straightedge at $\frac{3}{4}$.
- On the "eighths" stick, the straightedge touches the edge of the sixth piece, which is $\frac{6}{8}$.

So, $\frac{3}{4} = \frac{6}{8}$.

- On the "twelfths" stick, the straightedge touches the edge of the ninth piece, which is $\frac{9}{12}$.

So, $\frac{3}{4} = \frac{9}{12}$.

- On the "sixteenths" stick, the straightedge touches the edge of the twelfth piece, which is $\frac{12}{16}$.

So, $\frac{3}{4} = \frac{12}{16}$.

- The straightedge doesn't line up with an edge of any other sticks on the chart, so $\frac{3}{4}$ cannot be written as an equivalent fraction using those sticks.

CHECK YOUR UNDERSTANDING

Use the Fraction-Stick Chart to find equivalent fractions.

1. $\frac{1}{2}$ **2.** $\frac{1}{3}$ **3.** $\frac{5}{6}$

Check your answers on page 387.

Methods for Finding Equivalent Fractions

Here are two methods for finding equivalent fractions.

Using Multiplication

If the numerator and the denominator of a fraction are both multiplied by the same number (not 0), the result is a fraction that is equivalent to the original fraction.

> **EXAMPLE** Rename $\frac{3}{7}$ as a fraction with the denominator 21.
>
> Multiply the numerator and the denominator of $\frac{3}{7}$ by 3.
>
> In symbols, you can write $\frac{3}{7} = \frac{3 * 3}{7 * 3} = \frac{9}{21}$
>
> So, $\frac{3}{7}$ is equivalent to $\frac{9}{21}$.

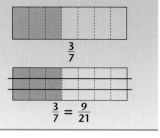

Using Division

If the numerator and the denominator of a fraction are both divided by the same number (not 0), the result is a fraction that is equivalent to the original fraction.

To understand why division works, think about "undoing" the multiplication. Since division "undoes" multiplication, divide the numerator and the denominator by the same number to find an equivalent fraction.

> **EXAMPLE** $\frac{6}{15} = \frac{6 \div 3}{15 \div 3} = \frac{2}{5}$

CHECK YOUR UNDERSTANDING

1. Use multiplication to find an equivalent for each fraction.

   a. $\frac{3}{4}$ **b.** $\frac{5}{8}$ **c.** $\frac{4}{5}$ **d.** $\frac{2}{7}$

2. Use division to find an equivalent for each fraction.

   a. $\frac{9}{12}$ **b.** $\frac{15}{25}$ **c.** $\frac{24}{36}$ **d.** $\frac{75}{100}$

Check your answers on page 387.

Table of Equivalent Fractions

Simplest Name	Equivalent Fraction Name								
0 (zero)	$\frac{0}{1}$	$\frac{0}{2}$	$\frac{0}{3}$	$\frac{0}{4}$	$\frac{0}{5}$	$\frac{0}{6}$	$\frac{0}{7}$	$\frac{0}{8}$	$\frac{0}{9}$
1 (one)	$\frac{1}{1}$	$\frac{2}{2}$	$\frac{3}{3}$	$\frac{4}{4}$	$\frac{5}{5}$	$\frac{6}{6}$	$\frac{7}{7}$	$\frac{8}{8}$	$\frac{9}{9}$
$\frac{1}{2}$	$\frac{2}{4}$	$\frac{3}{6}$	$\frac{4}{8}$	$\frac{5}{10}$	$\frac{6}{12}$	$\frac{7}{14}$	$\frac{8}{16}$	$\frac{9}{18}$	$\frac{10}{20}$
$\frac{1}{3}$	$\frac{2}{6}$	$\frac{3}{9}$	$\frac{4}{12}$	$\frac{5}{15}$	$\frac{6}{18}$	$\frac{7}{21}$	$\frac{8}{24}$	$\frac{9}{27}$	$\frac{10}{30}$
$\frac{2}{3}$	$\frac{4}{6}$	$\frac{6}{9}$	$\frac{8}{12}$	$\frac{10}{15}$	$\frac{12}{18}$	$\frac{14}{21}$	$\frac{16}{24}$	$\frac{18}{27}$	$\frac{20}{30}$
$\frac{1}{4}$	$\frac{2}{8}$	$\frac{3}{12}$	$\frac{4}{16}$	$\frac{5}{20}$	$\frac{6}{24}$	$\frac{7}{28}$	$\frac{8}{32}$	$\frac{9}{36}$	$\frac{10}{40}$
$\frac{3}{4}$	$\frac{6}{8}$	$\frac{9}{12}$	$\frac{12}{16}$	$\frac{15}{20}$	$\frac{18}{24}$	$\frac{21}{28}$	$\frac{24}{32}$	$\frac{27}{36}$	$\frac{30}{40}$
$\frac{1}{5}$	$\frac{2}{10}$	$\frac{3}{15}$	$\frac{4}{20}$	$\frac{5}{25}$	$\frac{6}{30}$	$\frac{7}{35}$	$\frac{8}{40}$	$\frac{9}{45}$	$\frac{10}{50}$
$\frac{2}{5}$	$\frac{4}{10}$	$\frac{6}{15}$	$\frac{8}{20}$	$\frac{10}{25}$	$\frac{12}{30}$	$\frac{14}{35}$	$\frac{16}{40}$	$\frac{18}{45}$	$\frac{20}{50}$
$\frac{3}{5}$	$\frac{6}{10}$	$\frac{9}{15}$	$\frac{12}{20}$	$\frac{15}{25}$	$\frac{18}{30}$	$\frac{21}{35}$	$\frac{24}{40}$	$\frac{27}{45}$	$\frac{30}{50}$
$\frac{4}{5}$	$\frac{8}{10}$	$\frac{12}{15}$	$\frac{16}{20}$	$\frac{20}{25}$	$\frac{24}{30}$	$\frac{28}{35}$	$\frac{32}{40}$	$\frac{36}{45}$	$\frac{40}{50}$
$\frac{1}{6}$	$\frac{2}{12}$	$\frac{3}{18}$	$\frac{4}{24}$	$\frac{5}{30}$	$\frac{6}{36}$	$\frac{7}{42}$	$\frac{8}{48}$	$\frac{9}{54}$	$\frac{10}{60}$
$\frac{5}{6}$	$\frac{10}{12}$	$\frac{15}{18}$	$\frac{20}{24}$	$\frac{25}{30}$	$\frac{30}{36}$	$\frac{35}{42}$	$\frac{40}{48}$	$\frac{45}{54}$	$\frac{50}{60}$
$\frac{1}{8}$	$\frac{2}{16}$	$\frac{3}{24}$	$\frac{4}{32}$	$\frac{5}{40}$	$\frac{6}{48}$	$\frac{7}{56}$	$\frac{8}{64}$	$\frac{9}{72}$	$\frac{10}{80}$
$\frac{3}{8}$	$\frac{6}{16}$	$\frac{9}{24}$	$\frac{12}{32}$	$\frac{15}{40}$	$\frac{18}{48}$	$\frac{21}{56}$	$\frac{24}{64}$	$\frac{27}{72}$	$\frac{30}{80}$
$\frac{5}{8}$	$\frac{10}{16}$	$\frac{15}{24}$	$\frac{20}{32}$	$\frac{25}{40}$	$\frac{30}{48}$	$\frac{35}{56}$	$\frac{40}{64}$	$\frac{45}{72}$	$\frac{50}{80}$
$\frac{7}{8}$	$\frac{14}{16}$	$\frac{21}{24}$	$\frac{28}{32}$	$\frac{35}{40}$	$\frac{42}{48}$	$\frac{49}{56}$	$\frac{56}{64}$	$\frac{63}{72}$	$\frac{70}{80}$
$\frac{1}{12}$	$\frac{2}{24}$	$\frac{3}{36}$	$\frac{4}{48}$	$\frac{5}{60}$	$\frac{6}{72}$	$\frac{7}{84}$	$\frac{8}{96}$	$\frac{9}{108}$	$\frac{10}{120}$
$\frac{5}{12}$	$\frac{10}{24}$	$\frac{15}{36}$	$\frac{20}{48}$	$\frac{25}{60}$	$\frac{30}{72}$	$\frac{35}{84}$	$\frac{40}{96}$	$\frac{45}{108}$	$\frac{50}{120}$
$\frac{7}{12}$	$\frac{14}{24}$	$\frac{21}{36}$	$\frac{28}{48}$	$\frac{35}{60}$	$\frac{42}{72}$	$\frac{49}{84}$	$\frac{56}{96}$	$\frac{63}{108}$	$\frac{70}{120}$
$\frac{11}{12}$	$\frac{22}{24}$	$\frac{33}{36}$	$\frac{44}{48}$	$\frac{55}{60}$	$\frac{66}{72}$	$\frac{77}{84}$	$\frac{88}{96}$	$\frac{99}{108}$	$\frac{110}{120}$

NOTE

Each fraction in the first column is in **simplest form**. A fraction is in simplest form if no equivalent fraction can be obtained by dividing the numerator and the denominator by a whole number. Every fraction is either in simplest form or is equivalent to a fraction in simplest form.

Lowest terms means the same as *simplest form*.

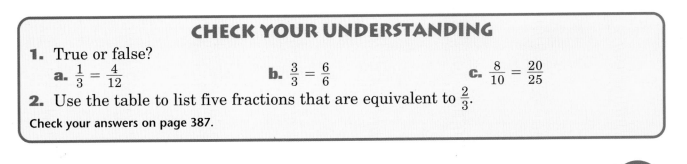

CHECK YOUR UNDERSTANDING

1. True or false?
   a. $\frac{1}{3} = \frac{4}{12}$
   b. $\frac{3}{3} = \frac{6}{6}$
   c. $\frac{8}{10} = \frac{20}{25}$
2. Use the table to list five fractions that are equivalent to $\frac{2}{3}$.

Check your answers on page 387.

Mixed Numbers and Improper Fractions

Numbers like $1\frac{1}{2}$, $2\frac{3}{5}$, and $4\frac{3}{8}$ are called **mixed numbers.** A mixed number has a whole number part and a fraction part. In the mixed number $4\frac{3}{8}$, the whole number part is 4 and the fraction part is $\frac{3}{8}$. The value of the mixed number is the sum of the whole number part and the fraction part: $4\frac{3}{8} = 4 + \frac{3}{8}$. Mixed numbers are used in many of the same ways as fractions.

An **improper fraction** is a fraction that is greater than or equal to 1. Fractions like $\frac{4}{3}$, $\frac{5}{5}$, and $\frac{125}{10}$ are improper fractions. In a **proper fraction,** the numerator is smaller than the denominator; in an improper fraction, the numerator is greater than or equal to the denominator.

N O T E

Even though they are called *improper*, there is nothing wrong or inappropriate about improper fractions. You shouldn't feel that they should be avoided.

Renaming Mixed Numbers as Improper Fractions

Mixed numbers can be renamed as improper fractions. For example, if a circle is the ONE, then $3\frac{1}{2}$ is three whole circles and $\frac{1}{2}$ of a fourth circle.

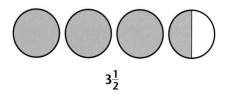

$$3\frac{1}{2}$$

If you divide the three whole circles into halves, then you can see that $3\frac{1}{2} = \frac{7}{2}$.

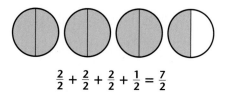

$$\frac{2}{2} + \frac{2}{2} + \frac{2}{2} + \frac{1}{2} = \frac{7}{2}$$

To change a mixed number to a fraction, rename the whole number as a fraction with the same denominator as the fraction part, and add the numerators.

EXAMPLE Rename $3\frac{1}{2}$ as a fraction.

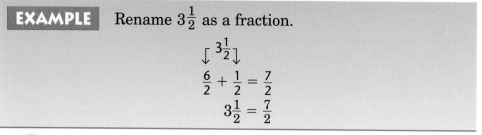

$$\underset{\downarrow\downarrow}{3\frac{1}{2}}$$

$$\frac{6}{2} + \frac{1}{2} = \frac{7}{2}$$

$$3\frac{1}{2} = \frac{7}{2}$$

Renaming Improper Fractions as Mixed Numbers

An improper fraction can be renamed as a mixed number or a whole number.

EXAMPLE Rename $\frac{19}{4}$ as a mixed number.

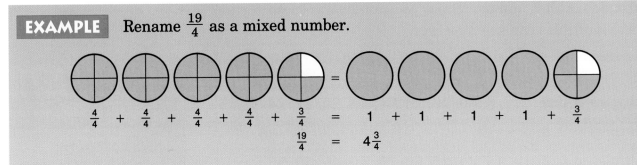

$$\frac{4}{4} + \frac{4}{4} + \frac{4}{4} + \frac{4}{4} + \frac{3}{4} = 1 + 1 + 1 + 1 + \frac{3}{4}$$

$$\frac{19}{4} = 4\frac{3}{4}$$

Shortcut:

Divide the numerator, 19, by the denominator, 4: 19 / 4 gives 4 R3.

- The quotient, 4, is the whole-number part of the mixed number.
  It tells how many wholes there are in $\frac{19}{4}$.

$$\begin{array}{r} 4\overline{)19} \\ -16 \end{array} \begin{array}{|l} \\ 4 \\ \hline 4 \end{array}$$
$$3$$

- The remainder, 3, is the numerator of the fraction part of the mixed number.
  It tells how many fourths are left that cannot be made into wholes.

$$\frac{19}{4} = 4\frac{3}{4}$$

Some calculators have a special key for renaming fractions as whole numbers or mixed numbers.

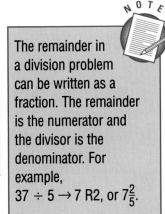

NOTE

The remainder in a division problem can be written as a fraction. The remainder is the numerator and the divisor is the denominator. For example,
$37 \div 5 \rightarrow 7$ R2, or $7\frac{2}{5}$.

EXAMPLE Rename $\frac{19}{4}$ as a mixed number.

Key in: 19 (n) 4 (d) (U$\frac{n}{d}$↔$\frac{n}{d}$) (Enter) Answer: $4\frac{3}{4}$

See if you can do this on your calculator.

CHECK YOUR UNDERSTANDING

Write each mixed number as an improper fraction.

1. $3\frac{3}{4}$ **2.** $5\frac{1}{3}$ **3.** $4\frac{3}{5}$

Write each improper fraction as a mixed number.

4. $\frac{26}{3}$ **5.** $\frac{39}{5}$ **6.** $\frac{73}{4}$

Check your answers on page 387.

Least Common Multiples

Multiples

When you skip-count by a number, your counts are the **multiples** of that number. Since you can always count further, lists of multiples can go on forever.

> **EXAMPLES** Find multiples of 2, 3, and 5.
>
> Multiples of 2: 2, 4, 6, 8, 10, 12, 14, 16, 18, 20, 22, 24, ...
>
> Multiples of 3: 3, 6, 9, 12, 15, 18, 21, 24, 27, 30, 33, 36, ...
>
> Multiples of 5: 5, 10, 15, 20, 25, 30, 35, 40, 45, 50, 55, ...

NOTE

The three dots, ..., mean that the lists can go on in the same way forever.

Common Multiples

On lists of multiples for numbers, some numbers are on more than one list. These numbers are called **common multiples.**

> **EXAMPLES** Find common multiples of 2 and 3.
>
> Multiples of 2: 2, 4, **6,** 8, 10, **12,** 14, 16, **18,** 20, 22, **24,** ...
>
> Multiples of 3: 3, **6,** 9, **12,** 15, **18,** 21, **24,** 27, ...
>
> Common multiples of 2 and 3: 6, 12, 18, 24, ...

Least Common Multiples

The **least common multiple** of two numbers is the smallest number that is a multiple of both numbers.

> **EXAMPLE** Find the least common multiple of 6 and 8.
>
> Multiples of 6: 6, 12, 18, **24,** 30, 36, 42, **48,** 54, ...
>
> Multiples of 8: 8, 16, **24,** 32, 40, **48,** 56, ...
>
> 24 and 48 are common multiples. 24 is the smallest common multiple.
>
> 24 is the least common multiple for 6 and 8. It is the smallest number that can be divided evenly by both 6 and 8.

CHECK YOUR UNDERSTANDING

Find the least common multiple of each pair of numbers.

1. 6 and 12   **2.** 4 and 10   **3.** 9 and 15

Check your answers on page 387.

Common Denominators

Adding, subtracting, comparing, and dividing are easier with fractions that have the same denominator. For this reason, people often rename fractions so they will have the same denominator, called a **common denominator.**

There are different methods to rename fractions with a common denominator.

EXAMPLES Rename $\frac{3}{4}$ and $\frac{1}{6}$ with a common denominator.

Method 1: Equivalent Fractions Method

List equivalent fractions for $\frac{3}{4}$ and $\frac{1}{6}$.

$$\frac{3}{4} = \frac{6}{8} = \frac{9}{12} = \frac{12}{16} = \frac{15}{20} = \frac{18}{24} = \frac{21}{28} = \frac{24}{32} = \frac{27}{36} = \cdots$$

$$\frac{1}{6} = \frac{2}{12} = \frac{3}{18} = \frac{4}{24} = \frac{5}{30} = \frac{6}{36} = \frac{7}{42} = \frac{8}{48} = \frac{9}{54} = \cdots$$

Both $\frac{3}{4}$ and $\frac{1}{6}$ can be renamed as fractions with the common denominator 12.

$$\frac{3}{4} = \frac{9}{12} \text{ and } \frac{1}{6} = \frac{2}{12}$$

Method 2: The Multiplication Method

Multiply the numerator and the denominator of each fraction by *the denominator of the other fraction.*

$$\frac{3}{4} = \frac{3*6}{4*6} = \frac{18}{24} \qquad \frac{1}{6} = \frac{1*4}{6*4} = \frac{4}{24}$$

Method 3: Least Common Multiple Method

Find the least common multiple of the denominators.
Multiples of 4: 4, 8, **12**, 16, 20, …
Multiples of 6: 6, **12**, 18, 24, …
The least common multiple of 4 and 6 is 12.

Rename the fractions so that their denominator is the least common multiple.

$$\frac{3}{4} = \frac{3*3}{4*3} = \frac{9}{12} \qquad \frac{1}{6} = \frac{1*2}{6*2} = \frac{2}{12}$$

This method gives fractions with the **least common denominator.**

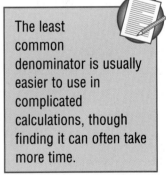

The Multiplication Method gives what *Everyday Mathematics* calls the **quick common denominator.** The quick common denominator can be used with variables, so it is common in algebra.

The least common denominator is usually easier to use in complicated calculations, though finding it can often take more time.

CHECK YOUR UNDERSTANDING

Rename each pair of fractions as fractions with a common denominator.

1. $\frac{2}{3}$ and $\frac{1}{6}$ **2.** $\frac{1}{2}$ and $\frac{2}{5}$ **3.** $\frac{3}{10}$ and $\frac{3}{4}$

Check your answers on page 387.

Comparing Fractions

When you compare fractions, pay attention to both the numerator and the denominator.

Like Denominators

Fractions with the same denominator are also said to have **like denominators.** The fractions $\frac{1}{4}$ and $\frac{3}{4}$ have like denominators. To compare fractions that have like denominators, just compare the numerators. The fraction with the larger numerator is larger.

The denominator tells how many parts the whole has been divided into. If the denominators of two fractions are the same, then the parts are the same size.

<	is less than
>	is greater than
=	is equal to

EXAMPLE Compare $\frac{5}{8}$ and $\frac{3}{8}$.

For both fractions, the ONE has been divided into the same number of parts. Therefore, the parts for both fractions are the same size.

The fraction with the greater number of parts is larger.

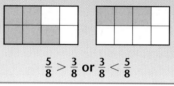

$$\frac{5}{8} > \frac{3}{8} \text{ or } \frac{3}{8} < \frac{5}{8}$$

Like Numerators

If the numerators of two fractions are the same, then the fraction with the smaller denominator is larger.

EXAMPLE Compare $\frac{2}{3}$ and $\frac{2}{5}$.

The ONE for $\frac{2}{3}$ has been divided into fewer parts than the ONE for $\frac{2}{5}$. So, the parts in $\frac{2}{3}$ are larger than the parts in $\frac{2}{5}$.

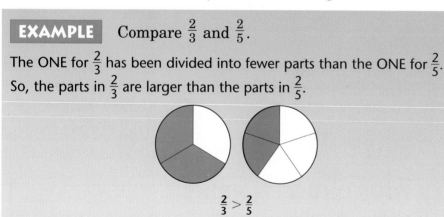

$$\frac{2}{3} > \frac{2}{5}$$

Therefore, $\frac{2}{3}$ is more than $\frac{2}{5}$.

Unlike Numerators and Unlike Denominators

Here are several strategies that can help when both the numerators and the denominators are different.

Comparing to $\frac{1}{2}$

Notice that $\frac{5}{7}$ is more than $\frac{1}{2}$ and $\frac{3}{8}$ is less than $\frac{1}{2}$. So, $\frac{3}{8} < \frac{5}{7}$.

0        $\frac{3}{8}$ $\frac{1}{2}$ $\frac{5}{7}$ 1

Comparing to 0 and 1

$\frac{7}{8}$ is $\frac{1}{8}$ away from 1 and $\frac{3}{4}$ is $\frac{1}{4}$ away from 1. Since eighths are smaller than fourths, $\frac{7}{8}$ is closer to 1 than $\frac{3}{4}$. So, $\frac{7}{8} > \frac{3}{4}$.

0        $\frac{1}{2}$ $\frac{3}{4}$ $\frac{7}{8}$ 1

Common Denominators

Rename both fractions with a common denominator. The fraction with the larger numerator is larger.

> **EXAMPLE**   Compare $\frac{5}{8}$ and $\frac{3}{5}$.
>
> A common denominator for $\frac{5}{8}$ and $\frac{3}{5}$ is 40.
>
> $\frac{5}{8} = \frac{5 * 5}{8 * 5} = \frac{25}{40}$ $\frac{3}{5} = \frac{3 * 8}{5 * 8} = \frac{24}{40}$ $\frac{25}{40} > \frac{24}{40}$
>
> So, $\frac{5}{8} > \frac{3}{5}$.

Decimal Equivalents

To compare $\frac{2}{5}$ and $\frac{3}{8}$, use a calculator to rename both fractions as decimals:

$\frac{2}{5}$: Key in: 2 ÷ 5 (Enter)   Answer: 0.4

$\frac{3}{8}$: Key in: 3 ÷ 8 (Enter)   Answer: 0.375

Since $0.4 > 0.375$, you know that $\frac{2}{5} > \frac{3}{8}$.

CHECK YOUR UNDERSTANDING

Compare. Use $<$, $>$, or $=$.

1. $\frac{1}{7} \square \frac{1}{9}$ **2.** $\frac{3}{7} \square \frac{5}{9}$ **3.** $\frac{1}{4} \square \frac{3}{12}$ **4.** $\frac{5}{8} \square \frac{2}{3}$ **5.** $\frac{5}{9} \square \frac{2}{3}$

Check your answers on page 387.

Addition and Subtraction of Fractions

Like Denominators

To add or subtract fractions that have the same denominator, just add or subtract the numerators. The denominator does not change. After you find the sum or difference, you can use the division rule to put it in simplest form.

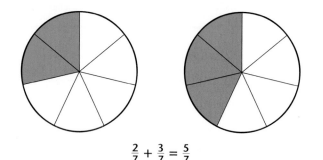

$$\frac{2}{7} + \frac{3}{7} = \frac{5}{7}$$

EXAMPLES	$\frac{3}{8} + \frac{2}{8} = ?$	$\frac{7}{10} - \frac{3}{10} = ?$

$$\frac{3}{8} + \frac{2}{8} = \frac{3+2}{8} = \frac{5}{8}$$

$$\frac{7}{10} - \frac{3}{10} = \frac{7-3}{10} = \frac{4}{10} = \frac{2}{5}$$

Unlike Denominators

To add or subtract fractions that have unlike denominators, first rename the fractions with a common denominator.

EXAMPLE $\frac{5}{12} + \frac{2}{3} = ?$

To rename $\frac{5}{12}$ and $\frac{2}{3}$ with a common denominator, you can multiply both the numerator and the denominator of each fraction by the other fraction's denominator.

$$\frac{5}{12} = \frac{5*3}{12*3} = \frac{15}{36}$$

$$\frac{2}{3} = \frac{2*12}{3*12} = \frac{24}{36}$$

So, $\frac{5}{12} + \frac{2}{3} = \frac{15}{36} + \frac{24}{36} = \frac{39}{36}$.

Sometimes an answer like $\frac{39}{36}$ is fine as the solution to a problem. Other times you may want to change it to a mixed number in simplest form.

$$\frac{39}{36} = 1\frac{3}{36} = 1\frac{1}{12}$$

Using a Slide Rule

In Fifth Grade *Everyday Mathematics,* you are given a paper
slide rule to help you add and subtract some fractions.

EXAMPLE Find $\frac{3}{4} + \frac{1}{2}$.

Step 1: Place the fraction side of the slider inside
the fraction side of the holder.

Step 2: Line up the 0-mark on the slider with the
mark for $\frac{3}{4}$ on the holder.

Step 3: Find the mark for $\frac{1}{2}$ on the slider. It is lined
up with the mark for $1\frac{1}{4}$ on the holder.
That is the answer to the problem.

$$\frac{3}{4} + \frac{1}{2} = 1\frac{1}{4}$$

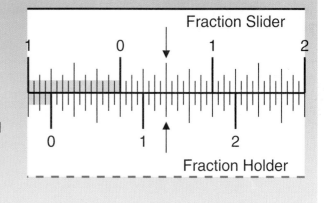

EXAMPLE Find $2\frac{1}{4} - \frac{1}{2}$.

Step 1: Line up the 0-mark on the slider with the
mark for $2\frac{1}{4}$ on the holder.

Step 2: Find the mark for $\frac{1}{2}$ on the negative part
of the slider. It is lined up with the mark
for $1\frac{3}{4}$ on the holder. This is the answer
to the problem.

$$2\frac{1}{4} - \frac{1}{2} = 1\frac{3}{4}$$

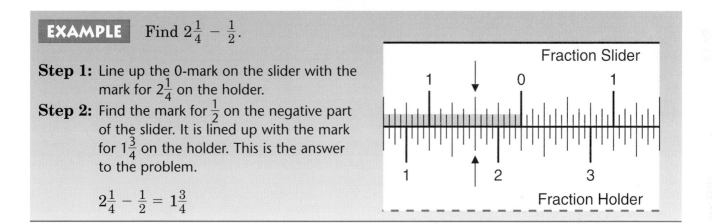

Using a Calculator

Some calculators can be used to add and subtract fractions.

EXAMPLE $\frac{3}{8} + \frac{1}{4} = ?$

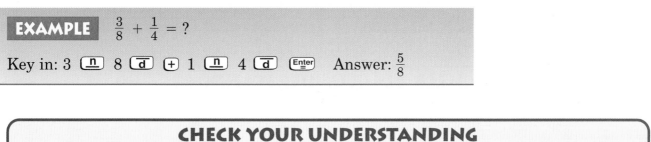

Key in: 3 ⃞n 8 ⃞d ⃞+ 1 ⃞n 4 ⃞d ⃞Enter   Answer: $\frac{5}{8}$

CHECK YOUR UNDERSTANDING

Add or subtract.

1. $\frac{5}{8} - \frac{1}{3}$ **2.** $\frac{7}{8} - \frac{1}{2}$ **3.** $\frac{5}{12} - \frac{1}{4}$ **4.** $\frac{5}{12} + \frac{1}{4}$ **5.** $\frac{5}{8} + \frac{1}{3}$

Check your answers on page 387.

Addition of Mixed Numbers

One way to add mixed numbers is to add the whole numbers and the fractions separately. You will have to rename the fractions' sum if it is more than 1. If the fractions in the mixed numbers have unlike denominators, you should first rename them using a common denominator.

EXAMPLE Find $3\frac{3}{4} + 5\frac{2}{3}$.

Rename the fractions with a common denominator.

$$3\ \frac{3}{4} \qquad (3\tfrac{3}{4} = 3\tfrac{9}{12}) \qquad 3\ \frac{9}{12}$$
$$+\ 5\ \frac{2}{3} \qquad (5\tfrac{2}{3} = 5\tfrac{8}{12}) \qquad +\ 5\ \frac{8}{12}$$

Add the fractions.

$$3\ \frac{9}{12}$$
$$+\ 5\ \frac{8}{12}$$
$$\overline{\frac{17}{12}}$$

Add the whole numbers.

$$3\ \frac{9}{12}$$
$$+\ 5\ \frac{8}{12}$$
$$\overline{8\ \frac{17}{12}}$$

Rename the sum.

$$8\tfrac{17}{12} \ = \ 8 + \tfrac{12}{12} + \tfrac{5}{12}$$
$$= \ 8 + 1 + \tfrac{5}{12}$$
$$= \ 9 + \tfrac{5}{12}$$
$$= \ 9\tfrac{5}{12}$$
$$3\tfrac{3}{4} + 5\tfrac{2}{3} \ = \ 9\tfrac{5}{12}$$

Some calculators have special keys for entering and renaming mixed numbers. See pages 235 and 236.

CHECK YOUR UNDERSTANDING

Add.

1. $1\frac{1}{2} + 2\frac{3}{4}$

2. $3\frac{2}{3} + 5\frac{1}{4}$

3. $7\frac{5}{6} + 2\frac{1}{2}$

Check your answers on page 387.

Subtraction of Mixed Numbers

Here is one way to subtract a mixed number from a mixed number:

First, subtract the fraction parts of the mixed numbers.

- If the fractions have unlike denominators, rename them using a common denominator.

- If necessary, rename the larger mixed number so the fraction part is large enough to subtract from.

Second, subtract the whole number parts.

EXAMPLE   Find $5\frac{1}{4} - 3\frac{2}{3}$.

Rename the fractions using a common denominator.

$$5\ \frac{1}{4} \qquad (5\tfrac{1}{4} = 5\tfrac{3}{12}) \qquad\qquad 5\ \frac{3}{12}$$
$$-\ 3\ \frac{2}{3} \qquad (3\tfrac{2}{3} = 3\tfrac{8}{12}) \qquad\qquad -\ 3\ \frac{8}{12}$$

Rename the larger mixed number so the numerator of the fraction part is large enough to subtract from. (Remember that 1 can be renamed as a fraction with the same numerator and denominator.)

$$\mathbf{5}\ \frac{3}{12} = 4 + 1 + \frac{3}{12} = 4 + \frac{12}{12} + \frac{3}{12} = \mathbf{4}\ \frac{15}{12}$$
$$-\ 3\ \frac{8}{12} \qquad\qquad\qquad\qquad\qquad -\ 3\ \frac{8}{12}$$

Subtract the fractions.

$$4\ \frac{15}{12}$$
$$-\ 3\ \frac{8}{12}$$
$$\overline{\frac{7}{12}}$$

Subtract the whole numbers.

$$\mathbf{4}\ \frac{15}{12}$$
$$-\ \mathbf{3}\ \frac{8}{12}$$
$$\overline{\mathbf{1}\ \frac{7}{12}}$$

$$5\tfrac{1}{4} - 3\tfrac{2}{3} = 1\tfrac{7}{12}$$

EXAMPLE Find $5 - 2\frac{2}{3}$.

Rename the whole number as a mixed number.

$$5 = 4 + 1 = 4 + \frac{3}{3} = 4\frac{3}{3} = \mathbf{4\,\frac{3}{3}}$$
$$-\,2\,\frac{2}{3} \qquad\qquad\qquad\qquad -\,2\,\frac{2}{3}$$

Subtract the fractions.   Subtract the whole numbers.

$$\begin{array}{r} 4\ \frac{3}{3} \\ -\ 2\ \frac{2}{3} \\ \hline 2\ \frac{1}{3} \end{array} \qquad\qquad \begin{array}{r} \mathbf{4}\ \frac{3}{3} \\ -\ \mathbf{2}\ \frac{2}{3} \\ \hline \mathbf{2}\ \frac{1}{3} \end{array}$$

$$5 - 2\frac{2}{3} = 2\frac{1}{3}$$

Another way to subtract (or add) mixed numbers is to rename the mixed numbers as improper fractions.

EXAMPLE Find $4\frac{1}{6} - 2\frac{2}{3}$.

Rename the mixed numbers as fractions. $4\frac{1}{6} = \frac{25}{6}$ $2\frac{2}{3} = \frac{8}{3}$

Rename the fractions with a common denominator. Subtract.

$$\begin{array}{r} \frac{25}{6} \\ -\ \frac{8}{3} \\ \hline \end{array} \qquad \left(\frac{8}{3} = \frac{16}{6}\right) \qquad \begin{array}{r} \frac{25}{6} \\ -\ \frac{16}{6} \\ \hline \frac{9}{6} \end{array}$$

Rename the result as a mixed number. $\frac{9}{6} = 1\frac{3}{6} = 1\frac{1}{2}$

So, $4\frac{1}{6} - 2\frac{2}{3} = 1\frac{1}{2}$.

CHECK YOUR UNDERSTANDING

Subtract.

1. $4\frac{1}{2} - 1\frac{1}{4}$ **2.** $3\frac{2}{5} - \frac{4}{5}$ **3.** $5\frac{1}{2} - 2\frac{5}{6}$

Check your answers on page 387.

Multiplying Fractions and Whole Numbers

There are several ways to show the multiplication of a whole number and a fraction.

Area Model

EXAMPLE Find $\frac{2}{3} * 2$.

Notice that the number of rectangles equals the whole number.
Both rectangles are divided into thirds.
$\frac{2}{3}$ of each rectangle is shaded.
In each rectangle, there are 3 parts; 2 of them are shaded.
In the 2 rectangles, there are 4 shaded thirds altogether.
So, $\frac{2}{3} * 2 = \frac{4}{3}$ or $1\frac{1}{3}$.

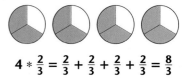

Number Line Model

Another way to multiply a fraction and a whole number is to think about "hops" on a number line. The whole number tells how many hops to make, and the fraction tells how long each hop should be. For example, to find $5 * \frac{2}{3}$, imagine taking 5 hops on a number line, each $\frac{2}{3}$ unit long.

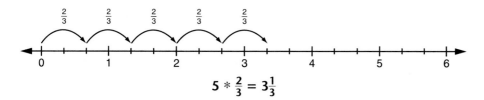

$$5 * \frac{2}{3} = 3\frac{1}{3}$$

Addition

Another way is to use addition. For example, to find $4 * \frac{2}{3}$, draw 4 models of $\frac{2}{3}$.

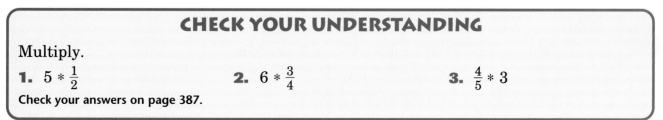

$$4 * \frac{2}{3} = \frac{2}{3} + \frac{2}{3} + \frac{2}{3} + \frac{2}{3} = \frac{8}{3}$$

CHECK YOUR UNDERSTANDING

Multiply.

1. $5 * \frac{1}{2}$

2. $6 * \frac{3}{4}$

3. $\frac{4}{5} * 3$

Check your answers on page 387.

Finding a Fraction of a Number

Many problems with fractions involve finding a fraction of a number.

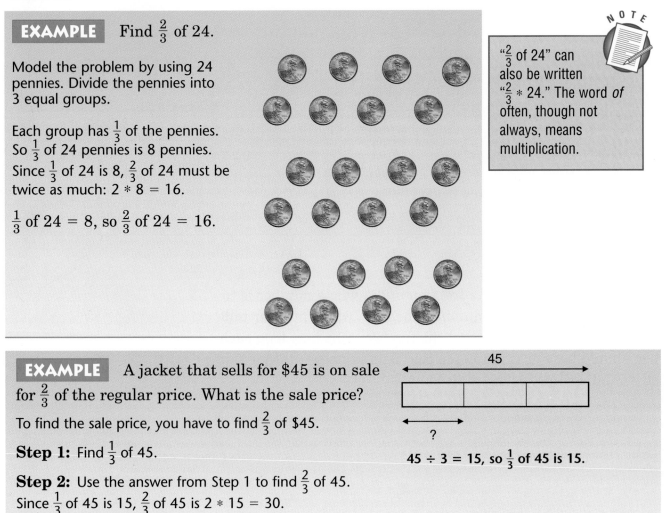

EXAMPLE Find $\frac{2}{3}$ of 24.

Model the problem by using 24 pennies. Divide the pennies into 3 equal groups.

Each group has $\frac{1}{3}$ of the pennies. So $\frac{1}{3}$ of 24 pennies is 8 pennies. Since $\frac{1}{3}$ of 24 is 8, $\frac{2}{3}$ of 24 must be twice as much: $2 * 8 = 16$.

$\frac{1}{3}$ of 24 = 8, so $\frac{2}{3}$ of 24 = 16.

NOTE "$\frac{2}{3}$ of 24" can also be written "$\frac{2}{3} * 24$." The word *of* often, though not always, means multiplication.

EXAMPLE A jacket that sells for $45 is on sale for $\frac{2}{3}$ of the regular price. What is the sale price?

To find the sale price, you have to find $\frac{2}{3}$ of $45.

Step 1: Find $\frac{1}{3}$ of 45.

$45 \div 3 = 15$, so $\frac{1}{3}$ of 45 is 15.

Step 2: Use the answer from Step 1 to find $\frac{2}{3}$ of 45. Since $\frac{1}{3}$ of 45 is 15, $\frac{2}{3}$ of 45 is $2 * 15 = 30$.

The sale price is $30.

CHECK YOUR UNDERSTANDING

Solve each problem.

1. $\frac{1}{4}$ of 36
2. $\frac{3}{4}$ of 36
3. $\frac{4}{5}$ of 20
4. Rita and Hunter earned $15 raking lawns. Since Rita did most of the work, they decided that Rita should get $\frac{2}{3}$ of the money. How much does each person get?

Check your answers on page 387.

Using a Unit Fraction to Find the Whole

A fraction with 1 in the numerator is called a **unit fraction.**
The fractions $\frac{1}{2}$, $\frac{1}{3}$, $\frac{1}{4}$, and $\frac{1}{5}$ are unit fractions. Unit fractions can often be helpful in solving problems with fractions.

EXAMPLE Alex collects sports cards. Seventy of his cards feature basketball players. These 70 cards are $\frac{2}{3}$ of Alex's collection. How many sports cards does Alex have?

$\frac{2}{3}$ of the collection is 70 cards. So $\frac{1}{3}$ of the collection is 35 cards. The whole collection ($\frac{3}{3}$) is $3 * 35 = 105$.

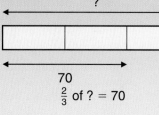

$\frac{2}{3}$ of ? = 70

Alex has 105 cards in his whole collection.

EXAMPLE Alicia baked cookies. She gave away 24 cookies, which was $\frac{3}{5}$ of the total she baked. How many cookies did Alicia bake?

$\frac{3}{5}$ of Alicia's cookies is 24 cookies. So $\frac{1}{5}$ of Alicia's cookies is 8 cookies. The whole batch of cookies ($\frac{5}{5}$) is $5 * 8 = 40$ cookies.

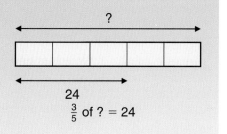

$\frac{3}{5}$ of ? = 24

Alicia baked 40 cookies.

CHECK YOUR UNDERSTANDING

Solve each problem.

1. $\frac{1}{2}$ of a package is 24 cookies. How many cookies are in the whole package?

2. $\frac{2}{3}$ of a package is 4 cookies. How many cookies are in the whole package?

3. $\frac{3}{4}$ of a package is 18 cookies. How many cookies are in the whole package?

Check your answers on page 387.

Multiplying Fractions

When you multiply two fractions, thinking about area can help.

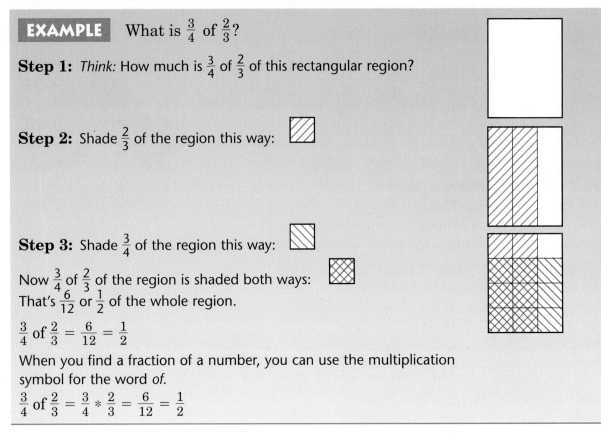

EXAMPLE   What is $\frac{3}{4}$ of $\frac{2}{3}$?

Step 1: *Think:* How much is $\frac{3}{4}$ of $\frac{2}{3}$ of this rectangular region?

Step 2: Shade $\frac{2}{3}$ of the region this way:

Step 3: Shade $\frac{3}{4}$ of the region this way:

Now $\frac{3}{4}$ of $\frac{2}{3}$ of the region is shaded both ways:
That's $\frac{6}{12}$ or $\frac{1}{2}$ of the whole region.

$$\frac{3}{4} \text{ of } \frac{2}{3} = \frac{6}{12} = \frac{1}{2}$$

When you find a fraction of a number, you can use the multiplication symbol for the word *of*.

$$\frac{3}{4} \text{ of } \frac{2}{3} = \frac{3}{4} * \frac{2}{3} = \frac{6}{12} = \frac{1}{2}$$

Multiplication of Fractions Property

The problem above is an example of the following general pattern: To multiply fractions, simply multiply the numerators, and multiply the denominators.
This pattern can be expressed as follows:

$$\frac{a}{b} * \frac{c}{d} = \frac{a * c}{b * d} \qquad (b \text{ and } d \text{ may not be } 0)$$

N O T E
Check page 235 to see how a calculator can be used to multiply fractions.

EXAMPLE $\frac{3}{4} * \frac{2}{3} = ?$

$$\frac{3}{4} * \frac{2}{3} = \frac{3 * 2}{4 * 3} = \frac{6}{12} = \frac{1}{2}$$

CHECK YOUR UNDERSTANDING

Multiply.

1. $\frac{1}{3} * \frac{1}{2}$

2. $\frac{3}{5} * \frac{1}{4}$

3. $\frac{5}{6} * \frac{3}{10}$

Check your answers on page 387.

Multiplying Fractions, Whole Numbers, and Mixed Numbers

Multiplying Whole Numbers and Fractions

The Multiplication of Fractions Property can be used to multiply a whole number and a fraction. First, rename the whole number as a fraction with 1 in the denominator.

EXAMPLE Find $5 * \frac{2}{3}$.

$$5 * \frac{2}{3} = \frac{5}{1} * \frac{2}{3} = \frac{5 * 2}{1 * 3} = \frac{10}{3} = 3\frac{1}{3}$$
$$5 * \frac{2}{3} = 3\frac{1}{3}$$

Multiplying Mixed Numbers by Renaming as Improper Fractions

One way to multiply two mixed numbers is to rename each mixed number as an improper fraction, multiply the fractions, and rename the product as a mixed number.

EXAMPLE Find $3\frac{1}{4} * 1\frac{5}{6}$.

Rename the mixed numbers as fractions.
Multiply the fractions.

$$3\frac{1}{4} * 1\frac{5}{6} = \frac{13}{4} * \frac{11}{6}$$
$$= \frac{13 * 11}{4 * 6}$$
$$= \frac{143}{24}$$

Rename the product as a mixed number.

$$\begin{array}{r} 24\overline{)143} \\ -120 \\ \hline 23 \end{array}$$

$\frac{143}{24} = 5\frac{23}{24}$

So, $3\frac{1}{4} * 1\frac{5}{6} = 5\frac{23}{24}$.

Multiplying Mixed Numbers by Using Partial Products

Another way to multiply mixed numbers is to find partial products and add them.

EXAMPLES Find $7\frac{1}{2} * 2\frac{3}{5}$.

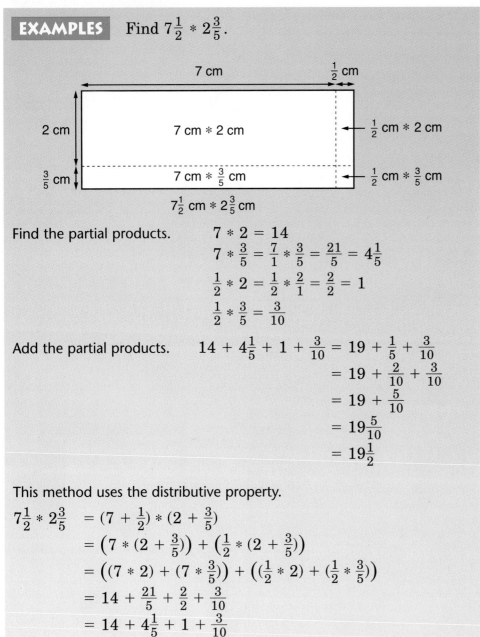

Find the partial products.

$$7 * 2 = 14$$
$$7 * \frac{3}{5} = \frac{7}{1} * \frac{3}{5} = \frac{21}{5} = 4\frac{1}{5}$$
$$\frac{1}{2} * 2 = \frac{1}{2} * \frac{2}{1} = \frac{2}{2} = 1$$
$$\frac{1}{2} * \frac{3}{5} = \frac{3}{10}$$

Add the partial products.

$$14 + 4\frac{1}{5} + 1 + \frac{3}{10} = 19 + \frac{1}{5} + \frac{3}{10}$$
$$= 19 + \frac{2}{10} + \frac{3}{10}$$
$$= 19 + \frac{5}{10}$$
$$= 19\frac{5}{10}$$
$$= 19\frac{1}{2}$$

This method uses the distributive property.

$$7\frac{1}{2} * 2\frac{3}{5} = (7 + \frac{1}{2}) * (2 + \frac{3}{5})$$
$$= \left(7 * (2 + \frac{3}{5})\right) + \left(\frac{1}{2} * (2 + \frac{3}{5})\right)$$
$$= \left((7 * 2) + (7 * \frac{3}{5})\right) + \left((\frac{1}{2} * 2) + (\frac{1}{2} * \frac{3}{5})\right)$$
$$= 14 + \frac{21}{5} + \frac{2}{2} + \frac{3}{10}$$
$$= 14 + 4\frac{1}{5} + 1 + \frac{3}{10}$$
$$= 19\frac{1}{2}$$

> **NOTE**
> See page 235 for using a calculator to multiply mixed numbers.

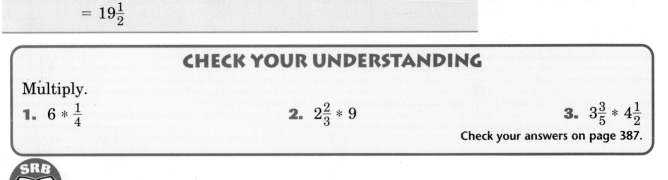

CHECK YOUR UNDERSTANDING

Multiply.

1. $6 * \frac{1}{4}$

2. $2\frac{2}{3} * 9$

3. $3\frac{3}{5} * 4\frac{1}{2}$

Check your answers on page 387.

Division of Fractions

Dividing a number by a fraction often gives a quotient that is larger than the dividend. For example, $4 \div \frac{1}{2} = 8$. To understand why this is, it's helpful to think about what division means.

There are 8 halves in 4 wholes.

Equal Groups

A division problem like $a \div b = ?$ is asking "How many b's are there in a?" For example, the problem $6 \div 3 = ?$ asks, "How many 3s are there in 6?" The figure at the right shows that there are two 3s in 6, so $6 \div 3 = 2$.

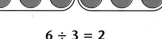

$6 \div 3 = 2$

A division problem like $6 \div \frac{1}{3} = ?$ is asking, "How many $\frac{1}{3}$s are there in 6?" The figure at the right shows that there are 18 thirds in 6, so $6 \div \frac{1}{3} = 18$.

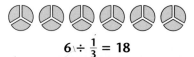

$6 \div \frac{1}{3} = 18$

> **EXAMPLE** Frank has 5 pounds of rice. A cup of rice is about $\frac{1}{2}$ pound. How many cups of rice does Frank have?
>
> This problem is solved by finding how many $\frac{1}{2}$s are in 5, which is the same as $5 \div \frac{1}{2}$.
>
> $\frac{1}{2}$lb + $\frac{1}{2}$lb + $\frac{1}{2}$lb + $\frac{1}{2}$lb + $\frac{1}{2}$lb + $\frac{1}{2}$lb + $\frac{1}{2}$lb + $\frac{1}{2}$lb + $\frac{1}{2}$lb + $\frac{1}{2}$lb = 5 lb
>
> So Frank has about 10 cups of rice.

Common Denominators

One way to solve a fraction division problem is to rename both the dividend and the divisor as fractions with a common denominator. Then divide the numerators and the denominators.

> **EXAMPLE** Find $6 \div \frac{2}{3}$.
>
> Rename 6 as $\frac{18}{3}$.
>
> Divide the numerators and the denominators.
>
> $$6 \div \frac{2}{3} = \frac{18}{3} \div \frac{2}{3}$$
> $$= \frac{18 \div 2}{3 \div 3}$$
> $$= \frac{9}{1} \text{ or } 9$$
>
> $6 \div \frac{2}{3} = 9$
>
> To see why this method works, imagine putting the 18 thirds in groups of $\frac{2}{3}$s each. There would be 9 groups.

EXAMPLE   Jake has 8 pounds of sugar. He wants to put it in packages that hold $\frac{2}{3}$ of a pound each. How many packages can he make?

Solve $8 \div \frac{2}{3}$.

Rename 8 as $\frac{24}{3}$.

Divide.

$$8 \div \frac{2}{3} = \frac{24}{3} \div \frac{2}{3}$$
$$= \frac{24 \div 2}{3 \div 3}$$
$$= \frac{12}{1} \text{ or } 12$$

The 24 thirds can be put in 12 groups of $\frac{2}{3}$s each.

So Jake can make 12 packages.

Missing Factors

A division problem is equivalent to a multiplication problem with a missing factor. A problem like $6 \div \frac{1}{2} = \square$ is equivalent to $\frac{1}{2} * \square = 6$. And $\frac{1}{2} * \square = 6$ is the same as asking "$\frac{1}{2}$ of what number equals 6?" Since $\frac{1}{2}$ of 12 is 6, you know that $\frac{1}{2} * 12 = 6$ and $6 \div \frac{1}{2} = 12$.

EXAMPLE   Find $6 \div \frac{2}{3}$.

This problem is equivalent to $\frac{2}{3} * \square = 6$, which means "$\frac{2}{3}$ of what number is 6?"

?

6

$\frac{2}{3}$ of ? = 6

The diagram above shows that $\frac{2}{3}$ of the missing number is 6. So $\frac{1}{3}$ must be 3. The missing number, $\frac{3}{3}$, is $3 * 3 = 9$.

So, $\frac{2}{3}$ of $9 = 6$, which is equivalent to $\frac{2}{3} * 9 = 6$. This means that $6 \div \frac{2}{3} = 9$.

CHECK YOUR UNDERSTANDING

Solve. Write a division number model for each problem.

1. Richard has 6 pizzas. If each person can eat $\frac{1}{2}$ of a pizza, how many people can Richard serve?

2. Maya has 8 yards of plastic strips for making bracelets. She needs $\frac{1}{2}$ yard for each bracelet. How many bracelets can she make?

3. 5 is $\frac{1}{2}$ of a number. What is the number?

Check your answers on page 387.

Rational Numbers

Counting is almost as old as the human race and has been used in some form by every human society. Long ago, people found that the **counting numbers** (1, 2, 3 and so on) did not meet all their needs.

- Counting numbers cannot be used to express measures between two consecutive whole numbers, such as $2\frac{1}{2}$ inches and 1.6 kilometers.

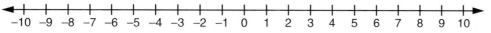

- With the counting numbers, division problems such as 8 / 5 and 3 / 7 do not have an answer.

Positive rational numbers were invented to meet these needs. Positive rational numbers can be expressed as fractions, decimals, and percents. With the invention of the positive rational numbers, it became possible to express rates and ratios, to name many more points on the number line, and to solve any division problem involving whole numbers (except division by 0).

Even the positive rational numbers did not meet every need. For example, problems such as $5 - 7$ and $2\frac{3}{4} - 5\frac{1}{4}$ could not be answered. This led to the invention of the **negative rational numbers.** Negative numbers serve several purposes in mathematics and everyday life.

- Negative numbers can be used to express locations such as temperatures below zero on a thermometer and depths below sea level.

- Negative numbers can be used to express changes such as yards lost in a football game and decreases in weight.

- Negative numbers allow the number line to be extended to less than zero.

- Negative numbers allow answers to many subtraction problems.

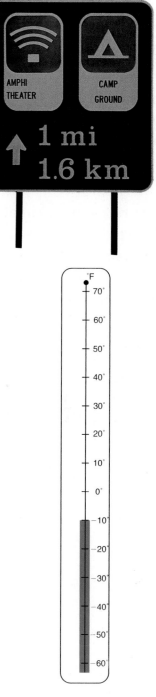

Rational numbers are made up of all the positive and negative rational numbers and zero.

Integers are a special kind of rational number. The set of integers consists of all counting numbers, all the opposites of counting numbers, and zero. Rational numbers are called *rational* because they can be written as ratios of integers. This means that every rational number can be written as a fraction using only integers in the numerator and the denominator.

There are other numbers that are called **irrational numbers.** Some of these, like the number π, you have used before. Irrational numbers cannot be written as ratios of integers, which is why they are called *irrational.* You will learn more about irrational numbers when you study algebra.

The rational and irrational numbers together make up the **real numbers.** The real numbers complete the number line: every point on the number line corresponds to a real number, and every real number has a point on the number line.

Counting Numbers: 1, 2, 3, 4, 5, ...

Positive Rational Numbers: $5, \frac{1}{2}, 2, 7.08, 40\%$

Negative Rational Numbers: $-6, -(\frac{3}{8}), -0.006, -1\frac{1}{2}$

Integers: $12, 0, -37$

Irrational Numbers $\sqrt{2}, \tan 30°$

Real Numbers: All of the examples above.

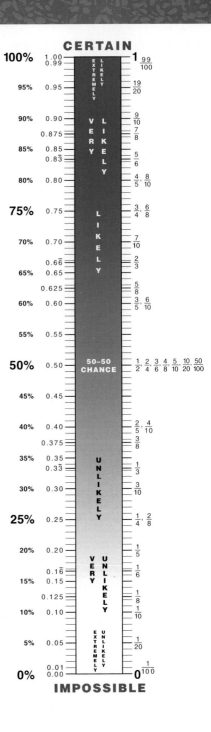

Renaming Fractions as Decimals

Fractions, decimals, and percents are different ways to write numbers. Sometimes it's easier to work with a fraction instead of a decimal or with a percent instead of a fraction, so it's good to know how to rename fractions, decimals, and percents in whatever way you want.

Any fraction that names a rational number can always be renamed as a decimal. Sometimes the decimal will end after a certain number of places, but sometimes the decimal will have one or more digits that repeat in a pattern forever. Decimals that end are called **terminating decimals;** those that repeat forever are called **repeating decimals.** The fraction $\frac{1}{2}$ is equivalent to the terminating decimal 0.5. The fraction $\frac{1}{3}$ is equivalent to the repeating decimal 0.3333....

There are several ways to rename a fraction as a decimal. One way is just to memorize the decimal equivalent: $\frac{1}{2} = 0.5$, $\frac{1}{4} = 0.25$, $\frac{1}{8} = 0.125$, and so on. But this only works for a few simple fractions, unless you have a very good memory.

Another way to find a decimal equivalent for a fraction is to use logical thinking. For example, if $\frac{1}{8} = 0.125$, then $\frac{3}{8} = 0.125 + 0.125 + 0.125 = 0.375$. Logical thinking and a few memorized equivalents will help you rename many common fractions as decimals.

Sometimes you can rename a fraction as a decimal by finding an equivalent fraction with a denominator such as 10, 100, or 1,000.

For other fractions, you can find decimal equivalents by using the Fraction-Stick Chart on page 357.

Finally, you can rename any fraction as a decimal by dividing the numerator by the denominator. You can do the division either with paper and pencil or with a calculator.

> **NOTE**
>
> All fractions in this book are assumed to be rational numbers unless stated otherwise.

Equivalent Fractions Method

One way to rename a fraction as a decimal is to find an equivalent fraction with a denominator that is a power of 10, such as 10, 100, or 1,000. This method works only for some fractions.

EXAMPLE

The solid lines divide the square into 5 equal parts. Each part is $\frac{1}{5}$ of the square. $\frac{3}{5}$ of the square is shaded.

The dashed lines divide each fifth into 2 equal parts. Each part is $\frac{1}{10}$, or 0.1, of the square. $\frac{6}{10}$, or 0.6, of the square is shaded.

$$\frac{3}{5} = \frac{6}{10} = 0.6$$

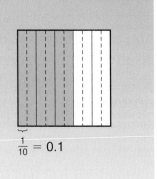

$\frac{1}{10} = 0.1$

EXAMPLE

The solid lines divide the square into 4 equal parts. Each part is $\frac{1}{4}$ of the square. $\frac{3}{4}$ of the square is shaded.

The dashed lines divide each fourth into 25 equal parts. Each part is $\frac{1}{100}$, or 0.01, of the square. $\frac{75}{100}$, or 0.75, of the square is shaded.

$$\frac{3}{4} = \frac{75}{100} = 0.75$$

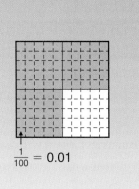

$\frac{1}{100} = 0.01$

CHECK YOUR UNDERSTANDING

Rename each fraction as a decimal.

1. $\frac{1}{4}$ **2.** $\frac{4}{5}$ **3.** $\frac{5}{2}$ **4.** $\frac{13}{20}$

Check your answers on page 387.

Using the Fraction-Stick Chart

The Fraction-Stick Chart below, and also on page 357, can also be used to rename fractions as decimals. Note that the result is often not exact.

EXAMPLE Rename $\frac{2}{3}$ as a decimal.

1. Locate $\frac{2}{3}$ on the "thirds" stick.
2. Place one edge of a straightedge at $\frac{2}{3}$.
3. Find where the straightedge crosses the number line.

The straightedge crosses the number line between 0.66 and 0.67:

So $\frac{2}{3}$ is equivalent to about 0.66 or 0.67.

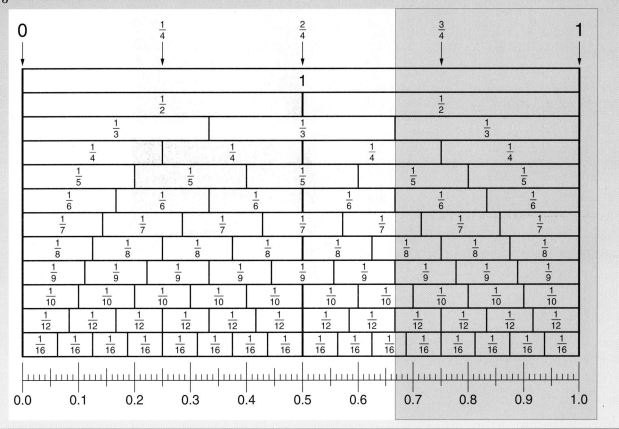

CHECK YOUR UNDERSTANDING

Use the chart above to find an approximate decimal name for each fraction or mixed number.

1. $\frac{3}{10}$ 2. $\frac{7}{8}$ 3. $4\frac{1}{3}$ 4. $\frac{12}{16}$

Check your answers on page 387.

Using Division

Another way to rename a fraction as a decimal is to divide its numerator by its denominator. This can usually be done easily on a calculator, but it can also be done by division.

EXAMPLE   Change $\frac{7}{8}$ to a decimal by division.

First, estimate the answer.
Since $\frac{7}{8}$ is more than $\frac{1}{2}$ but less than 1, the decimal equivalent will be more than 0.5 and less than 1.0.

Next, decide how many decimal places you want.
Two or three decimal places are usually enough for solving everyday problems. Rename $\frac{7}{8}$ as a decimal with three decimal places.
In order to get three decimal places, write the 7 in $\frac{7}{8}$ as 7.000.

Then, use partial-quotients division to divide 7.000 by 8.
Remember, ignore the decimal point for now, and divide 7000 by 8.

```
8)7000
 − 6400 | 800
    600
  − 560 | 70
     40
   − 40 |   5
      0   875
```

Finally, use the estimate from the first step to place the decimal point so that the decimal equivalent of $\frac{7}{8}$ is between 0.5 and 1.0.
0.875 is between 0.5 and 1.0.
So $\frac{7}{8}$ = 0.875.

In the example above, there was no remainder.

When there is a remainder, you may want to round the quotient.

EXAMPLE   Rename $\frac{2}{3}$ as a decimal using division.

Estimate.
Since $\frac{2}{3}$ is more than $\frac{1}{2}$ and less than 1, the decimal equivalent should be between 0.5 and 1.0.

Decide how many decimal places you want and rewrite the numerator accordingly.

Rename $\frac{2}{3}$ as a decimal to 2 decimal places. Write 2 as 2.00.

Use partial-quotients division to divide 200 by 3.

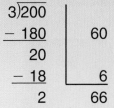

```
  3)200
  − 180  │   60
     20  │
  −  18  │    6
      2  │   66
```

The algorithm shows that 200 / 3 = $66\frac{2}{3}$, which you can round to 67.

Use the estimate to place the decimal point. The estimate was between 0.5 and 1.0, so 0.67 is between 0.5 and 1.0.

So, $\frac{2}{3}$ = 0.67, rounded to the nearest hundredth.

CHECK YOUR UNDERSTANDING

Use division to find decimal equivalents for these fractions.

1. $\frac{3}{8}$ (to nearest thousandth)

2. $\frac{1}{6}$ (to nearest thousandth)

3. $\frac{5}{9}$ (to nearest hundredth)

Check your answers on page 387.

Using a Calculator

You can also rename a fraction as a decimal by dividing the numerator by the denominator using a calculator.

> **EXAMPLES** Rename as a decimal.
>
> For $\frac{2}{3}$, key in: 2 $\div$ 3 [Enter]
>
> $\frac{2}{3} = 0.6666666667$
>
> Answer: 0.6666666667
>
> For $\frac{5}{6}$, key in: 5 $\div$ 6 [Enter]
>
> $\frac{5}{6} = 0.8333333333$
>
> Answer: 0.8333333333

In some cases, the decimal takes up the entire calculator display. If one or more digits repeat, the decimal can be written by writing the repeating digit or digits just once and putting a bar over whatever repeats.

> **EXAMPLES**
>
> | Fraction | Key in: | Calculator Answer | Decimal |
> |----------|---------|-------------------|---------|
> | $\frac{1}{3}$ | 1 $\div$ 3 [Enter] | 0.3333333333 | $0.\overline{3}$ |
> | $\frac{4}{9}$ | 4 $\div$ 9 [Enter] | 0.4444444444 | $0.\overline{4}$ |
> | $\frac{6}{11}$ | 6 $\div$ 11 [Enter] | 0.5454545455 | $0.\overline{54}$ |
> | $\frac{7}{12}$ | 7 $\div$ 12 [Enter] | 0.5833333333 | $0.58\overline{3}$ |

Decimals in which one or more digits repeat according to a pattern are called **repeating decimals.** In a repeating decimal, the pattern of repeating digits goes on forever. For example, suppose you converted $\frac{2}{3}$ to a decimal using a calculator with a display that could show 1,000 digits. The display would show a 0 and 999 sixes: 0.6666666666.... A calculator that shows 0.6666666667 for $\frac{2}{3}$ rounds the last digit in the display.

238–239

A decimal that does not have a repeating pattern is called a **terminating decimal.** For example, 0.625 is a terminating decimal.

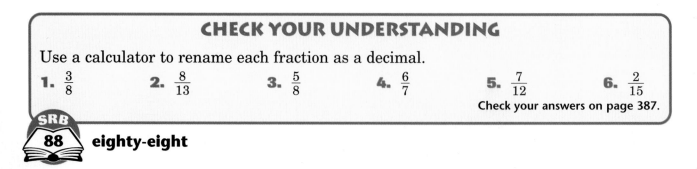

> ## CHECK YOUR UNDERSTANDING
>
> Use a calculator to rename each fraction as a decimal.
>
> **1.** $\frac{3}{8}$ **2.** $\frac{8}{13}$ **3.** $\frac{5}{8}$ **4.** $\frac{6}{7}$ **5.** $\frac{7}{12}$ **6.** $\frac{2}{15}$
>
> Check your answers on page 387.

Renaming Fractions, Decimals, and Percents

The previous pages described several ways to rename fractions as decimals. Here we discuss how to change fractions to percents, decimals to fractions, and so on.

Renaming a Decimal as a Fraction

Most decimals can be renamed as fractions whose denominator is a power of 10. To change a decimal to a fraction, use the place value of the rightmost digit as the denominator.

EXAMPLES   Write as fractions.

0.5   The rightmost digit is 5, which is in the 0.1s place.

So $0.5 = \frac{5}{10}$ or, in simplest form, $\frac{1}{2}$.

0.307   The rightmost digit is 7, which is in the 0.001s place.

So $0.307 = \frac{307}{1000}$.

4.75   The rightmost digit is 5, which is in the 0.01s place.

So $4.75 = \frac{475}{100}$. You can simplify $\frac{475}{100}$ as $4\frac{75}{100}$ or $4\frac{3}{4}$.

Some calculators have a special key for renaming decimals as fractions.

EXAMPLE   Rename 0.32 as a fraction.

To rename 0.32 as a fraction, key in: ⊡ 32 (Enter) (F↔D).
Answer: $\frac{32}{100}$

To simplify the fraction, key in: (Simp) (Enter) (Simp) (Enter).
Answer: $\frac{8}{25}$

Renaming Fractions as Percents

The best way to change a fraction to a percent is by memory. If you have a good memory, you may be able to remember almost all of the equivalents in the table of percent and decimal equivalents of "easy" fractions on page 356.

If you can't remember the percent equivalent for a fraction, usually the best thing to do is change the fraction to a decimal and then multiply the decimal by 100.

EXAMPLE   Use a calculator to rename $\frac{3}{8}$ as a percent.

Key in: 3 ÷ 8 × 100 (Enter). Answer: 37.5

Therefore, $\frac{3}{8} = 37.5\%$.

Renaming Percents as Fractions

A percent can always be written as a fraction with a denominator of 100. Simply remove the % symbol and write the number as a fraction with a denominator of 100. The fraction can be renamed in simplest form.

EXAMPLES $40\% = \frac{40}{100} = \frac{2}{5}$ $85\% = \frac{85}{100} = \frac{17}{20}$ $150\% = \frac{150}{100} = \frac{3}{2} = 1\frac{1}{2}$

Renaming a Percent as a Decimal

A percent can be written as a decimal by dividing by 100.

EXAMPLES $45\% = 45 / 100 = 0.45$ $120\% = 120 / 100 = 1.2$ $1\% = 1 / 100 = 0.01$

Renaming a Decimal as a Percent

To rename a decimal as a percent, just multiply by 100.

EXAMPLES $0.45 = (0.45 * 100)\% = 45\%$ $1.2 = (1.2 * 100)\% = 120\%$

$0.01 = (0.01 * 100)\% = 1\%$

CHECK YOUR UNDERSTANDING

Copy and complete this table.

Fraction	Decimal	Percent
$\frac{1}{4}$	0.25	25%
		33%
$\frac{1}{2}$		
	0.67	
		10%
$\frac{4}{5}$		

Check your answers on page 387.

Uses of Negative Numbers

You have probably used positive and negative numbers before. For example, 20 degrees above zero can be written as $+20°$ and 5 degrees below zero as $-5°$.

Many other real-world situations have zero as a starting point. Numbers go in opposite directions from zero. The numbers greater than zero are called **positive numbers;** the numbers less than zero are called **negative numbers.**

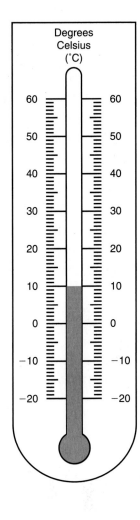

Degrees Celsius (°C)

EXAMPLES			
Situation	**Negative (−)**	**Zero (0)**	**Positive (+)**
Temperature	below zero	zero	above zero
Business	loss	break even	profit
Bank account	withdrawal	unchanged	deposit
Time	past; before	present; now	future; after
Game	behind	tied; even	ahead
Elevation	below sea level	at sea level	above sea level
Gauges, dials, dipsticks	below correct level	at correct level	above correct level

A number line may be used to show both positive and negative numbers. Some number lines may be horizontal, others vertical. A timeline is usually shown as a horizontal number line. A thermometer and the oil dipstick in an automobile can be thought of as vertical number lines.

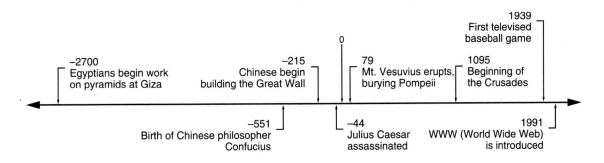

Addition and Subtraction of Positive and Negative Numbers

Number-Line Walking

One way to add and subtract positive and negative numbers is to imagine walking on a number line.

- The first number tells you where to start.
- The operation sign (+ or −) tells you which way to face:

  + means face towards the positive end of the number line.
  − means face towards the negative end of the number line.

- If the second number is negative (has a − sign), then you will walk backward. Otherwise, walk forward.
- The second number tells you how many steps to take.
- The number where you end up is the answer.

EXAMPLE $-3 + 5 = ?$

Start at −3.
The operation sign is +, so face the positive end of the number line.
The second number is positive, so walk forward 5 steps.
You end up at 2.

So, $-3 + 5 = 2$.

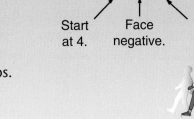

−3 + 5

Start at −3.   Face positive.   Walk forward 5 steps.

EXAMPLE $4 - (-3) = ?$

Start at 4.
The operation sign is −, so face the negative end of the number line.
The second number is negative, so walk backward 3 steps.
You end up at 7.

So, $4 - (-3) = 7$.

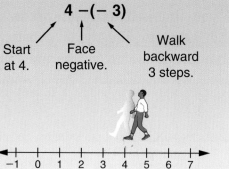

4 −(− 3)

Start at 4.   Face negative.   Walk backward 3 steps.

CHECK YOUR UNDERSTANDING

Add or subtract.

1. $3 + (-5)$ **2.** $-4 - 2$ **3.** $-5 - (-8)$ **4.** $-3 + (-5)$

Check your answers on page 387.

Using a Slide Rule

In *Fifth Grade Everyday Mathematics* there is a special slide rule that can be used for adding and subtracting positive and negative numbers. (The other side of the slide rule can be used for adding and subtracting fractions; see page 69.)

Addition with a Slide Rule

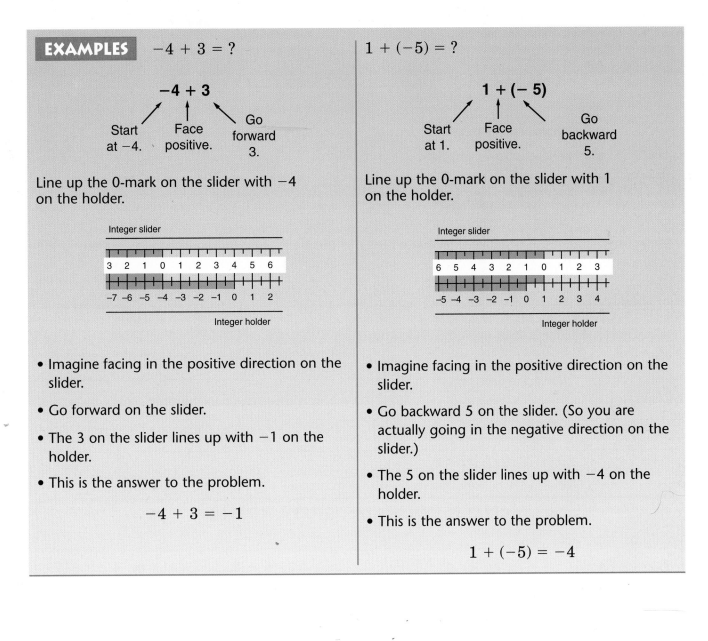

EXAMPLES $-4 + 3 = ?$

−4 + 3

Start at −4.   Face positive.   Go forward 3.

Line up the 0-mark on the slider with −4 on the holder.

Integer slider

3 2 1 0 1 2 3 4 5 6

−7 −6 −5 −4 −3 −2 −1 0 1 2

Integer holder

- Imagine facing in the positive direction on the slider.
- Go forward on the slider.
- The 3 on the slider lines up with −1 on the holder.
- This is the answer to the problem.

$$-4 + 3 = -1$$

$1 + (-5) = ?$

1 + (− 5)

Start at 1.   Face positive.   Go backward 5.

Line up the 0-mark on the slider with 1 on the holder.

Integer slider

6 5 4 3 2 1 0 1 2 3

−5 −4 −3 −2 −1 0 1 2 3 4

Integer holder

- Imagine facing in the positive direction on the slider.
- Go backward 5 on the slider. (So you are actually going in the negative direction on the slider.)
- The 5 on the slider lines up with −4 on the holder.
- This is the answer to the problem.

$$1 + (-5) = -4$$

Subtraction with a Slide Rule

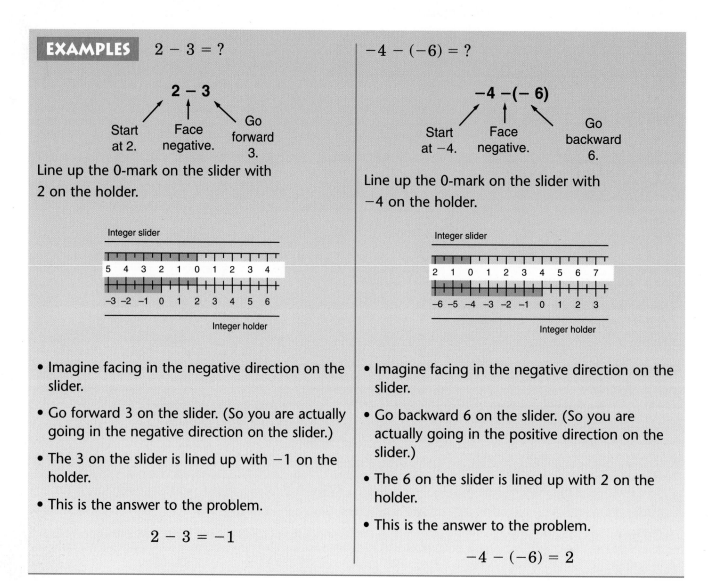

EXAMPLES $2 - 3 = ?$

2 − 3

Start at 2.   Face negative.   Go forward 3.

Line up the 0-mark on the slider with 2 on the holder.

Integer slider

5 4 3 2 1 0 1 2 3 4

−3 −2 −1 0 1 2 3 4 5 6

Integer holder

- Imagine facing in the negative direction on the slider.

- Go forward 3 on the slider. (So you are actually going in the negative direction on the slider.)

- The 3 on the slider is lined up with −1 on the holder.

- This is the answer to the problem.

$$2 - 3 = -1$$

$-4 - (-6) = ?$

−4 −(− 6)

Start at −4.   Face negative.   Go backward 6.

Line up the 0-mark on the slider with −4 on the holder.

Integer slider

2 1 0 1 2 3 4 5 6 7

−6 −5 −4 −3 −2 −1 0 1 2 3

Integer holder

- Imagine facing in the negative direction on the slider.

- Go backward 6 on the slider. (So you are actually going in the positive direction on the slider.)

- The 6 on the slider is lined up with 2 on the holder.

- This is the answer to the problem.

$$-4 - (-6) = 2$$

CHECK YOUR UNDERSTANDING

Add or subtract.

1. $-3 + (-5)$ **2.** $4 - (-7)$ **3.** $5 - 9$ **4.** $4 + (-17)$

Check your answers on page 387.

Rates, Ratios, & Proportions

Rates

The easiest fractions to understand are fractions that name parts of wholes and fractions used in measurement. In working with such fractions, it's important to know what the ONE, or whole, is. For example, if a mile is the ONE, then $\frac{3}{4}$ mile describes 3 parts of a mile that has been divided into 4 equal parts.

Not all fractions name parts of wholes. Some fractions compare two different amounts, where one amount is not part of the other. For example, a store might sell apples at 3 apples for 75 cents, or a car's gas mileage might be 160 miles per 8 gallons. These can be written as fractions: $\frac{3 \text{ apples}}{75¢}$, $\frac{160 \text{ miles}}{8 \text{ gallons}}$. These fractions do not name parts of wholes: The apples are *not* part of the money; the miles are *not* part of the gallons of gasoline.

Fractions like $\frac{160 \text{ miles}}{8 \text{ gallons}}$ show rates. A **rate** tells how many of one thing there are for a certain number of another thing. Rates often contain the word **per,** meaning "for each," "for every," or something similar.

> **EXAMPLES** Alex rode her bicycle 10 miles in 1 hour. Her rate was 10 miles per hour. This rate describes the distance Alex traveled and the time it took her. The rate "10 miles per hour" is often written as 10 mph. The fraction for this rate is $\frac{10 \text{ miles}}{1 \text{ hour}}$.
>
> Here are some other rates:
>
> | typing speed | 50 words per minute | $\frac{50 \text{ words}}{1 \text{ minute}}$ |
> |---|---|---|
> | price | 14 cents per ounce | $\frac{14¢}{1 \text{ ounce}}$ |
> | scoring average | 17 points per game | $\frac{17 \text{ points}}{1 \text{ game}}$ |
> | exchange rate | 5.4 French francs for each U.S. dollar | $\frac{5.4 \text{ French francs}}{1 \text{ U.S. dollar}}$ |
> | allowance | $5.00 per week | $\frac{\$5.00}{1 \text{ week}}$ |
> | baby-sitting | $4.00 per hour | $\frac{\$4.00}{1 \text{ hour}}$ |

Per-Unit Rates

A **per-unit rate** is a rate with 1 in the denominator. Per-unit rates tell how many of one thing there are for a single one of another thing. We say that "2 dollars per gallon" is a **per-gallon rate,** "12 miles per hour" is a **per-hour rate,** and "4 words per minute" is a **per-minute rate.** The fractions for these per-unit rates each have a 1 in the denominator: $\frac{\$2}{1 \text{ gallon}}$, $\frac{12 \text{ miles}}{1 \text{ hour}}$, and $\frac{4 \text{ words}}{1 \text{ minute}}$.

Any rate can be renamed as a per-unit rate by dividing the numerator and the denominator by the denominator.

A gas pump displays the per-gallon rate, the number of gallons pumped, and the total cost of the gas.

> **EXAMPLES** Change each rate to a per-unit rate.
>
> $$\frac{36 \text{ in.}}{3 \text{ ft}} = \frac{36 \text{ in.} \div 3}{3 \text{ ft} \div 3} \qquad \frac{72¢}{12 \text{ eggs}} = \frac{72¢ \div 12}{12 \text{ eggs} \div 12}$$
> $$\qquad\quad = \frac{12 \text{ in.}}{1 \text{ ft}} \qquad\qquad\qquad = \frac{6¢}{1 \text{ egg}}$$

A rate can also have 1 in the numerator. A food stand might sell apples at a rate of 1 apple for 25¢ or $\frac{1 \text{ apple}}{25¢}$. Conversions between inches and centimeters are at a rate of 1 inch to 2.54 centimeters or $\frac{1 \text{ in.}}{2.54 \text{ cm}}$. Rates with 1 in the numerator or in the denominator are often easier to work with than other rates.

Rate Tables

Rate information can be used to make a **rate table.**

> **EXAMPLE** Write a fraction and make a rate table for the statement, "A computer printer prints 4 pages per minute."
>
> 4 pages per minute = $\frac{4 \text{ pages}}{1 \text{ minute}}$
> This is the per-unit rate.
>
> | pages | 4 | 8 | 12 | 16 | 20 | 24 | 28 |
> |---|---|---|---|---|---|---|---|
> | minutes | 1 | 2 | 3 | 4 | 5 | 6 | 7 |
>
> The table shows that if a printer prints 4 pages per minute, it will print 8 pages in 2 minutes, 12 pages in 3 minutes, and so on.
>
> Each rate in a rate table is **equivalent** to each of the other rates in the table.

CHECK YOUR UNDERSTANDING

Write each rate as a fraction and make a rate table showing 4 equivalent rates.

1. Joan baby-sits for 5 dollars per hour. **2.** Water weighs about 8 pounds per gallon.

Check your answers on page 388.

Solving Rate Problems

In many problems that involve rates, a rate is given and you need to find an equivalent rate. These problems can be solved in more than one way.

EXAMPLES Bill's car can travel 35 miles on 1 gallon of gasoline. At this rate, how far can the car travel on 7 gallons?

Solution 1: Using a rate table

First, set up a rate table, and enter what you know. Write a question mark in place of what you are trying to find.

miles	35					?
gallons	1					7

Next, work from what you know to what you need to find. In this case, by doubling, you can find how far Bill could travel on 2 gallons, 4 gallons, and 8 gallons of gasoline.

miles	35	70	140	280			?
gallons	1	2	4	8			7

There are two different ways to use the rate table to answer the question. You will find that Bill can travel 245 miles.

- By adding the distances for 1 gallon, 2 gallons, and 4 gallons: 35 miles + 70 miles + 140 miles = 245 miles.
- By subtracting the distance for 1 gallon from the distance for 8 gallons: 280 miles − 35 miles = 245 miles.

Solution 2: Using multiplication

If the car can travel 35 miles on 1 gallon, then it can travel 7 times as far on 7 gallons.

$7 * 35 = 245$, so the car can travel 245 miles on 7 gallons of gas.

Sometimes, a rate is given and you need to find the equivalent per-unit rate. You can solve these problems by using a rate table or by division.

EXAMPLES   Keisha receives an allowance of $20 for 4 weeks. At this rate, how much does she get per week?

Solution 1: Using a rate table

First, set up a table and enter what you know. Next, work from what you know to what you need to find. By halving $20, you can find how much Keisha gets for 2 weeks. By halving again, you can find what she makes for 1 week.

allowance	$20				?
weeks	4				1

allowance	$20	$10	$5		?
weeks	4	2	1		1

So, Keisha gets $5 for 1 week.

Solution 2: Using division

If Keisha receives $20 for 4 weeks, she receives $\frac{1}{4}$ as much for 1 week.

$$\frac{20}{4} = 5$$

So, Keisha receives $5 per week.

Sometimes a rate that is not a per-unit rate is given and you need to find an equivalent rate that is not a per-unit rate.

• First find the equivalent per-unit rate.
• Then use the per-unit rate to find the rate asked for in the problem.

A rate table can help you organize your work.

EXAMPLE   A gray whale's heart beats 24 times in 3 minutes. At this rate, how many times does it beat in 2 minutes?

If the whale's heart beats 24 times in 3 minutes, it beats $\frac{1}{3}$ of 24 times in 1 minute (24 / 3 = 8). Double this to find how many times it beats in 2 minutes (2 * 8 = 16).

heartbeats	24	8	16		?
minutes	3	1	2		2

The whale's heart beats 16 times in 2 minutes.

CHECK YOUR UNDERSTANDING

Solve.

1. There are 3 feet in 1 yard. How many feet are there in 5 yards?

2. Ashley baby-sat for 5 hours. She was paid $25. How much did she earn per hour?

3. Bob saved $300 last year. How much did he save per month?

4. A carton of 12 eggs costs 72 cents. At this rate, how much do 8 eggs cost?

Check your answers on page 388.

Proportions

A **proportion** is a number sentence which states that two fractions are equal.

> **EXAMPLES** $\frac{1}{2} = \frac{3}{6}$ $\frac{2}{3} = \frac{8}{12}$ $\frac{7}{8} = \frac{14}{16}$

If you know any three numbers in a proportion, you can find the fourth number. Finding the fourth number is like finding a missing number in a pair of equivalent fractions.

> **EXAMPLES**   Solve each proportion.
>
> $\frac{2}{3} = \frac{n}{9}$ $\frac{3}{4} = \frac{30}{k}$ $\frac{x}{5} = \frac{6}{15}$ $\frac{1}{z} = \frac{6}{24}$
>
> $n = 6$ $k = 40$ $x = 2$ $z = 4$

Proportions are useful in problem solving. Writing a proportion can help you organize the numbers in a problem, then help you decide whether to multiply or divide to find the answer.

> **EXAMPLE**   Jack earned $12. He bought a can of tennis balls that cost $\frac{1}{3}$ of his earnings. How much did he spend?
>
> Write a proportion for the cost of the tennis balls and Jack's earnings.
>
> $\frac{\text{cost of tennis balls}}{\text{total earnings}} = \frac{1}{3}$
>
> Jack's total earnings were $12. Substitute 12 for "earnings" in the proportion.
>
> $\frac{\text{cost of tennis balls}}{\$12} = \frac{1}{3}$
>
> These two fractions are equivalent.
> To rename $\frac{1}{3}$ as an equivalant fraction with a denominator 12, multiply the numerator and denominator of $\frac{1}{3}$ by 4.
>
> $\overset{*4}{\underset{*4}{\frac{\text{cost}}{\$12} = \frac{1}{3}}}$
>
> The cost of the tennis balls was $4.

EXAMPLE Jacqueline has 45 baseball cards in her collection. $\frac{3}{5}$ of her cards are for National League players. How many of Jacqueline's cards are for National League players?

Write a proportion for the number of cards for National League players (#NL) and the total number of cards in Jacqueline's collection.

$$\frac{\#NL}{total} = \frac{3}{5}$$

Jacqueline has 45 cards altogether. Substitute 45 for "total" in the proportion.

$$\frac{\#NL}{45} = \frac{3}{5}$$

These fractions are equivalent.

$$\frac{\#NL}{45} = \frac{3}{5}$$

The number of cards for National League players is 27.

EXAMPLE Ms. Griffith spends \$1,000 a month. This amount is $\frac{4}{5}$ of her monthly earnings. How much does she earn per month?

Write a proportion for Ms. Griffith's spending and earnings.

$$\frac{spending}{earnings} = \frac{4}{5}$$

Ms. Griffith's spending is \$1,000 each month. Substitute 1,000 for "spending" in the proportion.

$$\frac{1,000}{earnings} = \frac{4}{5}$$

These fractions are equivalent.

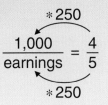

$$\frac{1,000}{earnings} = \frac{4}{5}$$

Ms. Griffith earns \$1,250 each month.

CHECK YOUR UNDERSTANDING

Solve.

1. Francine earned \$24 mowing lawns. She spent $\frac{2}{3}$ of her money on CDs. How much did she spend on CDs?

2. $\frac{3}{4}$ of Frank's cousins are girls. Frank has 12 girl cousins. How many cousins does he have in all?

Check your answers on page 388.

Ratios

A **ratio** is a comparison that uses division to compare two counts or measures having the same unit. Some ratios compare part of a collection of things to the total number of things in the collection. For example, the statement "1 out of 6 students in the class is absent" compares the number of absent students to the total number of students in the class. This ratio can be expressed in many ways.

In *words:* For every 6 students enrolled in the class, 1 student is absent. One in 6 students is absent. The ratio of absent students to all students is 1 to 6.

With a *fraction:* $\frac{1}{6}$ of the students are absent.

With a *percent:* About 16.7% of the students are absent.

With a *colon* between the two numbers: The ratio of absent students to all students is 1:6 (read as: "one to six").

In a *proportion:* $\frac{\text{number of absent students}}{\text{number of students}} = \frac{1}{6}$

If you know the total number of students in the class, you can use this ratio to find the number of students who are absent.

EXAMPLE There are 12 students in the class. $\frac{1}{6}$ of the students are absent.

$\frac{\text{absent students}}{12} = \frac{1}{6} \rightarrow$ absent students = 2

Two of the students are absent.

If you know the number of students who are absent, you can also use the ratio to find the total number of students in the class.

EXAMPLE There are 5 students absent. $\frac{1}{6}$ of the students are absent.

$\frac{5}{\text{total students}} = \frac{1}{6} \rightarrow$ total students = 30

There is a total of 30 students in the class.

NOTE

All of the following are statements of ratios:

- It is estimated that by the year 2020, there will be *5 times as many* people at least 100 years old as there were in 1990.
- Elementary school students make up about *14%* of the U.S. population.
- On an average evening, about $\frac{1}{3}$ *of* the U.S. population watches TV.
- The chances of winning a lottery can be less than *1 in 1 million.*
- A common scale for doll houses is *1 inch to 12 inches.*

NOTE

A ratio with 1 in the denominator is known as an *n*-to-1 ratio.

CHECK YOUR UNDERSTANDING

Last month, Mark received an allowance of $20. He spent $12 and saved the rest.

1. What is the ratio of the money he spent to his total allowance?

2. What is the ratio of the money he saved to the money he spent?

3. What percent of his allowance did he save?

Check your answers on page 388.

Using Ratios to Describe Size Changes

Many situations produce a **size change.** A magnifying glass, a microscope, and an overhead projector all enlarge the original image. Most copying machines can create a variety of size changes—both enlargements and reductions of the original document.

Similar figures are figures that have the same shape but not necessarily the same size. In the examples of size changes above, the enlargements or reductions are **similar** to the originals; that is, they have the same shapes as the originals.

The **size-change factor** is a number that tells the amount of enlargement or reduction that takes place. For example, if you use a copy machine to make a 2X change in size, then every length in the copy is twice the size of the original. The size-change factor is 2. If you make a 0.5X change in size, then every length in the copy is half the size of the original. The size-change factor is $\frac{1}{2}$, or 0.5.

You can think of the size-change factor as a ratio. For a 2X size change, the ratio of a length in the copy to the corresponding length in the original is 2 to 1.

size-change factor 2: $\frac{\text{copy size}}{\text{original size}} = \frac{2}{1}$

For a 0.5X size change, the ratio of a length in the copy to a corresponding length in the original is 0.5 to 1.

size-change factor 0.5: $\frac{\text{copy size}}{\text{original size}} = \frac{0.5}{1}$

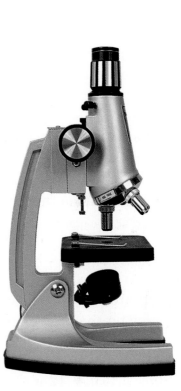

Scale Models

A model that is a careful copy of an actual object is called a
scale model. You have probably seen scale models of cars,
trains, and airplanes. The size-change factor in scale
models is usually called the **scale factor.**

Doll houses often have a scale factor of $\frac{1}{12}$. You
can write this scale factor as "$\frac{1}{12}$ of actual
size," "scale 1:12," "$\frac{1}{12}$ scale," or as a proportion:

$$\frac{\text{doll house length}}{\text{real house length}} = \frac{1 \text{ inch}}{12 \text{ inches}}$$

Every part of the real house is 12 times as long as the
corresponding part of the doll house.

Maps

The size-change factor for maps and scale drawings is usually
called the **scale.** If a map scale is 1:25,000, then every length
on the map is $\frac{1}{25,000}$ of the actual length, and any real distance
is 25,000 times the distance shown on the map.

$$\frac{\text{map distance}}{\text{real distance}} = \frac{1}{25,000}$$

Scale Drawings

If an architect's scale drawing shows "scale $\frac{1}{4}$ inch:1 foot," then
$\frac{1}{4}$ inch on the drawing represents 1 foot of actual length.

$$\frac{\text{drawing length}}{\text{real length}} = \frac{\frac{1}{4} \text{ inch}}{1 \text{ foot}}$$

Since 1 foot = 12 inches, we can rename $\frac{\frac{1}{4} \text{ inch}}{1 \text{ foot}}$ as $\frac{\frac{1}{4} \text{ inch}}{12 \text{ inches}}$.

Multiply by 4 to change this to an easier fraction:

$\frac{\frac{1}{4} \text{ inch} * 4}{12 \text{ inches} * 4} = \frac{1 \text{ inch}}{48 \text{ inches}}$. The drawing is $\frac{1}{48}$ of the actual size.

> **N O T E**
>
> You may see
> scales written
> with an equal sign,
> such as
> "$\frac{1}{4}$ inch = 1 foot."
> But $\frac{1}{4}$ inch is certainly
> not equal to 1 foot, so
> this is not
> mathematically correct.
> This scale is intended to
> mean that $\frac{1}{4}$ inch on the
> map or scale drawing
> stands for 1 foot in the
> real world.

CHECK YOUR UNDERSTANDING

Solve.

1. The diameter of a circle is 3 centimeters.
   A copier is used to make an
   enlargement of the circle. The size
   change factor is 2. What is the diameter
   of the enlarged circle?

2. Two cities are 3 inches apart on the
   map. The map scale is

   $$\frac{\text{map distance}}{\text{real distance}} = \frac{1 \text{ inch}}{250 \text{ miles}}.$$

   What is the real distance between the
   two cities?

   Check your answers on page 388.

Value of Pi

Measurements are *always* estimates. But if circles could be measured exactly, the ratio of the circumference to the diameter would be the same for every circle. This ratio is called **"pi"** and is written as the Greek letter π.

$$\frac{\text{circumference}}{\text{diameter}} = \pi$$

Since ancient times, mathematicians have worked to find the value of π. Here are some of the earliest results.

Date	Source	Approximate Value of π
c. 1800–1650 B.C.	Babylonians	$3\frac{1}{8}$
c. 1650 B.C.	Rhind Papyrus (Egypt)	3.16
c. 950 B.C.	Bible (I Kings 7:23)	3
c. 240 B.C.	Archimedes (Greece)	Between $3\frac{10}{71}$ and $3\frac{1}{7}$
c. A.D. 470	Tsu Ch'ung Chi (China)	$\frac{355}{113}$ (3.1415929...) correct to 6 decimal places
c. A.D. 510	Aryabhata (India)	$\frac{62,832}{20,000}$ (3.1415) less than 0.0001 different from π
c. A.D. 800	al'Khwarizmi (Persia)	3.1416

NOTE: *c.* stands for *circa*, a Latin word which means "about."

Today, computers are used to calculate the value of π. In 1949, π was calculated to 37,000 decimal places on ENIAC, one of the first computers. Later, π was computed to 100,000 digits on an IBM 7090 computer, and in 1981 to 2 million digits on an NEC supercomputer. In the years that followed, these calculations were extended to 17.5 million digits, then to 34 million digits, then past 200 million digits. In 1999, they went to more than 206 billion digits!

It's not possible to write π exactly with digits, because the decimal for π goes on forever. No pattern has ever been found in this decimal.

$\pi = 3.14159265358979323846264338327950288419716939937 51...$

Calculating with π

The number π is so important that most scientific calculators have a π key. If you use the π key on your calculator, be sure to round your results. Results shouldn't be more precise than the original measurements. One or two decimal places are usually enough.

If you don't have a calculator, you can use an approximation for π. Since few measures are more precise than hundredths, an approximation like 3.14 or $\frac{22}{7}$ is usually close enough.

EXAMPLE   A circle has a diameter of 5 inches. What is its circumference?

Method 1: Use the π key on your calculator.

$c = \pi * d$
Key in: π ✕ 5 Enter F↔D
Answer: 15.70796327
$c \approx 15.70796327$ in.

Method 2: Use the 3.14 as an approximation for π.

$c = \pi * d$ $c \approx 3.14 * 5 \text{ in.} = 15.7 \text{ in.}$

Depending on how precise you think the 5-inch measurement is, round this result to 16 in., 15.7 in., or 15.71 in.

What a Memory!

In April 1995, the Xinhua News Agency in southern China reported that Zhang Zhuo, a 12-year-old boy, set a record by reciting the value of pi from memory to 4,000 decimal places. He needed 25 minutes and 30 seconds to accomplish this amazing feat. His error rate was 0.2 percent.

His performance broke the previous record of 1,000 digits set by another Chinese boy many years ago.

CHECK YOUR UNDERSTANDING

Use a calculator to find each answer.

1. What is the circumference of a circle with a diameter of 3 inches?

2. What is the diameter of a circle with a circumference of 6 inches?

Check your answers on page 388.

Data & Probability

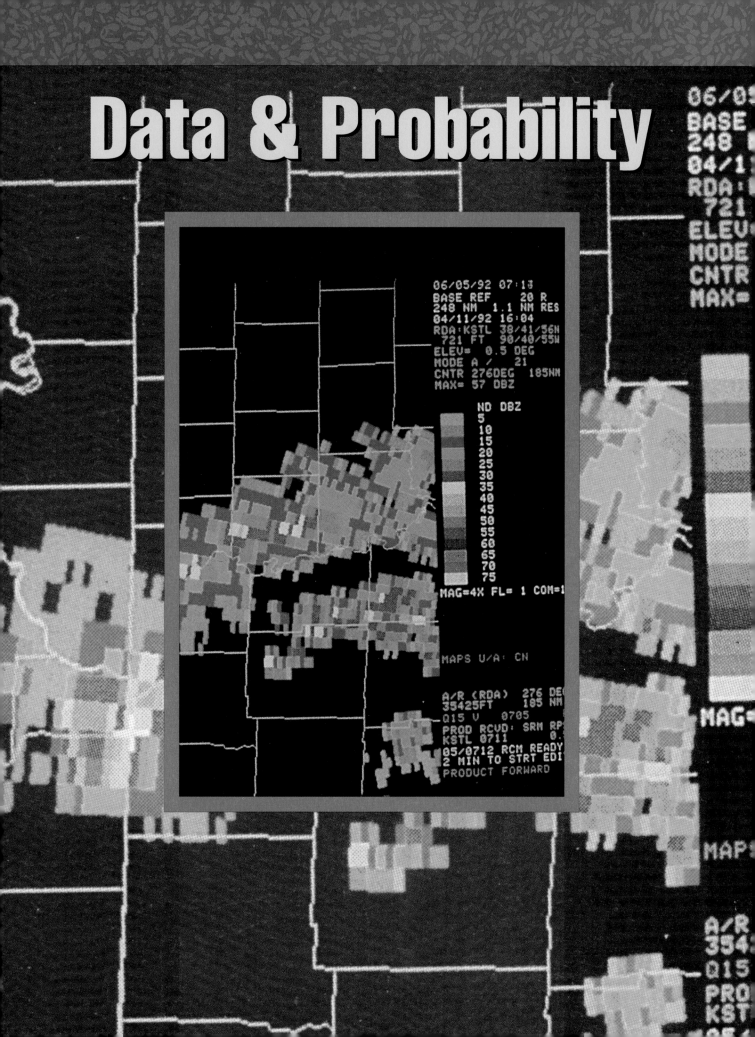

Collecting Data

There are different ways to collect information about something. You can count, measure, ask questions, or observe and describe what you see.

The information you collect is called **data.**

Surveys

Much of the information used to make decisions comes from **surveys.** Many surveys collect data about people. Stores survey their customers to find out what products they should carry. Television stations survey viewers to learn what programs are popular. Politicians survey people to learn how they plan to vote in elections.

The survey data about people is collected in several ways. These include face-to-face interviews, telephone interviews, written questionnaires that are returned by mail, and group discussions (often called *focus groups*).

However, not all surveys gather information about people. For example, there are surveys about cars and animal groups.

EXAMPLE

A bird survey is conducted during December and January each year in the Chicago area. Bird watchers list the different bird species they see. Then they count the number of each species observed. The lists are combined to create a final data set.

From the 1999–2000 Chicago Bird Survey

Species	Number of Birds Seen
crow	1,335
mallard duck	2,134
mourning dove	213
song sparrow	15

Some surveys collect data in other ways than interviews or questionnaires.

EXAMPLE Highway engineers sometimes make videotapes of vehicles and drivers along a street or highway. They use the video data to analyze vehicle speeds and driving patterns.

Samples

The **population** is a group of people or things that is being studied. Because the population may be very large, it may not be possible to collect data from every member. Therefore, data are collected only from a sample group to provide information that is probably valid about the entire population. A **sample** is a part of the population that is chosen to represent the whole population.

Large samples give more dependable estimates than small ones. For example, if you want to estimate the percentage of adults who drive to work, a sample of 100 persons provides a better estimate than a sample of 10.

EXAMPLE

A survey of teenagers needs data on people aged 13 to 19. There are about 27 million teenagers in the United States. Therefore, it would be impossible to collect data from every teenager. Instead, data are collected from a large sample of teenagers.

The results from a recent survey of teens:

Reason for Playing Sports	
Love of game	50%
Love to compete and win	24%
Be with friends	14%
Earn college scholarship	6%
Because I'm good at it	4%
Recognition	2%

Source: Reported in the *Chicago Sun-Times*, 1/16/00.

The decennial (every 10 years) census is an example of a survey that includes *all* the people in the United States. Every household is required to fill out a census form. But certain questions are asked only in a sample of 1 in 6 households.

A **random sample** is a sample that gives all members of the population the same chance of being selected. Random samples give more dependable information than those which are not random.

EXAMPLE   Suppose you want to estimate what percentage of the population will vote for Mr. Jones.

If you use a sample of 100 best friends of Mr. Jones, the sample is *not* a random sample. People who do not know Mr. Jones have no chance of being selected. A sample of best friends will not fairly represent the entire population. It will not furnish a dependable estimate of how the entire population will vote.

Student Survey Data

Information was collected from samples of students at Lee Middle School. Three questions were asked.

1. Entertainment Data

Students were asked to select their favorite form of entertainment. They were given four possible choices:

TV: Watch TV/videos   **Games:** Play video/computer games

Music: Listen to radio/CDs   **Read:** Read books, magazines

Twenty-four students responded (answered the survey). Here are their data.

TV	TV	Read	TV	Games	TV	Music	Games
Games	TV	Read	Music	TV	TV	Music	TV
Games	Games	Music	TV	TV	Games	TV	Read

2. Favorite Sports Data

Students were asked to select their TWO favorite sports from this list.

Baseball	Basketball	Bicycle riding
Bowling	Soccer	Swimming

Twenty students responded. The data below includes 40 answers because each student named two sports.

Basketball	Bicycle	Swimming	Soccer	Basketball
Swimming	Baseball	Swimming	Bicycle	Swimming
Bicycle	Swimming	Soccer	Bicycle	Soccer
Bowling	Soccer	Bicycle	Swimming	Bicycle
Bicycle	Swimming	Baseball	Bowling	Bicycle
Baseball	Bowling	Basketball	Basketball	Swimming
Basketball	Swimming	Soccer	Soccer	Baseball
Bicycle	Soccer	Bicycle	Swimming	Bicycle

3. Shower/Bath Time Data

A sample of 40 students was asked to estimate the number of minutes they usually spend taking a shower or bath. Here are the data.

3	20	10	5	8	4	10	7	5	5
25	5	3	25	20	17	5	30	14	35
9	20	15	7	5	10	16	40	10	15
10	5	15	10	15	5	12	22	3	9

Organizing Data

Once the data have been collected, it helps to organize them in order to make them easier to understand. **Line plots** and **tally charts** are two methods of organizing data.

EXAMPLE Ms. Barton's class got the following scores on a 20-word spelling test. Make a line plot and a tally chart to show the data below.

20 15 18 17 20 12 15 17 19 18 20 16 16
17 14 15 19 18 18 15 10 20 19 18 15 18

Scores on a 20-Word Spelling Test

Number
of
Students

```
                                        X
                        X               X
                        X               X           X
                        X       X   X   X   X
                        X   X   X   X   X   X
    X       X       X   X   X   X   X   X   X
```
    10 11 12 13 14 15 16 17 18 19 20
              Number Correct

Scores on a 20-Word Spelling Test	
Number Correct	Number of Students
10	/
11	
12	/
13	
14	/
15	#####
16	//
17	///
18	##### /
19	///
20	////

In the line plot, there are 5 Xs above 15.
In the tally chart, there are 5 tallies to the right of 15.

Both the line plot and the tally chart help to organize the data. They make it easier to describe the data. For example,

- 4 students had 20 correct (a perfect score).
- 18 correct is the score that came up most often.
- 10, 12, and 14 correct are scores that came up least often.
- 0–9, 11, and 13 correct are scores that did not occur at all.

CHECK YOUR UNDERSTANDING

Here are the numbers of hits made by 12 players in a baseball game. 3 2 4 0 2 2 1 0 2 2 0 3

Organize the data.

1. Make a tally chart.   **2.** Make a line plot.

Check your answers on page 388.

Sometimes the data are spread over a wide range of numbers. This makes a tally chart and a line plot difficult to draw. In such cases, you can make a tally chart in which the results are grouped. Or, you may organize the data by making a **stem-and-leaf plot.**

For a science project, the students in Ms. Beck's class took each other's pulse rates. (A *pulse rate* is the number of heartbeats per minute.) These were the results:

75	86	108	94	75	88	86	99	78	86
90	94	70	94	78	75	90	102	65	94
92	72	90	86	102	78	88	75	72	
70	94	85	88	105	86	78	82		

Tally Chart of Grouped Data

The data have been sorted or grouped into intervals of 10.

The chart shows that most of the students had a pulse rate from 70 to 99. More students had a pulse rate in the 70s than in any other interval.

Pulse Rates of Students

Number of Heartbeats	Number of Students
60–69	/
70–79	₩₩₩ ₩₩₩ //
80–89	₩₩₩ ₩₩₩
90–99	₩₩₩ ₩₩₩
100–109	////

Stem-and-Leaf Plot

In a stem-and-leaf plot, the digit or digits in the left column (the **stem**) are combined with a single digit in the right column (the **leaf**) to form a numeral.

Each row has as many entries as there are digits in the right column. For example, the row with 9 in the left column has ten entries: 94, 99, 90, 94, 94, 90, 94, 92, 90, and 94.

Pulse Rates of Students

Stems (10s)	Leaves (1s)
6	5
7	5 5 8 0 8 5 2 8 5 2 0 8
8	6 8 6 6 6 8 2 5 8 6
9	4 9 0 4 4 0 4 2 0 4
10	8 2 2 5

CHECK YOUR UNDERSTANDING

Michael Jordan played in 12 games of the 1996 NBA Playoffs. He scored the following number of points:

35 29 26 44 28 46 27 35 21 35 17 45

Organize the data.

1. Make a tally chart of grouped data.

2. Make a stem-and-leaf plot.

Check your answers on page 388.

Statistical Landmarks

The **landmarks** for a set of data are used to describe the data.

- The **minimum** is the smallest value.
- The **maximum** is the largest value.
- The **range** is the difference between the maximum and the minimum.
- The **mode** is the value or values that occur most often.
- The **median** is the middle value.

EXAMPLE   Here is a record of children's absences for one week at Medgar Evers School.

Monday	Tuesday	Wednesday	Thursday	Friday
25	15	10	14	14

Find the landmarks for the data.

Minimum (lowest) number: 10

Range of numbers: 25 − 10 = 15

Maximum (highest) number: 25

Mode (most frequent number): 14

To find the median (middle value):

- List the numbers in order from smallest to largest or from largest to smallest.

  10 14 14 15 25

- Cross out one number from each end of the list.

  1̶0̶ 14 14 15 2̶5̶

- Continue to cross out one more number from each end of the list.

  1̶0̶ 1̶4̶ 14 1̶5̶ 2̶5̶
            ↑
         median

- The median is the number that remains after all others have been crossed out.

CHECK YOUR UNDERSTANDING

Here are the math quiz scores (number correct) for 11 students:

1 2 0 4 2 4 3 2 4 1 2

Find the landmarks for the data.

1. Find the minimum.   **2.** Find the maximum.   **3.** Find the range.

4. Find the mode.   **5.** Find the median.

Check your answers on page 388.

EXAMPLE The **line plot** shows students' scores on a
20-word spelling test. Find the landmarks for the data.

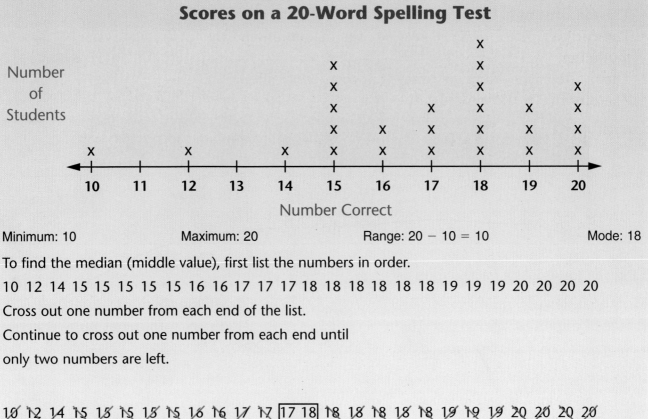

Scores on a 20-Word Spelling Test

Minimum: 10   Maximum: 20   Range: 20 − 10 = 10   Mode: 18

To find the median (middle value), first list the numbers in order.

10 12 14 15 15 15 15 15 16 16 17 17 17 18 18 18 18 18 18 19 19 19 20 20 20 20

Cross out one number from each end of the list.

Continue to cross out one number from each end until

only two numbers are left.

10̸ 1̸2̸ 1̸4̸ 1̸5̸ 1̸5̸ 1̸5̸ 1̸5̸ 1̸5̸ 1̸6̸ 1̸6̸ 1̸7̸ 1̸7̸ |17 18| 1̸8̸ 1̸8̸ 1̸8̸ 1̸8̸ 1̸8̸ 1̸9̸ 1̸9̸ 1̸9̸ 2̸0̸ 2̸0̸ 2̸0̸ 2̸0̸

middle scores

The two numbers remaining are the middle scores.
There are two middle scores, 17 and 18.
The median is 17.5, which is the number halfway between 17 and 18.

CHECK YOUR UNDERSTANDING

1. Here are the math quiz scores (number correct) for 12 students:

0 1 3 2 4 3 4 2 1 2 4 3.

Find the minimum, maximum, range, mode, and median for this set of data.

2. Find the median for this set of numbers: 33 12 8 21 16 33 16 9 8 12

Check your answers on page 388.

The Mean (or Average)

The **mean** of a set of numbers is often called the *average*.
To find the mean, do the following:

Step 1: Add the numbers.
Step 2: Then divide the sum by the number of addends.

> **NOTE**
>
> The mean and the median are often the same or almost the same. Both the mean and the median can be thought of as a "typical" number for the data set.

> **EXAMPLE**   On a 4-day trip, Lisa's family drove 240, 100, 200, and 160 miles. What is the mean number of miles they drove per day?
> **Step 1:** Add the numbers: 240 + 100 + 200 + 160 = 700.
> **Step 2:** Divide by the number of addends: 700 ÷ 4 = 175.
> The mean is 175 miles. They drove an average of 175 miles per day. You can use a calculator:
>
> Add the miles. Key in: 240 ⊕ 100 ⊕ 200 ⊕ 160 (Enter)
>
> Answer: 700
>
> Divide the sum by 4. Key in: 700 ÷ 4 (Enter)   Answer: 175

Sometimes you will calculate the mean for a set of numbers where many of the numbers are repeated. The shortcut explained below could save you time.

> **EXAMPLE**   Calculate the mean for this set of eight numbers:
>
> 80 80 80 90 90 90 90 90
>
> You could add the eight numbers, then divide by 8.
> 80 + 80 + 80 + 90 + 90 + 90 + 90 + 90 = 690; 690 ÷ 8 = 86.25
> Or, you could use this shortcut.
>
> - Multiply each data value by the number of times it occurs.
> - Add these products.
> - Divide by the number of addends.
>
>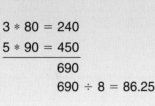
>
> 3 * 80 = 240
> 5 * 90 = 450
> 690
> 690 ÷ 8 = 86.25
>
> The mean is 86.25.

CHECK YOUR UNDERSTANDING

Jason received these scores on math tests: 80 75 85 75 85 90 80 70 80 90 80.

Use your calculator to find Jason's mean score.

Check your answers on page 388.

Bar Graphs

A **bar graph** is a drawing that uses bars to represent numbers. Bar graphs display information in a way that makes it easy to show comparisons.

The title of a bar graph describes the information in the graph. Each bar has a label. Units are given to show how something was counted or measured. When possible, the graph gives the source of the information.

EXAMPLE This is a **vertical bar graph.**

- Each bar represents the mean (average) length of the animal named beneath the bar.
- It is easy to compare animal lengths by comparing the bars. The whale is about 3 times as long as the python. The python, tapeworm, and shark are about the same length.

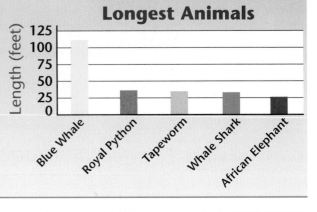

EXAMPLE This is a **horizontal bar graph.**

The purpose of this graph is to compare the fat content of several kinds of food.

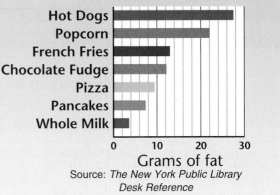

CHECK YOUR UNDERSTANDING

The table at the right shows the average number of vacation days per year for three countries. Make a bar graph to show this information.

Vacation Days per Year

Country	Average Number of Days
Canada	26
Italy	42
United States	13

Check your answers on page 388.

Side-by-Side and Stacked Bar Graphs

Sometimes there are two or more bar graphs that are related to the same situation. Related bar graphs are often combined into a single graph. The combined graph saves space and makes it easier to compare the data. The examples below show two different ways to draw combined bar graphs.

EXAMPLE One bar graph shows road miles from Los Angeles to different cities. A second bar graph shows air miles.

The graphs are combined into a **side-by-side bar graph** by drawing the related bars side-by-side in different colors. It is easy to compare road miles and air miles on the side-by-side graph.

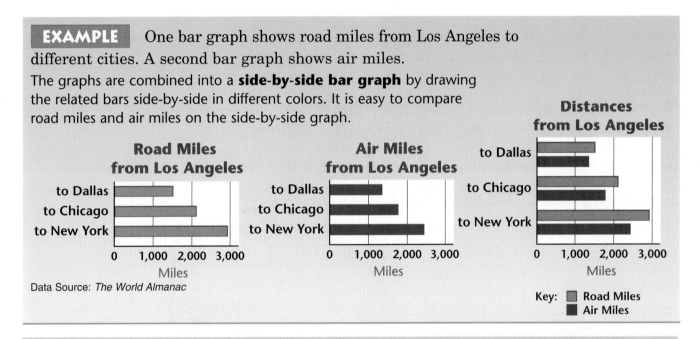

Data Source: *The World Almanac*

EXAMPLE The bar graphs below show the number of sports teams that boys and girls joined during a 1-year period.

The bars within each graph can be stacked on top of one another. The **stacked bar graph** includes each of the stacked bars.

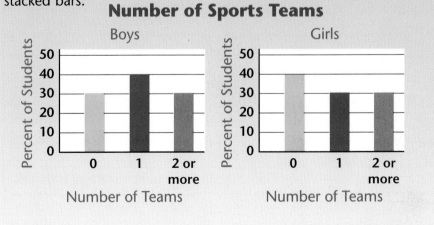

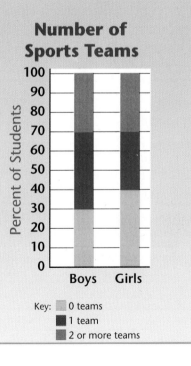

Line Graphs

Line graphs are used to display information that shows trends. They often show how something has changed over a period of time.

Line graphs are often called **broken-line graphs.** Line segments connect the points on the graph. The segments joined end-to-end look like a broken line.

Line graphs have a horizontal and a vertical scale. Each of these scales is called an **axis** (plural: **axes**). Each axis is labeled to show what is being measured and what the unit of measure is.

When looking at a line graph, try to determine the purpose of the graph. See what conclusions you can draw from the graph.

Broken-Line Graph

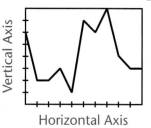

Joined end-to-end, the segments look like a broken line.

EXAMPLE   The broken-line graph at the right shows average temperatures for one year in Anchorage, Alaska.

The horizontal axis shows each month of the year. The average temperature for a month is shown with a dot above the label for that month. The labels on the vertical axis at the left are used to estimate the temperature represented by that dot.

July is the warmest month (58°F). January is the coldest month (15°F). The largest change in temperature from one month to the next is a 14°F decrease from October to November.

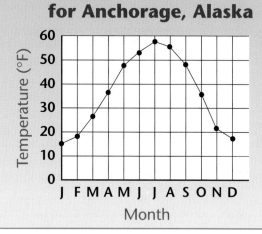

Average Temperatures for Anchorage, Alaska

CHECK YOUR UNDERSTANDING

The following table shows average temperatures for Phoenix, Arizona.

Make a line graph to show this information.

Average Temperatures for Phoenix, Arizona

Month	Jan	Feb	Mar	Apr	May	Jun	Jul	Aug	Sep	Oct	Nov	Dec
Temperature (°F)	54	58	62	70	79	88	94	92	86	75	62	54

Check your answers on page 388.

How to Use the Percent Circle

A **compass** is a device for drawing circles. You can also use some of the shapes on your **Geometry Template** to draw circles.

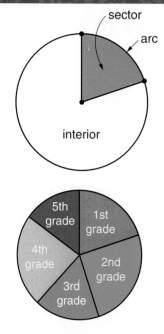

An **arc** is a piece of a circle. If you mark two points on a circle, these points and the part of the circle between them form an arc.

The region inside a circle is called its **interior.**

A **sector** is a wedge-shaped piece of a circle and its interior. A sector consists of two radii (singular: radius), the arc determined by their endpoints, and the part of the interior of the circle bounded by the radii and the arc.

A **circle graph** is sometimes called a **pie graph** because it looks like a pie that has been cut into several pieces. Each "piece" is a sector of the circle.

You can use the **Percent Circle** on your Geometry Template to find what percent of the circle graph each sector represents. Here are two methods for using the Percent Circle.

The circle graph shows the distribution of students in grades 1 to 5 at Elm Place School.

Method 1: Direct Measure
- Place the center of the Percent Circle over the center of the circle graph.
- Rotate the template so that the 0% mark is aligned with one side (line segment) of the sector you are measuring.
- Read the percent at the mark on the Percent Circle located over the other side of the sector. This tells what percent the sector represents.

The sector for first grade represents 20%.

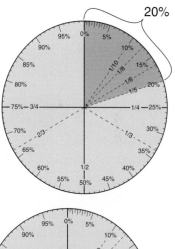

Method 2: Difference Comparison
- Place the center of the Percent Circle over the center of the circle graph.
- Note the percent reading for one side of the sector you are measuring.
- Find the percent reading for the other side of the sector.
- Find the difference between these readings.

The sector for second grade represents 45% – 20%, or 25%.

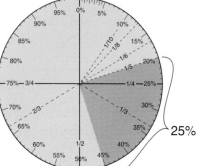

CHECK YOUR UNDERSTANDING
What percents are represented by the other three sectors in the above circle graph?
Check your answers on page 389.

How to Draw a Circle Graph Using a Percent Circle

EXAMPLE Draw a circle graph to show the following information. The students in Ms. Ahmad's class were asked to name their favorite colors: 9 students chose blue, 7 students chose green, 4 students chose yellow, and 5 chose red.

Step 1: Find what percent of the total each part represents. The total number of students who voted is $9 + 7 + 4 + 5 = 25$.

- 9 out of 25 chose blue.

  $\frac{9}{25} = \frac{36}{100} = 36\%$, so 36% chose blue.

- 7 out of 25 chose green.

  $\frac{7}{25} = \frac{28}{100} = 28\%$, so 28% chose green.

- 4 out of 25 chose yellow.

  $\frac{4}{25} = \frac{16}{100} = 16\%$, so 16% chose yellow.

- 5 out of 25 chose red.

  $\frac{5}{25} = \frac{20}{100} = 20\%$, so 20% chose red.

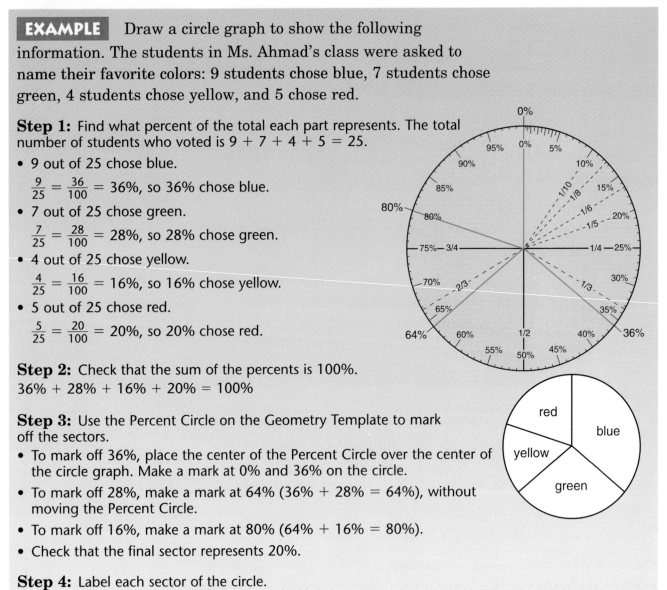

Step 2: Check that the sum of the percents is 100%.
$36\% + 28\% + 16\% + 20\% = 100\%$

Step 3: Use the Percent Circle on the Geometry Template to mark off the sectors.

- To mark off 36%, place the center of the Percent Circle over the center of the circle graph. Make a mark at 0% and 36% on the circle.
- To mark off 28%, make a mark at 64% ($36\% + 28\% = 64\%$), without moving the Percent Circle.
- To mark off 16%, make a mark at 80% ($64\% + 16\% = 80\%$).
- Check that the final sector represents 20%.

Step 4: Label each sector of the circle.

CHECK YOUR UNDERSTANDING

Draw a circle graph to display the following information:
- The Hot Shots basketball team scored 30 points in one game.
- Sally scored 15 points. • Drew and Bonita each scored 6 points.
- Damon scored 3 points.

Check your answers on page 389.

How to Draw a Circle Graph Using a Protractor

EXAMPLE   Draw a circle graph to show the following information:

In the month of June, there were 19 sunny days, 6 partly-cloudy days, and 5 cloudy days.

Step 1: Find out what fraction or percent of the total each part represents. June has 30 days.

- 5 out of 30 were cloudy days.
  $\frac{5}{30} = \frac{1}{6}$, so $\frac{1}{6}$ of the days were cloudy.

- 6 out of 30 were partly-cloudy days.
  $\frac{6}{30} = \frac{1}{5}$, so $\frac{1}{5}$ of the days were partly cloudy.

- 19 out of 30 were sunny days.
  $\frac{19}{30} = 0.633 \ldots = 63.3\%$, so 63.3% of the days were sunny.

Step 2: Calculate the degree measure of the sector for each piece of data.

- The number of cloudy days in June was $\frac{1}{6}$ of the total number of days. Therefore, the degree measure of the sector for cloudy days is $\frac{1}{6}$ of 360°. $\frac{1}{6}$ of 360° = 60°.

- The number of partly-cloudy days in June was $\frac{1}{5}$ of the total number of days. Therefore, the degree measure of the sector for partly-cloudy days is $\frac{1}{5}$ of 360°. $\frac{1}{5}$ of 360° = 72°.

- The number of sunny days in June was 63.3% of the total number of days. Therefore, the degree measure of the sector for sunny days is 63.3% of 360°. 0.633 * 360° = 228°, rounded to the nearest degree.

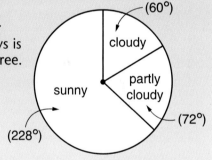

Step 3: Check that the sum of the degree measures of the sectors is 360°.
$$60° + 72° + 228° = 360°$$

Step 4: Measure each sector with a protractor. Draw and label the sector.

CHECK YOUR UNDERSTANDING

Use your protractor to make a circle graph to display the information in the chart. What is the degree measure of each sector?

Favorite Subjects

Subject	Number of Students
Reading	6
Social Studies	2
Math	4
Music	1
Science	2
Art	5

Check your answers on page 389.

Chance and Probability

Chance

Things that happen are called **events.** There are many events that you can be sure about:

- You are **certain** that the sun will set today.
- It is **impossible** for you to grow to be 10 feet tall.

There are also many events that you *cannot* be sure about.

- You cannot be sure that you will get a letter tomorrow.
- You cannot be sure whether it will be sunny next Friday.

You might sometimes talk about the **chance** that something will happen. If Paul is a good chess player, you may say, "Paul has a *good chance* of winning the game." If Paul is a poor player, you may say, "It is *very unlikely* that Paul will win."

Probability

Sometimes a number is used to tell the chance of something happening. This number is called a **probability.** It is a number from 0 to 1. The closer a probability is to 1, the more likely it is that an event will happen.

- A probability of 0 means the event is *impossible.* The probability is 0 that you will live to the age of 150.
- A probability of 1 means that the event is *certain.* The probability is 1 that the sun will rise tomorrow.
- A probability of $\frac{1}{2}$ means that in the long run, an event will happen about 1 in 2 times (half of the time or 50% of the time.) The probability a tossed coin will land heads up is $\frac{1}{2}$. We often say that the coin has a "50–50 chance" of landing heads up.

A probability can be written as a fraction, a decimal, or a percent. The **Probability Meter** is often used to record probabilities. It is marked to show fractions, decimals, and percents between 0 (or 0%) and 1 (or 100%).

The phrases printed on the bar of the Probability Meter may be used to describe probabilities in words. For example, suppose that the probability of snow tomorrow is 70%. The 70% mark falls within that part of the bar where "LIKELY" is printed. So you can say that "Snow is *likely* tomorrow," instead of stating the probability as 70%.

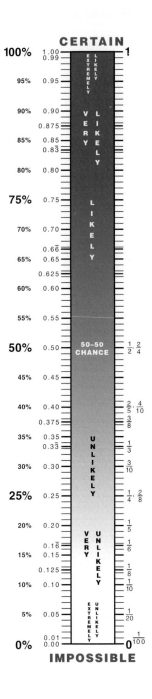

Calculating a Probability

Four common ways for finding probabilities are shown below.

Make a Guess	Vince guesses that he has a 10% chance (a 1 in 10 chance) of returning home by 9 o'clock.
Conduct an Experiment	Elizabeth dropped 100 tacks: 60 landed point up and 40 landed point down. The chance of a tack landing point up is $\frac{60}{100}$, or 60%.
Use a Data Table	Kenny got 48 hits in his last 100 times at bat. He estimates the probability that he will get a hit the next time at bat is $\frac{48}{100}$, or 48%.
Assume that All Possible Results Have the Same Chance	A die has 6 faces. Each face has the same chance of coming up. The probability of rolling a 4 is $\frac{1}{6}$. The probability of rolling a 4 or a 3 is double this—$\frac{2}{6}$, or $\frac{1}{3}$.

For the Data Table example:

Hits	48
Walks	11
Outs	41
Total	100

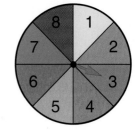

The spinner is divided into 8 equal sections. Each section, and each number from 1 through 8, has the same chance ($\frac{1}{8}$ or 12.5%) of being landed on. The sections numbered 1 through 8 are **equally likely.**

> **EXAMPLES**   What is the probability that the spinner shown at the right will land on an even number? On a number greater than 5?
>
> The spinner will land on an even number if it lands on 2, 4, 6, or 8. Each of these numbers is likely to come up $\frac{1}{8}$ of the time. So the total chance that one of these numbers will come up is $\frac{1}{8} + \frac{1}{8} + \frac{1}{8} + \frac{1}{8}$, or $\frac{4}{8}$.
>
> The probability of landing on an even number is $\frac{4}{8}$, $\frac{1}{2}$, or 50%.
>
> The spinner will land on a number greater than 5 if it lands on 6, 7, or 8. Each of these numbers has a probability of $\frac{1}{8}$ of coming up.
>
> The probability that a number greater than 5 will come up is $\frac{1}{8} + \frac{1}{8} + \frac{1}{8} = \frac{3}{8}$, or 37.5%.

CHECK YOUR UNDERSTANDING

Use the spinner above to find the probability of the following:

1. landing on a number less than 7

2. landing on a prime number

Check your answers on page 389.

Tree Diagrams and the Multiplication Counting Principle

Many situations require two or more choices. Here is an example of a simple situation that involves two choices.

Suppose Vince is buying a new shirt. He must choose among three colors—white, blue, and green. He must also decide between long or short sleeves. How many different combinations of color and sleeve length are there?

One way to count the different combinations and see what they are is by making a **tree diagram** like the one shown at the right. The paths drawn look like the branches of a tree.

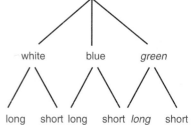

- The 3 top branches of the diagram are labeled white, blue, and green to show the color choices.
- The 2 branches below each color show the sleeve-length choices that are possible.

Each possible way to choose a shirt is found by following a path from the top to the bottom of the diagram. One possible choice is shown in italics: *green–long*. Counting shows that there are six different paths. Six different shirt choices are possible.

Multiplication is used to solve many types of counting problems that involve two or more choices.

Multiplication Counting Principle

Suppose you can make a first choice in m ways and a second choice in n ways. There are $m * n$ ways of making the first choice followed by the second choice.

> **EXAMPLE**   Vince has shirts in 8 different colors and pants in 4 different colors. How many different color combinations for shirts and pants can Vince choose from?
>
> Use the Multiplication Counting Principle: **8 * 4 = 32**. There are 32 different color combinations that Vince could choose from.

Cases with three or more choices can be counted in the same way.

CHECK YOUR UNDERSTANDING

Draw a tree diagram that shows all 32 combinations for the example.

Check your answers on page 389.

Geometry & Constructions

Geometry in Our World

The world is filled with geometry. There are angles, segments, lines, and curves everywhere you look. There are 2-dimensional and 3-dimensional shapes of every type.

Many wonderful geometric patterns can be seen in nature. You can find patterns in flowers, spider webs, leaves, seashells, even your own face and body.

The ideas of geometry are also found in the things people create. Think of the games you play. Checkers is played with round pieces. The gameboard is covered with squares. Basketball and tennis are played with spheres. They are played on rectangular courts that are painted with straight and curved lines. The next time you play or watch a game, notice how geometry is important to the way the game is played.

The places we live in are built from plans that use geometry. Buildings almost always have rectangular rooms. They often have triangular roofs. Archways are sometimes curved. Staircases may be straight or spiral. Buildings and rooms are often decorated with beautiful patterns. You see these decorations on doors and windows; on walls, floors, and ceilings; and on railings of staircases.

The clothes people wear are often decorated with geometric shapes. So are the things they use every day. Everywhere in the world, people create things using geometric patterns. Examples include quilts, pottery, baskets, and tile patterns. Some patterns are shown here. Which are your favorites?

 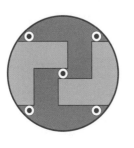  

Make a practice of noticing geometric shapes around you. Pay attention to bridges, buildings, and other structures. Look at the ways in which simple shapes such as triangles, rectangles, and circles are combined. Notice interesting designs. Share these with your classmates and your teacher.

In this section, you will study geometric shapes and learn how to construct them. As you learn, try to create your own beautiful designs.

Angles

An **angle** is formed by 2 rays or 2 line segments that share the same endpoint.

angle formed by 2 rays　　　　**angle formed by 2 segments**

The endpoint where the rays or segments meet is called the **vertex** of the angle. The rays or segments are called the **sides** of the angle.

Naming Angles

The symbol for an angle is ∠. An angle can be named in two ways:

1. Name the vertex. The angle shown above is angle *S*. Write this as ∠*S*.

2. Name 3 points: the vertex and one point on each side of the angle. The angle above can be named angle *DSC* (∠*DSC*) or angle *CSD* (∠*CSD*). The vertex must always be listed in the middle, between the points on the sides.

Measuring Angles

The **protractor** is a tool used to measure angles. Angles are measured in **degrees.** A degree is the unit of measure for the size of an angle.

The **degree symbol** ° is often used in place of the word *degrees*. The measure of ∠*S* above is 30 degrees, or 30°.

Sometimes there is confusion about which angle should be measured. The small curved arrow in each picture shows which angle opening should be measured.

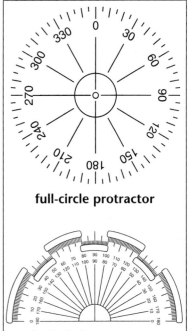

full-circle protractor

half-circle protractor

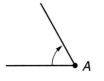　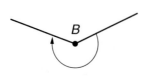　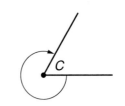

Measure of ∠*A* is 60°.　　Measure of ∠*B* is 225°.　　Measure of ∠*C* is 300°.

Classifying Angles According to Size

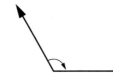

A right angle measures 90°.

An acute angle measures between 0° and 90°.

An obtuse angle measures between 90° and 180°.

A straight angle measures 180°.

Classifying Pairs of Angles

Vertical angles are angles that are opposite each other when two lines intersect. If two angles are vertical angles, they have the same measure in degrees.

Adjacent angles are angles that are next to each other. They have a common side but no other overlap.

Supplementary angles are two angles whose measures add up to 180°.

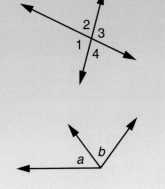

A reflex angle measures between 180° and 360°.

EXAMPLE When two lines intersect, the angles formed have special properties.

For the figures at the right, the following statements are true.
- Angles 1 and 3 are vertical angles. They have the same measure. Angles 2 and 4 are vertical angles. They have the same measure.
- There are four pairs of adjacent angles:
  ∠1 and ∠2   ∠2 and ∠3   ∠3 and ∠4   ∠4 and ∠1
- There are four pairs of supplementary angles:
  ∠1 and ∠2   ∠2 and ∠3   ∠3 and ∠4   ∠4 and ∠1
- Angles a and b are adjacent angles. They are *not* supplementary angles because their measures don't add up to 180°.

CHECK YOUR UNDERSTANDING

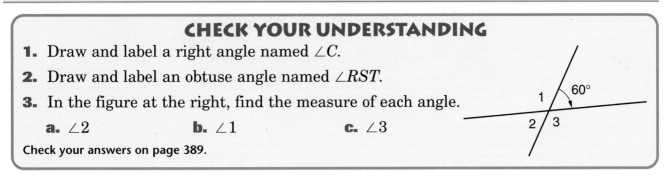

1. Draw and label a right angle named ∠C.
2. Draw and label an obtuse angle named ∠RST.
3. In the figure at the right, find the measure of each angle.
   a. ∠2   **b.** ∠1   **c.** ∠3

Check your answers on page 389.

Parallel Lines and Segments

Parallel lines are lines on a flat surface that never meet. Think of a railroad track that goes on forever. The two rails are parallel lines. They never meet or cross and are always the same distance apart.

Parallel line segments are segments that are always the same distance apart. The top and bottom edges of this page are parallel segments because they are always about 11 inches apart.

The symbol for *parallel* is a pair of vertical lines ∥. If $\overline{BF}$ and $\overline{TG}$ are parallel, write $\overline{BF} \parallel \overline{TG}$.

If lines or segments cross each other, they **intersect**. Lines or segments that intersect and form right angles are called **perpendicular** lines or segments.

The symbol for *perpendicular* is ⊥, which looks like an upside-down letter T. If $\overleftrightarrow{TS}$ and $\overleftrightarrow{XY}$ are perpendicular, write $\overleftrightarrow{TS} \perp \overleftrightarrow{XY}$.

EXAMPLES

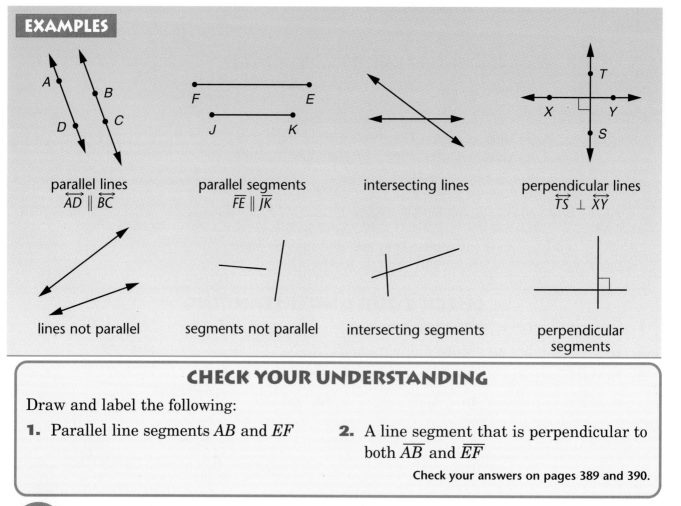

parallel lines
$\overleftrightarrow{AD} \parallel \overleftrightarrow{BC}$

parallel segments
$\overline{FE} \parallel \overline{JK}$

intersecting lines

perpendicular lines
$\overleftrightarrow{TS} \perp \overleftrightarrow{XY}$

lines not parallel

segments not parallel

intersecting segments

perpendicular segments

CHECK YOUR UNDERSTANDING

Draw and label the following:

1. Parallel line segments *AB* and *EF*

2. A line segment that is perpendicular to both $\overline{AB}$ and $\overline{EF}$

Check your answers on pages 389 and 390.

Line Segments, Rays, Lines, and Angles

Figure	Name or Symbol	Description
• A	A	**point:** A location in space.
C B endpoints	$\overline{BC}$ or $\overline{CB}$	**line segment:** A straight path between 2 points, called its endpoints.
N M endpoint	$\overrightarrow{MN}$	**ray:** A straight path that goes on forever in one direction from an endpoint.
T S	$\overleftrightarrow{ST}$ or $\overleftrightarrow{TS}$	**line:** A straight path that goes on forever in both directions.
vertex S T P	$\angle T$ or $\angle STP$ or $\angle PTS$	**angle:** Two rays or line segments with a common endpoint called the vertex.
B A D C	$\overleftrightarrow{AB} \parallel \overleftrightarrow{CD}$ $\overline{AB} \parallel \overline{CD}$	**parallel lines:** Lines that never meet and are everywhere the same distance apart. **parallel line segments:** Segments that are everywhere the same distance apart.
R E D S	none none	**intersecting lines:** Lines that meet. **intersecting line segments:** Segments that meet.
B E F C	$\overleftrightarrow{BC} \perp \overleftrightarrow{EF}$ $\overline{BC} \perp \overline{EF}$	**perpendicular lines:** Lines that intersect at right angles. **perpendicular line segments:** Segments that intersect at right angles.

CHECK YOUR UNDERSTANDING

Draw and label each of the following.

1. point H **2.** $\overrightarrow{JK}$ **3.** $\angle CAT$ **4.** $\overline{TU}$ **5.** $\overline{PR} \parallel \overline{JK}$ **6.** $\overrightarrow{EF}$

Check your answers on page 390.

Polygons

A **polygon** is a flat, 2-dimensional figure made up of line segments called **sides.** A polygon can have any number of sides, as long as it has at least three. The **interior** (inside) of the polygon is not a part of the polygon.

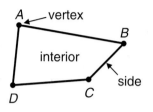

* The sides of a polygon are connected end-to-end and make a closed path.

* The sides of a polygon do not cross (intersect).

Each endpoint where two sides meet is called a **vertex.** The plural of vertex is **vertices.**

Figures that Are Polygons

| 4 sides, 4 vertices | 3 sides, 3 vertices | 7 sides, 7 vertices |

Figures that Are NOT Polygons

All sides of a polygon must be line segments. Curved lines are not line segments.

The sides of a polygon must form a closed path.

A polygon must have at least 3 sides.

The sides of a polygon must not cross.

Polygons are named after the number of sides they have. The prefix for a polygon's name tells the number of sides it has.

Prefixes

tri-	3
quad-	4
penta-	5
hexa-	6
hepta-	7
octa-	8
nona-	9
deca-	10
dodeca-	12

Convex Polygons

A **convex** polygon is a polygon in which all the sides are pushed outward. The polygons below are convex.

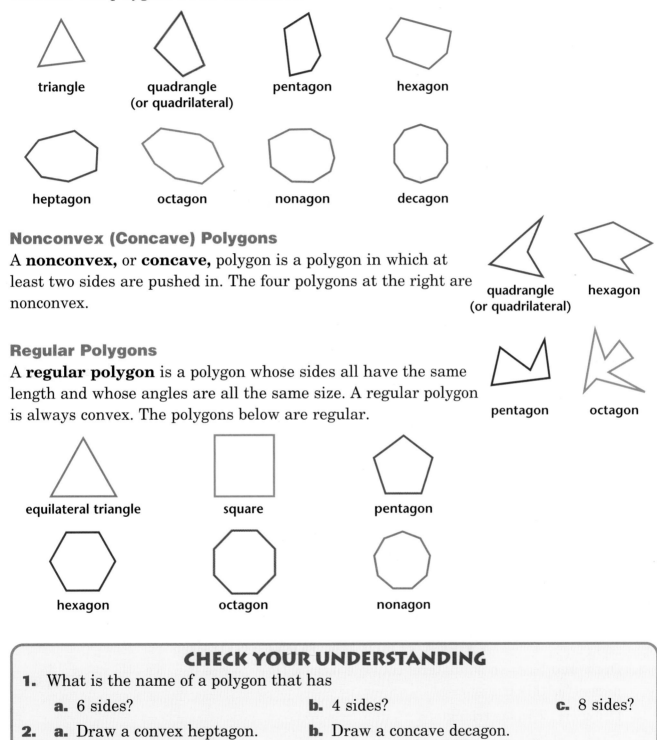

triangle

quadrangle
(or quadrilateral)

pentagon

hexagon

heptagon

octagon

nonagon

decagon

Nonconvex (Concave) Polygons

A **nonconvex,** or **concave,** polygon is a polygon in which at least two sides are pushed in. The four polygons at the right are nonconvex.

quadrangle
(or quadrilateral)

hexagon

Regular Polygons

A **regular polygon** is a polygon whose sides all have the same length and whose angles are all the same size. A regular polygon is always convex. The polygons below are regular.

pentagon

octagon

equilateral triangle

square

pentagon

hexagon

octagon

nonagon

CHECK YOUR UNDERSTANDING

1. What is the name of a polygon that has
    a. 6 sides?   b. 4 sides?   c. 8 sides?
2. a. Draw a convex heptagon.   b. Draw a concave decagon.
3. Explain why the cover of your journal is not a regular polygon.

Check your answers on page 390.

Triangles

Triangles are the simplest type of polygon. The prefix *tri-* means *three*. All triangles have 3 vertices, 3 sides, and 3 angles.

For the triangle shown here:

- The vertices are the points *B*, *C*, and *A*.
- The sides are $\overline{BC}$, $\overline{BA}$, and $\overline{CA}$.
- The angles are ∠*B*, ∠*C*, and ∠*A*.

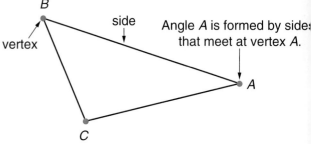

side

vertex

Angle *A* is formed by sides that meet at vertex *A*.

Triangles have 3-letter names. You name a triangle by listing in order the letter names for the vertices. The triangle above has 6 possible names: triangle *BCA, BAC, CAB, CBA, ABC,* or *ACB.*

Triangles may be classified according to the length of their sides.

A **scalene triangle** is a triangle whose sides all have different lengths.

An **isosceles triangle** is a triangle that has two sides of the same length.

An **equilateral triangle** is a triangle whose sides are all the same length.

A **right triangle** is a triangle with one right angle (square corner). Right triangles have many different shapes and sizes.

Some right triangles are scalene triangles, and some right triangles are isosceles triangles. But a right triangle cannot be an equilateral triangle because the side opposite the right angle is always longer than each of the other two sides.

CHECK YOUR UNDERSTANDING

1. Draw and label an equilateral triangle named *DEF*. Write the five other possible names for this triangle.

2. Draw an isosceles triangle.

3. Draw a right scalene triangle.

Check your answers on page 390.

Quadrangles

A **quadrangle** is a polygon that has 4 sides. Another name for quadrangle is **quadrilateral.** The prefix *quad-* means *four*. All quadrangles have 4 vertices, 4 sides, and 4 angles.

For the quadrangle shown here:

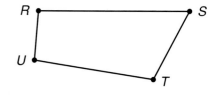

- The sides are $\overline{RS}$, $\overline{ST}$, $\overline{TU}$, and $\overline{UR}$.

- The vertices are *R*, *S*, *T*, and *U*.

- The angles are $\angle R$, $\angle S$, $\angle T$, and $\angle U$.

A quadrangle is named by listing in order the letter names for the vertices. The quadrangle above has 8 possible names:

RSTU, RUTS, STUR, SRUT, TURS, TSRU, URST, UTSR

Some quadrangles have two pairs of parallel sides. These quadrangles are called **parallelograms.**

Reminder: Two sides are parallel if they are the same distance apart everywhere.

Figures that Are Parallelograms

Opposite sides are parallel in each figure.

Figures that Are NOT Parallelograms

 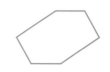

No parallel sides.

Only 1 pair of parallel sides.

3 pairs of parallel sides. A parallelogram must have exactly 2 pairs of parallel sides.

CHECK YOUR UNDERSTANDING

1. Draw and label a quadrangle named *QUAD* that has exactly one pair of parallel sides.

2. Is *QUAD* a parallelogram?

3. Write the seven other possible names for this quadrangle.

Check your answers on page 390.

Special types of quadrangles have been given names. Some of these are parallelograms, others are not.

The tree diagram at the right shows how the different types of quadrangles are related. For example, quadrangles are divided into two major groups— "parallelograms" and "not parallelograms." The special types of parallelograms include "rectangles," "rhombuses," and "squares."

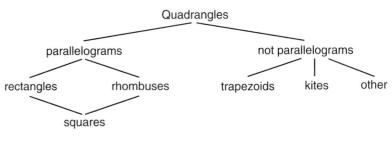

Quadrangles that Are Parallelograms

rectangle		**Rectangles** are parallelograms. A rectangle has 4 right angles (square corners). The sides do not all have to be the same length.
rhombus		**Rhombuses** are parallelograms. A rhombus has 4 sides that are all the same length. The angles of a rhombus are usually not right angles, but they may be.
square		**Squares** are parallelograms. A square has 4 right angles (square corners). Its 4 sides are all the same length. *All* squares are rectangles. *All* squares are also rhombuses.

Quadrangles that Are NOT Parallelograms

trapezoid		**Trapezoids** have exactly 1 pair of parallel sides. The 4 sides of a trapezoid can all have different lengths.
kite		A **kite** is a quadrangle with 2 pairs of equal sides. The equal sides are next to each other. The 4 sides cannot all have the same length. (A rhombus is not a kite.)
other		Any closed figure with 4 sides that is not a parallelogram, a trapezoid, or a kite.

CHECK YOUR UNDERSTANDING

What is the difference between the quadrangles in each pair below?

1. a square and a rectangle   **2.** a kite and a rhombus   **3.** a trapezoid and a parallelogram

Check your answers on page 390.

Geometric Solids

Polygons and circles are flat, **2-dimensional** figures. The surfaces they enclose take up a certain amount of area, but they do not have any thickness and do not take up any volume.

Three-dimensional shapes have length, width, *and* thickness. They take up volume. Boxes, pails, books, cans, and balls are all examples of 3-dimensional shapes.

A **geometric solid** is the surface or surfaces that surround a 3-dimensional shape. The surfaces of a geometric solid may be flat or curved or both. Despite its name, a geometric solid is hollow; it does not include the points within its interior.

- A **flat surface** of a solid is called a **face.**
- A **curved surface** of a solid does not have any special name.

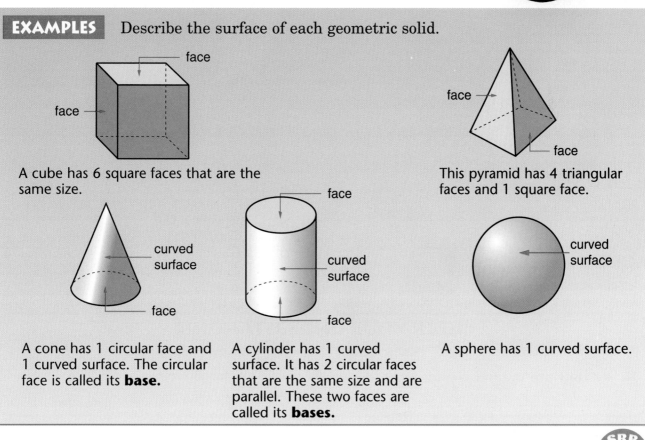

EXAMPLES   Describe the surface of each geometric solid.

face

face

A cube has 6 square faces that are the same size.

face

curved surface

face

A cone has 1 circular face and 1 curved surface. The circular face is called its **base.**

face

curved surface

face

A cylinder has 1 curved surface. It has 2 circular faces that are the same size and are parallel. These two faces are called its **bases.**

face

face

This pyramid has 4 triangular faces and 1 square face.

curved surface

A sphere has 1 curved surface.

The **edges** of a geometric solid are the line segments or curves where surfaces meet.

A corner of a geometric solid is called a **vertex** (plural *vertices*).

A vertex is usually a point at which edges meet. The vertex of a cone is an isolated corner completely separated from the edge of the cone.

A cone has 1 edge and 1 vertex. The vertex opposite the circular base is called the **apex.**

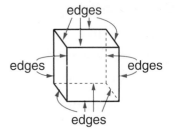

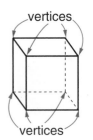

A cube has 12 edges and 8 vertices.

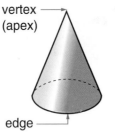

The pyramid shown here has 8 edges and 5 vertices. The vertex opposite the rectangular base is called the **apex.**

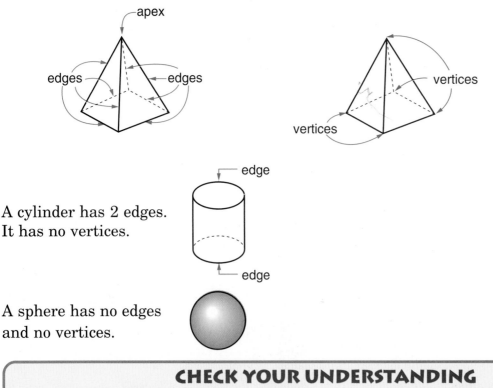

A cylinder has 2 edges. It has no vertices.

A sphere has no edges and no vertices.

CHECK YOUR UNDERSTANDING

1. a. How are cylinders and cones alike? **b.** How do they differ?

2. a. How are pyramids and cones alike? **b.** How do they differ?

Check your answers on page 391.

Polyhedrons

A **polyhedron** is a geometric solid whose surfaces are all formed by polygons. These surfaces are the faces of the polyhedron. A polyhedron does not have any curved surfaces.

Two important groups of polyhedrons are shown below. These are **pyramids** and **prisms.**

Pyramids

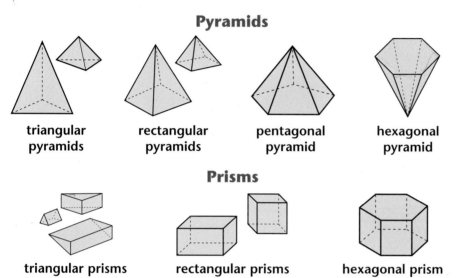

triangular pyramids

rectangular pyramids

pentagonal pyramid

hexagonal pyramid

Prisms

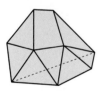

triangular prisms

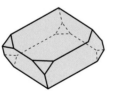

rectangular prisms

hexagonal prism

Many polyhedrons are not pyramids or prisms. Some examples are shown below.

Polyhedrons that Are NOT Pyramids or Prisms

To find out why these are neither pyramids nor prisms, read pages 140 and 141.

CHECK YOUR UNDERSTANDING

1. a. How many faces does a rectangular pyramid have?

   b. How many faces have a rectangular shape?

2. a. How many faces does a rectangular prism have?

   b. How many faces have a rectangular shape?

3. Which solid has more faces, a triangular pyramid or a triangular prism?

Check your answers on page 391.

Prisms

All of the geometric solids below are **prisms.**

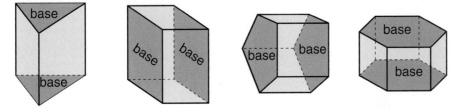

triangular prism rectangular prism pentagonal prism hexagonal prism

The two shaded faces of each prism are called **bases.**

• The bases have the same size and shape.
• The bases are parallel. This means that they are the same distance apart everywhere.
• All edges that connect the bases are parallel to each other.

The shape of its bases is used to name a prism. If the bases are triangular shapes, it is called a **triangular prism.** If the bases are rectangular shapes, it is called a **rectangular prism.** Rectangular prisms have three possible pairs of bases.

The number of faces, edges, and vertices that a prism has depends on the shape of the base.

EXAMPLE   The triangular prism shown here has 5 faces—3 rectangular faces and 2 triangular bases. It has 9 edges and 6 vertices.

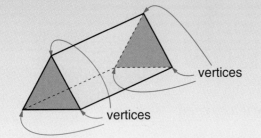

vertices

vertices

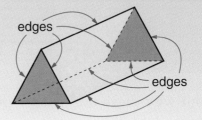

edges

edges

CHECK YOUR UNDERSTANDING

1. a. How many faces does a hexagonal prism have?

 b. How many edges?

 c. How many vertices?

2. What is the name of a prism that has 10 faces?

Check your answers on page 391.

Pyramids

All of the geometric solids below are **pyramids.**

triangular pyramid

square pyramid

pentagonal pyramid

hexagonal pyramid

The shaded face of each of these pyramids is called the **base** of the pyramid.

- The polygon that forms the base can have any number of sides.
- The faces that are not a base all have a triangular shape.
- The faces that are not a base all meet at the same vertex.

The shape of its base is used to name a pyramid. If the base is a triangle shape, it is called a **triangular pyramid.** If the base is a square shape, it is called a **square pyramid.**

The pyramids of Egypt have square bases. They are square pyramids.

The number of faces, edges, and vertices that a pyramid has depends on the shape of the base.

EXAMPLE The hexagonal pyramid shown here has 7 faces—6 triangular faces and a hexagonal base.

It has 12 edges. Six edges surround the hexagonal base. The other 6 edges meet at the apex (tip) of the pyramid.

apex

It has 7 vertices. Six vertices are on the hexagonal base. The remaining vertex is the apex of the pyramid.

The apex is the vertex opposite the base.

CHECK YOUR UNDERSTANDING

1. **a.** How many faces does a triangular pyramid have?

   b. How many edges?

   c. How many vertices?

2. What is the name of a pyramid that has 10 edges?

3. **a.** How are prisms and pyramids alike?   **b.** How do they differ?

Check your answers on page 391.

Regular Polyhedrons

A polyhedron is **regular** if:

- Each face is formed by a regular polygon.

- The faces all have the same size and shape.

- Every vertex looks exactly the same as every other vertex.

There are only five kinds of regular polyhedrons.

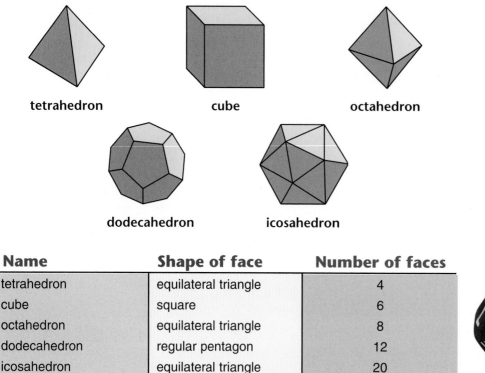

tetrahedron   cube   octahedron

dodecahedron   icosahedron

Name	Shape of face	Number of faces
tetrahedron	equilateral triangle	4
cube	square	6
octahedron	equilateral triangle	8
dodecahedron	regular pentagon	12
icosahedron	equilateral triangle	20

CHECK YOUR UNDERSTANDING

1. Which regular polyhedrons have faces that are formed by equilateral triangles?

2. a. How many edges does an octahedron have?

   b. How many vertices?

3. a. How are tetrahedrons and octahedrons alike?

   b. How are they different?

Check your answers on page 391.

Circles

A **circle** is a curved line that forms a closed path on a flat surface. All of the points on a circle are the same distance from the **center of the circle**.

The center is not part of the circle. The interior is not part of the circle.

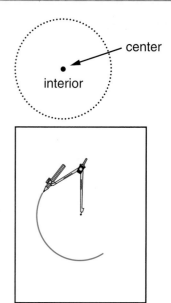

center

interior

The **compass** is a tool used to draw circles.

- The point of a compass, called the **anchor,** is placed at the center of the circle.

- The pencil in a compass traces out a circle. Every point on the circle is the same distance from the anchor.

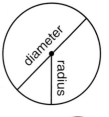

The **radius** of a circle is any line segment that connects the center of the circle with any point on the circle. The word *radius* can also refer to the length of this segment.

The **diameter** of a circle is any line segment that passes through the center of the circle and has both of its endpoints on the circle. The word *diameter* can also refer to the length of this segment.

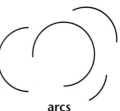

diameter

radius

An **arc** is part of a circle, from one point on the circle to another. For example, a **semicircle** is an arc: its endpoints are the endpoints of a diameter of the circle.

All circles are similar because they have the same shape, but circles do not all have the same size.

arcs

EXAMPLES   Many pizzas have a circular shape. You can order pizza by saying the diameter that you want.

A "12-inch pizza" means a pizza with a 12-inch diameter.

A "16-inch pizza" means a pizza with a 16-inch diameter.

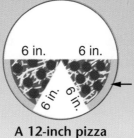

6 in.   6 in.

6 in.   6 in.

A 12-inch pizza

The pizza is 12 inches wide. The diameter is 12 inches.

Each slice is a wedge that has 6-inch long sides.

Spheres

A **sphere** is a geometric solid that has a single curved surface shaped like a ball, a marble, or a globe. All of the points on the surface of the sphere are the same distance from the **center of the sphere.**

All spheres have the same shape. But spheres do not all have the same size. The size of a sphere is the distance across its center.

- The line segment *RS* passes through the center of the sphere. This line segment is called a **diameter of the sphere.**

- The length of line segment *RS* is also called the diameter of the sphere.

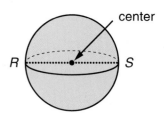

Globes and basketballs are examples of spheres that are hollow. The interior of each is empty. The hollow interior is not part of the sphere. The sphere includes only the points on the curved surface.

Marbles and baseballs are examples of spheres that have solid interiors. In cases like these, think of the solid interior as part of the sphere.

EXAMPLE The Earth is shaped very nearly like a sphere.

The diameter of the Earth is about 8,000 miles.

The distance from the Earth's surface to the center of the Earth is about 4,000 miles.

Every point on the Earth's surface is about 4,000 miles from the center of the Earth.

Layers Inside the Earth

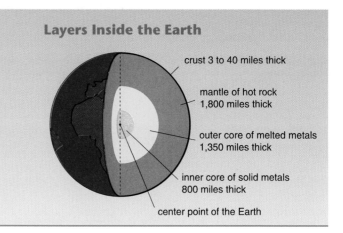

crust 3 to 40 miles thick

mantle of hot rock 1,800 miles thick

outer core of melted metals 1,350 miles thick

inner core of solid metals 800 miles thick

center point of the Earth

Congruent Figures

It sometimes happens that figures have the same shape and size. They are **congruent.** Figures are congruent if they match exactly when one figure is placed on top of the other.

EXAMPLE Line segments are congruent if they have the same length.

$\overline{EF}$ and $\overline{CD}$ are both 3 centimeters long.

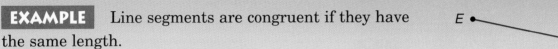

EXAMPLE Angles are congruent if they have the same degree measure.

Angle S and angle T are both right angles. They have the same shape, and they each measure 90°. The angle openings match exactly when one angle is placed on top of the other.

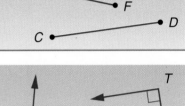

EXAMPLE Circles are congruent if their diameters are the same length.

The circles here have $\frac{1}{2}$-inch diameters. They have the same shape and the same size. The three circles are congruent.

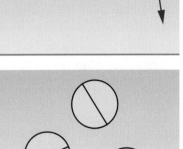

EXAMPLE A copy machine was used to copy the pentagon *RSTUV*.

If you cut out the copy, it will match exactly when placed on top of the original. The sides will match exactly. All the angles will match exactly. The original figure and the copy are congruent.

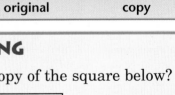

original   copy

CHECK YOUR UNDERSTANDING

Which of these methods could you use to make a congruent copy of the square below?

a. Use a copy machine to copy the square.

b. Use tracing paper and trace over the square.

c. Cut out the square and trace around it.

d. Measure the sides with a ruler, then draw the sides at right angles to each other using a protractor.

Check your answers on page 391.

Similar Figures

Figures that have exactly the same shape are called **similar figures.** Usually, one figure is an enlargement or reduction of the other. The **size-change factor** tells the amount of enlargement or reduction. Congruent figures are similar because they have the same shape.

EXAMPLES If a copy machine is used to copy a drawing or picture, the copy will be similar to the original.

original   copy   original   copy   original   copy

Exact copy
Copy machine set to 100%.
Size-change factor is 1X.

Enlargement
Copy machine set to 200%.
Size-change factor is 2X.

Reduction
Copy machine set to 50%.
Size-change factor is $\frac{1}{2}$X.

EXAMPLE The triangles *CAT* and *DOG* are similar. The larger triangle is an enlargement of the smaller triangle.

Each side and its enlargement form a pair of sides called **corresponding sides.** These sides are marked with the same number of slash marks.

The size-change factor is 2X. Each side in the larger triangle is twice the size of the corresponding side in the smaller triangle. The size of the angles is the same for both triangles. For example, ∠T and ∠G have the same degree measure.

EXAMPLE Quadrangles *ABCD* and *MNOP* are similar. How long is side *MN*? How long is side *AD*?

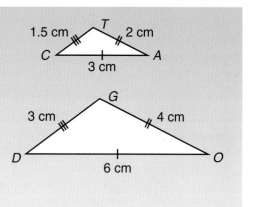

$\overline{NO}$ is $\frac{1}{3}$ as long as $\overline{BC}$. $\overline{OP}$ is $\frac{1}{3}$ as long as side *CD*.
So, the size-change factor is $\frac{1}{3}$X.
$\overline{AB}$ and $\overline{MN}$ are corresponding sides. $\overline{AB}$ is 15 feet long.
So, $\overline{MN}$ must be $\frac{1}{3} * 15 = 5$ feet long.

$\overline{AD}$ and $\overline{MP}$ are corresponding sides.
$\overline{MP}$ is $\frac{1}{3}$ as long as $\overline{AD}$ and equals 7 feet.

So, $\overline{AD}$ must be 21 feet long.

Reflections, Translations, and Rotations

In geometry, a figure can be moved from one place to another.
Three different ways to move a figure are shown below.

- A **reflection** moves a figure by "flipping" it over a line.

- A **translation** moves a figure by "sliding" it to a new location.

- A **rotation** moves a figure by "turning" it around a point.

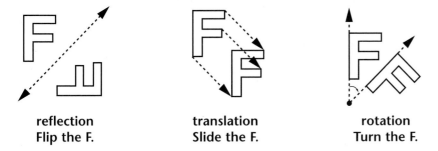

| reflection | translation | rotation |
| Flip the F. | Slide the F. | Turn the F. |

The original figure, before it has been moved, is called the
preimage. The new figure produced by the move is called
the **image.**

Each point of the preimage is moved to a new point of the image
called its **matching point.** A point and its matching point are
also called **corresponding points.**

For each of the moves shown above, the image has the same
size and shape as the preimage. The image and preimage are
congruent shapes.

Reflections

A reflection is a "flipping" motion of a figure. The line that
the figure is flipped over is called the **line of reflection.**
The preimage and the image are on opposite sides of the
line of reflection.

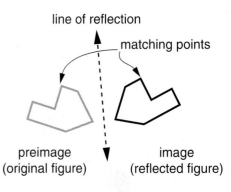

For any reflection:

- The preimage and the image have the same size
  and shape.

- The preimage and the image are reversed.

- Each point and its matching point are the same distance
  from the line of reflection.

Translations

A translation is a "sliding" motion of a figure. Each point of the figure slides the same distance in the same direction. Imagine a drawing of the letter T on grid paper.

- If each point of the letter T slides 6 grid squares to the right, the result is a *horizontal translation*.

- If each point of the letter T slides 8 grid squares upward, the result is a *vertical translation*.

- Suppose that each point of the letter T slides 6 grid squares to the right, then 8 grid squares upward. The result is the same as a *diagonal translation*.

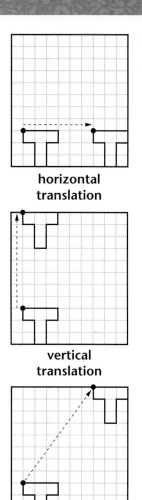

horizontal
translation

vertical
translation

diagonal
translation

Rotations

When a figure is rotated, it is turned a certain number of degrees around a particular point.

A figure can be rotated *clockwise* (the direction in which clock hands move). A figure can also be rotated *counterclockwise* (the opposite direction of the way clock hands move).

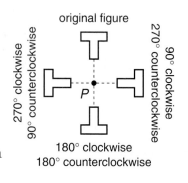

original figure

270° clockwise
90° counterclockwise

90° clockwise
270° counterclockwise

180° clockwise
180° counterclockwise

CHECK YOUR UNDERSTANDING

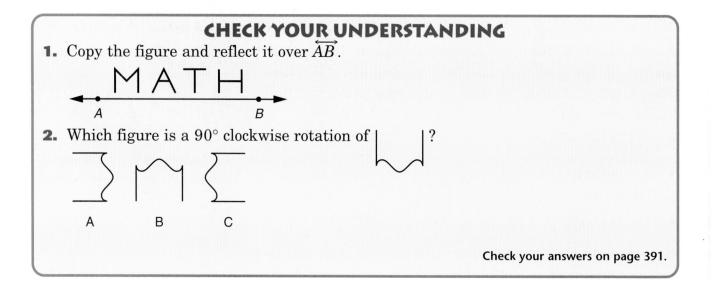

1. Copy the figure and reflect it over $\overleftrightarrow{AB}$.

MATH

A   B

2. Which figure is a 90° clockwise rotation of ⌐⌐ ?

A   B   C

Check your answers on page 391.

Line Symmetry

A dashed line is drawn through the figure at the right. The line divides the figure into two parts. Both parts look exactly alike, but are facing in opposite directions.

The figure is **symmetric about a line.** The dashed line is called a **line of symmetry** for the figure.

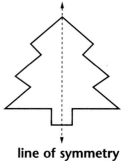

line of symmetry

You can use a reflection to get the figure shown at the right.

* Think of the line of symmetry as a line of reflection.

* Reflect the left side of the figure over the line.

* The left side and its reflection (the right side) together form the figure.

An easy way to check whether a figure has *line symmetry* is to fold it in half. If the two halves match exactly, then the figure is symmetric. The fold line is the line of symmetry.

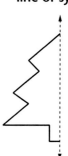

Reflect the left side to get the figure above.

EXAMPLES The letters T, V, E, and X are symmetric. The lines of symmetry are drawn for each letter.

The letter X has two lines of symmetry. If you could fold along either line, the two halves would match exactly.

The figures below are all symmetric. The line of symmetry is drawn for each figure. If there is more than one line of symmetry, they are all drawn.

flag of Jamaica   butterfly   human body   ellipse   rectangle   square

CHECK YOUR UNDERSTANDING

1. Trace each pattern-block (PB) shape on your Geometry Template onto a sheet of paper. Draw the lines of symmetry for each shape.

2. How many lines of symmetry does a circle have?

Check your answers on page 391.

Tessellations

A **tessellation** is a pattern of closed shapes that completely covers a surface.

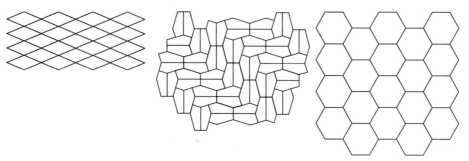

• The shapes in a tessellation do not overlap.

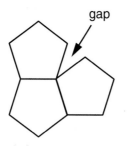

overlap

• There are no gaps between shapes.

gap

A **vertex point** of a tessellation is a point where vertices of the shapes meet.

• The sum of the measures of the angles around a vertex point must be exactly 360°.

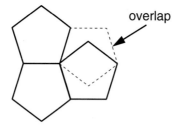

vertex point

120° 60°
60° 120°

120° + 60° + 120° + 60° = 360°

• If the sum is less than 360°, there will be gaps between the shapes. The pattern is not a tessellation.

• If the sum is greater than 360°, the shapes will overlap. The pattern is not a tessellation.

Regular Tessellations

A tessellation made by repeating congruent copies of one kind of regular polygon is called a **regular tessellation.**

For example, a regular tessellation can be made up of regular hexagons.

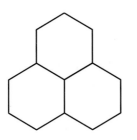

In a regular tessellation—

- All of the polygons are **congruent.** (They are the same size and shape.)

- Vertices of at least three polygons meet at each vertex point.

- There are at least three angles around each vertex point.

There are exactly three possible regular tessellations. The regular hexagon tessellation is shown above. Can you find the other two regular tessellations?

Semiregular Tessellations

Tessellations may involve more than one type of shape.

A tessellation is called a **semiregular tessellation** if it satisfies these conditions—

- It uses at least two different shapes.

- The shapes used are regular polygons.

- The same combination of regular polygons meets in the same order at each vertex.

The example shown here is a semiregular tessellation made up of squares and equilateral triangles. As you move clockwise around any vertex point, there are 2 triangles, 1 square, 1 triangle, and 1 square.

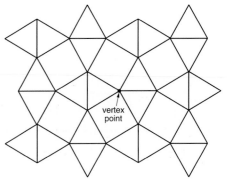

vertex point

The Geometry Template

The **Geometry Template** has many uses.

The template has two rulers. The inch scale measures in inches and fractions of an inch. The centimeter scale measures in centimeters or millimeters. Use either side of the template as a straightedge for drawing line segments.

There are 17 different geometric figures on the template. The figures labeled "PB" are **pattern-block shapes.** These are half the size of real pattern blocks. There is a hexagon, a trapezoid, two different rhombuses, an equilateral triangle, and a square. These will come in handy for some of the activities you do this year.

Each triangle on the template is labeled with a T and a number. Triangle "T1" is an equilateral triangle whose sides all have the same length. Triangles "T2" and "T5" are right triangles. Triangle "T3" has sides that all have different lengths. Triangle "T4" has two sides of the same length.

The remaining shapes are circles, squares, a regular octagon, a regular pentagon, a kite, a rectangle, a parallelogram, and an ellipse.

The two circles near the inch scale can be used as ring-binder holes so you can store your template in your notebook.

Use the **half-circle** and **full-circle protractors** at the bottom of the template to measure and draw angles. Use the **Percent Circle** at the top of the template to construct and measure circle graphs. The Percent Circle is divided into 1% intervals, and some common fractions of the circle are marked.

Notice the tiny holes near the 0-, $\frac{1}{4}$-, $\frac{2}{4}$-, and $\frac{3}{4}$-inch marks of the inch scale and at each inch mark from 1 to 7. On the centimeter side, the holes are placed at each centimeter mark from 0 to 10. These holes can be used to draw circles.

EXAMPLE   Draw a circle with a 4-inch radius.

Place one pencil point in the hole at 0. Place another pencil point in the hole at 4 inches. Hold the pencil at 0 inches steady while rotating the pencil at 4 inches (along with the template) to draw the circle.

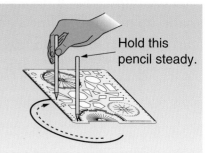

Hold this pencil steady.

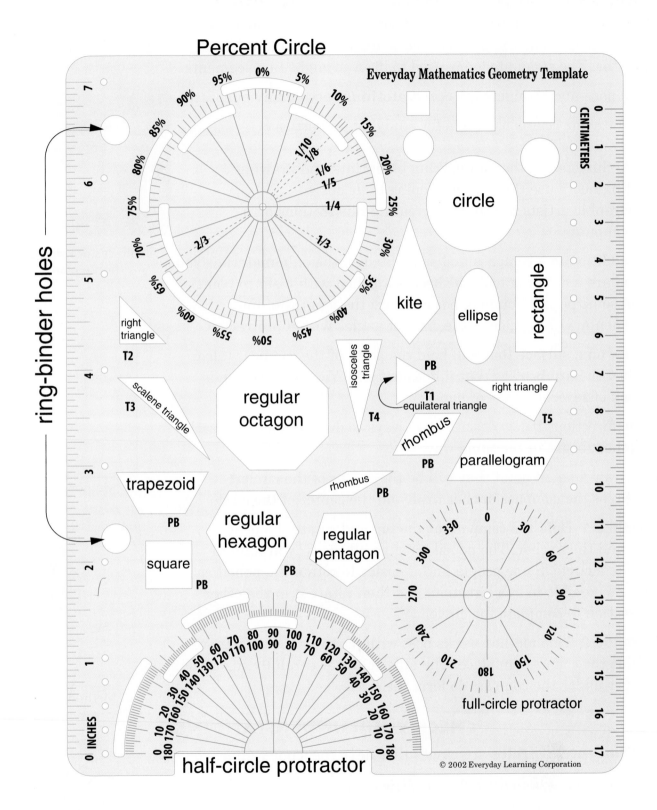

Percent Circle

Everyday Mathematics Geometry Template

circle

kite

ellipse

rectangle

right triangle
T2

scalene triangle
T3

regular octagon

isosceles triangle

PB
T1
equilateral triangle

right triangle
T5

rhombus
PB

parallelogram

trapezoid
PB

rhombus
PB

regular hexagon
PB

regular pentagon
PB

square
PB

full-circle protractor

half-circle protractor

ring-binder holes

© 2002 Everyday Learning Corporation

Compass-and-Straightedge Constructions

Many geometric figures can be drawn using only a compass and straightedge. The compass is used to draw circles and mark off lengths. The straightedge is used to draw straight line segments.

Compass-and-straightedge **constructions** serve many purposes.

- Mathematicians use them for studying properties of geometric figures.
- Architects use them in making blueprints and drawings.
- Engineers use them in developing their designs.
- Graphic artists use them in creating illustrations on a computer.

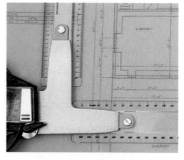

Architect's drawing of a house plan

In addition to a compass and straightedge, the only materials you need are a drawing tool (the best is a pencil with a sharp point) and some paper. You may not measure the lengths of line segments with a ruler or the sizes of angles with a protractor.

Draw on a surface that will hold the point of the compass (also called the **anchor**) so that it does not slip. You can draw on a stack of several sheets of paper.

The directions below describe two ways to draw circles. For each method, begin in the same way.

- Draw a small point that will be the center of the circle.
- Press the compass anchor firmly on the center of the circle.

Method 1

Method 1 Hold the compass at the top and rotate the pencil around the anchor. The pencil must go all the way around to make a circle. Some people find it easier to rotate the pencil as far as possible in one direction, and then rotate it in the other direction to complete the circle.

Method 2 This method works best with partners. One partner holds the compass in place. The other partner carefully turns the paper under the compass to form the circle.

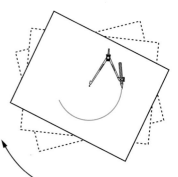

Method 2

CHECK YOUR UNDERSTANDING

Concentric circles are circles that have the same center.

Use a compass to draw 3 concentric circles.

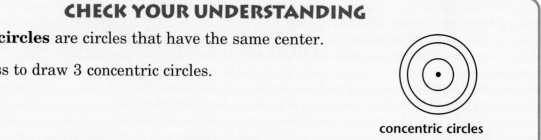

concentric circles

Copying a Line Segment
Follow each step carefully. Use a clean sheet of paper.

Step 1: Draw line segment *AB*.

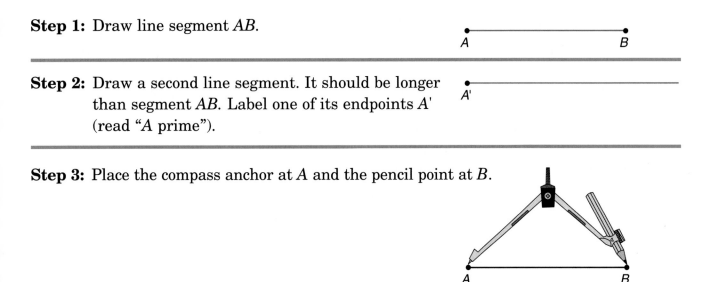

Step 2: Draw a second line segment. It should be longer than segment *AB*. Label one of its endpoints *A'* (read "A prime").

Step 3: Place the compass anchor at *A* and the pencil point at *B*.

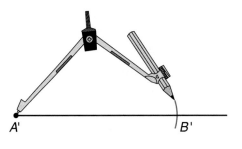

Step 4: Without changing your compass opening, place the compass anchor on *A'* and draw a small arc that crosses the line segment. Label the point where the arc crosses the line segment point *B'*.

The segments *A'B'* and *AB* have the same length.

Line segment *A'B'* is **congruent** to line segment *AB*.

CHECK YOUR UNDERSTANDING
1. Draw a line segment. Using a compass and straightedge only, copy the line segment.
2. After you make your copy, measure the segments with a ruler to see how accurately you copied the original line segment.

Copying a Triangle

Follow each step carefully. Use a clean sheet of paper.

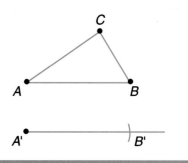

Step 1: Draw a triangle *ABC*. Draw a line segment that is longer than line segment *AB*. Copy line segment *AB* onto the segment you just drew. (See page 155.) Label the end points of the copy *A'* and *B'* (read as "*A* prime" and "*B* prime").

Step 2: Place the compass anchor at *A* and the pencil point at *C*. Without changing your compass opening, place the compass anchor on *A'* and draw an arc.

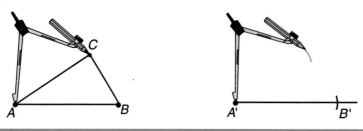

Step 3: Place the compass anchor at *B* and the pencil point at *C*. Without changing your compass opening, place the compass anchor on *B'* and draw another arc. Label the point where the arcs intersect *C'*.

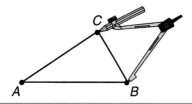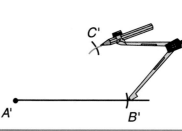

Step 4: Draw line segments *A'C'* and *B'C'*.

Triangles *ABC* and *A'B'C'* are congruent. That is, they are the same size and shape.

CHECK YOUR UNDERSTANDING

Draw a triangle. Using a compass and straightedge, copy the triangle. Cut out the copy and place it on top of the original triangle to check that the triangles are congruent.

Constructing a Parallelogram

Follow each step carefully. Use a clean sheet of paper.

Step 1: Draw an angle *ABC*.

Step 2: Place the compass anchor at *B* and the pencil point at *C*. Without changing your compass opening, place the compass anchor on point *A* and draw an arc.

Step 3: Place the compass anchor at *B* and the pencil point at *A*. Without changing your compass opening, place the compass anchor on point *C* and draw another arc that crosses the first arc. Label the point where the two arcs cross point *D*.

Step 4: Draw line segments *AD* and *CD*.

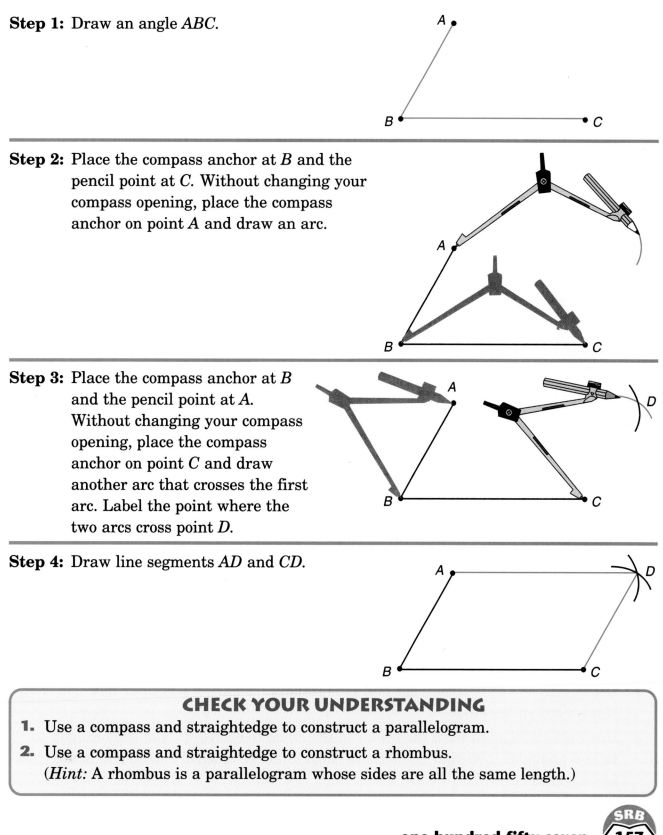

CHECK YOUR UNDERSTANDING

1. Use a compass and straightedge to construct a parallelogram.
2. Use a compass and straightedge to construct a rhombus.
   (*Hint:* A rhombus is a parallelogram whose sides are all the same length.)

Constructing a Regular Inscribed Hexagon

Follow each step carefully. Use a clean sheet of paper.

Step 1: Draw a circle and keep the same compass opening. Make a dot on the circle. Place the compass anchor on the dot and make a mark with the pencil point on the circle. Keep the same compass opening for Steps 2 and 3.

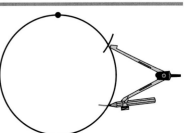

Step 2: Place the compass anchor on the mark you just made. Make another mark with the pencil point on the circle.

Step 3: Do this four more times to divide the circle into 6 equal parts. The 6th mark should be on the dot you started with or very close to it.

Step 4: With your straightedge, connect the 6 marks on the circle to form a regular hexagon.

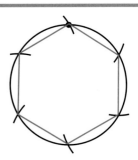

Use your compass to check that the sides of the hexagon are the same length.

The hexagon is **inscribed** in the circle because each vertex of the hexagon is on the circle.

CHECK YOUR UNDERSTANDING

1. Draw a circle. Using a compass and straightedge, construct a regular hexagon that is inscribed in the circle.

2. Draw a line segment from the center of the circle to each vertex of the hexagon to form 6 triangles. Use your compass to check that the sides of each triangle are the same length.

Constructing an Inscribed Square

Follow each step carefully. Use a clean sheet of paper.

Step 1: Draw a circle with a compass.

Step 2: Draw a line segment through the center of the circle with endpoints on the circle. Label the endpoints point *A* and point *B*.

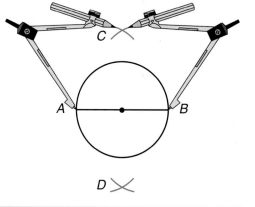

Step 3: Increase the compass opening. Place the compass anchor on point *A*. Draw an arc above the center of the circle and another arc below the center of the circle.

Step 4: Without changing the compass opening, place the compass anchor on point *B*. Draw arcs that cross the arcs you drew in Step 3. Label the points where the arcs intersect point *C* and point *D*.

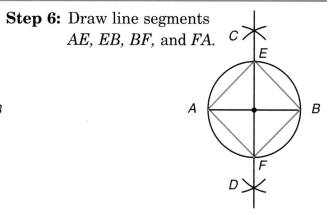

Step 5: Draw a line through points *C* and *D*.

Label the points where line *CD* intersects the circle as point *E* and point *F*.

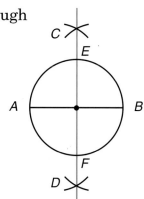

Step 6: Draw line segments *AE*, *EB*, *BF*, and *FA*.

Check with your compass that all four line segments are the same length. Check with the corner of your straightedge or some other square corner that all four angles are right angles.

The square is **inscribed** in the circle because all vertices of the square are on the circle.

CHECK YOUR UNDERSTANDING

Use a compass and straightedge to construct an inscribed square.

Bisecting a Line Segment

Follow each step carefully. Use a clean sheet of paper.

Step 1: Draw line segment AB.

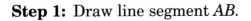

Step 2: Open your compass so that the compass opening is greater than half the distance between point A and point B. Place the compass anchor on point A. Draw a small arc above $\overline{AB}$ and another small arc below $\overline{AB}$.

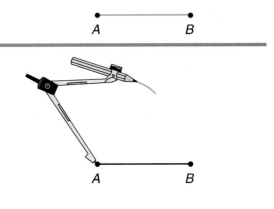

Step 3: Without changing the compass opening, place the compass anchor on point B. Draw an arc above $\overline{AB}$ and another arc below $\overline{AB}$, so that the arcs cross the first arcs you drew. Label the points where pairs of arcs intersect M and N.

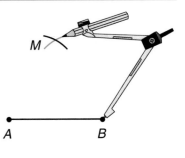

Step 4: Draw a line through point M and point N. Label the point where $\overleftrightarrow{MN}$ intersects $\overline{AB}$ as point O.

We say that line segment MN bisects line segment AB at point O. The distance from A to O is the same as the distance from B to O.

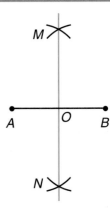

CHECK YOUR UNDERSTANDING

Draw a line segment. Use a compass and straightedge to bisect it. Then measure to check that the line segment has been divided into two equal parts.

Constructing a Perpendicular Line Segment (Part 1)

You can construct a line segment that is perpendicular to another line segment through a point *on* the line segment.

Follow each step carefully. Use a clean sheet of paper.

Step 1: Draw line segment *AB*. Make a dot on $\overline{AB}$ and label it point *P*.

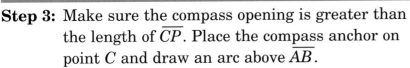

Step 2: Place the compass anchor on *P*, and draw an arc that crosses $\overline{AB}$ at point *C*.

Keeping the compass anchor on point *P* and the same compass opening, draw another arc that crosses $\overline{AB}$ at point *D*.

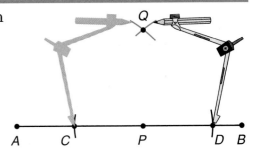

Step 3: Make sure the compass opening is greater than the length of $\overline{CP}$. Place the compass anchor on point *C* and draw an arc above $\overline{AB}$.

Keeping the same compass opening, place the compass anchor on point *D* and draw another arc above $\overline{AB}$ that crosses the first arc.

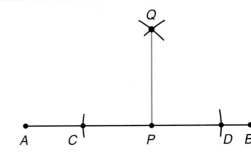

Label the point where the two arcs cross point *Q*.

Step 4: Draw $\overline{QP}$.

$\overline{QP}$ is **perpendicular** to $\overline{AB}$.

CHECK YOUR UNDERSTANDING

Draw a line segment. Draw a point on the segment and label it point *R*.

R

Use a compass and straightedge. Construct a line segment through point *R* that is perpendicular to the segment you drew. Use a protractor to check that the segments are perpendicular.

Constructing a Perpendicular Line Segment (Part 2)

You can construct a line segment perpendicular to another line segment from a point *not on* the line segment.

Follow each step carefully. Use a clean sheet of paper.

Step 1: Draw line segment *PQ*.
Draw a point *M* not on $\overline{PQ}$.

Step 2: Place the compass anchor on point *M* and draw an arc that crosses $\overline{PQ}$ at two points.

Step 3: Place the compass anchor on one of the points and draw an arc below $\overline{PQ}$.

Step 4: Keeping the same compass opening, place the compass anchor on the other point and draw another arc that crosses the first arc.

Label the point where the two arcs cross point *N*. Then draw the line segment *MN*.

$\overline{MN}$ is **perpendicular** to $\overline{PQ}$.

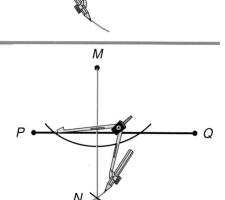

CHECK YOUR UNDERSTANDING

1. Draw a line segment *HI* and a point *G* above the line segment. Using a compass and straightedge, construct a line segment from point *G* that is perpendicular to $\overline{HI}$.

2. Use the Geometry Template to draw a parallelogram. Then construct a line segment to show the height of the parallelogram.

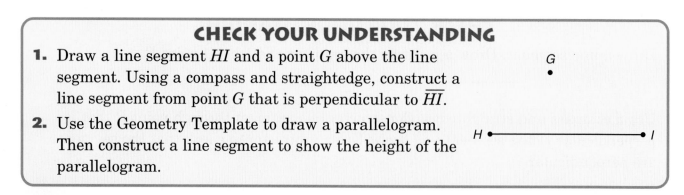

Copying an Angle

Follow each step carefully. Use a clean sheet of paper.

Step 1: Draw an angle B.

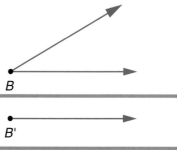

Step 2: To start copying the angle, draw a ray. Label the endpoint of the ray B'.

Step 3: Place the compass anchor on point B. Draw an arc that crosses both sides of angle B. Label the point where the arc crosses one side as point A. Label the point where the arc crosses the other side as point C.

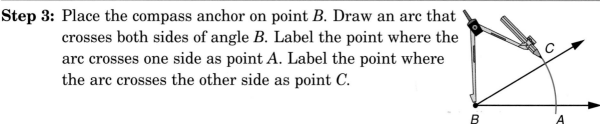

Step 4: Without changing the compass opening, place the compass anchor on point B'. Draw an arc about the same size as the one you drew in Step 3. Label the point where the arc crosses the ray as A'.

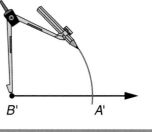

Step 5: Place the compass anchor on point A and the pencil point on point C.

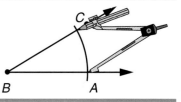

Step 6: Without changing the compass opening, place the compass anchor on point A'. Draw a small arc where the pencil point crosses the larger arc and label it as point C'.

Step 7: Draw a ray from point B' through point C'. $\angle A'B'C'$ is **congruent** to $\angle ABC$. That is, the two angles have the same degree measure.

CHECK YOUR UNDERSTANDING

Draw an angle. Use a compass and straightedge to copy the angle. Then measure the two angles with a protractor to check that they are the same size.

Copying a Quadrangle

Follow each step carefully. Use a clean sheet of paper.

Before you can copy a quadrangle with compass and straightedge, you need to know how to copy line segments and angles. Those constructions are described on pages 155 and 163.

Step 1: Draw a quadrangle *ABCD*. Copy ∠*BAD*. Label the vertex of the new angle *A'*. The sides of your new angle should be longer than $\overline{AB}$ and $\overline{AD}$.

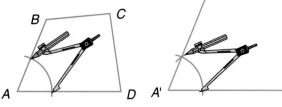

Step 2: Mark off the distance from point *A* to point *D* on the horizontal side of your new angle. Label the endpoint *D'*.

Mark off the distance from point *A* to point *B* on the other side of your new angle. Label the endpoint *B'*.

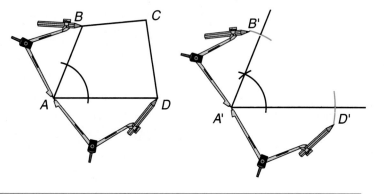

Step 3: Place the compass anchor on point *B* and the pencil point on point *C*. Without changing the compass opening, place the compass anchor on point *B'* and make an arc.

Step 4: Place the compass anchor on point *D* and the pencil point on point *C*. Without changing the compass opening, place the compass anchor on point *D'* and make an arc that crosses the arc you made in Step 3. Label the point where the two arcs meet point *C'*.

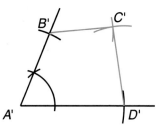

Step 5: Draw $\overline{B'C'}$ and $\overline{D'C'}$.

Quadrangle *A'B'C'D'* is **congruent** to quadrangle *ABCD*.

The two quadrangles are the same size and shape.

CHECK YOUR UNDERSTANDING

Draw a quadrangle. Use a compass and straightedge to copy the quadrangle.

Measurement

Natural Measures and Standard Units

Systems of weights and measures have been used in many parts of the world since ancient times. People measured lengths and weights long before they had rulers and scales.

Ancient Measures of Weight

Shells and grains such as wheat or rice were often used as units of weight. For example, a small item might be said to weigh 300 grains. Large weights were often compared to the load that could be carried by a man or a pack animal.

Ancient Measures of Length

People used **natural measures** based on the body to measure length and distance. Some of these units are shown below.

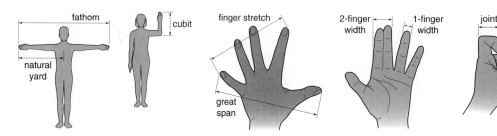

Standard Units of Length and Weight

Using shells and grains to measure weight is not exact. Even if the shells and grains are of the same type, they vary in size and weight.

Using body lengths to measure length is also not exact. The body measures used depend upon the person who is doing the measuring. The problem is that different persons have hands and arms of different lengths.

One way to solve this problem is to make **standard units** of length and weight. Most rulers are marked off with inches and centimeters as standard units. Bath scales are marked off using pounds and kilograms as standard units. The standard units never change and are the same for everyone. If two people measure the same object using standard units, their measurements will be the same or almost the same.

The Metric System and the U.S. Customary System

About 200 years ago, a system of weights and measures called the **metric system** was developed. It uses standard units for length, weight, and temperature. In the metric system:

- The **meter** is the standard unit for length. The symbol for a meter is **m.** A meter is about the width of a front door.
- The **gram** is the standard unit for weight. The symbol for a gram is **g.** A paper clip weighs about $\frac{1}{2}$ gram.
- The **Celsius degree** is the standard unit for temperature. The symbol for degrees Celsius is °**C.** Water freezes at 0°C and boils at 100°C. Room temperature is about 20°C.

Scientists almost always use the metric system to measure. The metric system is easy to use because it is a base-ten system. Larger and smaller units are defined by multiplying or dividing the units given above by powers of ten—10, 100, 1,000, and so on.

EXAMPLES   All metric units of length are based on the meter. Each unit is defined by multiplying or dividing the meter by a power of 10.

Units of Length Based on the Meter

	Prefix	Meaning
1 decimeter (dm) = $\frac{1}{10}$ meter	deci-	$\frac{1}{10}$
1 centimeter (cm) = $\frac{1}{100}$ meter	centi-	$\frac{1}{100}$
1 millimeter (mm) = $\frac{1}{1,000}$ meter	milli-	$\frac{1}{1,000}$
1 kilometer (km) = 1,000 meters	kilo-	1,000

The metric system is used in most countries around the world. In the United States, the **U.S. customary system** is used for everyday purposes. The U.S. customary system uses standard units like the **inch, foot, yard, mile, ounce, pound,** and **ton.**

> **NOTE**
>
> The U.S. customary system is not based on powers of 10. This makes it more difficult to use than the metric system. For example, in order to change inches to yards, you must know that 36 inches equals 1 yard.

CHECK YOUR UNDERSTANDING

1. Which units in the list below are units in the metric system?

foot   millimeter   pound   inch   gram   meter   centimeter   yard

2. What does the prefix "milli-" mean?   **3.** 2 grams = ? milligrams

Check your answers on page 391.

Converting Units of Length

The table below shows how different units of length in the metric system compare. You can use this table to rewrite a length using a different unit.

Comparing Metric Units of Length

Symbols for Units of Length

1 cm = 10 mm	1 m = 1,000 mm	1 m = 100 cm	1 km = 1,000 m
1 mm = $\frac{1}{10}$ cm	1 mm = $\frac{1}{1,000}$ m	1 cm = $\frac{1}{100}$ m	1 m = $\frac{1}{1,000}$ km

mm = millimeter	cm = centimeter
m = meter	km = kilometer

EXAMPLES   Use the table to rewrite each length using a different unit. Replace the unit given first with an equal length that uses the new unit.

Problem	Solution
38 centimeters = ? millimeters	38 cm = 38 ∗ 10 mm = 380 mm
38 centimeters = ? meters	38 cm = 38 ∗ $\frac{1}{100}$ m = 0.38 m
7.4 kilometers = ? meters	7.4 km = 7.4 ∗ 1,000 m = 7,400 m
8.6 meters = ? centimeters	8.6 m = 8.6 ∗ 100 cm = 860 cm

The table below shows how different units of length in the U.S. customary system compare. You can use this table to rewrite a length using a different unit.

Comparing U.S. Customary Units of Length

Symbols for Units of Length

1 ft = 12 in.	1 yd = 36 in.	1 yd = 3 ft	1 mi = 5,280 ft
1 in. = $\frac{1}{12}$ ft	1 in. = $\frac{1}{36}$ yd	1 ft = $\frac{1}{3}$ yd	1 ft = $\frac{1}{5,280}$ mi

in. = inch	ft = foot
yd = yard	mi = mile

EXAMPLES   Use the table to rewrite each length using a different unit. Replace the unit given first with an equal length that uses the new unit.

Problem	Solution
8 feet = ? inches	8 ft = 8 ∗ 12 in. = 96 in.
9 feet = ? yards	9 ft = 9 ∗ $\frac{1}{3}$ yd = $\frac{9}{3}$ yd = 3 yd
4 miles = ? feet	4 mi = 4 ∗ 5,280 ft = 21,120 ft
108 inches = ? yards	108 in. = 108 ∗ $\frac{1}{36}$ yd = $\frac{108}{36}$ yd = 3 yd

Personal References for Units of Length

Sometimes it is hard to remember just how long a centimeter or a yard is, or how a kilometer and a mile compare. You may not have a ruler, yardstick, or tape measure handy. When this happens, you can estimate lengths by using the lengths of common objects and distances that you do know.

Some examples of personal references for length are given below. A good personal reference is something that you see or use often, so you don't forget it. A good personal reference doesn't change size. For example, a wooden pencil is not a good personal reference for length, because it gets shorter as it is sharpened.

Personal References for Metric Units of Length

About 1 millimeter	About 1 centimeter
Thickness of a dime	Thickness of a crayon
Thickness of the point of a thumbtack	Width of the head of a thumbtack
Thickness of the thin edge of a paper match	Thickness of a pattern block
About 1 meter	**About 1 kilometer**
One big step (for an adult)	1,000 big steps (for an adult)
Width of a front door	Length of 10 football fields
Tip of the nose to tip of the thumb, with arm extended (for an adult)	

Personal References for U.S. Customary Units of Length

About 1 inch	About 1 foot
Length of a paper clip	A man's shoe length
Width (diameter) of a quarter	Length of a license plate
Width of a man's thumb	Length of this book
About 1 yard	**About 1 mile**
One big step (for an adult)	2,000 average-size steps (for an adult)
Width of a front door	
Tip of the nose to tip of the thumb, with arm extended (for an adult)	Length of 15 football fields (including the end zones)

NOTE

The personal references for 1 meter can also be used for 1 yard.
1 yard = 36 inches while 1 meter is about 39.37 inches. One meter is often called a "fat yard," which means one yard plus one hand width.

Perimeter

Sometimes we want to know the **distance around** a shape, which is called the **perimeter.** To measure perimeter, use units of length such as inches, meters, or miles.

To find the perimeter of a polygon, add the lengths of its sides. Remember to name the unit of length used to measure the shape.

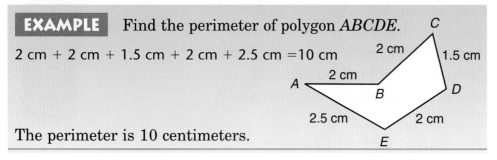

EXAMPLE   Find the perimeter of polygon *ABCDE*.

2 cm + 2 cm + 1.5 cm + 2 cm + 2.5 cm = 10 cm

The perimeter is 10 centimeters.

Perimeter Formulas

Rectangles	Squares
$p = 2 * (l + w)$	$p = 4 * s$
p is the perimeter, *l* is the length, *w* is the width of the rectangle.	*p* is the perimeter, *s* is the length of one of the sides of the square.

EXAMPLES   Find the perimeter of each polygon.

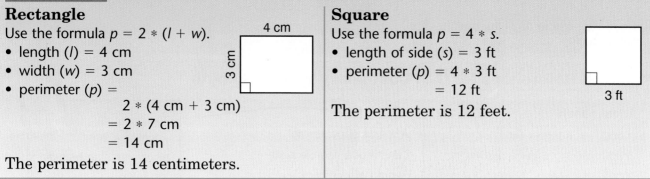

Rectangle
Use the formula $p = 2 * (l + w)$.
• length (*l*) = 4 cm
• width (*w*) = 3 cm
• perimeter (*p*) =
$$2 * (4 \text{ cm} + 3 \text{ cm})$$
$$= 2 * 7 \text{ cm}$$
$$= 14 \text{ cm}$$
The perimeter is 14 centimeters.

Square
Use the formula $p = 4 * s$.
• length of side (*s*) = 3 ft
• perimeter (*p*) = 4 * 3 ft
$$= 12 \text{ ft}$$
The perimeter is 12 feet.

CHECK YOUR UNDERSTANDING

1. Find the perimeter of a rectangle whose dimensions are 3 feet 3 inches and 7 feet 8 inches.

2. Measure the sides of this book to the nearest half-inch. What is the perimeter of the book?

Check your answers on page 391.

Circumference

The perimeter of a circle is the **distance around** the circle.
The perimeter of a circle has a special name. It is called the
circumference of the circle.

start
end

EXAMPLE   Most food cans are cylinders. Their tops and bottoms
have circular shapes. The circumference of a circular can top is how far
a can opener turns in opening the can.

The **diameter** of a circle is any line segment that passes through the
center of the circle and has both endpoints on the circle.

The length of a diameter segment is also called the diameter.

If you know the diameter, there is a simple formula for finding
the circumference.

circumference = pi ∗ diameter   or $c = \pi * d$

c is the circumference and d is the diameter of the circle. The
Greek letter π is called **pi**. It is approximately equal to 3.14.
In your work with the number π, you can either use 3.14 or
$3\frac{1}{7}$ as approximate values for π, or a calculator with a π key.

EXAMPLE   Find the circumference of the circle.

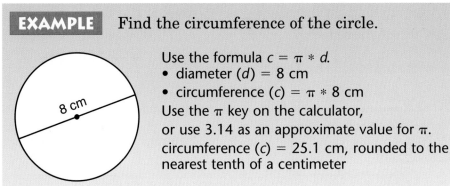

Use the formula $c = \pi * d$.
• diameter (d) = 8 cm
• circumference (c) = $\pi * 8$ cm
Use the π key on the calculator,
or use 3.14 as an approximate value for π.
circumference (c) = 25.1 cm, rounded to the
nearest tenth of a centimeter

The circumference of the circle is 25.1 cm.

CHECK YOUR UNDERSTANDING

1. Measure the diameter of the quarter in millimeters.

2. Find the circumference of the quarter in millimeters.

3. What is the circumference of a pizza whose diameter is 14 inches?

Check your answers on page 391.

Area

Area is a measure of the amount of surface inside a closed boundary. You can find the area by counting the number of squares of a certain size that cover the region inside the boundary. The squares must cover the entire region. They must not overlap, have any gaps, or extend outside the boundary.

Sometimes a region cannot be covered by an exact number of squares. In that case, first count the number of whole squares, then the fractions of squares that cover the region.

Area is reported in square units. Units of area for small regions are square inches (in.^{2}), square feet (ft^2), square yards (yd^2), square centimeters (cm^2), and square meters (m^2). For large areas, square miles (mi^2) are used in the United States, while square kilometers (km^2) are used in other countries.

You may report area using any of the square units. But you should choose a square unit that makes sense for the region being measured.

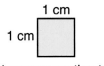

1 square centimeter
(actual size)

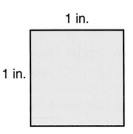

1 square inch
(actual size)

EXAMPLES The area of a field-hockey field is reported below in three different ways.

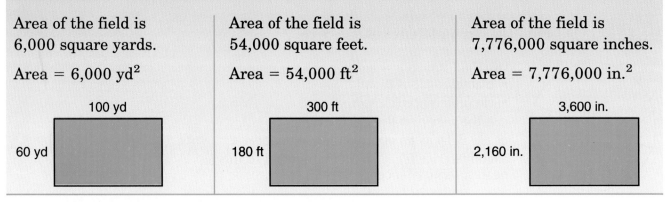

Area of the field is 6,000 square yards.

Area = 6,000 yd^2

100 yd / 60 yd

Area of the field is 54,000 square feet.

Area = 54,000 ft^2

300 ft / 180 ft

Area of the field is 7,776,000 square inches.

Area = 7,776,000 in.^{2}

3,600 in. / 2,160 in.

Although each of the measurements above is correct, giving the area in square inches really doesn't give a good idea about the size of the field. It is hard to imagine 7,776,000 of anything!

Area of Rectangles

When you cover a rectangular shape with unit squares, the squares can be arranged into rows. Each row contains the same number of squares and fractions of squares.

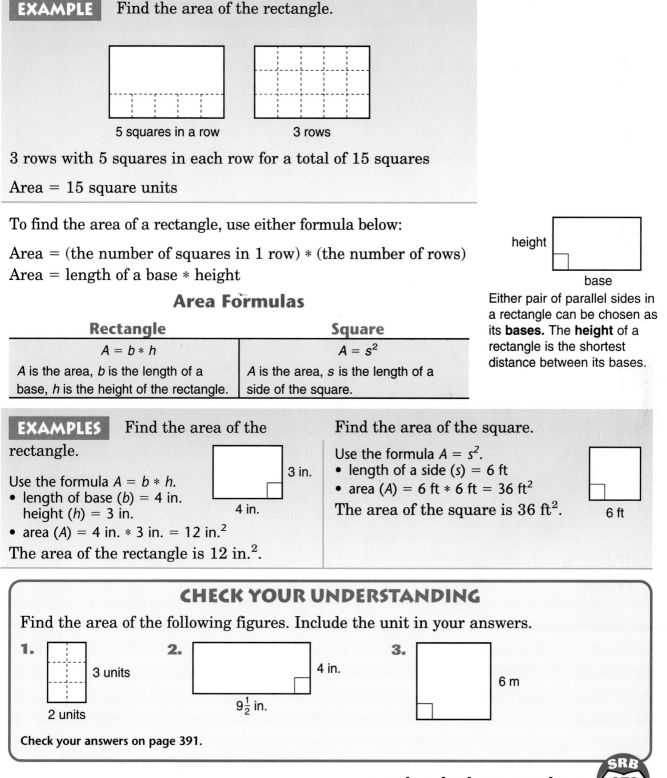

EXAMPLE Find the area of the rectangle.

5 squares in a row   3 rows

3 rows with 5 squares in each row for a total of 15 squares

Area = 15 square units

To find the area of a rectangle, use either formula below:

Area = (the number of squares in 1 row) * (the number of rows)
Area = length of a base * height

Area Formulas

Rectangle	Square
$A = b * h$	$A = s^2$
A is the area, b is the length of a base, h is the height of the rectangle.	A is the area, s is the length of a side of the square.

height

base

Either pair of parallel sides in a rectangle can be chosen as its **bases**. The **height** of a rectangle is the shortest distance between its bases.

EXAMPLES Find the area of the rectangle.

Use the formula $A = b * h$.
• length of base (b) = 4 in.
  height (h) = 3 in.
• area (A) = 4 in. * 3 in. = 12 in.^{2}

The area of the rectangle is 12 in.^{2}.

3 in.

4 in.

Find the area of the square.

Use the formula $A = s^2$.
• length of a side (s) = 6 ft
• area (A) = 6 ft * 6 ft = 36 ft^2

The area of the square is 36 ft^2.

6 ft

CHECK YOUR UNDERSTANDING

Find the area of the following figures. Include the unit in your answers.

1. 3 units

2 units

2. 4 in.

$9\frac{1}{2}$ in.

3. 6 m

Check your answers on page 391.

The Rectangle Method of Finding Area

Many times you will need to find the area of a polygon that is not a rectangle. Unit squares will not fit neatly inside the figure, and you won't be able to use the formula for the area of a rectangle.

One approach that works well in cases such as these is called the **rectangle method.** Rectangles are used to surround the figure or parts of the figure. Then the only areas that you must calculate are for rectangles and triangular halves of rectangles.

EXAMPLE   What is the area of triangle *JKL*?

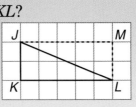

Draw a rectangle around the triangle.
Rectangle *JKLM* surrounds the triangle.

The area of rectangle *JKLM* is 10 square units.
The segment *JL* divides the rectangle into two congruent triangles that have the same area.
The area of triangle *JKL* is 5 square units.

EXAMPLE   What is the area of triangle *ABC*?

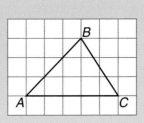

Step 1: Divide triangle *ABC* into two parts.

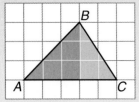

Step 2: Draw a rectangle around the left shaded part. The area of the rectangle is 9 square units. The shaded area is $4\frac{1}{2}$ square units.

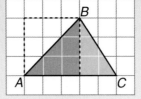

Step 3: Draw a rectangle around the right shaded part. The area of the rectangle is 6 square units. The shaded area is 3 square units.

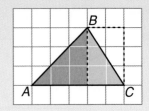

Step 4: Add the areas of the two shaded parts: $4\frac{1}{2} + 3 = 7\frac{1}{2}$ square units.

The area of triangle *ABC* is $7\frac{1}{2}$ square units.

EXAMPLE What is the area of
triangle *XYZ*?

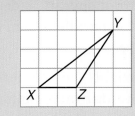

Step 1: Draw a rectangle
around the triangle.

Step 2: The area of rectangle
XRYS is 12 square units. So,
the area of triangle *XRY* is
6 square units.

Step 3: Draw a rectangle
around triangle *ZSY*. The area
of the rectangle is 6 square
units, so the area of triangle
ZSY is 3 square units.

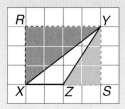

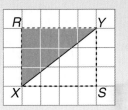

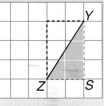

Step 4: Subtract the areas of the two shaded triangles from the area of rectangle *XRYS*.
12 − 6 − 3 = 3 square units.

The area of triangle *XYZ* is 3 square units.

CHECK YOUR UNDERSTANDING

Use the rectangle method to find the area of each figure below.

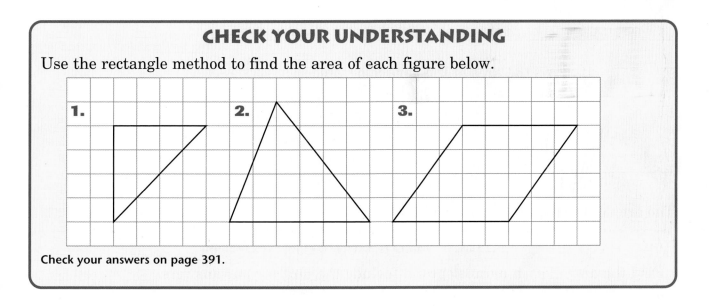

Check your answers on page 391.

Area of Parallelograms

In a parallelogram, either pair of opposite sides can be chosen as its **bases.** The **height** of the parallelogram is the shortest distance between the two bases.

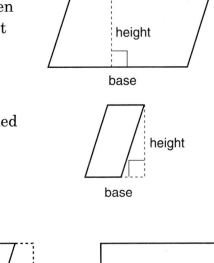

In the parallelograms at the right, the height is shown by a dashed line that is **perpendicular** (at a right angle) to the base. In the second parallelogram, the base has been extended and the dashed height falls outside the parallelogram.

Any parallelogram can be cut into two pieces and the pieces rearranged to form a rectangle whose base and height are the same as the base and height of the parallelogram. The rectangle has the same area as the parallelogram. So you can find the area of the parallelogram in the same way you find the area of the rectangle—by multiplying the length of the base by the height.

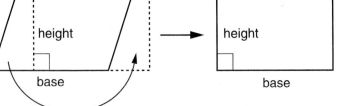

Formula for the Area of Parallelograms

$$A = b * h$$

A is the area, b is the length of the base, h is the height of the parallelogram.

EXAMPLE   Find the area of the parallelogram.

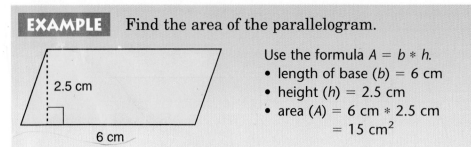

Use the formula $A = b * h$.
- length of base (b) = 6 cm
- height (h) = 2.5 cm
- area (A) = 6 cm * 2.5 cm
  = 15 cm^2

The area of the parallelogram is 15 cm^2.

CHECK YOUR UNDERSTANDING

Find the area of each parallelogram. Include the unit in your answers.

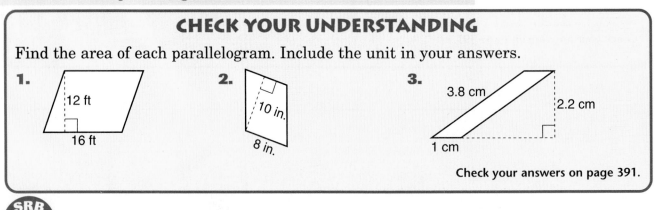

1. 12 ft   16 ft

2. 10 in.   8 in.

3. 3.8 cm   2.2 cm   1 cm

Check your answers on page 391.

Area of Triangles

Any of the sides of a triangle can be chosen as its **base.** The **height** of the triangle (for that base) is the shortest distance between the base and the **vertex** opposite the base. The height is always perpendicular to the base.

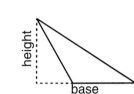

In the triangles at the right, the height is shown by a dashed line that is **perpendicular** (at a right angle) to the base. In one of the triangles, the base has been extended and the dashed height falls outside the triangle.

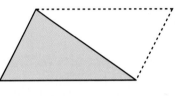

Any triangle can be combined with a second triangle of the same size and shape to form a parallelogram. Each triangle at the right has the same size base and height as the parallelogram. The area of each triangle is half the area of the parallelogram. Therefore, the area of a triangle is half the product of the base multiplied by the height.

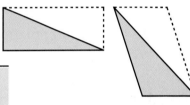

Area Formulas

Parallelograms	Triangles
$A = b * h$	$A = \frac{1}{2} * (b * h)$
A is the area, b is the length of a base, h is the height.	A is the area, b is the length of a base, h is the height.

EXAMPLE   Find the area of the triangle.

4 in.

7 in.

Use the formula $A = \frac{1}{2} * (b * h)$.
- length of base (b) = 7 in.
- height (h) = 4 in.
- area (A) = $\frac{1}{2} * (7$ in. $* 4$ in.$)$
  $= \frac{1}{2} * 28$ in.$^2 = 14$ in.^{2}

So, the area of the triangle is 14 in.^{2}.

CHECK YOUR UNDERSTANDING

Find the area of each triangle. Include the unit in your answers.

1.
6 in.   10 in.
8 in.

2.
9 cm
6 cm

3.
4.8 yd
4.5 yd

Check your answers on page 392.

Area of Circles

The **radius** of a circle is any line segment that connects the center of the circle with any point on the circle. The length of a radius segment is also called the radius.

The **diameter** of a circle is any segment that passes through the center of the circle and has both endpoints on the circle. The length of a diameter segment is also called the diameter.

If you know either the radius or the diameter, you can find the other length. Use the following formulas.

$$\text{diameter} = 2 * \text{radius} \qquad \text{radius} = \tfrac{1}{2} * \text{diameter}$$

If you know the radius, there is a simple formula for finding the area of a circle:

$$\text{Area} = \text{pi} * (\text{radius squared}) \qquad \text{or} \qquad A = \pi * r^2$$

A is the area, and r is the radius of the circle. The Greek letter π is called **pi,** and it is approximately equal to 3.14. You can either use 3.14 or $3\tfrac{1}{7}$ as approximate values for π, or a calculator with a π key.

EXAMPLE Find the area of the circle.

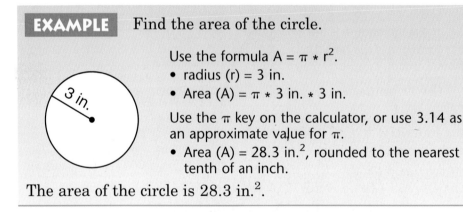

Use the formula $A = \pi * r^2$.
- radius (r) = 3 in.
- Area (A) = $\pi * 3$ in. $* 3$ in.

Use the π key on the calculator, or use 3.14 as an approximate value for π.
- Area (A) = 28.3 in.^{2}, rounded to the nearest tenth of an inch.

The area of the circle is 28.3 in.^{2}.

CHECK YOUR UNDERSTANDING

1. Measure the diameter of the dime in millimeters.
2. What is the radius of the dime?
3. Find the area of the dime in square millimeters.

Check your answers on page 392.

Volume and Capacity

Volume

The **volume** of a solid object such as a brick or a ball is a measure of how much *space the object takes up.* The volume of a container such as a freezer is a measure of *how much the container will hold.*

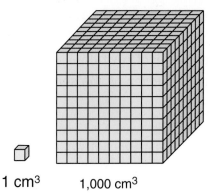

1 cm³   1,000 cm³

Volume is measured in **cubic units,** such as cubic inches (in.³), cubic feet (ft³), and cubic centimeters (cm³). It is easy to find the volumes of objects that are shaped like cubes or other rectangular prisms. For example, picture a container in the shape of a 10-centimeter cube (that is, a cube that is 10 cm by 10 cm by 10 cm). It can be filled with exactly 1,000 centimeter cubes. Therefore, the volume of a 10-centimeter cube is 1,000 cubic centimeters (1,000 cm³).

To find the volume of a rectangular prism, all you need to know are the length and width of its base and its height. The length, width, and height are called the **dimensions** of the prism.

The Dimensions of
a Rectangular Prism

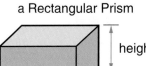

You can also find the volume of other solids, such as triangular prisms, pyramids, cones, and spheres, by measuring their dimensions. It is even possible to find the volume of irregular objects such as rocks or your own body.

Capacity

We often measure things that can be poured into or out of containers, such as liquids, grains, salt, and so on. The volume of a container that is filled with a liquid or a solid that can be poured is often called its **capacity.**

Capacity is usually measured in units such as **gallons, quarts, pints, cups, fluid ounces, liters,** and **milliliters.**

The tables at the right compare different units of capacity. These units of capacity are not cubic units, but liters and milliliters are easily converted to cubic units:

1 milliliter = 1 cm³   1 liter = 1,000 cm³

Metric Units

1 liter (L) = 1,000 milliliters (mL)
1 milliliter = $\frac{1}{1,000}$ liter
1 liter = 1,000 cubic centimeters
1 milliliter = 1 cubic centimeter

U.S. Customary Units

1 gallon (gal) = 4 quarts (qt)
1 gallon = 2 half-gallons
1 half-gallon = 2 quarts
1 quart = 2 pints (pt)
1 pint = 2 cups (c)
1 cup = 8 fluid ounces (fl oz)
1 pint = 16 fluid ounces
1 quart = 32 fluid ounces
1 half-gallon = 64 fluid ounces
1 gallon = 128 fluid ounces

Volume of Geometric Solids

You can think of the volume of a geometric solid as the total number of unit cubes and fractions of unit cubes needed to fill the interior of the solid without any gaps or overlaps.

Prisms and Cylinders

In a prism or cylinder, the cubes can be arranged in layers that each contain the same number of cubes or fractions of cubes.

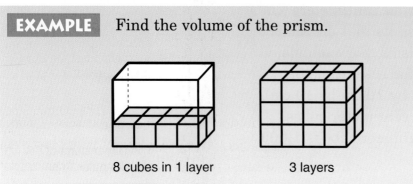

EXAMPLE Find the volume of the prism.

8 cubes in 1 layer   3 layers

3 layers with 8 cubes in each layer makes a total of 24 cubes.

Volume = 24 cubic units

The **height** of a prism or cylinder is the shortest distance between its **bases.** The volume of a prism or cylinder is the product of the area of the base (the number of cubes in one layer) multiplied by its height (the number of layers).

Pyramids and Cones

The height of a pyramid or cone is the shortest distance between its base and the vertex opposite its base.

If a prism and a pyramid have the same size base and height, then the volume of the pyramid is one-third the volume of the prism. If a cylinder and a cone have the same size base and height, then the volume of the cone is one-third the volume of the cylinder.

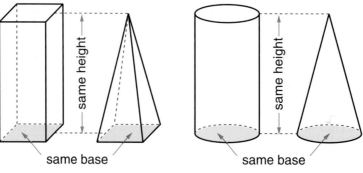

Volume of Rectangular and Triangular Prisms

Volume of Prisms	Area of Rectangles	Area of Triangles
$V = B * h$	$A = b * h$	$A = \frac{1}{2} * (b * h)$
V is the volume, B is the area of the base, h is the height of the prism.	A is the area, b is the length of the base, h is the height of the rectangle.	A is the area, b is the length of the base, h is the height of the triangle.

EXAMPLE Find the volume of the rectangular prism.

Step 1: Find the area of the base (B). Use the formula $A = b * h$.
- length of the rectangular base (b) = 8 cm
- width of the rectangular base (h) = 5 cm
- area of base (B) = 8 cm * 5 cm = 40 cm^2

Step 2: Multiply the area of the base by the height of the rectangular prism. Use the formula $V = B * h$.
- area of base (B) = 40 cm^2
- height of prism (h) = 6 cm
- volume (V) = 40 cm^2 * 6 cm = 240 cm^3

So, the volume of the rectangular prism is 240 cm^3.

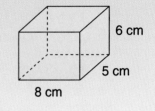

EXAMPLE Find the volume of the triangular prism.

Step 1: Find the area of the base (B). Use the formula $A = \frac{1}{2} * (b * h)$.
- length of the triangular base (b) = 5 in.
- height of the triangular base (h) = 4 in.
- area of base (B) = $\frac{1}{2}$ * (5 in. * 4 in.) = 10 in.^{2}

Step 2: Multiply the area of the base by the height of the triangular prism. Use the formula $V = B * h$
- area of base (B) = 10 in.^{2}
- height of prism (h) = 6 in.
- volume (V) = 10 in.^{2} * 6 in. = 60 in.^{3}

So, the volume of the triangular prism is 60 in.^{3}.

CHECK YOUR UNDERSTANDING

Find the volume of each prism. Be sure to include the unit in your answers.

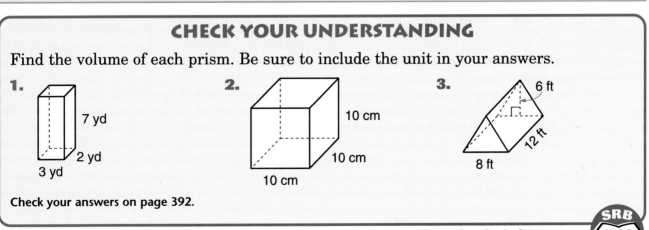

1. 7 yd, 2 yd, 3 yd

2. 10 cm, 10 cm, 10 cm

3. 6 ft, 12 ft, 8 ft

Check your answers on page 392.

Volume of Cylinders and Cones

Volume of Cylinders	Volume of Cones	Area of Circles
$V = B * h$	$V = \frac{1}{3} * (B * h)$	$A = \pi * r^2$
V is the volume, B is the area of the base, h is the height of the cylinder.	V is the volume, B is the area of the base, h is the height of the cone.	A is the area, r is the radius of the base.

EXAMPLE   Find the volume of the cylinder.

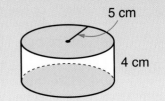

Step 1: Find the area of the base (B).
Use the formula $A = \pi * r^2$.
- radius of base (r) = 5 cm
- area of base (B) = $\pi * 5$ cm $* 5$ cm

Use the π key on a calculator or 3.14 as an approximate value for π.
- area of base (B) = 78.5 cm^2, rounded to the nearest tenth of a square centimeter.

Step 2: Multiply the area of the base by the height of the cylinder.
Use the formula $V = B * h$.
- area of base (B) = 78.5 cm^2
- height of cylinder (h) = 4 cm
- volume (V) = 78.5 cm^2 $* 4$ cm = 314.0 cm^3

The volume of the cylinder is 314.0 cm^3.

EXAMPLE   Find the volume of the cone.

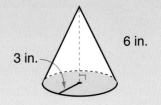

Step 1: Find the area of the base (B).
Use the formula $A = \pi * r^2$.
- radius of base (r) = 3 in.
- area of base (B) = $\pi * 3$ in. $* 3$ in.
Use the π key on a calculator or 3.14 as an approximate value for π.
- area of base (B) = 28.3 in.^{2}, rounded to the nearest tenth of a square inch.

Step 2: Find $\frac{1}{3}$ of the product of the area of the base multiplied by the height of the cone.
Use the formula $V = \frac{1}{3} * (B * h)$.
- area of base (B) = 28.3 in.^{2}
- height of cone (h) = 6 in.
- volume (V) = $\frac{1}{3} * 28.3$ in.^{2} $* 6$ in.= 56.6 in.^{3}

The volume of the cone is 56.6 in.^{3}.

Volume of Rectangular and Triangular Pyramids

Volume of Pyramids	Area of Rectangles	Area of Triangles
$V = \frac{1}{3} * (B * h)$	$A = b * h$	$A = \frac{1}{2} * (b * h)$
V is the volume, B is the area of the base, h is the height of the pyramid.	A is the area, b is the length of the base, h is the height of the rectangle.	A is the area, b is the length of the base, h is the height of the triangle.

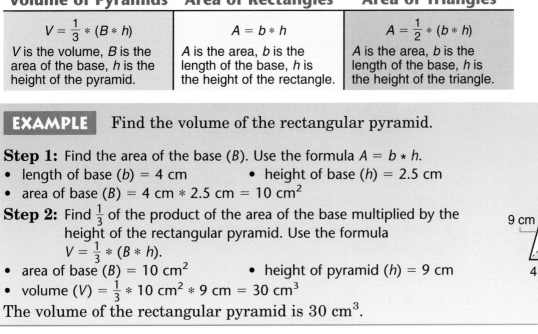

EXAMPLE   Find the volume of the rectangular pyramid.

Step 1: Find the area of the base (B). Use the formula $A = b * h$.
• length of base (b) = 4 cm   • height of base (h) = 2.5 cm
• area of base (B) = 4 cm $*$ 2.5 cm = 10 cm^2

Step 2: Find $\frac{1}{3}$ of the product of the area of the base multiplied by the height of the rectangular pyramid. Use the formula
   $V = \frac{1}{3} * (B * h)$.
• area of base (B) = 10 cm^2 • height of pyramid (h) = 9 cm
• volume (V) = $\frac{1}{3} * 10$ cm^2 $* 9$ cm = 30 cm^3

The volume of the rectangular pyramid is 30 cm^3.

EXAMPLE   Find the volume of the triangular pyramid.

Step 1: Find the area of the base (B). Use the formula $A = \frac{1}{2} * (b * h)$.
• length of base (b) = 10 in.   • height of base (h) = 6 in.
• area of base (B) = $\frac{1}{2} * (10$ in. $* 6$ in.) = 30 in.^{2}

Step 2: Find $\frac{1}{3}$ of the product of the area of the base multiplied by the height of the triangular pyramid. Use the formula
   $V = \frac{1}{3} * (B * h)$.
• area of base (B) = 30 in.^{2} • height of pyramid (h) = $4\frac{1}{2}$ in.
• volume (V) = $\frac{1}{3} * 30$ in.^{2} $* 4\frac{1}{2}$ in. = 45 in.^{3}

The volume of the triangular pyramid is 45 in.^{3}.

CHECK YOUR UNDERSTANDING

Find the volume of each pyramid. Be sure to include the unit in your answers.

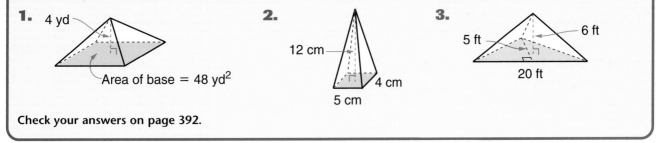

1. 4 yd — Area of base = 48 yd^2

2. 12 cm — 4 cm — 5 cm

3. 5 ft — 6 ft — 20 ft

Check your answers on page 392.

Surface Area of Rectangular Prisms

A rectangular prism has six flat surfaces, or **faces.** The **surface area** of a rectangular prism is the sum of the areas of all six faces of the prism. One way to find the surface area of a rectangular prism is to think of the six faces as three pairs of opposite, parallel faces. Since opposite faces have the same area, you can find the area of one face in each pair of opposite faces. Then find the sum of these three areas, and double the result.

The dimensions of a rectangular prism are its length (l), width (w), and height (h), as shown in the prism at the right. You can find the surface area of rectangular prisms, as follows:

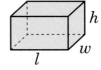

Step 1: Find the area of one face in each pair of opposite faces.

area of	area of front	area of side
base = $l * w$	face $= l * h$	face $= w * h$

Step 2: Find the sum of the areas of the three faces.
- sum of areas $= (l * w) + (l * h) + (w * h)$

Step 3: Multiply the sum of the three areas by 2.
- surface area of prism $= 2 * ((l * w) + (l * h) + (w * h))$

Surface Area of Rectangular Prisms

$$S = 2 * ((l * w) + (l * h) + (w * h))$$

S is the surface area, l the length of the base, w the width of the base, h the height of the prism.

EXAMPLE Find the surface area of the rectangular prism.

Use the formula $S = 2 * ((l * w) + (l * h) + (w * h))$.
- length (l) = 4 in.   width (w) = 3 in.   height (h) = 2 in.
- surface area (S) = 2 * ((4 in. * 3 in.) + (4 in. * 2 in.) + (3 in. * 2 in.))
  = 2 * (12 in.^{2} + 8 in.^{2} + 6 in.^{2}) = 2 * 26 in.^{2} = 52 in.^{2}

The surface area of the rectangular prism is 52 in.^{2}.

CHECK YOUR UNDERSTANDING

Find the surface area of each prism. Be sure to include the unit in your answer.

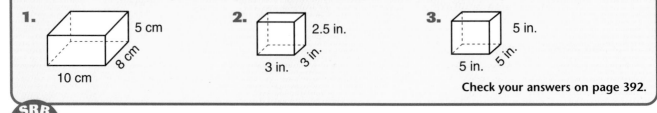

1. 5 cm, 8 cm, 10 cm

2. 2.5 in., 3 in., 3 in.

3. 5 in., 5 in., 5 in.

Check your answers on page 392.

Surface Area of Cylinders

A cylinder has two circular faces, which are called **bases.** The bases are connected by a curved surface. They are parallel and have the same area.

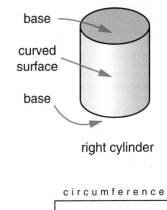

base

curved surface

base

right cylinder

To find the area of the curved surface of a cylinder, imagine a soup can with a label. If you cut the label perpendicular to the top and bottom of the can, peel it off, and lay it flat on a surface, you will get a rectangle. The length of the rectangle is the same as the circumference of the base of the cylinder. The width of the rectangle is the same as the height of the can. Therefore, the area of the curved surface is the product of the circumference of the base multiplied by the height of the can.

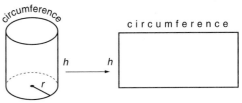

circumference

circumference

h   h

r

circumference of base = $2 * \pi * r$
area of curved surface = $(2 * \pi * r) * h$

The surface area of a cylinder is the sum of the areas of the two bases $(2 * \pi * r^2)$ and the curved surface.

Surface Area of Cylinders

$$S = (2 * \pi * r^2) + ((2 * \pi * r) * h)$$

S is the surface area, r is the radius of the base, h is the height of the cylinder.

EXAMPLE   Find the surface area of the cylinder.

Use the formula $S = (2 * \pi * r^2) + ((2 * \pi * r) * h)$.
- radius of base = 3 cm
- height = 5 cm
Use the π key on the calculator or 3.14 as an approximate value for π.
- surface area = $(2 * \pi * 3 \text{ cm} * 3 \text{ cm}) + ((2 * \pi * 3 \text{ cm}) * 5 \text{ cm})$
  = $(\pi * 18 \text{ cm}^2) + (\pi * 30 \text{ cm}^2)$
  = 150.8 cm², rounded to the nearest tenth of a square centimeter

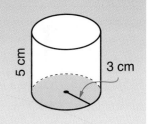

5 cm

3 cm

CHECK YOUR UNDERSTANDING

Find the surface area of the cylinder to the nearest tenth of a square inch. Be sure to include the unit in your answer.

2 in.

3 in.

Check your answers on page 392.

SRB

Weight

Today, in the United States, two different sets of standard units are used to measure weight.

- The standard unit for weight in the metric system is the **gram.** A small, plastic base-10 cube weighs about 1 gram. Heavier weights are measured in **kilograms.** One kilogram equals 1,000 grams.

- Two standard units for weight in the U.S. customary system are the **ounce** and the **pound.** Heavier weights are measured in pounds. One pound equals 16 ounces. Some weights are reported in both pounds and ounces. For example, we might say that "the suitcase weighs 14 pounds 6 ounces."

Metric Units	U.S. Customary Units
1 gram (g) = 1,000 milligrams (mg)	1 pound (lb) = 16 ounces (oz)
1 milligram = $\frac{1}{1,000}$ gram	1 ounce = $\frac{1}{16}$ pound
1 kilogram (kg) = 1,000 grams	1 ton (t) = 2,000 pounds
1 gram = $\frac{1}{1,000}$ kilogram	1 pound = $\frac{1}{2,000}$ ton
1 metric ton (t) = 1,000 kilograms	
1 kilogram = $\frac{1}{1,000}$ metric ton	

Rules of Thumb	Exact Equivalents
1 ounce equals about 30 grams.	1 ounce = 28.35 grams
1 kilogram weighs about 2 pounds.	1 kilogram = 2.205 pounds

EXAMPLES   A bicycle weighs 14 kilograms. How many pounds is that?

Rough Solution: Use the Rule of Thumb. Since 1 kg equals about 2 lb, 14 kg weighs about 14 * 2 = 28 lb.

Exact Solution: Use the exact equivalent.
Since 1 kg = 2.205 lb, 14 kg = 14 * 2.205 = 30.87 lb.

> N O T E
>
> The Rules of Thumb table shows how units of weight in the metric system relate to units in the U.S. customary system. You can use this table to convert ounces to grams and kilograms to pounds. For most everyday purposes, you need only remember the simple Rules of Thumb.

CHECK YOUR UNDERSTANDING

Solve each problem.

1. A softball weighs 6 ounces. How many grams is that? Use a Rule of Thumb and an exact equivalent.

2. Andy's brother weighs 34 pounds 11 ounces. How many ounces is that?

Check your answers on page 392.

Temperature

Temperature is a measure of the hotness or coldness of something. To read a temperature in degrees, you need a reference frame that begins with a zero point and has an interval for the scale. The two most commonly used temperature scales, Fahrenheit and Celsius, have different zero points.

Fahrenheit

This scale was invented in the early 1700s by the German physicist G.D. Fahrenheit. Pure water freezes at 32°F and boils at 212°F. A salt-water solution freezes at 0°F (the zero point) at sea level. The normal temperature for the human body is 98.6°F. The Fahrenheit scale is used primarily in the United States.

Celsius

This scale was developed in 1742 by the Swedish astronomer Anders Celsius. The zero point (0 degrees Celsius or 0°C) is the freezing point of pure water. Pure water boils at 100°C. The Celsius scale divides the interval between these two points into 100 equal parts. For this reason, it is sometimes called the *centigrade* scale. The normal temperature for the human body is 37°C. The Celsius scale is the standard for most people outside of the United States and for scientists everywhere.

A **thermometer** measures temperature. The common thermometer is a glass tube that contains a liquid. When the temperature goes up, the liquid expands and moves up the tube. When the temperature goes down, the liquid shrinks and moves down the tube.

Here are two formulas for converting from degrees Fahrenheit (°F) to degrees Celsius (°C) and vice versa:

$$C = \frac{5}{9} * (F - 32) \quad \text{and} \quad F = \frac{9}{5} * C + 32.$$

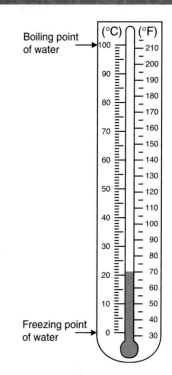

The thermometer is marked to show both the Fahrenheit and Celsius scales. Key reference temperatures, such as the boiling and freezing points of water, are indicated. This thermometer shows a reading of 70°F (or about 21°C), which is normal room temperature.

EXAMPLE   Find the Celsius equivalent of 82°F.

Use the formula $C = \frac{5}{9} * (F - 32)$ and replace F with 82:
$C = \frac{5}{9} * (82 - 32)$
So, $C = \frac{5}{9} * (50) = 27.77$, or about 28°C.

Measuring and Drawing Angles

Angles are measured in **degrees.** When writing the measure of an angle, a small raised circle (°) is used as a symbol for the word degree.

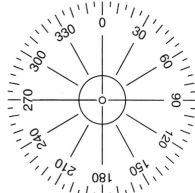

Angles are measured with a tool called a **protractor.** You will find both a full-circle and a half-circle protractor on your Geometry Template. Since there are 360 degrees in a circle, a 1° angle marks off $\frac{1}{360}$ of a circle.

The **full-circle protractor** on the Geometry Template is marked off in 5° intervals from 0° to 360°. It can be used to measure angles, but it cannot be used to draw angles of a given measure.

The **half-circle protractor** on the Geometry Template is marked off in 1° intervals from 0° to 180°.

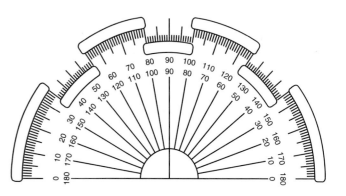

It has two scales, each of which starts at 0°. One scale is read clockwise, the other is read counterclockwise.

The half-circle protractor can be used both to measure angles and to draw angles of a given measure.

Two rays starting from the same endpoint form two angles. The smaller angle measures between 0° and 180°. The larger angle is called a **reflex angle.** It measures between 180° and 360°. The sum of the measures of the smaller angle and the reflex angle is 360°.

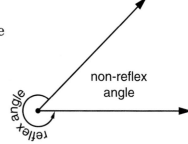

non-reflex angle

reflex angle

Measuring an Angle with a Full-Circle Protractor

Think of the angle as a rotation of the minute hand of a clock.
One side of the angle represents the minute hand at the
beginning of a time interval. The other side of the angle
represents the minute hand some time later.

EXAMPLE   To measure angle *IJK* with a full-circle
protractor:

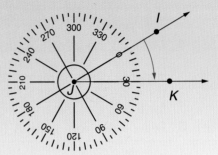

Step 1: Place the center of the protractor over the vertex
of the angle, point *J*.

Step 2: Line up the 0° mark on the protractor with $\overrightarrow{JI}$.

Step 3: Read the degree measure where $\overrightarrow{JK}$ crosses the
edge of the protractor.

The measure of angle *IJK* = 30°.

EXAMPLE   To measure reflex angle *EFG*:

Step 1: Place the center of the protractor over point *F*.

Step 2: Line up the 0° mark on the protractor with $\overrightarrow{FG}$.

Step 3: Read the degree measure where $\overrightarrow{FE}$ crosses the
edge of the protractor.

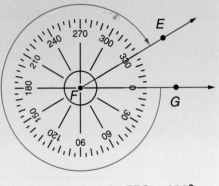

The measure of angle *EFG* = 330°.

Measuring Angles with a Half-Circle Protractor

EXAMPLE   To measure angle *PQR* with a half-circle protractor:

Step 1: Lay the baseline of the protractor on $\overrightarrow{QR}$.

Step 2: Slide the protractor so that the
center of the baseline is over the
vertex of the angle, point *Q*.

Step 3: Read the degree measure where
$\overrightarrow{QP}$ crosses the edge of the
protractor. There are two scales
on the protractor. Use the scale
that makes sense for the size of
the angle you are measuring.

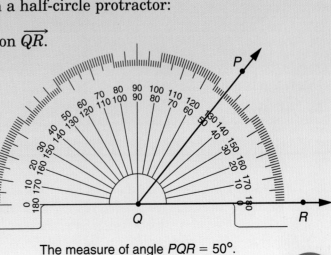

The measure of angle *PQR* = 50°.

Drawing Angles with a Half-Circle Protractor

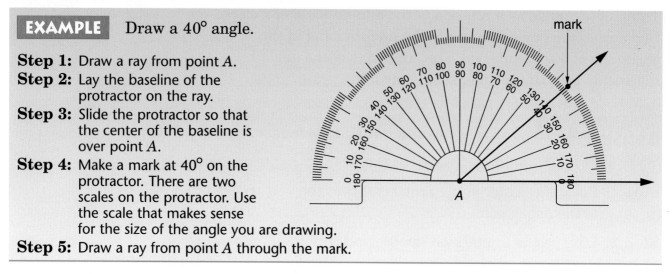

EXAMPLE   Draw a 40° angle.

Step 1: Draw a ray from point *A*.
Step 2: Lay the baseline of the
protractor on the ray.
Step 3: Slide the protractor so that
the center of the baseline is
over point *A*.
Step 4: Make a mark at 40° on the
protractor. There are two
scales on the protractor. Use
the scale that makes sense
for the size of the angle you are drawing.
Step 5: Draw a ray from point *A* through the mark.

To draw a reflex angle using the half-circle protractor, subtract
the measure of the reflex angle from 360°. Use this as the
measure of the smaller angle.

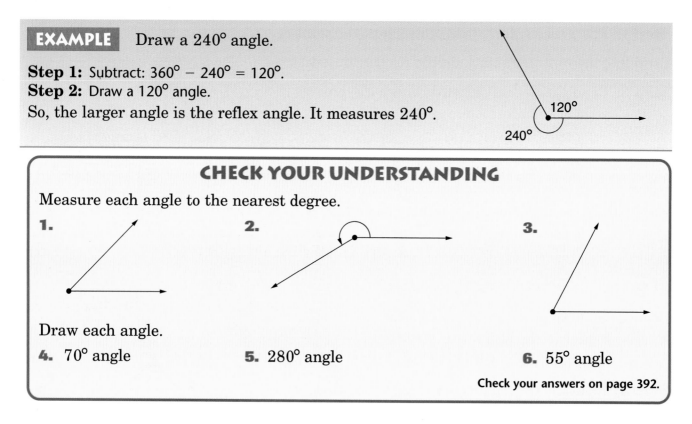

EXAMPLE   Draw a 240° angle.

Step 1: Subtract: 360° − 240° = 120°.
Step 2: Draw a 120° angle.
So, the larger angle is the reflex angle. It measures 240°.

CHECK YOUR UNDERSTANDING

Measure each angle to the nearest degree.

1.

2.

3.

Draw each angle.

4. 70° angle

5. 280° angle

6. 55° angle

Check your answers on page 392.

The Measures of the Angles of Polygons

Any polygon can be divided into triangles.

- The measures of the three angles of each triangle add up to 180°.
- To find the sum of the measures of all the angles of a polygon, multiply: (number of triangles in the polygon) * 180°.

EXAMPLE What is the sum of the measures of the angles of a hexagon?

Step 1: Draw any hexagon, then divide it into triangles. This hexagon can be divided into four triangles.

Step 2: Multiply the number of triangles by 180°.

Since the measures of the angles of each triangle add up to 180°, the sum of the measures of the angles = 4 * 180° = 720°.

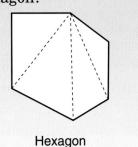

Hexagon

Finding the Measure of an Angle of a Regular Polygon

All the angles of a regular polygon have the same measure. So the measure of an angle is equal to the sum of the measures of the angles of the polygon, divided by the number of angles.

EXAMPLE What is the measure of an angle of a regular hexagon?

The sum of the measures of the angles of any hexagon is 720°. A regular hexagon has 6 congruent angles.

Therefore, the measure of an angle of a regular hexagon is $\frac{720}{6} = 120°$.

Regular Hexagon
(6 congruent sides and 6 congruent angles)

CHECK YOUR UNDERSTANDING

1. Into how many triangles can you divide

   a. a quadrilateral? **b.** a pentagon? **c.** an octagon? **d.** a 12-sided polygon?

2. What is the sum of the measures of the angles of a pentagon?

3. What is the measure of an angle of a regular octagon?

4. Suppose that you know the number of sides of a polygon. Without drawing a picture, how can you calculate the number of triangles into which it can be divided?

Check your answers on page 392.

Plotting Ordered Number Pairs

A **rectangular coordinate grid** is used to name points in the plane. It is made up of two number lines, called **axes**, that meet at right angles at their zero points. The point where the two lines meet is called the **origin.**

Every point on a coordinate grid can be named by an **ordered number pair.** The two numbers that make up an ordered number pair are called the **coordinates** of the point. The first coordinate is always the *horizontal* distance of the point from the vertical axis. The second coordinate is always the *vertical* distance of the point from the horizontal axis. For example, the ordered pair (3,5) names point *A* on the grid at the right. The numbers 3 and 5 are the coordinates of point *A*.

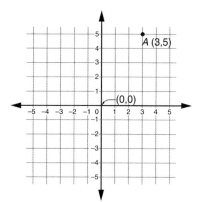

The ordered pair (0,0) names the origin.

EXAMPLE   Plot the ordered number pair (5,3).

Step 1: Locate 5 on the horizontal axis.
Step 2: Locate 3 on the vertical axis.
Step 3: Draw a vertical line from point 5 on the horizontal axis and a horizontal line from point 3 on the vertical axis. The point (5,3) is located at the intersection of the two lines. Note that the order of the numbers in an ordered pair is important. The ordered pair (5,3) does not name the same point as the ordered pair (3,5).

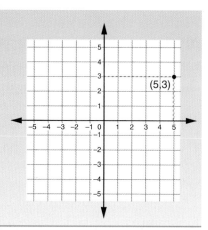

EXAMPLE   Locate $(-2,3)$, $(-4,-1)$, and $(3\frac{1}{2},0)$.

For each ordered pair, locate the first coordinate on the horizontal axis and the second coordinate on the vertical axis. Draw intersecting lines from these two points.

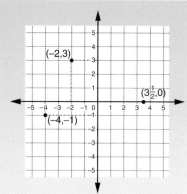

CHECK YOUR UNDERSTANDING

Draw a coordinate grid on graph paper and plot the following points.

1. (2,4)   **2.** $(-1,-3)$ **3.** (0,5)   **4.** $(-2,2)$

Check your answers on page 392.

Latitude and Longitude

The Earth is almost a perfect **sphere.** All points on Earth are about the same distance from its center. The Earth rotates on an **axis,** which is an imaginary line connecting the **North Pole** and the **South Pole.**

Reference lines are drawn on globes and maps to make places easier to find. Lines that go east and west around the Earth are called **lines of latitude.** The **equator** is a special line of latitude. Every point on the equator is the same distance from the North Pole and the South Pole. The lines of latitude are often called **parallels** because each one is a circle that is parallel to the equator.

Lines of latitude are measured in **degrees.** (The symbol for degrees is (°).) Lines north of the equator are labeled °N (degrees north), lines south of the equator are labeled °S (degrees south). The number of degrees tells how far north or south of the equator a place is. The area north of the equator is called the **Northern Hemisphere.** The area south of the equator is called the **Southern Hemisphere.**

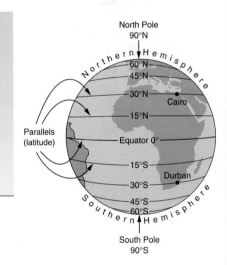

> **EXAMPLES**   The latitude of the North Pole is 90°N. The latitude of the South Pole is 90°S. The poles are the points farthest north and farthest south on Earth.
>
> The latitude of Cairo, Egypt, is 30°N. We say that Cairo is 30 degrees north of the equator.
>
> The latitude of Durban, South Africa, is 30°S. Durban is in the Southern Hemisphere.

A second set of lines runs from north to south. These are semicircles (half-circles) that connect the poles. They are called **lines of longitude** or **meridians.** The meridians are not parallel, since they meet at the poles.

The **prime meridian** is the special meridian labeled 0°. The prime meridian crosses near London, England. Another special meridian is the **international date line.** This meridian is labeled 180° and is exactly opposite the prime meridian on the other side of the world.

Longitude is measured in degrees. Lines west of the prime meridian are labeled °W. Lines east of the prime meridian are labeled °E. The number of degrees tells how far west or east of the prime meridian a place is. The area west of the prime meridian is called the **Western Hemisphere.** The area east of the prime meridian is called the **Eastern Hemisphere.**

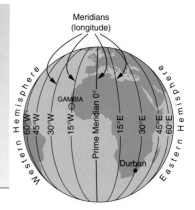

EXAMPLES   The longitude of London is 0° because London lies on the prime meridian.

The longitude of Durban, South Africa, is 30°E. Durban is in the Eastern Hemisphere.

The longitude of Gambia (a small country in Africa) is about 15°W. Gambia is 15 degrees west of the prime meridian.

When lines of both latitude and longitude are shown on a globe or map, they form a pattern of crossing lines called a **grid.** The grid can help you locate places on the map. Any place on the map can be located by naming its latitude and longitude.

EXAMPLES   The map may be used to find the approximate latitude and longitude for the cities shown. For example, Denver, Colorado is about 40° North and 105° West.

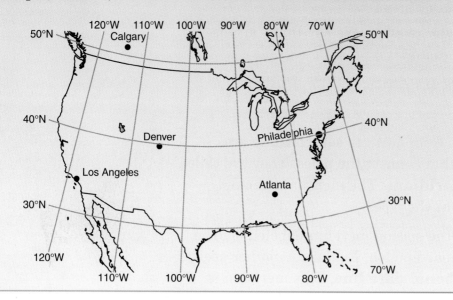

Map Scales and Distances

Map Scales

Mapmakers show large areas of land and water on small pieces of paper. Places that are actually thousands of miles apart may be only inches apart on a map. When you use a map, you can estimate real distances by using a **map scale.**

Different maps use different scales. On one map, 1 inch may represent 10 miles in the real world. On another map, 1 inch may represent 100 miles.

On the map scale here, the bar is 2 inches long. Two inches on the map represent 2,000 real miles. One inch on the map represents 1,000 real miles.

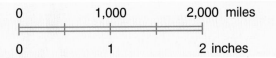

Sometimes you see a map scale written as "2 inches = 2,000 miles." This statement is not mathematically correct because 2 inches is not equal to 2,000 miles. What is meant is that a 2 inch distance on the map represents 2,000 miles in the real world.

Measuring Distances on a Map

There are many ways to measure distances on a map. Here are several.

Use a Ruler

Sometimes the distance you want to measure is along a straight line. Measure the straight line distance with a ruler. Then use the map scale to change the map distance to the real distance.

EXAMPLE   Use the map and scale shown below to find the air distance from Denver to Chicago. The air distance is the straight-line distance between the two cities.

The line segment connecting Denver and Chicago is 3 inches long. The map scale shows that 1 inch represents 300 miles. So 3 inches must represent 3 * 300 miles, or 900 miles. The air distance from Denver to Chicago is 900 miles.

Measurement

Use String and a Ruler

Sometimes you may need to find the length of a curved path, such as a road or river. You can use a piece of string, a ruler, and the map scale to find the length.

- Lay a string along the path you want to measure. Mark the beginning and ending points on the string.
- Straighten out the string. Be careful not to stretch it. Use a ruler to measure between the beginning and ending points.
- Use the map scale to change the map distance into the real distance.

Use a Compass

Sometimes map scales are not in inches or centimeters, so a ruler is not much help. In these cases you can use a compass to find distances. Using a compass can also be easier than using a ruler, especially if you are measuring a curved path and you do not have string.

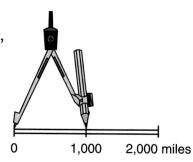

Step 1: Adjust the compass so that the distance between the anchor point and the pencil point is the same as a distance on the map scale.

0   1,000   2,000 miles

Step 2: Imagine a path connecting the starting point and ending point of the distance you want to measure. Put the anchor point of the compass at the starting point. Use the pencil point to make an arc on the path. Move the anchor point to the spot where the arc and the path meet. Continue walking the compass along the path until you reach or pass the ending point. Be careful not to change the opening of the compass.

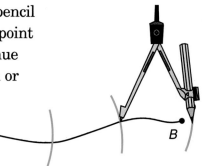

Step 3: Keep track of how many times you swing the compass. Each swing stands for the distance on the map scale. To estimate total distance, multiply the number of swings by the distance each swing stands for.

If you use a compass to measure distance along a curved path, your estimate will be less than the actual distance. The distance along a straight line between two points is less than the distance along a curved path between the same two points.

Perpetual Calendar

The **perpetual calendar** consists of 14 different one-year calendars. It shows all the possible one-year calendars. The calendar for a year is determined by which day is January 1. There are 7 calendars for years with 365 days. There are another 7 calendars for years with 366 days.

Years that have 366 days are called **leap years**. They occur every four years. The extra day is added to February. Years that are divisible by 4 are leap years, except for years that are multiples of 100. Those years (1600, 1700, 1800, 1900, 2000, and so on) are leap years only if they are divisible by 400. The years 1600 and 2000 are leap years, but years 1700, 1800, and 1900 are not leap years.

Calendar to use for years 1899 to 2028

Year	No.	Year	No.	Year	No.	Year	No.	Year	No.
1899	1	1925	5	1951	2	1977	7	2003	4
1900	2	1926	6	1952	10	1978	1	2004	12
1901	3	1927	7	1953	5	1979	2	2005	7
1902	4	1928	8	1954	6	1980	10	2006	1
1903	5	1929	3	1955	7	1981	5	2007	2
1904	13	1930	4	1956	8	1982	6	2008	10
1905	1	1931	5	1957	3	1983	7	2009	5
1906	2	1932	13	1958	4	1984	8	2010	6
1907	3	1933	1	1959	5	1985	3	2011	4
1908	11	1934	2	1960	13	1986	4	2012	8
1909	6	1935	3	1961	1	1987	5	2013	3
1910	7	1936	11	1962	2	1988	13	2014	4
1911	1	1937	6	1963	3	1989	1	2015	5
1912	9	1938	7	1964	11	1990	2	2016	13
1913	4	1939	1	1965	6	1991	3	2017	1
1914	5	1940	9	1966	7	1992	11	2018	2
1915	6	1941	4	1967	1	1993	6	2019	3
1916	14	1942	5	1968	9	1994	7	2020	11
1917	2	1943	6	1969	4	1995	1	2021	6
1918	3	1944	14	1970	5	1996	9	2022	7
1919	4	1945	2	1971	6	1997	4	2023	1
1920	12	1946	3	1972	14	1998	5	2024	9
1921	7	1947	4	1973	2	1999	6	2025	4
1922	1	1948	12	1974	3	2000	14	2026	5
1923	2	1949	7	1975	4	2001	2	2027	6
1924	10	1950	1	1976	12	2002	3	2028	14

Calendar 1

```
JANUARY                 FEBRUARY                MARCH                   APRIL
 S  M  T  W  T  F  S     S  M  T  W  T  F  S     S  M  T  W  T  F  S     S  M  T  W  T  F  S
 1  2  3  4  5  6  7                 1  2  3  4              1  2  3  4                       1
 8  9 10 11 12 13 14     5  6  7  8  9 10 11     5  6  7  8  9 10 11     2  3  4  5  6  7  8
15 16 17 18 19 20 21    12 13 14 15 16 17 18    12 13 14 15 16 17 18     9 10 11 12 13 14 15
22 23 24 25 26 27 28    19 20 21 22 23 24 25    19 20 21 22 23 24 25    16 17 18 19 20 21 22
29 30 31                26 27 28                26 27 28 29 30 31       23 24 25 26 27 28 29
                                                                       30

MAY                     JUNE                    JULY                    AUGUST
 S  M  T  W  T  F  S     S  M  T  W  T  F  S     S  M  T  W  T  F  S     S  M  T  W  T  F  S
    1  2  3  4  5  6                 1  2  3                       1           1  2  3  4  5
 7  8  9 10 11 12 13     4  5  6  7  8  9 10     2  3  4  5  6  7  8     6  7  8  9 10 11 12
14 15 16 17 18 19 20    11 12 13 14 15 16 17     9 10 11 12 13 14 15    13 14 15 16 17 18 19
21 22 23 24 25 26 27    18 19 20 21 22 23 24    16 17 18 19 20 21 22    20 21 22 23 24 25 26
28 29 30 31             25 26 27 28 29 30       23 24 25 26 27 28 29    27 28 29 30 31
                                                30 31

SEPTEMBER               OCTOBER                 NOVEMBER                DECEMBER
 S  M  T  W  T  F  S     S  M  T  W  T  F  S     S  M  T  W  T  F  S     S  M  T  W  T  F  S
                1  2     1  2  3  4  5  6  7                 1  2  3  4                 1  2
 3  4  5  6  7  8  9     8  9 10 11 12 13 14     5  6  7  8  9 10 11     3  4  5  6  7  8  9
10 11 12 13 14 15 16    15 16 17 18 19 20 21    12 13 14 15 16 17 18    10 11 12 13 14 15 16
17 18 19 20 21 22 23    22 23 24 25 26 27 28    19 20 21 22 23 24 25    17 18 19 20 21 22 23
24 25 26 27 28 29 30    29 30 31                26 27 28 29 30          24 25 26 27 28 29 30
                                                                       31
```

Calendar 2

```
JANUARY                 FEBRUARY                MARCH                   APRIL
 S  M  T  W  T  F  S     S  M  T  W  T  F  S     S  M  T  W  T  F  S     S  M  T  W  T  F  S
    1  2  3  4  5  6                 1  2  3                 1  2  3     1  2  3  4  5  6  7
 7  8  9 10 11 12 13     4  5  6  7  8  9 10     4  5  6  7  8  9 10     8  9 10 11 12 13 14
14 15 16 17 18 19 20    11 12 13 14 15 16 17    11 12 13 14 15 16 17    15 16 17 18 19 20 21
21 22 23 24 25 26 27    18 19 20 21 22 23 24    18 19 20 21 22 23 24    22 23 24 25 26 27 28
28 29 30 31             25 26 27 28             25 26 27 28 29 30 31    29 30

MAY                     JUNE                    JULY                    AUGUST
 S  M  T  W  T  F  S     S  M  T  W  T  F  S     S  M  T  W  T  F  S     S  M  T  W  T  F  S
       1  2  3  4  5                 1  2        1  2  3  4  5  6  7                 1  2  3  4
 6  7  8  9 10 11 12     3  4  5  6  7  8  9     8  9 10 11 12 13 14     5  6  7  8  9 10 11
13 14 15 16 17 18 19    10 11 12 13 14 15 16    15 16 17 18 19 20 21    12 13 14 15 16 17 18
20 21 22 23 24 25 26    17 18 19 20 21 22 23    22 23 24 25 26 27 28    19 20 21 22 23 24 25
27 28 29 30 31          24 25 26 27 28 29 30    29 30 31                26 27 28 29 30 31

SEPTEMBER               OCTOBER                 NOVEMBER                DECEMBER
 S  M  T  W  T  F  S     S  M  T  W  T  F  S     S  M  T  W  T  F  S     S  M  T  W  T  F  S
                   1        1  2  3  4  5  6                 1  2  3                       1
 2  3  4  5  6  7  8     7  8  9 10 11 12 13     4  5  6  7  8  9 10     2  3  4  5  6  7  8
 9 10 11 12 13 14 15    14 15 16 17 18 19 20    11 12 13 14 15 16 17     9 10 11 12 13 14 15
16 17 18 19 20 21 22    21 22 23 24 25 26 27    18 19 20 21 22 23 24    16 17 18 19 20 21 22
23 24 25 26 27 28 29    28 29 30 31             25 26 27 28 29 30       23 24 25 26 27 28 29
30                                                                     30 31
```

Calendar 3

```
JANUARY                 FEBRUARY                MARCH                   APRIL
 S  M  T  W  T  F  S     S  M  T  W  T  F  S     S  M  T  W  T  F  S     S  M  T  W  T  F  S
       1  2  3  4  5                    1  2                    1  2        1  2  3  4  5  6
 6  7  8  9 10 11 12     3  4  5  6  7  8  9     3  4  5  6  7  8  9     7  8  9 10 11 12 13
13 14 15 16 17 18 19    10 11 12 13 14 15 16    10 11 12 13 14 15 16    14 15 16 17 18 19 20
20 21 22 23 24 25 26    17 18 19 20 21 22 23    17 18 19 20 21 22 23    21 22 23 24 25 26 27
27 28 29 30 31          24 25 26 27 28          24 25 26 27 28 29 30    28 29 30
                                                31

MAY                     JUNE                    JULY                    AUGUST
 S  M  T  W  T  F  S     S  M  T  W  T  F  S     S  M  T  W  T  F  S     S  M  T  W  T  F  S
             1  2  3  4                       1     1  2  3  4  5  6                 1  2  3
 5  6  7  8  9 10 11     2  3  4  5  6  7  8     7  8  9 10 11 12 13     4  5  6  7  8  9 10
12 13 14 15 16 17 18     9 10 11 12 13 14 15    14 15 16 17 18 19 20    11 12 13 14 15 16 17
19 20 21 22 23 24 25    16 17 18 19 20 21 22    21 22 23 24 25 26 27    18 19 20 21 22 23 24
26 27 28 29 30 31       23 24 25 26 27 28 29    28 29 30 31             25 26 27 28 29 30 31
                        30

SEPTEMBER               OCTOBER                 NOVEMBER                DECEMBER
 S  M  T  W  T  F  S     S  M  T  W  T  F  S     S  M  T  W  T  F  S     S  M  T  W  T  F  S
 1  2  3  4  5  6  7           1  2  3  4  5                    1  2     1  2  3  4  5  6  7
 8  9 10 11 12 13 14     6  7  8  9 10 11 12     3  4  5  6  7  8  9     8  9 10 11 12 13 14
15 16 17 18 19 20 21    13 14 15 16 17 18 19    10 11 12 13 14 15 16    15 16 17 18 19 20 21
22 23 24 25 26 27 28    20 21 22 23 24 25 26    17 18 19 20 21 22 23    22 23 24 25 26 27 28
29 30                   27 28 29 30 31          24 25 26 27 28 29 30    29 30 31
```

Calendar 4

```
JANUARY                 FEBRUARY                MARCH                   APRIL
 S  M  T  W  T  F  S     S  M  T  W  T  F  S     S  M  T  W  T  F  S     S  M  T  W  T  F  S
             1  2  3  4                       1                       1        1  2  3  4  5
 5  6  7  8  9 10 11     2  3  4  5  6  7  8     2  3  4  5  6  7  8     6  7  8  9 10 11 12
12 13 14 15 16 17 18     9 10 11 12 13 14 15     9 10 11 12 13 14 15    13 14 15 16 17 18 19
19 20 21 22 23 24 25    16 17 18 19 20 21 22    16 17 18 19 20 21 22    20 21 22 23 24 25 26
26 27 28 29 30 31       23 24 25 26 27 28       23 24 25 26 27 28 29    27 28 29 30
                                                30 31

MAY                     JUNE                    JULY                    AUGUST
 S  M  T  W  T  F  S     S  M  T  W  T  F  S     S  M  T  W  T  F  S     S  M  T  W  T  F  S
             1  2  3     1  2  3  4  5  6  7           1  2  3  4  5                    1  2
 4  5  6  7  8  9 10     8  9 10 11 12 13 14     6  7  8  9 10 11 12     3  4  5  6  7  8  9
11 12 13 14 15 16 17    15 16 17 18 19 20 21    13 14 15 16 17 18 19    10 11 12 13 14 15 16
18 19 20 21 22 23 24    22 23 24 25 26 27 28    20 21 22 23 24 25 26    17 18 19 20 21 22 23
25 26 27 28 29 30 31    29 30                   27 28 29 30 31          24 25 26 27 28 29 30
                                                                       31

SEPTEMBER               OCTOBER                 NOVEMBER                DECEMBER
 S  M  T  W  T  F  S     S  M  T  W  T  F  S     S  M  T  W  T  F  S     S  M  T  W  T  F  S
    1  2  3  4  5  6                 1  2  3  4                       1        1  2  3  4  5  6
 7  8  9 10 11 12 13     5  6  7  8  9 10 11     2  3  4  5  6  7  8     7  8  9 10 11 12 13
14 15 16 17 18 19 20    12 13 14 15 16 17 18     9 10 11 12 13 14 15    14 15 16 17 18 19 20
21 22 23 24 25 26 27    19 20 21 22 23 24 25    16 17 18 19 20 21 22    21 22 23 24 25 26 27
28 29 30                26 27 28 29 30 31       23 24 25 26 27 28 29    28 29 30 31
                                                30
```

Calendar 5

```
JANUARY                 FEBRUARY                MARCH                   APRIL
 S  M  T  W  T  F  S     S  M  T  W  T  F  S     S  M  T  W  T  F  S     S  M  T  W  T  F  S
             1  2  3     1  2  3  4  5  6  7     1  2  3  4  5  6  7                 1  2  3  4
 4  5  6  7  8  9 10     8  9 10 11 12 13 14     8  9 10 11 12 13 14     5  6  7  8  9 10 11
11 12 13 14 15 16 17    15 16 17 18 19 20 21    15 16 17 18 19 20 21    12 13 14 15 16 17 18
18 19 20 21 22 23 24    22 23 24 25 26 27 28    22 23 24 25 26 27 28    19 20 21 22 23 24 25
25 26 27 28 29 30 31                            29 30 31                26 27 28 29 30

MAY                     JUNE                    JULY                    AUGUST
 S  M  T  W  T  F  S     S  M  T  W  T  F  S     S  M  T  W  T  F  S     S  M  T  W  T  F  S
                1  2        1  2  3  4  5  6                 1  2  3  4                       1
 3  4  5  6  7  8  9     7  8  9 10 11 12 13     5  6  7  8  9 10 11     2  3  4  5  6  7  8
10 11 12 13 14 15 16    14 15 16 17 18 19 20    12 13 14 15 16 17 18     9 10 11 12 13 14 15
17 18 19 20 21 22 23    21 22 23 24 25 26 27    19 20 21 22 23 24 25    16 17 18 19 20 21 22
24 25 26 27 28 29 30    28 29 30                26 27 28 29 30 31       23 24 25 26 27 28 29
31                                                                     30 31

SEPTEMBER               OCTOBER                 NOVEMBER                DECEMBER
 S  M  T  W  T  F  S     S  M  T  W  T  F  S     S  M  T  W  T  F  S     S  M  T  W  T  F  S
       1  2  3  4  5                 1  2  3     1  2  3  4  5  6  7           1  2  3  4  5
 6  7  8  9 10 11 12     4  5  6  7  8  9 10     8  9 10 11 12 13 14     6  7  8  9 10 11 12
13 14 15 16 17 18 19    11 12 13 14 15 16 17    15 16 17 18 19 20 21    13 14 15 16 17 18 19
20 21 22 23 24 25 26    18 19 20 21 22 23 24    22 23 24 25 26 27 28    20 21 22 23 24 25 26
27 28 29 30             25 26 27 28 29 30 31    29 30                   27 28 29 30 31
```

6

JANUARY

S	M	T	W	T	F	S
					1	2
3	4	5	6	7	8	9
10	11	12	13	14	15	16
17	18	19	20	21	22	23
24	25	26	27	28	29	30
31						

FEBRUARY

S	M	T	W	T	F	S
	1	2	3	4	5	6
7	8	9	10	11	12	13
14	15	16	17	18	19	20
21	22	23	24	25	26	27
28						

MARCH

S	M	T	W	T	F	S
	1	2	3	4	5	6
7	8	9	10	11	12	13
14	15	16	17	18	19	20
21	22	23	24	25	26	27
28	29	30	31			

APRIL

S	M	T	W	T	F	S
				1	2	3
4	5	6	7	8	9	10
11	12	13	14	15	16	17
18	19	20	21	22	23	24
25	26	27	28	29	30	

MAY

S	M	T	W	T	F	S
						1
2	3	4	5	6	7	8
9	10	11	12	13	14	15
16	17	18	19	20	21	22
23	24	25	26	27	28	29
30	31					

JUNE

S	M	T	W	T	F	S
		1	2	3	4	5
6	7	8	9	10	11	12
13	14	15	16	17	18	19
20	21	22	23	24	25	26
27	28	29	30			

JULY

S	M	T	W	T	F	S
				1	2	3
4	5	6	7	8	9	10
11	12	13	14	15	16	17
18	19	20	21	22	23	24
25	26	27	28	29	30	31

AUGUST

S	M	T	W	T	F	S
1	2	3	4	5	6	7
8	9	10	11	12	13	14
15	16	17	18	19	20	21
22	23	24	25	26	27	28
29	30	31				

SEPTEMBER

S	M	T	W	T	F	S
			1	2	3	4
5	6	7	8	9	10	11
12	13	14	15	16	17	18
19	20	21	22	23	24	25
26	27	28	29	30		

OCTOBER

S	M	T	W	T	F	S
					1	2
3	4	5	6	7	8	9
10	11	12	13	14	15	16
17	18	19	20	21	22	23
24	25	26	27	28	29	30
31						

NOVEMBER

S	M	T	W	T	F	S
	1	2	3	4	5	6
7	8	9	10	11	12	13
14	15	16	17	18	19	20
21	22	23	24	25	26	27
28	29	30				

DECEMBER

S	M	T	W	T	F	S
			1	2	3	4
5	6	7	8	9	10	11
12	13	14	15	16	17	18
19	20	21	22	23	24	25
26	27	28	29	30	31	

7

JANUARY

S	M	T	W	T	F	S
						1
2	3	4	5	6	7	8
9	10	11	12	13	14	15
16	17	18	19	20	21	22
23	24	25	26	27	28	29
30	31					

FEBRUARY

S	M	T	W	T	F	S
		1	2	3	4	5
6	7	8	9	10	11	12
13	14	15	16	17	18	19
20	21	22	23	24	25	26
27	28					

MARCH

S	M	T	W	T	F	S
		1	2	3	4	5
6	7	8	9	10	11	12
13	14	15	16	17	18	19
20	21	22	23	24	25	26
27	28	29	30	31		

APRIL

S	M	T	W	T	F	S
					1	2
3	4	5	6	7	8	9
10	11	12	13	14	15	16
17	18	19	20	21	22	23
24	25	26	27	28	29	30

MAY

S	M	T	W	T	F	S
1	2	3	4	5	6	7
8	9	10	11	12	13	14
15	16	17	18	19	20	21
22	23	24	25	26	27	28
29	30	31				

JUNE

S	M	T	W	T	F	S
			1	2	3	4
5	6	7	8	9	10	11
12	13	14	15	16	17	18
19	20	21	22	23	24	25
26	27	28	29	30		

JULY

S	M	T	W	T	F	S
					1	2
3	4	5	6	7	8	9
10	11	12	13	14	15	16
17	18	19	20	21	22	23
24	25	26	27	28	29	30
31						

AUGUST

S	M	T	W	T	F	S
	1	2	3	4	5	6
7	8	9	10	11	12	13
14	15	16	17	18	19	20
21	22	23	24	25	26	27
28	29	30	31			

SEPTEMBER

S	M	T	W	T	F	S
				1	2	3
4	5	6	7	8	9	10
11	12	13	14	15	16	17
18	19	20	21	22	23	24
25	26	27	28	29	30	

OCTOBER

S	M	T	W	T	F	S
						1
2	3	4	5	6	7	8
9	10	11	12	13	14	15
16	17	18	19	20	21	22
23	24	25	26	27	28	29
30	31					

NOVEMBER

S	M	T	W	T	F	S
		1	2	3	4	5
6	7	8	9	10	11	12
13	14	15	16	17	18	19
20	21	22	23	24	25	26
27	28	29	30			

DECEMBER

S	M	T	W	T	F	S
				1	2	3
4	5	6	7	8	9	10
11	12	13	14	15	16	17
18	19	20	21	22	23	24
25	26	27	28	29	30	31

8

JANUARY

S	M	T	W	T	F	S
1	2	3	4	5	6	7
8	9	10	11	12	13	14
15	16	17	18	19	20	21
22	23	24	25	26	27	28
29	30	31				

FEBRUARY

S	M	T	W	T	F	S
			1	2	3	4
5	6	7	8	9	10	11
12	13	14	15	16	17	18
19	20	21	22	23	24	25
26	27	28	29			

MARCH

S	M	T	W	T	F	S
				1	2	3
4	5	6	7	8	9	10
11	12	13	14	15	16	17
18	19	20	21	22	23	24
25	26	27	28	29	30	31

APRIL

S	M	T	W	T	F	S
1	2	3	4	5	6	7
8	9	10	11	12	13	14
15	16	17	18	19	20	21
22	23	24	25	26	27	28
29	30					

MAY

S	M	T	W	T	F	S
		1	2	3	4	5
6	7	8	9	10	11	12
13	14	15	16	17	18	19
20	21	22	23	24	25	26
27	28	29	30	31		

JUNE

S	M	T	W	T	F	S
					1	2
3	4	5	6	7	8	9
10	11	12	13	14	15	16
17	18	19	20	21	22	23
24	25	26	27	28	29	30

JULY

S	M	T	W	T	F	S
1	2	3	4	5	6	7
8	9	10	11	12	13	14
15	16	17	18	19	20	21
22	23	24	25	26	27	28
29	30	31				

AUGUST

S	M	T	W	T	F	S
			1	2	3	4
5	6	7	8	9	10	11
12	13	14	15	16	17	18
19	20	21	22	23	24	25
26	27	28	29	30	31	

SEPTEMBER

S	M	T	W	T	F	S
						1
2	3	4	5	6	7	8
9	10	11	12	13	14	15
16	17	18	19	20	21	22
23	24	25	26	27	28	29
30						

OCTOBER

S	M	T	W	T	F	S
	1	2	3	4	5	6
7	8	9	10	11	12	13
14	15	16	17	18	19	20
21	22	23	24	25	26	27
28	29	30	31			

NOVEMBER

S	M	T	W	T	F	S
				1	2	3
4	5	6	7	8	9	10
11	12	13	14	15	16	17
18	19	20	21	22	23	24
25	26	27	28	29	30	

DECEMBER

S	M	T	W	T	F	S
						1
2	3	4	5	6	7	8
9	10	11	12	13	14	15
16	17	18	19	20	21	22
23	24	25	26	27	28	29
30	31					

9

JANUARY

S	M	T	W	T	F	S
	1	2	3	4	5	6
7	8	9	10	11	12	13
14	15	16	17	18	19	20
21	22	23	24	25	26	27
28	29	30	31			

FEBRUARY

S	M	T	W	T	F	S
				1	2	3
4	5	6	7	8	9	10
11	12	13	14	15	16	17
18	19	20	21	22	23	24
25	26	27	28	29		

MARCH

S	M	T	W	T	F	S
					1	2
3	4	5	6	7	8	9
10	11	12	13	14	15	16
17	18	19	20	21	22	23
24	25	26	27	28	29	30
31						

APRIL

S	M	T	W	T	F	S
	1	2	3	4	5	6
7	8	9	10	11	12	13
14	15	16	17	18	19	20
21	22	23	24	25	26	27
28	29	30				

MAY

S	M	T	W	T	F	S
			1	2	3	4
5	6	7	8	9	10	11
12	13	14	15	16	17	18
19	20	21	22	23	24	25
26	27	28	29	30	31	

JUNE

S	M	T	W	T	F	S
						1
2	3	4	5	6	7	8
9	10	11	12	13	14	15
16	17	18	19	20	21	22
23	24	25	26	27	28	29
30						

JULY

S	M	T	W	T	F	S
	1	2	3	4	5	6
7	8	9	10	11	12	13
14	15	16	17	18	19	20
21	22	23	24	25	26	27
28	29	30	31			

AUGUST

S	M	T	W	T	F	S
				1	2	3
4	5	6	7	8	9	10
11	12	13	14	15	16	17
18	19	20	21	22	23	24
25	26	27	28	29	30	31

SEPTEMBER

S	M	T	W	T	F	S
1	2	3	4	5	6	7
8	9	10	11	12	13	14
15	16	17	18	19	20	21
22	23	24	25	26	27	28
29	30					

OCTOBER

S	M	T	W	T	F	S
		1	2	3	4	5
6	7	8	9	10	11	12
13	14	15	16	17	18	19
20	21	22	23	24	25	26
27	28	29	30	31		

NOVEMBER

S	M	T	W	T	F	S
					1	2
3	4	5	6	7	8	9
10	11	12	13	14	15	16
17	18	19	20	21	22	23
24	25	26	27	28	29	30

DECEMBER

S	M	T	W	T	F	S
1	2	3	4	5	6	7
8	9	10	11	12	13	14
15	16	17	18	19	20	21
22	23	24	25	26	27	28
29	30	31				

10

JANUARY

S	M	T	W	T	F	S
		1	2	3	4	5
6	7	8	9	10	11	12
13	14	15	16	17	18	19
20	21	22	23	24	25	26
27	28	29	30	31		

FEBRUARY

S	M	T	W	T	F	S
					1	2
3	4	5	6	7	8	9
10	11	12	13	14	15	16
17	18	19	20	21	22	23
24	25	26	27	28	29	

MARCH

S	M	T	W	T	F	S
						1
2	3	4	5	6	7	8
9	10	11	12	13	14	15
16	17	18	19	20	21	22
23	24	25	26	27	28	29
30	31					

APRIL

S	M	T	W	T	F	S
		1	2	3	4	5
6	7	8	9	10	11	12
13	14	15	16	17	18	19
20	21	22	23	24	25	26
27	28	29	30			

MAY

S	M	T	W	T	F	S
				1	2	3
4	5	6	7	8	9	10
11	12	13	14	15	16	17
18	19	20	21	22	23	24
25	26	27	28	29	30	31

JUNE

S	M	T	W	T	F	S
1	2	3	4	5	6	7
8	9	10	11	12	13	14
15	16	17	18	19	20	21
22	23	24	25	26	27	28
29	30					

JULY

S	M	T	W	T	F	S
		1	2	3	4	5
6	7	8	9	10	11	12
13	14	15	16	17	18	19
20	21	22	23	24	25	26
27	28	29	30	31		

AUGUST

S	M	T	W	T	F	S
					1	2
3	4	5	6	7	8	9
10	11	12	13	14	15	16
17	18	19	20	21	22	23
24	25	26	27	28	29	30
31						

SEPTEMBER

S	M	T	W	T	F	S
	1	2	3	4	5	6
7	8	9	10	11	12	13
14	15	16	17	18	19	20
21	22	23	24	25	26	27
28	29	30				

OCTOBER

S	M	T	W	T	F	S
			1	2	3	4
5	6	7	8	9	10	11
12	13	14	15	16	17	18
19	20	21	22	23	24	25
26	27	28	29	30	31	

NOVEMBER

S	M	T	W	T	F	S
						1
2	3	4	5	6	7	8
9	10	11	12	13	14	15
16	17	18	19	20	21	22
23	24	25	26	27	28	29
30						

DECEMBER

S	M	T	W	T	F	S
	1	2	3	4	5	6
7	8	9	10	11	12	13
14	15	16	17	18	19	20
21	22	23	24	25	26	27
28	29	30	31			

11

JANUARY

S	M	T	W	T	F	S
			1	2	3	4
5	6	7	8	9	10	11
12	13	14	15	16	17	18
19	20	21	22	23	24	25
26	27	28	29	30	31	

FEBRUARY

S	M	T	W	T	F	S
						1
2	3	4	5	6	7	8
9	10	11	12	13	14	15
16	17	18	19	20	21	22
23	24	25	26	27	28	29

MARCH

S	M	T	W	T	F	S
1	2	3	4	5	6	7
8	9	10	11	12	13	14
15	16	17	18	19	20	21
22	23	24	25	26	27	28
29	30	31				

APRIL

S	M	T	W	T	F	S
			1	2	3	4
5	6	7	8	9	10	11
12	13	14	15	16	17	18
19	20	21	22	23	24	25
26	27	28	29	30		

MAY

S	M	T	W	T	F	S
					1	2
3	4	5	6	7	8	9
10	11	12	13	14	15	16
17	18	19	20	21	22	23
24	25	26	27	28	29	30
31						

JUNE

S	M	T	W	T	F	S
	1	2	3	4	5	6
7	8	9	10	11	12	13
14	15	16	17	18	19	20
21	22	23	24	25	26	27
28	29	30				

JULY

S	M	T	W	T	F	S
			1	2	3	4
5	6	7	8	9	10	11
12	13	14	15	16	17	18
19	20	21	22	23	24	25
26	27	28	29	30	31	

AUGUST

S	M	T	W	T	F	S
						1
2	3	4	5	6	7	8
9	10	11	12	13	14	15
16	17	18	19	20	21	22
23	24	25	26	27	28	29
30	31					

SEPTEMBER

S	M	T	W	T	F	S
		1	2	3	4	5
6	7	8	9	10	11	12
13	14	15	16	17	18	19
20	21	22	23	24	25	26
27	28	29	30			

OCTOBER

S	M	T	W	T	F	S
				1	2	3
4	5	6	7	8	9	10
11	12	13	14	15	16	17
18	19	20	21	22	23	24
25	26	27	28	29	30	31

NOVEMBER

S	M	T	W	T	F	S
1	2	3	4	5	6	7
8	9	10	11	12	13	14
15	16	17	18	19	20	21
22	23	24	25	26	27	28
29	30					

DECEMBER

S	M	T	W	T	F	S
		1	2	3	4	5
6	7	8	9	10	11	12
13	14	15	16	17	18	19
20	21	22	23	24	25	26
27	28	29	30	31		

12

JANUARY

S	M	T	W	T	F	S
				1	2	3
4	5	6	7	8	9	10
11	12	13	14	15	16	17
18	19	20	21	22	23	24
25	26	27	28	29	30	31

FEBRUARY

S	M	T	W	T	F	S
1	2	3	4	5	6	7
8	9	10	11	12	13	14
15	16	17	18	19	20	21
22	23	24	25	26	27	28
29						

MARCH

S	M	T	W	T	F	S
	1	2	3	4	5	6
7	8	9	10	11	12	13
14	15	16	17	18	19	20
21	22	23	24	25	26	27
28	29	30	31			

APRIL

S	M	T	W	T	F	S
				1	2	3
4	5	6	7	8	9	10
11	12	13	14	15	16	17
18	19	20	21	22	23	24
25	26	27	28	29	30	

MAY

S	M	T	W	T	F	S
						1
2	3	4	5	6	7	8
9	10	11	12	13	14	15
16	17	18	19	20	21	22
23	24	25	26	27	28	29
30	31					

JUNE

S	M	T	W	T	F	S
		1	2	3	4	5
6	7	8	9	10	11	12
13	14	15	16	17	18	19
20	21	22	23	24	25	26
27	28	29	30			

JULY

S	M	T	W	T	F	S
				1	2	3
4	5	6	7	8	9	10
11	12	13	14	15	16	17
18	19	20	21	22	23	24
25	26	27	28	29	30	31

AUGUST

S	M	T	W	T	F	S
1	2	3	4	5	6	7
8	9	10	11	12	13	14
15	16	17	18	19	20	21
22	23	24	25	26	27	28
29	30	31				

SEPTEMBER

S	M	T	W	T	F	S
			1	2	3	4
5	6	7	8	9	10	11
12	13	14	15	16	17	18
19	20	21	22	23	24	25
26	27	28	29	30		

OCTOBER

S	M	T	W	T	F	S
					1	2
3	4	5	6	7	8	9
10	11	12	13	14	15	16
17	18	19	20	21	22	23
24	25	26	27	28	29	30
31						

NOVEMBER

S	M	T	W	T	F	S
	1	2	3	4	5	6
7	8	9	10	11	12	13
14	15	16	17	18	19	20
21	22	23	24	25	26	27
28	29	30				

DECEMBER

S	M	T	W	T	F	S
			1	2	3	4
5	6	7	8	9	10	11
12	13	14	15	16	17	18
19	20	21	22	23	24	25
26	27	28	29	30	31	

13

JANUARY

S	M	T	W	T	F	S
					1	2
3	4	5	6	7	8	9
10	11	12	13	14	15	16
17	18	19	20	21	22	23
24	25	26	27	28	29	30
31						

FEBRUARY

S	M	T	W	T	F	S
	1	2	3	4	5	6
7	8	9	10	11	12	13
14	15	16	17	18	19	20
21	22	23	24	25	26	27
28	29					

MARCH

S	M	T	W	T	F	S
		1	2	3	4	5
6	7	8	9	10	11	12
13	14	15	16	17	18	19
20	21	22	23	24	25	26
27	28	29	30	31		

APRIL

S	M	T	W	T	F	S
					1	2
3	4	5	6	7	8	9
10	11	12	13	14	15	16
17	18	19	20	21	22	23
24	25	26	27	28	29	30

MAY

S	M	T	W	T	F	S
1	2	3	4	5	6	7
8	9	10	11	12	13	14
15	16	17	18	19	20	21
22	23	24	25	26	27	28
29	30	31				

JUNE

S	M	T	W	T	F	S
			1	2	3	4
5	6	7	8	9	10	11
12	13	14	15	16	17	18
19	20	21	22	23	24	25
26	27	28	29	30		

JULY

S	M	T	W	T	F	S
					1	2
3	4	5	6	7	8	9
10	11	12	13	14	15	16
17	18	19	20	21	22	23
24	25	26	27	28	29	30
31						

AUGUST

S	M	T	W	T	F	S
	1	2	3	4	5	6
7	8	9	10	11	12	13
14	15	16	17	18	19	20
21	22	23	24	25	26	27
28	29	30	31			

SEPTEMBER

S	M	T	W	T	F	S
				1	2	3
4	5	6	7	8	9	10
11	12	13	14	15	16	17
18	19	20	21	22	23	24
25	26	27	28	29	30	

OCTOBER

S	M	T	W	T	F	S
						1
2	3	4	5	6	7	8
9	10	11	12	13	14	15
16	17	18	19	20	21	22
23	24	25	26	27	28	29
30	31					

NOVEMBER

S	M	T	W	T	F	S
		1	2	3	4	5
6	7	8	9	10	11	12
13	14	15	16	17	18	19
20	21	22	23	24	25	26
27	28	29	30			

DECEMBER

S	M	T	W	T	F	S
				1	2	3
4	5	6	7	8	9	10
11	12	13	14	15	16	17
18	19	20	21	22	23	24
25	26	27	28	29	30	31

14

JANUARY

S	M	T	W	T	F	S
						1
2	3	4	5	6	7	8
9	10	11	12	13	14	15
16	17	18	19	20	21	22
23	24	25	26	27	28	29
30	31					

FEBRUARY

S	M	T	W	T	F	S
		1	2	3	4	5
6	7	8	9	10	11	12
13	14	15	16	17	18	19
20	21	22	23	24	25	26
27	28	29				

MARCH

S	M	T	W	T	F	S
			1	2	3	4
5	6	7	8	9	10	11
12	13	14	15	16	17	18
19	20	21	22	23	24	25
26	27	28	29	30	31	

APRIL

S	M	T	W	T	F	S
						1
2	3	4	5	6	7	8
9	10	11	12	13	14	15
16	17	18	19	20	21	22
23	24	25	26	27	28	29
30						

MAY

S	M	T	W	T	F	S
	1	2	3	4	5	6
7	8	9	10	11	12	13
14	15	16	17	18	19	20
21	22	23	24	25	26	27
28	29	30	31			

JUNE

S	M	T	W	T	F	S
				1	2	3
4	5	6	7	8	9	10
11	12	13	14	15	16	17
18	19	20	21	22	23	24
25	26	27	28	29	30	

JULY

S	M	T	W	T	F	S
						1
2	3	4	5	6	7	8
9	10	11	12	13	14	15
16	17	18	19	20	21	22
23	24	25	26	27	28	29
30	31					

AUGUST

S	M	T	W	T	F	S
		1	2	3	4	5
6	7	8	9	10	11	12
13	14	15	16	17	18	19
20	21	22	23	24	25	26
27	28	29	30	31		

SEPTEMBER

S	M	T	W	T	F	S
					1	2
3	4	5	6	7	8	9
10	11	12	13	14	15	16
17	18	19	20	21	22	23
24	25	26	27	28	29	30

OCTOBER

S	M	T	W	T	F	S
1	2	3	4	5	6	7
8	9	10	11	12	13	14
15	16	17	18	19	20	21
22	23	24	25	26	27	28
29	30	31				

NOVEMBER

S	M	T	W	T	F	S
			1	2	3	4
5	6	7	8	9	10	11
12	13	14	15	16	17	18
19	20	21	22	23	24	25
26	27	28	29	30		

DECEMBER

S	M	T	W	T	F	S
					1	2
3	4	5	6	7	8	9
10	11	12	13	14	15	16
17	18	19	20	21	22	23
24	25	26	27	28	29	30
31						

Algebra

Algebra

Algebra is arithmetic with letters (or other symbols such as blanks or question marks) as well as numbers. Much of algebra is about how to write and solve number sentences such as $8 + n = 13$ or $y = x + 3$.

In earlier times, algebra involved finding the value of a missing number (called an "unknown") in an equation. These unknowns were expressed with words: "Five plus some number equals eight." Then, in the late 1500s, François Viète began using letters, as in $5 + x = 8$, to stand for unknown quantities. Viète's invention made solving equations much easier and led to many discoveries in mathematics and science.

> **N O T E**
>
> Our word *algebra* comes from the title of a book written over 1,000 years ago by Muhammad ibn Musa al-Khwarizmi, a Persian mathematician who wrote in Arabic. But the origins of algebra can be traced back even farther to ancient Egypt and Babylon.

Variables and Unknowns

The letters that you sometimes see in number sentences are called **variables.**

Variables Can Be Used to Stand for Unknown Numbers.

For example, in the number sentence $5 + x = 8$, the variable x stands for an unknown number. To make the sentence true, the correct number for x must be found. People sometimes use other symbols such as question marks or blanks for unknown numbers.

The Rhind Papyrus, written almost 4,000 years ago

Variables Can Also Be Used to State Properties of Number Systems.

Properties of a number system are things that are true for all numbers. For example, any number multiplied by 1 is equal to itself. Variables are often used in statements that describe properties, as in $a * 1 = a$.

209

205–206

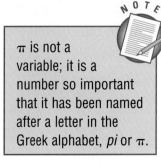

Variables Can Be Used in Formulas.

Formulas are used in everyday life, in science, in business, and in many other situations as an easy way to describe relationships. The formula for the area of a circle, for example, is $A = \pi * r^2$, where A is the area, r is the radius, and π is the number 3.1415.... The formula $A = \pi * r^2$ can also be written without a multiplication symbol: $A = \pi r^2$. Putting letters or variables next to each other like this means they are to be multiplied. The formula for the circumference of a circle is $c = \pi * d$, or $c = \pi d$.

Variables Can Be Used to Express General Relations or Functions.

Function machines and "What's My Rule?" tables have rules that tell you how to get the "out" numbers from the "in" numbers. These rules can be written using variables.

Rule

$y = 3 * x$

x	y
0	0
1	3
2	6
3	9
...	...

Variables Can Be Used in Computers and Calculators.

They are used in computer spreadsheets, which makes it possible to evaluate formulas quickly and efficiently. Variables are also used in writing computer programs. Computer programs are made up of a series of "commands" that contain variables, much like the variables in equations.

Certain calculators, especially graphing calculators, use variables to name calculator key functions.

CHECK YOUR UNDERSTANDING

For each problem, write a number sentence using a letter for the unknown.

1. Half of some number equals 32.

2. Some number equals 16 times 3.

Find the circumference of the circles below. Use the formula $c = \pi * d$. Use 3.14 for π.

3.

$d = 2$ cm

4.

$d = 3$ in.

Check your answers on page 392.

Algebraic Expressions

Variables can be used to express relationships between quantities.

EXAMPLE Claude earns $6 an hour. Use a variable to express the relationship between Claude's earnings and the amount of time worked.

If you use the variable *H* to stand for the number of hours Claude works, you can write his pay as *H* * 6.

H * 6 is an example of an **algebraic expression.** An algebraic expression uses operation symbols (+, −, *, and so on) to combine variables and numbers.

EXAMPLE Write the statement as an algebraic expression.

Statement	Algebraic Expression
Marshall is 5 years older than Carol.	If Carol is *C* years old, then Marshall's age in years is *C* + 5.

Evaluating Expressions

To **evaluate** something is to find out what it is worth. To evaluate an algebraic expression, first replace each variable with its value.

EXAMPLES Evaluate each algebraic expression.

6 * *H*	*x* * *x* * *x*
If *H* = 3, then 6 * *H* is 6 * 3, or 18.	If *x* = 3, then *x* * *x* * *x* is 3 * 3 * 3, or 27.

CHECK YOUR UNDERSTANDING

Write an algebraic expression for each situation using the suggested variable.

1. Alan is *A* inches tall. If Barbara is 4 inches shorter than Alan, what is Barbara's height in inches?

2. Toni runs 3 miles every day. How many miles will she run in *D* days?

What is the value of each expression when *k* = 2?

3. *k* + 3

4. *k* * *k*

5. *k* / 2

Check your answers on page 392.

Parentheses

The meaning of a number sentence is not always clear. For example, in $17 - 4 * 3 = n$, should you work from left to right or should you multiply 4 by 3 first, and then subtract the result from 17?

Working from left to right, you will get 39 as the answer. Multiplying first and then subtracting, you will get 5 as the answer. There is only one correct answer for the number sentence $17 - 4 * 3$.

You can use parentheses to make the meaning clear. The parentheses in the following examples tell you which operation to do first.

EXAMPLE $(17 - 4) * 3 = n$

The parentheses tell you to subtract $17 - 4$ first, and then multiply by 3.
$(17 - 4) * 3 = 39$

$$(17 - 4) * 3 = n$$
$$13 * 3 = n$$
$$39 = n$$

EXAMPLE $17 - (4 * 3) = n$

The parentheses tell you to multiply $4 * 3$ first, and then subtract.
$17 - (4 * 3) = 5$

$$17 - (4 * 3) = n$$
$$17 - 12 = n$$
$$5 = n$$

CHECK YOUR UNDERSTANDING

Solve.

1. $(5 * 5) + 20 = y$

2. $(100 - 80) * 30 = x$

3. $w = (15 - 11) + (5 * 4)$

4. $v = (10 - 3) * 8$

Insert parentheses to make each number sentence true.

5. $25 - 15 + 10 = 0$

6. $60 = 5 * 9 + 3$

7. $5 = 3 + 6 * 3 / 3 * 3$

8. $24 = 8 + 4 * 2$

Check your answers on page 392.

Order of Operations

In arithmetic and algebra, there are rules that tell you what to do first and what to do next. Without these rules, it may be hard to tell what the solution to a problem should be. For example, what is the answer to 8 + 4 * 3? Is the answer 36 or 20? You must know whether to multiply first or to add first.

Rules for the Order of Operations

1. Do operations inside **parentheses** first. Follow rules 2–4.
2. Calculate all expressions with **exponents**.
3. **Multiply** and **divide** in order, from left to right.
4. **Add** and **subtract** in order, from left to right.

Some people find it's easier to remember the order of operations by memorizing this sentence:

$\underline{P}$lease $\underline{E}$xcuse $\underline{M}$y $\underline{D}$ear $\underline{A}$unt $\underline{S}$ally.

$\underline{P}$arentheses $\underline{E}$xponents $\underline{M}$ultiplication $\underline{D}$ivision $\underline{A}$ddition $\underline{S}$ubtraction

---

EXAMPLE   Evaluate. 17 − 4 * 3 = ?

$$17 - 4 * 3 = ?$$

Multiply first and then subtract.
$$17 - 12 = 5$$

17 − 4 * 3 = 5

EXAMPLE   Evaluate. $5^2 + (3 * 4 - 2) / 5 = ?$

$$5^2 + (3 * 4 - 2) / 5 = ?$$

Clear parentheses first. $5^2 + 10 / 5 = ?$
Calculate exponents next. $25 + 10 / 5 = ?$
Divide, and then add. $25 + 2 = ?$

$5^2 + (3 * 4 - 2) / 5 = 27$

CHECK YOUR UNDERSTANDING

Evaluate each expression.

1. 12 − 4 / 2 + 3   **2.** 10 + (7 + 5) / 4   **3.** 5 (3 / 3 − 4 / 4) / 12 + 1

Check your answers on page 392.

Some Properties of Arithmetic

Certain facts are true of all numbers. Some of them are obvious—"every number equals itself," for example—but others are less obvious. Since you have been working with numbers for years, you probably already know most of these facts, or properties as they are called, although you probably don't know their mathematical names.

The Identity Properties

The sum of any number and 0 is that number. For example, $15 + 0 = 15$. The **identity** for addition is 0. Using variables, you write this as $a + 0 = a$, where a is any number.

The product of any number and 1 is that number. For example, $75 * 1 = 75$. The **identity** for multiplication is 1. Using variables, you write this as $a * 1 = a$, where a is any number.

The Commutative Properties

In addition, the order of the numbers makes no difference. For example, $8 + 5 = 5 + 8$. This is known as the **commutative property of addition.** Using variables, you write this as: $a + b = b + a$, where a and b are any numbers.

In multiplication, the order of the numbers also makes no difference. For example, $7 * 2 = 2 * 7$. This is known as the **commutative property of multiplication.** Using variables, you write this as: $a * b = b * a$, where a and b are any numbers.

The Associative Properties

When three numbers are added, it makes no difference which two are added first. For example, $(3 + 4) + 5 = 3 + (4 + 5)$. This is known as the **associative property of addition.** Using variables, you write this as: $(a + b) + c = a + (b + c)$, where a, b, and c are any numbers.

When three numbers are multiplied, it makes no difference which two are multiplied first. For example, $(3 * 4) * 5 = 3 * (4 * 5)$. This is known as the **associative property of multiplication.** Using variables, you write this as: $(a * b) * c = a * (b * c)$, where a, b, and c are any numbers.

The Distributive Property

When you play *Multiplication Wrestling* or multiply with the partial-products method, you use the **distributive property.**

For example, when you solve $60 * 38$ with partial products, you think of 38 as $30 + 8$ and multiply each part by 60.

$$
\begin{array}{r}
38 \\
* 60 \\
\hline
60 * 30 = 1800 \\
60 * 8 = \underline{\ \ 480} \\
60 * 38 = 2{,}280
\end{array}
$$

The distributive property says: $60 * (30 + 8) = (60 * 30) + (60 * 8)$.

EXAMPLE   Show how the distributive property works by finding the area of Rectangle A in two different ways.

Method 1 One way to find the area of Rectangle A is to find the total width of the rectangle, and multiply that by the height.

$$5 * (3 + 4) = 5 * 7$$
$$= 35$$

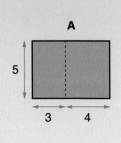

Method 2 Another way to find the area of Rectangle A is to find the area of the two smaller rectangles, then add them together.

$$(5 * 3) + (5 * 4) = 15 + 20$$
$$= 35$$

The area of Rectangle A is 35 square units.

Since both methods give the area of Rectangle A, you know that $5 * (3 + 4) = (5 * 3) + (5 * 4)$. This is an example of the distributive property.

The distributive property works with subtraction too.

EXAMPLE   Find the area of the shaded rectangle.

$$5 * (7 - 3) = 5 * 4 = 20, \text{ or}$$

$$(5 * 7) - (5 * 3) = 35 - 15 = 20$$

The area of the shaded rectangle is 20 square units.

CHECK YOUR UNDERSTANDING

Use the distributive property to fill in the blanks.

1. $7 * (13 + 11) = (7 * \underline{\ \ }) + (7 * \underline{\ \ })$ **2.** $(6 * 21) + (6 * 31) = 6 * (\underline{\ \ } + \underline{\ \ })$

3. $12 * (\underline{\ \ } - \underline{\ \ }) = (12 * 19) - (12 * 17)$

Check your answers on page 392.

Relations

A relation tells how two things compare. The table below shows the most common relations that compare numbers.

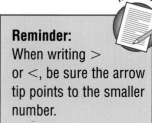

Symbol	Meaning
$=$	is equal to
$\neq$	is not equal to
$<$	is less than
$>$	is greater than
$\leq$	is less than or equal to
$\geq$	is greater than or equal to

Equations

Equality is the most important relation between numbers. Much of arithmetic is nothing more than finding equivalent names for numbers. For example, 75 is another name for $15 * 5$. The word *equivalent* is often used with fractions. For example, you say $\frac{1}{4}$ is equivalent to $\frac{4}{16}$.

Number sentences that contain the $=$ symbol are called **equations.** An equation may be true or it may be false.

EXAMPLES   Here are some equations:

$5 + 8 = 13$ $\qquad$ $(32 - 6) * 4 = 68$ $\qquad$ $58 = 58$

The first and third equations above are true. The second equation is false.

CHECK YOUR UNDERSTANDING

True or false?

1. $15 + 6 = 21$ $\qquad$ **2.** $84 = 8 * 12$ $\qquad$ **3.** $46 - (3 * 9) = 19$

4. $1{,}498 = 1{,}498$ $\qquad$ **5.** $6 * 9 - 3 = 36$ $\qquad$ **6.** $20 = 8 + 3 * 4$

Check your answers on page 392.

Inequalities

Number sentences that do not contain the = symbol are called
inequalities. Like equations, inequalities may be true or false.

> **EXAMPLES** Here are some inequalities:
>
> $5 + 6 < 15$ | $25 > 12 * 3$ | $36 \neq 7 * 6$
>
> The first and third inequalities above are true; the second
> inequality is false.

The symbols $\leq$ and $\geq$ combine two meanings. $\leq$ means "is less
than or equal to"; $\geq$ means "is greater than or equal to."

> **EXAMPLES** Here are some other inequalities:
>
> $5 \leq 5$ True | $300 \geq 350$ False | $5 + 8 \geq 10$ True
> $35 \geq 40 + 5$ False | $60 \leq 100 - 25$ True | $40 - 5 \leq 35$ True

Inequalities on the Number Line

For any pair of numbers on the number line, the number to the
left is less than the number to the right.

> **EXAMPLES** Use the number line to complete each statement. $-5 \;\square\; 2$ $3 \;\square\; -4$
>
>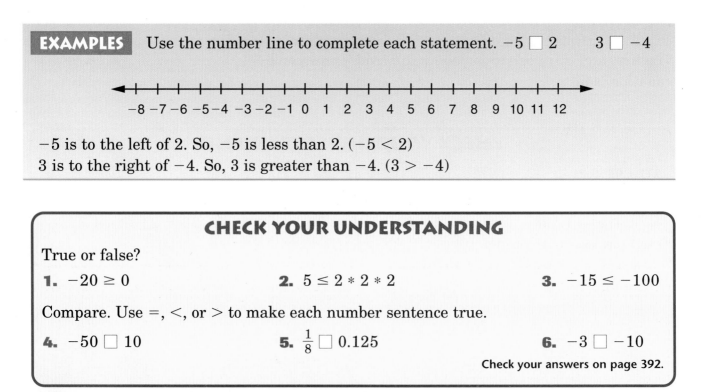
>
> -5 is to the left of 2. So, -5 is less than 2. $(-5 < 2)$
> 3 is to the right of -4. So, 3 is greater than -4. $(3 > -4)$

CHECK YOUR UNDERSTANDING

True or false?

1. $-20 \geq 0$ 　　　　　　**2.** $5 \leq 2 * 2 * 2$ 　　　　　　**3.** $-15 \leq -100$

Compare. Use =, <, or > to make each number sentence true.

4. $-50 \;\square\; 10$ 　　　　　**5.** $\frac{1}{8} \;\square\; 0.125$ 　　　　　**6.** $-3 \;\square\; -10$

Check your answers on page 392.

Number Sentences

Number sentences are made up of **mathematical symbols.**

Mathematical Symbols

Digits	Operation Symbols	Relation Symbols	Grouping Symbols
0, 1, 2, 3, 4, 5, 6, 7, 8, 9	+ −	= ≠	( )
	× *	< >	[ ]
	/ ÷	≤ ≥	

A number sentence must contain a **relation symbol.** Number sentences that contain the symbol = are called **equations.** Number sentences that contain the symbols ≠, <, >, ≤, or ≥ are called **inequalities.**

207–208

Recall that a number sentence may be **true,** or it may be **false.** For example, the number sentence $12 + 8 = 20$ is true; the number sentence $14 = 10$ is false.

Open Sentences

In some number sentences one or more of the numbers is missing. In place of the missing number (or numbers) there is a variable. These sentences are called **open sentences.**

200–201

Open sentences are neither true nor false. For example, $9 + x = 15$ is neither true nor false. If you replace x with a number, then you get a number sentence that is either true or false.

- If you replace x with 10, you get $9 + 10 = 15$, which is false.
- If you replace x with 6, you get $9 + 6 = 15$, which is true.

If a number used in place of the variable makes the number sentence true, that number is called a **solution** of the open sentence. For example, the number 6 is a solution of the open sentence $9 + x = 15$, because the number sentence $9 + 6 = 15$ is true. When you are being asked to solve a number sentence, you are being asked to find its solution(s).

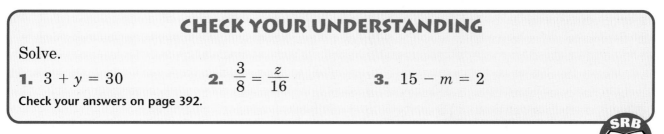

CHECK YOUR UNDERSTANDING

Solve.

1. $3 + y = 30$
2. $\dfrac{3}{8} = \dfrac{z}{16}$
3. $15 - m = 2$

Check your answers on page 392.

Mathematical Models

A good way to learn about something is to work with a model of it. A scale model of the human body can help you understand how the different systems in your own body work together.

Models are important in mathematics too. A mathematical model can be as simple as acting out a problem with chips or blocks. Other mathematical models use drawings or symbols. Mathematical models can help you understand and solve problems.

Situation Diagrams

EXAMPLE   Here are some examples of how you can use diagrams to model simple problems.

Problem	Diagram
Parts-and-Total Situation Kaitlin's class has 17 girls and 13 boys. How many students are there in all?	**Total**: ? **Part**: 17 **Part**: 13
Change Situation Jonathan had $20 and spent $13.49 on a CD. How much money did he have left?	**Start**: $20.00 **Change**: −$13.49 **End**: ?
Comparison Situation The average high temperature in Cairo, Egypt, in the summer is 95°F. The average high temperature in Reykjavik, Iceland, in the summer is 56°F. How much warmer is it in Cairo than in Reykjavik?	**Quantity**: 95°F **Quantity**: 56°F **Difference**: ?
Rate Situation Mitch bought 3 packages of pencils. There were 12 pencils in each package. How many pencils did Mitch buy?	**packages**: 3 **pencils per package**: 12 **pencils in all**: ?

The diagrams on page 210 work well for many simple problems, but for harder problems you need to use more powerful tools such as graphs, tables, and number models.

Number Models

Number sentences provide another way to model situations. In *Everyday Mathematics,* a number sentence that fits or describes some situation is called a **number model.** Often, two or more number models can fit a given situation.

Problem	Number Models
Kaitlin's class has 17 girls and 13 boys. How many students are there in all?	$17 + 13 = n$
Jonathan had $20 and spent $13.49 on a CD. How much did he have then?	$r = \$20 - \$13.49$ or $\$20 = \$13.49 + r$
The average summer high temperature in Cairo, Egypt, is 95°F. The average summer high temperature in Reykjavik, Iceland, is 56°F. How much warmer is it in Cairo than in Reykjavik?	$d = 95°F - 56°F$ or $95°F = 56°F + d$
Mitch bought 3 packages of pencils. There were 12 pencils in each package. How many pencils did Mitch buy?	$3 * 12 = n$

Number models can help you show the answer after you have solved the problem: $\$20 = \$13.49 + \$6.51$.

Number models can also help you solve problems. For example, the number sentence $\$20 = \$13.49 + r$ suggests counting up to find Jonathan's change from buying a $13.49 CD with a $20 bill.

CHECK YOUR UNDERSTANDING

Draw a diagram and write a number model for each problem. Then solve each problem.

1. Becky had $8.50. She wanted to buy a CD that cost $11.95. How much more did she need?

2. Dr. O'Malley's class is going to the museum on a field trip. The cost will be $4.25 for each of the 28 students. How much will the trip cost in all?

Check your answers on page 393.

Pan Balance Problems and Equations

If two different kinds of objects are placed in the pans of a balance so that they balance, then you can find the weight of one kind of object in terms of the other kind of object.

When you solve a pan balance problem, the pans must balance after each step. If you always do the same thing to the objects in both pans, then the pans will remain balanced. For example, you can remove the same number of the same kind of object from both pans. If the pans balanced before you removed the objects, they will remain balanced after you remove them.

EXAMPLE   How many paper clips balance 1 pen?

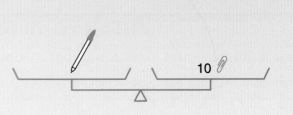

Step 1: Removing 10 paper clips from each pan will keep the pans balanced.

remove 10

40 📎

Step 2: Removing 2 pens from each pan will keep the pans balanced.

30 📎

Step 3: Removing $\frac{2}{3}$ of the objects from each pan will keep the pans balanced. ($\frac{2}{3}$ of 3 pens is 2 pens; $\frac{2}{3}$ of 30 paper clips is 20 clips.)

remove $\frac{2}{3}$ or 20 clips

30 📎

1 pen weighs the same as 10 paper clips.

10 📎

Pan Balance Equations

You can think of equations as models for pan balance problems. The example on page 212 can be modeled by the equation $5P + 10C = 2P + 40C$. (C stands for the weight of one paper clip; P stands for the weight of one pen.)

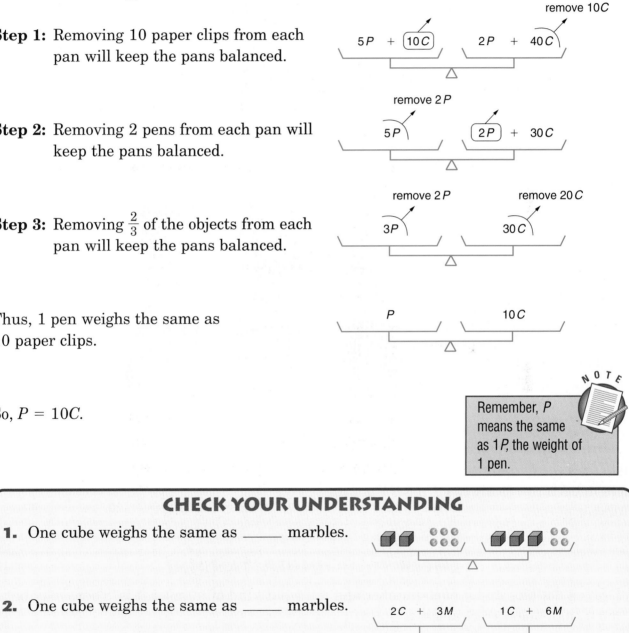

Step 1: Removing 10 paper clips from each pan will keep the pans balanced.

Step 2: Removing 2 pens from each pan will keep the pans balanced.

Step 3: Removing $\frac{2}{3}$ of the objects from each pan will keep the pans balanced.

Thus, 1 pen weighs the same as 10 paper clips.

So, $P = 10C$.

NOTE

Remember, P means the same as $1P$, the weight of 1 pen.

CHECK YOUR UNDERSTANDING

1. One cube weighs the same as _____ marbles.

2. One cube weighs the same as _____ marbles.

$2C + 3M$ $1C + 6M$

Check your answers on page 393.

Number Patterns

You can use dot pictures to explore number patterns.

Even Numbers

Even numbers are numbers that can be divided by 2 with a remainder of 0. One way to show even numbers with dots is shown at the right.

Odd Numbers

Odd numbers are numbers that have a remainder of 1 when they are divided by 2.

Triangular Numbers

Triangular numbers can be shown with dots arranged to form triangles.

Square Numbers

Square numbers can be shown with dots arranged in a square that has the same number of dots in each row and column. A square number is the product of a whole number multiplied by itself. For example, 16 is 4 * 4 or 4^2.

Rectangular Numbers

Rectangular numbers can be shown with dots arranged in a rectangle. The number of dots in each row is always 1 more than the number of rows.

CHECK YOUR UNDERSTANDING

Draw a dot picture for each number and tell what kind of number it is. There may be more than one correct answer.

1. 14   **2.** 25   **3.** 20   **4.** 15

Check your answers on page 393.

Function Machines and "What's My Rule?" Problems

A **function machine** is an imaginary machine that takes something in, works on it, and gives something else out. Function machines in *Everyday Mathematics* take numbers in, use rules to change those numbers, and give numbers out.

Here is a function machine with the rule "∗ 10 + 1." This machine will multiply any number put into it by 10, add 1, then give out the result.

If you put 3 into this "∗ 10 + 1" machine, it will multiply 3 ∗ 10 and then add 1. The number 31 will come out. If you put 60 into this machine, it will multiply 60 ∗ 10 and then add 1. The number 601 will come out.

To keep track of what goes in and what comes out, you can organize the "in" and "out" numbers in a table.

In previous grades, you solved many problems with function machines. You had to find the "out" numbers, or the "in" numbers, or a rule that fit the given "in" and "out" numbers. In *Everyday Mathematics,* these are called "What's My Rule?" problems.

3
↓

Rule

∗ 10 + 1

31

in	out
x	x ∗ 10 + 1
3	31
60	601
...	...
n	n ∗ 10 + 1

EXAMPLE Find the "out" numbers.

Rule

Add 7

in	out
2	
8	
22	
50	

The rule is: add 7 to each "in" number. Each "out" number must be 7 more than the "in" number.

2 went in, so 2 + 7 or 9 came out.

8 went in, so 8 + 7 or 15 came out.

22 went in, so 22 + 7 or 29 came out.

50 went in, so 50 + 7 or 57 came out.

EXAMPLE   Find the "in" numbers.

Rule

Subtract 10

in	out
r	r − 10
	2
	0
	−1

The rule is to subtract 10 from the "in" numbers.
So the "in" numbers must be 10 more than the
"out" numbers.

2 came out, so 10 + 2, or 12, went in.

0 came out, so 10 + 0, or 10, went in.

−1 came out, so 10 + (−1), or 9, went in.

EXAMPLE   Use the table to find the rule.

Rule

?

in	out
1	1
2	3
3	5

This table is easy to continue, since the "out" numbers
are just the odd numbers. But finding a rule that works
for any "in" number is harder.

One rule that works is "Double and subtract 1."

CHECK YOUR UNDERSTANDING

Copy and complete.

1.

Rule

Double and
add 1

in	out
v	2 ∗ v + 1
0	
1	
2	

2.

Rule

Multiply by 5

in	out
z	5z
	25
	45
	100

3.

Rule

?

in	out
10	5
20	10
2	1
100	50

Check your answers on page 393.

Rules, Tables, and Graphs

Relationships between variables can be shown by rules, in tables, or in graphs.

EXAMPLES Lauren earns $4 per hour. Use a rule, a table, and a graph to show the relationship between how many hours Lauren works and how much she earns.

Rule: Lauren's earnings equal $4 times the number of hours she works.

Table

Time (hours)	Earnings ($)
h	4 * h
0	0
1	4
2	8
3	12
4	16
...	...

Graph

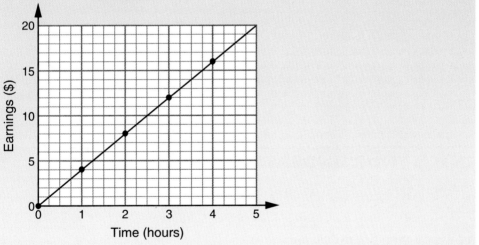

EXAMPLES   Use the table, the graph, and the rule to find how much Lauren earns if she works $3\frac{1}{2}$ hours.

One way to use the *table* to find Lauren's earnings is to think of $3\frac{1}{2}$ hours as 3 hours + $\frac{1}{2}$ hour. For 3 hours, Lauren earns $12. For $\frac{1}{2}$ hour, Lauren earns half of $4, or $2. In all, Lauren earns $12 + $2 = $14.

Another way to use the table is to note that $3\frac{1}{2}$ hours is halfway between 3 hours and 4 hours, so her earnings will be halfway between $12 and $16, which is $14.

To use the *graph,* first find $3\frac{1}{2}$ hours on the horizontal axis. Then go straight up to the line for Lauren's earnings. Turn left and go across to the vertical axis. You will end up at the same answer, $14, as you did when you used the table.

You can also use the *rule* to find Lauren's earnings:

earnings = 4 * number of hours worked

$= 4 * 3\frac{1}{2}$

$= 14$

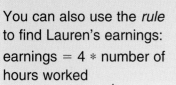

The answer, $14, agrees with the answer from the graph and the table, as it should.

CHECK YOUR UNDERSTANDING

1. Bakery cookies cost $4.00 a pound. Use the graph at the right to find the cost of $2\frac{1}{2}$ pounds.

2. Jim's average driving speed was 50 miles per hour on his trip to the mountains. Use the rule to find how far Jim drove in 6 hours.

   Rule: Distance = 50 miles * number of hours driving

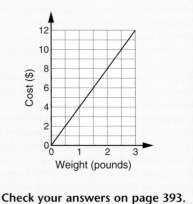

Check your answers on page 393.

Problem Solving

Mathematical Modeling

A **mathematical model** is something mathematical that fits something in the real world. A sphere, for example, is a model of a basketball. The number sentence $5.00 - (3 * 0.89) = 2.33$ is a model for buying three notebooks for 89¢ each with a $5 bill and getting $2.33 change. The graph at the right is a model for the average number of school days in several regions of the United States in 1900.

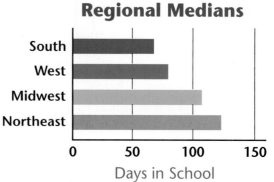

Days in School, 1900: Regional Medians

Days in School

You have used mathematical models to solve problems for many years. In Kindergarten and first grade, you probably used counters or drew pictures. In later grades, you learned to use other models such as situation diagrams, graphs, and number models. As you continue studying mathematics, you will learn to make and use more complicated and powerful mathematical models.

Everyday Mathematics has many different kinds of problems. Some problems ask you to find something. Other problems ask you to make something. When you get older, you will be asked to prove things, which means giving convincing reasons why something is true or correct.

Problems to Find	Problems to Make
1. The temperature at midnight was 5°F. The windchill temperature was −14°F. How much warmer was the actual temperature than the windchill temperature?	**3.** This is $\frac{1}{4}$ of a shape: Draw a picture of the whole shape.
2. What are the missing numbers? 1, 3, 7, 15, _____, 63, _____, 255	**4.** Use a compass and straightedge to make a triangle with each side equal in length to segment $\overline{AB}$ below: A _____ B

Problems you already know how to solve are often good practice for improving your skills. But the problems that will help you learn the most are the ones you can't solve right away. Learning to be a good problem solver means learning what to do when you don't know what to do.

A Guide for Solving Number Stories

Learning to solve problems is the main reason for studying mathematics. One way you learn to solve problems is by solving number stories. A **number story** is a story with a problem that can be solved with arithmetic.

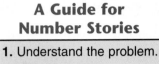

A Guide for Number Stories
1. Understand the problem.
2. Plan what to do.
3. Carry out the plan.
4. Look back.

1. Understand the problem.

- Read the problem. Can you retell it in your own words?
- What do you know?
- What do you want to find out?
- Do you have all the information needed to solve the problem?

2. Plan what to do.

- Is the problem like one you solved before?
- Is there a pattern you can use?
- Can you draw a picture or a diagram?
- Can you write a number model or make a table?
- Can you use counters, base-10 blocks, or some other tool?
- Can you estimate the answer and check if you're right?

3. Carry out the plan.

- After you decide what to do, do it. Be careful.
- Make a written record of what you do.
- Answer the question.

4. Look back.

- Does your answer make sense?
- Does your answer agree with your estimate?
- Can you write a number model for the problem?
- Can you solve the problem in another way?

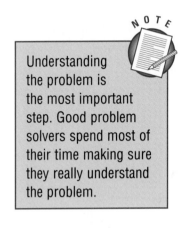

NOTE

Understanding the problem is the most important step. Good problem solvers spend most of their time making sure they really understand the problem.

NOTE

Sometimes it's easy to know what to do. Other times you need to be creative.

CHECK YOUR UNDERSTANDING

1. A store sells a certain brand of cereal in two sizes:
   - a 10-ounce box that costs $2.50
   - a 15-ounce box that costs $3.60

   Which box is the better buy? Why?

2. If you drive at an average speed of 50 miles per hour, how far will you travel for each length of time?

   a. 3 hours

   b. $\frac{1}{2}$ hour

   c. $2\frac{1}{2}$ hours

   d. 12 hours

Check your answers on page 393.

A Problem-Solving Diagram

Problems from everyday life, science, and business are often more complicated than number stories you solve in school. Sometimes the steps in the "Guide for Solving Number Stories" may not be helpful.

The diagram below shows another way to think about problem solving. This diagram is more complicated than a list, but it's more like what people do when they solve problems in science and business. The arrows connecting the boxes are meant to show that you don't always do things in the same order.

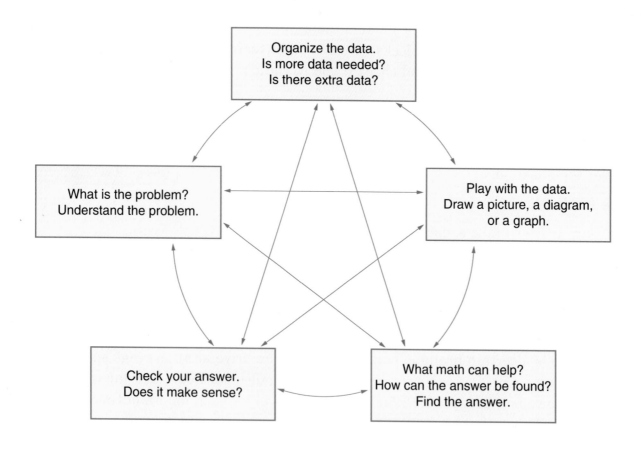

Thinking about the diagram on the previous page as you solve problems may help you be a better problem solver. Here are some things to try for each of the boxes in the diagram. Remember, these are not rules; they are only suggestions for things that might help.

• What is the problem? Can you retell it in your own words? What do you know? What do you want to find out? Try to imagine what an answer might look like. Try to understand the problem.

• Study the data you have. Look for more data if you need it. Get rid of data that you don't need. Organize the data in a list or in some other way.

• Play with the data. Try drawing a picture, a diagram, or a graph. Can you write a number model? Can you model the problem with counters or blocks?

• Do the math. Use arithmetic or geometry or other mathematics to find an answer. Label the answer with units.

• Check your answer. Does it make sense? Compare your answer to a friend's answer. Try the answer in the problem. Can you solve the problem another way?

CHECK YOUR UNDERSTANDING

Here is an up-and-down staircase that is 5 steps tall.

1. How many squares are needed for an up-and-down staircase that is 10 steps tall?

2. How many squares are needed for an up-and-down staircase that is 50 steps tall?

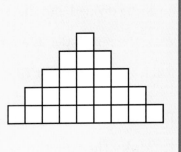

Check your answers on page 393.

Interpreting a Remainder in Division

Some number stories are solved by dividing whole numbers. You may need to decide what to do when there is a non-zero remainder.

There are three possible choices:

• Ignore the remainder. Just the quotient is the answer.
• Round the quotient up to the next whole number.
• Write the remainder as a fraction or decimal. The remainder is part of the answer.

EXAMPLES

• Suppose 3 people share 17 counters equally. How many counters will each person get?

17 / 3 → 5 R2

Ignore the remainder. The quotient is the answer.

Each person will have 5 counters, with 2 counters left over.

• Suppose 17 photos are placed in a photo album. How many pages are needed if 3 photos can fit on a page?

17 / 3 → 5 R2

You need to round the quotient up to the next whole number. The album will have 5 pages filled and another page only partially filled.

So, 6 pages are needed.

• Suppose three friends share a 17-inch-long string of licorice. How long is each piece if the friends receive equal shares?

17 / 3 → 5 R2

The answer, 5 R2, shows that if each person receives 5 inches of licorice, 2 inches remain to be divided. Imagine that this 2-inch remainder is divided into thirds. It can be divided into three $\frac{2}{3}$-inch pieces.

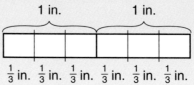

1 in.   1 in.

$\frac{1}{3}$ in. $\frac{1}{3}$ in. $\frac{1}{3}$ in. $\frac{1}{3}$ in. $\frac{1}{3}$ in. $\frac{1}{3}$ in.

Write the remainder as a fraction. The remainder is part of the answer.

Each friend will get $5\frac{2}{3}$-inch long piece of licorice.

To rewrite a remainder as a fraction:

1. Make the remainder the *numerator* of the fraction.
2. Make the divisor the *denominator* of the fraction.

Problem	Answer	Remainder Rewritten as a Fraction	Answer Written As a Mixed Number	Answer Written As a Decimal
367 / 4	91 R3	$\frac{3}{4}$	$91\frac{3}{4}$	91.75

Estimation

An **estimate** is an answer that is close to an exact answer. You make estimates every day.

- You estimate how long it will take to walk to school.
- You estimate how much money you will need to buy some things at the store.

Sometimes you must estimate because it is impossible to know the exact answer. When you predict the future, for example, you have to estimate since it's impossible to know exactly what will happen. A weather forecaster's prediction is an estimate of what will happen in the future.

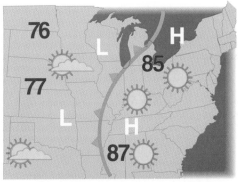

The weather will be sunny and about 85 degrees tomorrow.

Sometimes you will estimate because finding an exact answer is not practical. For example, the number of people in the United States is always an estimate. The count changes constantly because many people are born and die every day.

Sometimes you will estimate because finding an exact answer is not worth the trouble. You might estimate the cost of several items at the store, for example, to be sure you have enough money. There is no need to find an exact answer until you pay for the items.

Estimation in Problem Solving

Estimation can be useful even when you need to find an exact answer. Making an estimate when you first start working on a problem may help you understand the problem better. Estimating before you solve a problem is like making a rough draft of a writing assignment.

Estimation can also be useful after you have found an answer for a problem. You can use the estimate to check whether your answer makes sense. If your estimate is not close to the exact answer you found, then you need to check your work.

Leading-Digit Estimation

The best estimators are usually people who are experts. Someone who lays carpet for a living, for example, would probably be very good at estimating the size of rooms. A waiter would probably be very good at estimating the proper amount for a tip.

One way to estimate is to use only the first digit of a number. The other digits are replaced by zeros. This way of estimating is called **leading-digit** or **front-end estimation.**

Exact Number	Leading-Digit Estimate
429	400
6	6
8,578	8,000
68	60
125,718	100,000

EXAMPLE   What is the cost of 5 pounds of oranges at 74¢ per pound?

Use leading-digit estimation. The oranges cost about 70¢ per pound.

So, 5 pounds will cost about 5 * 70¢, or $3.50.

Leading-digit estimates are usually fairly rough. However, even a rough estimate can be useful for checking calculations. If the estimate and the exact answer are not close, you should look for a mistake in your work.

EXAMPLE   Elisa added 694 + 415 + 382 and got 1,025. Was she correct?

Since the leading-digit estimate is 1,300, which is not close to 1,025, Elisa is not correct. She should check her work.

Exact Number		Leading-Digit Estimate
694	→	600
415	→	400
+ 382	→	+ 300
		1,300

CHECK YOUR UNDERSTANDING

Use leading-digit estimation to decide if the answers are correct.

1. Emily added 921 + 345 + 618 and got 1,054.

2. Luis said that 893 / 45 is 197.

Check your answers on page 393.

Rounding

Rounding is a way to make numbers simpler so they are easier to work with. The simpler numbers you get from rounding usually give better estimates than you get with leading-digit estimation.

EXAMPLES

1. Round 4,538 to the nearest hundred.
3. Round 5,295 to the nearest ten.

2. Round 26,781 to the nearest thousand.
4. Round 3.573 to the nearest tenth.

	Step 1: Find the digit in the place you are rounding to.	**Step 2:** Rewrite the number, replacing all digits to the right of this digit with zeros. This is the lower number.	**Step 3:** Add 1 to the digit in the place you are rounding to. If the sum is 10, write 0 and add 1 to the digit to its left. This is the higher number.	**Step 4:** Is the number you are rounding closer to the lower number or to the higher number?	**Step 5:** Round to the closer of the two numbers. If it is halfway between the higher and the lower number, round to the higher number.
1.	4,5̲38	4,5̲00	4,6̲00	lower number	4,500
2.	2̲6,781	2̲6,000	2̲7,000	higher number	27,000
3.	5,29̲5	5,29̲0	5,30̲0	halfway	5,300
4.	3.5̲73	3.5̲00	3.6̲00	higher number	3.600 = 3.6

Thinking about a number line can also be helpful when you round numbers.

EXAMPLE   Round 7,385 to the nearest thousand.

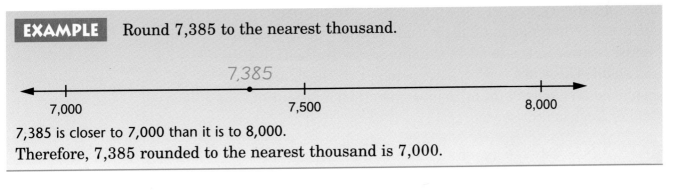

7,385 is closer to 7,000 than it is to 8,000.
Therefore, 7,385 rounded to the nearest thousand is 7,000.

CHECK YOUR UNDERSTANDING

Round 75,695 to the nearest:

1. hundred

2. ten thousand

3. ten

Check your answers on page 393.

Making Other Estimates
Interval Estimates

An **interval estimate** is made up of a range of possible values. The exact value falls between the lowest and the highest value in the range.

Here is one way to give an interval estimate:

- Name a number you are sure is *less than the exact value.*
- Name a number you are sure is *greater than the exact value.*

The smaller the difference between the upper and lower numbers, the more useful an interval estimate is likely to be.

An interval estimate can be stated in various ways.

EXAMPLES There are *at least* 30 [12s] in 427, but *not more than* 40 [12s].

The number of books in the school library is *greater than* 3,000 but *less than* 3,500.

Between 225 and 300 people live in my apartment building.

Magnitude Estimates

One kind of very rough estimate is called a **magnitude estimate.** When making a magnitude estimate, ask yourself: "Is the answer in the tens? In the hundreds? In the thousands?" and so on. These are good questions to ask to check answers displayed on a calculator or to judge whether information you read or hear makes sense.

EXAMPLE Make a magnitude estimate. 49,741 / 178

49,741 / 178 is about 50,000 / 200, which is the same as 500 / 2, or 250.

So, the answer to 49,741 / 178 is in the hundreds.

CHECK YOUR UNDERSTANDING
Make a magnitude estimate. Is the answer in the tens, hundreds, or thousands?

1. 289 * 35.7   **2.** 78,293 / 92   **3.** 2,398 / 1.23

Check your answers on page 393.

About Calculators

Throughout your study of mathematics you have used tools such as counters, rulers, tape measures, pattern blocks, compasses, protractors, and the Geometry Template. Since kindergarten, you have also used calculators. In earlier grades, you used calculators to help you learn to count. Now you use them for computations with whole numbers, fractions, decimals, and percents.

Although a calculator can help you compute quickly and accurately, you must know when and how to use it. You must decide whether it is best to solve a problem by using mental arithmetic, paper and pencil, or a calculator. When you choose to use a calculator, estimation should always be part of your work. You can use a magnitude estimate of the answer to check whether you have keyed in a wrong number or operation. Always ask yourself if the number in the display makes sense.

There are many different kinds of calculators. Simple four-function calculators do little more than add, subtract, multiply, and divide whole numbers and decimals. Other calculators also perform operations with fractions.

Rather than try to describe how various calculators work, we have chosen one calculator to which we refer throughout this book. If you have a different calculator, don't worry. There are many other calculators that work well with *Everyday Mathematics.* If the instructions in this book don't work for your calculator, you can refer to the directions that came with it, or you can ask your teacher for help.

A reminder: Just as carpenters, dentists, and people in many other occupations must take care of their tools if they expect them to work properly, you must take care of your calculator. Dropping it, leaving it in the sun, or other carelessness may break it or make it less reliable.

Basic Operations

Pressing a key on a calculator is called "keying in" or "entering." In this book, calculator keys, except numbers, are shown in rectangular boxes: ⊞ , (Enter) , ⊠ , and so on. A set of instructions for performing a calculation is called a "key sequence." The key sequences in this book are for the calculator shown on the previous page, but many of them also work for other calculators.

(On/Off) turns the calculator on and off. When you turn the calculator on, you will see a blinking triangle that looks like this: ◁. This is the cursor.

Simple Arithmetic: (On/Off) , ⊞ , ⊟ , ⊠ , ÷ , (Enter)

You probably already know how to use a calculator for basic arithmetic. Usually, you can just enter the numbers and operations and press (Enter) to see the answer. Solve each problem on your calculator.

Key	Problem	Key Sequence	Display
⊞	$4.7 + 6.8$	4 ⊡ 7 ⊞ 6 ⊡ 8 (Enter)	$4.7 + 6.8 = 11.5$
	$\frac{3}{8} + \frac{1}{4}$	3 (n) 8 (d) ⊞1 (n) 4 (d) (Enter)	$\frac{3}{8} + \frac{1}{4} = \frac{5}{8}$
⊟	$12.3 - 5.9$	12 ⊡ 3 ⊟ 5 ⊡ 9 (Enter)	$12.3 - 5.9 = 6.4$
	$\frac{7}{8} - \frac{1}{3}$	7 (n) 8 (d) ⊟ 1 (n) 3 (d) (Enter)	$\frac{7}{8} - \frac{1}{3} = \frac{13}{24}$
⊠	$3.5 * 7.4$	3 ⊡ 5 ⊠ 7 ⊡ 4 (Enter)	$3.5 \times 7.4 = 25.9$
	$\frac{4}{5} * \frac{3}{8}$	4 (n) 5 (d) ⊠ 3 (n) 8 (d) (Enter)	$\frac{4}{5} \times \frac{3}{8} = \frac{N}{D} \to \frac{n}{d} \frac{12}{40}$
÷	$24.9 / 1.6$	24 ⊡ 9 ÷ 1 ⊡ 6 (Enter)	$24.9 \div 1.6 = 15.5625$
	$\frac{5}{6} / \frac{1}{2}$	5 (n) 6 (d) ÷ 1 (n) 2 (d) (Enter)	$\frac{5}{6} \div \frac{1}{2} = \frac{N}{D} \to \frac{n}{d} 1\frac{4}{6}$

Correcting and Clearing: ⬅ , Clear , ⇐ , ⇒

⬅ erases the character to the left of the cursor.

EXAMPLE Enter 123.444. Change it to 123.456.

Key Sequence	Display
1 2 3 ⊙ 4 4 4	123.444
⬅ ⬅	123.4
5 6	123.456

You can use ⇐ and ⇒ to move the cursor to the left and right. This is useful for correcting mistakes in the middle of expressions you have entered.

EXAMPLES Enter 123.567. Change it to 123.4567.   Enter 123.4456. Change it to 123.456.

Key Sequence	Display
1 2 3 ⊙ 5 6 7	123.567
⇐ ⇐ ⇐ 4 Enter	123.4567 = 123.4567

Key Sequence	Display
1 2 3 ⊙ 4 4 5 6	123.4456
⇐ ⇐ ⇐ ⬅ Enter	123.456 = 123.456

Clear erases the entire display. If the cursor is in the middle of a display, you will need to press Clear twice to clear the entire display. Holding On/Off and Clear down together for a few moments will clear the calculator completely. Whenever you use the calculator, you should first clear it completely.

> **NOTE**
>
> The calculator remembers its settings and problems it has solved even when it is turned off. If you don't start by clearing it completely, it may not work properly.

Order of Operations and Parentheses: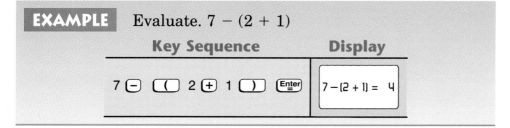

The calculator shown on page 230 follows the rules for the order of operations.

If you have a different calculator, check whether it follows the rules of the order of operations. To do so, key in 5 ⊕ 6 ⊗ 2 ⏎ (Enter). If your calculator follows the order of operations, it will multiply first, then add, and the display will show 17. A calculator that does not follow the order of operations will probably do the operations in the order they are entered, adding first, then multiplying, and will display 22.

If you want the calculator to do operations in an order different from the usual order, use ⌈(and)⌉ .

EXAMPLE Evaluate. $7 - (2 + 1)$

Key Sequence	Display
7 ⊖ ⌈(2 ⊕ 1)⌉ (Enter)	$7 - (2 + 1) = 4$

Sometimes expressions are given without all of the multiplication signs. Remember to press the multiplication key even when it is not written.

EXAMPLE Evaluate. $9 - 2(1 + 2)$

Key Sequence	Display
9 ⊖ 2 ⊗ ⌈(1 ⊕ 2)⌉ (Enter)	$9 - 2 \times (1 + 2) =$ 3

$9 - 2(1 + 2) = 3$

CHECK YOUR UNDERSTANDING

Use your calculator to evaluate each expression.

1. $34 - (5 + 8)$ **2.** $57 - 3(4 + 2)$ **3.** $8(7 + 4) - 23$ **4.** $3(54 - 6) + 25$

Check your answers on page 393.

Negative Numbers: (-)

Use (-) to enter a negative number.

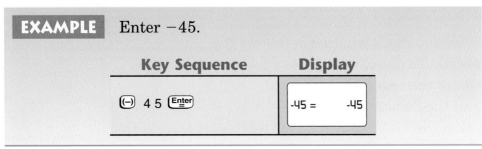

EXAMPLE Enter −45.

Key Sequence	Display
(-) 4 5 (Enter)	-45 = -45

Notice that (-) is not an operation. The key for subtraction is
(−). If you try to use (-) to do subtraction, you will get an error.

EXAMPLE 38 − 9 = ?

Key Sequence	Display
3 8 (-) 9 (Enter)	SYN ERROR
3 8 (−) 9 (Enter)	38 − 9 = 29

38 − 9 = 29

Division with Remainder: (Int÷)

The result of a division with whole numbers is often not a whole
number. Most calculators display such a result as a decimal.
Many calculators also have another division key, (Int÷), that
displays the results of a division as a whole number quotient
with a whole number remainder.

NOTE

Int stands for
integer. This
kind of division is
known as "integer
division."

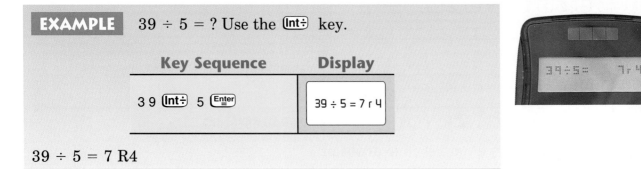

EXAMPLE 39 ÷ 5 = ? Use the (Int÷) key.

Key Sequence	Display
3 9 (Int÷) 5 (Enter)	39 ÷ 5 = 7 r 4

39 ÷ 5 = 7 R4

Integer division only works with whole numbers. If you try to
use a negative number or a fraction you will get an error.

Fractions and Percent

Certain calculators can handle fractions. Once fractions have been entered on such calculators, they can be added, subtracted, multiplied, and divided using the ⊕, ⊖, ⊗, or ⊘ keys.

Entering Fractions and Mixed Numbers: Ⓝ, Ⓓ, Unit, Uⁿ⁄ᵈ↔ⁿ⁄ᵈ 68–69

Use Ⓝ, Ⓓ, and Unit to enter fractions and mixed numbers.

EXAMPLE $\frac{3}{4} + \frac{7}{8} = ?$

Key Sequence	Display
3 Ⓝ 4 Ⓓ ⊕ 7 Ⓝ 8 Ⓓ Enter	$\frac{3}{4} + \frac{7}{8} = 1\frac{5}{8}$

> **NOTE**
> You do not need to press Ⓓ after you enter the denominator.

$\frac{3}{4} + \frac{7}{8} = 1\frac{5}{8}$

EXAMPLE $1\frac{1}{2} \div 2\frac{1}{2} = ?$

Key Sequence	Display
1 Unit 1 Ⓝ 2 Ⓓ ⊘ 2 Unit 1 Ⓝ 2 Ⓓ Enter	$\overset{\frac{N}{D}\to\frac{n}{d}}{1\frac{1}{2} \div 2\frac{1}{2} = \frac{6}{10}}$

79–80

$1\frac{1}{2} \div 2\frac{1}{2} = \frac{6}{10}$

Use Uⁿ⁄ᵈ↔ⁿ⁄ᵈ to change between mixed numbers and improper fractions.

EXAMPLE

Key Sequence	Display
4 5 Ⓝ 7 Ⓓ Enter	$\frac{45}{7} = 6\frac{3}{7}$
Uⁿ⁄ᵈ↔ⁿ⁄ᵈ	$\frac{45}{7}$
Uⁿ⁄ᵈ↔ⁿ⁄ᵈ	$6\frac{3}{7}$

62–63

Simplifying Fractions: (Simp), (Fac)

Ordinarily, the calculator on page 230 does not simplify fractions automatically. The message $\frac{N}{D} \to \frac{n}{d}$ in the display means that the fraction shown is not yet in simplest form.

Use (Simp) to simplify fractions. When you press (Simp) (Enter), the calculator divides the numerator and the denominator by a common factor. To see what number the calculator used, press (Fac). You may have to press (Simp) (Enter) several times to put a fraction in simplest form.

EXAMPLE Change $\frac{18}{24}$ to simplest form.

Key Sequence	Display
18 (n) 24 (d) (Simp) (Enter)	$\frac{18}{24} \triangleright \qquad \overset{\frac{N}{D} \to \frac{n}{d}}{\frac{9}{12}}$
(Simp) (Enter)	$\frac{9}{12} \triangleright \qquad \frac{3}{4}$
(Fac)	3

$\frac{18}{24} = \frac{3}{4}$

If you want to tell the calculator to divide the numerator and the denominator by a certain number, then enter that number after you press (Simp). If you use the greatest common factor of the numerator and the denominator, then you can simplify the fraction in one step.

EXAMPLE Change $\frac{18}{24}$ to simplest form in one step by dividing the numerator and the denominator by their greatest common factor, 6.

Key Sequence	Display
18 (n) 24 (d) (Simp) 6 (Enter)	$\frac{18}{24} \triangleright 6 \qquad \frac{3}{4}$
(Fac)	6

Percent: %, ▸%

On the calculator shown on page 230, % divides the number before it by 100. % can be used to change percents into decimals.

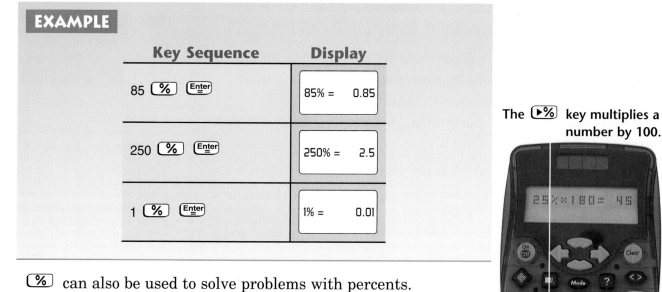

EXAMPLE	
Key Sequence	**Display**
85 % Enter	85% = 0.85
250 % Enter	250% = 2.5
1 % Enter	1% = 0.01

% can also be used to solve problems with percents.

EXAMPLE Find 25% of 180.

Key Sequence	**Display**
2 5 % × 1 8 0 Enter	25% × 180 = 45

25% of 180 = 45

The ▸% key multiplies a number by 100.

▸% does the opposite of %. That is, ▸% multiplies the number before it by 100. ▸% can be used to change a number into an equivalent percent.

The % key divides a number by 100.

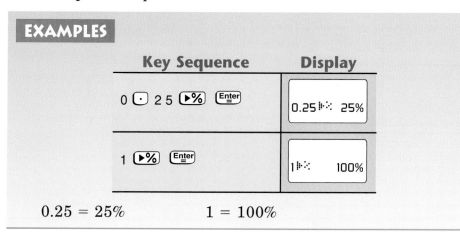

EXAMPLES	
Key Sequence	**Display**
0 · 2 5 ▸% Enter	0.25 ▸◦ 25%
1 ▸% Enter	1 ▸◦ 100%

0.25 = 25%   1 = 100%

Fraction/Decimal/Percent Conversions: F↔D

Calculators can be used to convert between fractions, decimals, and percents. Conversions of fractions to decimals and percents can be done on any calculator. For example, to rename $\frac{3}{5}$ as a decimal, simply enter 3 ÷ 5 Enter. The display will show 0.6. To rename a decimal as a percent, just multiply by 100.

Conversions of decimals and percents to fractions can only be done directly on calculators that have special keys to handle fractions. Such calculators usually have special keys for changing a fraction to its decimal equivalent or a decimal to an equivalent fraction.

Use F↔D to change between fractions and decimals. When decimals are changed to fractions, they may need to be simplified.

EXAMPLE Convert $\frac{3}{8}$ to a decimal and back to a fraction in simplest form.

Key Sequence	Display
3 ⎣n⎦ 8 ⎣d⎦ Enter	$\frac{3}{8} = \frac{3}{8}$
F↔D	0.375
F↔D	$\frac{N}{D} \to \frac{n}{d}$ $\frac{375}{1000}$
Simp Enter	$\frac{N}{D} \to \frac{n}{d}$ $\frac{375}{1000}$ ↦ $\frac{75}{200}$
Simp Enter	$\frac{N}{D} \to \frac{n}{d}$ $\frac{75}{200}$ ↦ $\frac{15}{40}$
Simp Enter	$\frac{15}{40}$ ↦ $\frac{3}{8}$

The table shows examples of various conversions. Although only one key sequence is shown for each conversion, there are other ways to do most of these conversions.

Conversion	Starting Number	Key Sequence	Display
Fraction to decimal	$\frac{3}{5}$	3 [n] 5 [d] [Enter] [F↔D]	0.6
Decimal to fraction	0.125	0 [·] 1 2 5 [Enter] [F↔D]	N→n D→d $\frac{125}{1000}$
Decimal to percent	0.75	0 [·] 7 5 [▶%] [Enter]	0.75 ▶∴ 75%
Percent to decimal	125%	1 2 5 [%] [Enter]	125% = 1.25
Fraction to percent	$\frac{5}{8}$	5 [n] 8 [d] [▶%] [Enter]	$\frac{5}{8}$ ▶∴ 62.5%
Percent to fraction	35%	3 5 [%] [Enter] [F↔D]	N→n D→d $\frac{35}{100}$

CHECK YOUR UNDERSTANDING

Use your calculator to convert between fractions, decimals, and percents.

1. $\frac{5}{12}$ to a decimal
2. 0.235 to a fraction
3. 0.72 to a percent
4. 365% to a decimal
5. $\frac{7}{8}$ to a percent
6. 95% to a fraction
7. $\frac{7}{13}$ to a decimal
8. 0.587 to a fraction
9. 0.98 to a percent
10. 475% to a decimal
11. $\frac{6}{8}$ to a percent
12. 25% to a fraction

Check your answers on page 393.

Advanced Operations

Your calculator can do more than simple arithmetic with whole numbers, fractions, and decimals. The following pages explain some of the other things your calculator can do.

Scrolling: ⬆ , ⬇

⬆ and ⬇ allow you to see previous entries and results. Moving up and down to previous displays is called **scrolling.** Small arrows in the display tell you which directions you can scroll.

You can use ⬆ and ⬇ to see problems you entered before. Then you can use ⬅, ➡, and ⊖ to change those problems if you wish.

⬆ and ⬇ are also used with menus.

Menus: (Mode)

The calculator shown here has several menus for changing how it works. In each menu, the current choice is underlined. Use ⬅ and ➡ to change what is underlined. Then press (Enter) to make your new choice active. If you don't press (Enter), then the old menu choice will still be active.

Most of the menus are reached by pressing (Mode). The fraction menus are reached by pressing (Frac).

Use the ⬆ and ⬇ keys to scroll through menus, entries, and results.

Use the (Mode) key to browse menus.

Key Sequence	Display	Purpose
(Mode)	N/d ÷	Controls whether quotients are shown as decimals or as mixed numbers.
(Mode) ⬇	+I ? OP	Controls whether the operation is shown or hidden when (Op1) and (Op2) are used.
(Mode) ⬇ ⬇	OPI OP2 CLEAR	Used for clearing a constant operation.
(Mode) ⬇ ⬇ ⬇	N Y RESET	Used for resetting the calculator.

EXAMPLE Divide. Find the quotient as a mixed number.

56 / 3 = ?

Key Sequence	Display
(Mode) ⟹ (Enter)	$\frac{n}{d}$ ÷ . $\underline{n/d}$ ÷
(Mode)	$\frac{n}{d}$ ÷
5 6 ÷ 3 (Enter)	$\frac{n}{d}$ ÷ $56 \div 3 = 18\frac{2}{3}$

$56 / 3 = 18\frac{2}{3}$

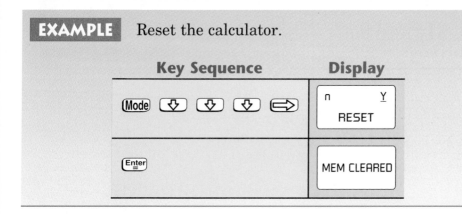

EXAMPLE Reset the calculator.

Key Sequence	Display
(Mode) ⬇ ⬇ ⬇ ⟹	n Y RESET
(Enter)	MEM CLEARED

Fraction Menus: (Frac)

There are two menus for changing how the calculator handles fractions. Use (Frac) to reach these menus. As with other menus, use ⟸ and ⟹ to change what is underlined. Then press (Enter) to make your new choice active. If you don't press (Enter), then the old choice will still be active.

Key Sequence	Display	Purpose
(Frac)	U n/d n/d	Controls whether results are shown as mixed numbers or improper fractions.
(Frac) ⬇	MAN AUTO	Controls whether simplifying fractions is done manually or automatically.

EXAMPLE Solve $\frac{4}{5} * \frac{1}{2}$ with the calculator in MAN mode and again in AUTO mode.

Key Sequence	Display
4 (n) 5 (d) (×) 1 (n) 2 (d) (Enter)	$\frac{4}{5} \times \frac{1}{2} = \frac{4}{10}$ $\frac{N}{D} \to \frac{n}{d}$
(Simp) (Enter)	$\frac{4}{10}$ ▶⋅⋯ $\frac{2}{5}$
(Frac) (⬇) (⮕) (Enter)	MAN **AUTO** Auto
(Frac) (Clear)	Auto
4 (n) 5 (d) (×) 1 (n) 2 (d) (Enter)	$\frac{4}{5} \times \frac{1}{2} = \frac{2}{5}$ Auto

$\frac{4}{5} * \frac{1}{2} = \frac{2}{5}$

EXAMPLE Change to improper fraction mode and solve $\frac{5}{2} + \frac{8}{3}$. Then change the answer to a mixed number.

Key Sequence	Display
(Frac) (⮕) (Enter)	U n/d n/d
5 (n) 2 (d) (+) 8 (n) 3 (d) (Enter)	$\frac{5}{2} + \frac{8}{3} = \frac{31}{6}$
(U n/d ↔ n/d)	$5\frac{1}{6}$

$\frac{5}{2} + \frac{8}{3} = 5\frac{1}{6}$

Rounding

To set the calculator to round, press (Fix) and one of the numbers on the red keys below the (Fix) key.

The calculator can be set to round to any place from thousands (1000.) to thousandths (0.001). To turn off rounding, press (Fix) (·).

EXAMPLE First set the calculator to round to hundreds. Then round 1,376, 79, and 23 to the nearest hundred.

Key Sequence	Display
(Fix) (100.)	Fix
1376 (Enter)	Fix 1376 = 1400.
79 (Enter)	Fix 79 = 100.
23 (Enter)	Fix 23 = 000.

EXAMPLE Solve 73 * 19 and 1,568 + 399. Find the exact answer. Then find the answer rounded to the nearest hundred.

Key Sequence	Display
7 3 (×) 1 9 (Enter)	73 × 19 = 1387
1 5 6 8 (+) 3 9 9 (Enter)	1568 + 399 = 1967

Key Sequence	Display
(Fix) (100.)	Fix
7 3 (×) 19 (Enter)	Fix 73 × 19 = 1400.
1 5 6 8 (+) 3 9 9 (Enter)	Fix 1568 + 399 = 2000.

CHECK YOUR UNDERSTANDING

Use your calculator to round 22,350 to the nearest:

1. ten   **2.** hundred   **3.** thousand

Check your answers on page 393.

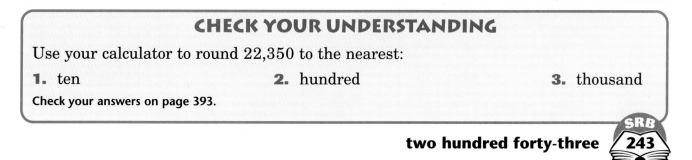

Powers and Square Roots: $\boxed{\wedge}$, $\boxed{\sqrt{}}$

$\boxed{\wedge}$ is used for raising numbers to powers on many calculators. Sometimes [y^x] or some other key is used. Negative exponents are allowed, but be careful to use $\boxed{(-)}$ when you enter a negative number. If you use $\boxed{-}$, you may get an error.

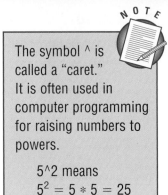

NOTE

The symbol ^ is called a "caret." It is often used in computer programming for raising numbers to powers.

$5\text{^}2$ means
$5^2 = 5 * 5 = 25$

EXAMPLES Find the value of 3^4 and 5^{-2}.

Problem	Key Sequence	Display
3^4	3 $\boxed{\wedge}$ 4 $\boxed{\text{Enter}}$	3 ^ 4 = 81
5^{-2}	5 $\boxed{\wedge}$ $\boxed{(-)}$ 2 $\boxed{\text{Enter}}$	5 ^ -2 = 0.04

To find the reciprocal of a number, raise the number to the -1 power.

EXAMPLES Find the reciprocals of 25 and $\frac{2}{3}$.

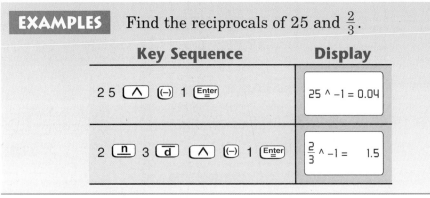

Key Sequence	Display
2 5 $\boxed{\wedge}$ $\boxed{(-)}$ 1 $\boxed{\text{Enter}}$	25 ^ –1 = 0.04
2 $\boxed{\text{n}}$ 3 $\boxed{\text{d}}$ $\boxed{\wedge}$ $\boxed{(-)}$ 1 $\boxed{\text{Enter}}$	$\frac{2}{3}$ ^ –1 = 1.5

Note: To see the reciprocal of $\frac{2}{3}$ as a fraction, key in $\boxed{\text{F↔D}}$, $\boxed{\text{Simp}}$, and $\boxed{\text{U}\frac{n}{d}↔\frac{n}{d}}$. The reciprocal of $\frac{2}{3}$ written as a fraction is $\frac{3}{2}$.

Many calculators have a special key for finding square roots. Notice that before you press $\boxed{\text{Enter}}$, you have to press $\boxed{)}$.

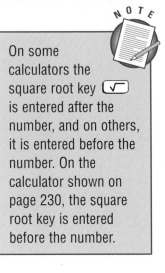

NOTE

On some calculators the square root key $\boxed{\sqrt{}}$ is entered after the number, and on others, it is entered before the number. On the calculator shown on page 230, the square root key is entered before the number.

EXAMPLES Find the square roots of 25 and 10,000.

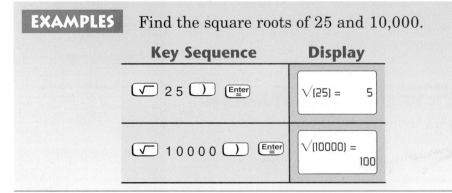

Key Sequence	Display
$\boxed{\sqrt{}}$ 2 5 $\boxed{)}$ $\boxed{\text{Enter}}$	$\sqrt{}$(25) = 5
$\boxed{\sqrt{}}$ 1 0 0 0 0 $\boxed{)}$ $\boxed{\text{Enter}}$	$\sqrt{}$(10000) = 100

Scientific Notation

On many calculators, numbers with more digits than will fit in the display are automatically shown in scientific notation. Calculators differ in the way they show scientific notation.

Scientific notation is a way of writing numbers in which a number is written as the product of a number and a power of 10. The number must be 1 or greater, but less than 10. In scientific notation, 900,000 is written as $9 * 10^5$.

Some calculators can display raised exponents, but most cannot. Some calculators that have scientific notation do not bother to display the base, which is always 10, and use a space or letter to show the exponent. Others, like the one on page 230, do show the base, but use a caret ^ to show the exponent.

EXAMPLES

Key Sequence	Display
7 ⊗ 1 0 ⟨∧⟩ 4 (Enter)	7 × 10 ^ 4 = 70000
4 ⟨·⟩ 3 5 ⊗ 1 0 ⟨∧⟩ 5 (Enter)	4.35 × 10 ^ 5 = 435000
4 ⊗ 1 0 ⟨∧⟩ ⟨(-)⟩ 3 (Enter)	4 × 10 ^ -3 = 0.004

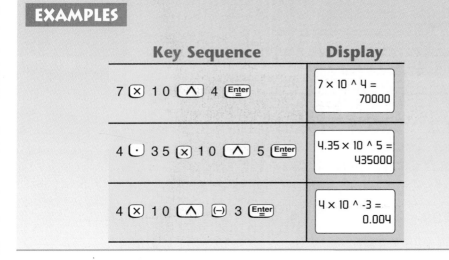

CHECK YOUR UNDERSTANDING

Use your calculator to convert the following to standard notation:

1. $6.5 * 10^{-3}$　　　**2.** $9.8 * 10^6$　　　**3.** $7.6 * 10^7$　　　**4.** $3.4 * 10^{-4}$

Check your answers on page 393.

Numbers with more than 10 digits can be entered in the calculator on page 230—the maximum number of digits allowed is 88—but answers with more than 10 digits are displayed in scientific notation.

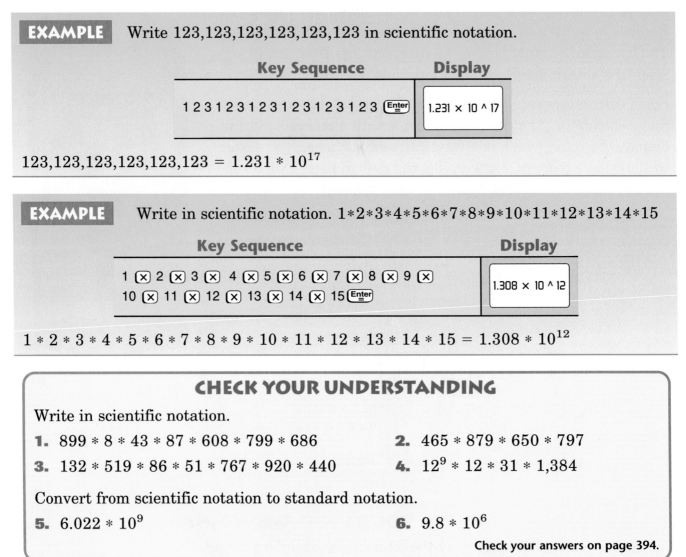

EXAMPLE Write 123,123,123,123,123,123 in scientific notation.

Key Sequence	Display
1 2 3 1 2 3 1 2 3 1 2 3 1 2 3 1 2 3 (Enter)	1.231 × 10 ^ 17

$123{,}123{,}123{,}123{,}123{,}123 = 1.231 * 10^{17}$

EXAMPLE Write in scientific notation. 1*2*3*4*5*6*7*8*9*10*11*12*13*14*15

Key Sequence	Display
1 (×) 2 (×) 3 (×) 4 (×) 5 (×) 6 (×) 7 (×) 8 (×) 9 (×) 10 (×) 11 (×) 12 (×) 13 (×) 14 (×) 15 (Enter)	1.308 × 10 ^ 12

$1 * 2 * 3 * 4 * 5 * 6 * 7 * 8 * 9 * 10 * 11 * 12 * 13 * 14 * 15 = 1.308 * 10^{12}$

CHECK YOUR UNDERSTANDING

Write in scientific notation.

1. $899 * 8 * 43 * 87 * 608 * 799 * 686$

2. $465 * 879 * 650 * 797$

3. $132 * 519 * 86 * 51 * 767 * 920 * 440$

4. $12^9 * 12 * 31 * 1{,}384$

Convert from scientific notation to standard notation.

5. $6.022 * 10^9$

6. $9.8 * 10^6$

Check your answers on page 394.

Pi: π

The formulas for the perimeter, area, and volume of many geometric figures involve pi (π). Pi is a number that is a little more than 3. The first few digits of π are 3.14159265.... Your calculator has a special key for pi, π . When you need to use π in a calculation, use π .

Note: To see a decimal for π, press π Enter F↔D .

EXAMPLE Find the area of a circle with a 4-foot radius. Use the formula $A = \pi r^2$.

Key Sequence	Display
π × 4 ∧ 2 Enter	Π × 4 ^ 2 = 16Π

Notice that the display answer is 16π. This is the exact area for a circle with a 4-foot radius. To see 16π as a decimal, press F↔D .

Key Sequence	Display
F↔D	50.26548246

This answer, 50.26548246 square feet, has more digits than are significant. Since you know the circle's radius only to one significant digit, it's not appropriate to have 10 digits in the area. You need to round the result to an appropriate number of decimal places. Here, you might say the area is 50 square feet or perhaps 50.3 square feet.

EXAMPLE Find the circumference of a circle with a 15-foot diameter. Use the formula $c = \pi d$.

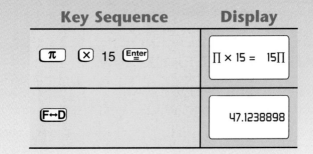

Key Sequence	Display
π × 15 Enter	Π × 15 = 15Π
F↔D	47.1238898

The circumference is about 47 feet.

Memory: ►M, MR/MC

The memory of a calculator is a place where a number can be stored while the calculator is working with other numbers. Later, when you need it, you can recall the number from memory. Most calculators display an M or similar symbol when there is a number other than 0 in the memory.

Key Sequence	Purpose
►M Enter	Stores the number in the display in the memory, *replacing* any number already in the memory.
MR/MC	Recalls the number stored in memory and shows it in the display.
MR/MC MR/MC	Clears the memory. (This really means that 0 is in the memory.)

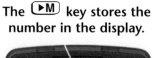

The ►M key stores the number in the display.

The calculator's memory only works with numbers that are the result of calculations. This means that you must press Enter before you can store a number in the memory.

EXAMPLE Store 25 in the memory.

Key Sequence	Display
2 5 ►M Enter	MEM ERROR
2 5 Enter ►M Enter	M 25 = 25
Clear	M
MR/MC	M 25

The MR/MC key recalls the number stored in the memory.

CHECK YOUR UNDERSTANDING

Store π in the memory. Clear the display. Then compute the area of a circle whose radius is 18, without pressing the π key. (Area $= \pi r^2$).

Check your answers on page 394.

EXAMPLE Compute a 15% tip on a $25 bill. Store the tip in the memory and then find the total bill.

Key Sequence	Display
15 [%] [×] 25 [Enter]	15% × 25 = 3.75
[▶M] [Enter]	M 15% × 25 = 3.75
25 [+] [MR/MC] [Enter]	M 25 + 3.75 = 28.75

To clear the memory, press [MR/MC] twice. Do not press [MR/MC] more than twice.

Key Sequence	Display	Number in Memory
5 [Enter] [▶M] [Enter]	M 5 = 5	5
[MR/MC]	M 5	5
[MR/MC]	5	0

NOTE

If you press [MR/MC] more than twice, the calculator will recall 0 from the memory.

CHECK YOUR UNDERSTANDING

Use your calculator to solve each problem.

1. Compute a 15% tip on a bill totaling $45.50.

2. Compute a 20% tip on a bill totaling $65.25.

Check your answers on page 394.

You can use the memory of a calculator to solve problems that have several steps.

EXAMPLE   Marguerite ordered the following food at the food court: 2 hamburgers at $1.49 each and 3 hot dogs at $0.89 each. How much change will she receive from a $10 bill?

Key Sequence	Display
2 × 1 · 4 9 Enter ▶M Enter	M 2 × 1.49 = 2.98
3 × · 8 9 Enter ▶M +	M 3 × .89 = 2.67
1 0 − MR/MC Enter	M 10 − 5.65 = 4.35

Marguerite will receive $4.35 cash back.

EXAMPLE   Mr. Beckman bought 2 adult tickets at $8.25 each and 3 child tickets at $4.75 each. He redeemed a $5 gift certificate. How much did he pay for the tickets?

Key Sequence	Display
2 × 8 · 2 5 Enter ▶M Enter	M 2 × 8.25 = 16.5
3 × 4 · 75 Enter ▶M +	M 3 × 4.75 = 14.25
MR/MC − 5 Enter	M 30.75 − 5 = 25.75

Mr. Beckman paid $25.75 for the tickets.

Repeating an Operation: Op1 , Op2

Most calculators have a way to let you repeat an operation. This is called the **constant function.** (*Constant* means *unchanging*.)

To use the constant function of your calculator, follow these steps.

1. Press Op1 .
2. Press the keys that define the constant function.
3. Press Op1 .
4. Enter a number.
5. Press Op1 .

You can repeat Steps 4 and 5 for as many different numbers as you wish.

The Op1 and Op2 keys allow you to program and repeat operations.

EXAMPLE Set up the calculator to multiply numbers by 7. Then multiply several numbers by 7.

Key Sequence	Display
Op1 ✕ 7 Op1	Opl ✕ 7
8 Op1	Opl 8 ✕ 7 1 56
20 Op1	Opl 20 ✕ 7 1 140

Use Mode to clear the constant operation(s).

Key Sequence	Display
Mode ⬇ ⬇ Enter	Opl Op2 CLEAR

In earlier grades, you may have used the constant function to practice counting by a certain number.

EXAMPLE   Count by 7s, starting at 3.

Key Sequence	Display
[Op1] [+] 7 [Op1]	Op1 + 7
3 [Op1]	Op1 3 + 7 1 10
[Op1]	Op1 10 + 7 2 17
[Op1]	Op1 17 + 7 3 24
[Op1]	Op1 24 +7 4 31
[Op1]	Op1 31 + 7 5 38

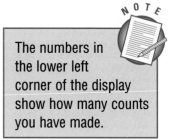

NOTE

The numbers in the lower left corner of the display show how many counts you have made.

You can use [Op2] to define a second constant operation. [Op2] works in exactly the same way as [Op1].

Other Features

The calculator shown on page 230 has several features not discussed in this book. Most of these have to do with the red keys: ◈, ▣, ?, and so on. Some of these keys are for place value. Others make the calculator give you problems so you can practice arithmetic. For details, ask your teacher or read the instructions that came with the calculator.

CHECK YOUR UNDERSTANDING

Use your calculator to do the following counts. Write five counts each.

1. Count by 5s, starting at 7.

2. Count by 12s, starting at 3.

Check your answers on page 394.

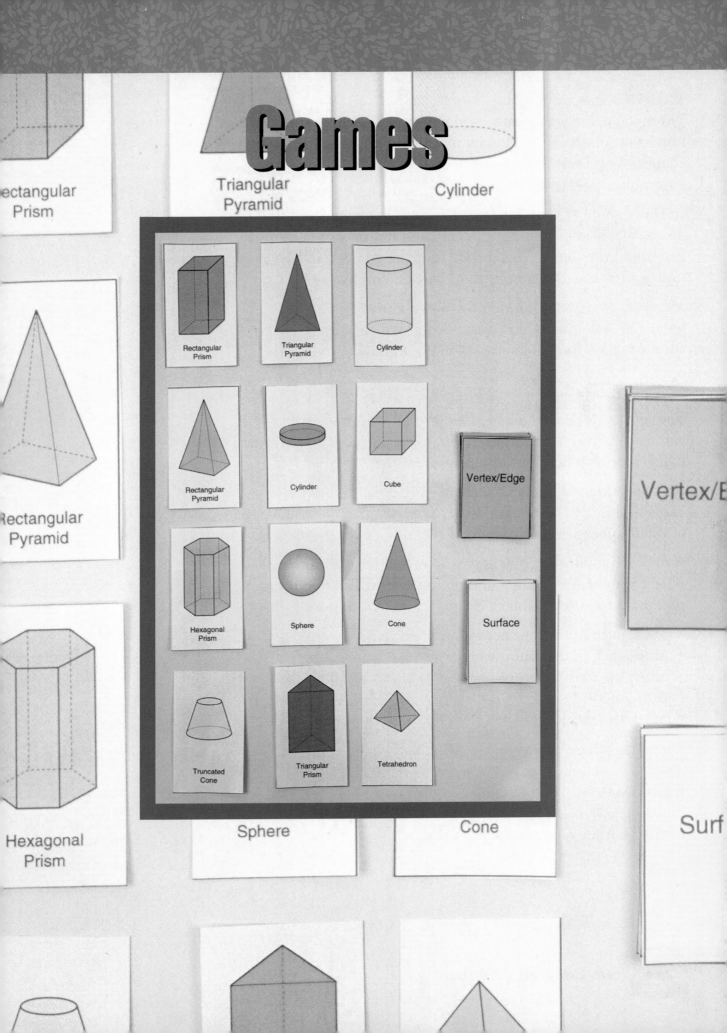

Games

Games

Throughout the year, you will play games that help you practice important math skills. Playing mathematics games gives you a chance to practice math skills in a way that is different and enjoyable.

In this section of your *Student Reference Book,* you will find the directions for many games. The numbers in most games are generated randomly. This means that the games can be played over and over without repeating the same problems.

Many students have created their own variations to these games to make them more interesting. We encourage you to do this. We hope that you will play often and have fun!

Materials

You need a deck of number cards for many of the games. You can use an Everything Math Deck, a regular deck of cards, or make your own deck out of index cards.

An Everything Math Deck includes 54 cards. There are four cards each for the numbers 0–10. And there is one card for each of the numbers 11–20.

A deck of playing cards includes 54 cards (52 regular cards, plus 2 jokers). To create a deck of number cards from it, use a permanent marker to mark cards in the following way:

- Mark each of the four aces with the number 1.
- Mark each of the four queens with the number 0.
- Mark the four jacks and four kings with the numbers 11 through 18.
- Mark the two jokers with the numbers 19 and 20.

For some games you will have to make a game board, or a score sheet, or a set of cards that are not number cards. The instructions for doing this are included with the game directions. More complicated game boards and card decks are available from your teacher.

Algebra Election

Materials
☐ 32 *First to 100* Problem Cards
  (*Math Masters*, pp. 46 and 47)
☐ Electoral Vote Map (*Math Masters*,
  pp. 48 and 49)
☐ 1 six-sided die
☐ 4 pennies or other small counters
☐ calculator

Players 2 teams, each with 2 players

Object of the game Players move their counters on a map of the United States. For each state, or the District of Columbia (D.C.), that a player lands on, the player tries to win that state's electoral votes by solving a problem. The first team to collect 270 or more votes wins the election. Winning-team members become President and Vice President.

Directions

1. Each player puts a counter on Iowa.
2. One member of each team rolls the die. The team with the higher roll goes first.
3. Alternate turns between teams and partners: Team 1, Player 1; Team 2, Player 1; Team 1, Player 2; Team 2, Player 2.
4. Shuffle the Problem Cards. Place them facedown in a pile.
5. The first player rolls the die. The result tells how many moves the player must make from the current state. Each new state counts as one move. Moves can be in any direction as long as they pass between states that share a common border. *Exceptions:* Players can get to and from Alaska by way of Washington state and to and from Hawaii by way of California. Once a player has been in a state, the player may not return to that state on the same turn.
6. The player makes the indicated number of moves and puts the counter on the last state moved to. The map names how many electoral votes the state has.
7. The player takes the top Problem Card. The state's number of electoral votes is substituted for the variable x in the problems on the card. The player solves the problem(s) and offers an answer. The other team checks the answer with a calculator.

How many inches are there in x feet? How many centimeters are there in x meters? **1**	How many quarts are there in x gallons? **2**	What is the smallest number of x's you can add to get a sum greater than 100? **3**	Is $50 * x$ greater than 1,000? Is $\frac{x}{10}$ less than 1? **4**
$\frac{1}{2}$ of $x = ?$ $\frac{1}{10}$ of $x = ?$ **5**	$1 - x = ?$ $x + 998 = ?$ **6**	If x people share 1,000 stamps equally, how many stamps will each person get? **7**	What time will it be x minutes from now? What time was it x minutes ago? **8**
It is 102 miles to your destination. You have gone x miles. How many miles are left? **9**	What whole or mixed number equals x divided by 2? **10**	Is x a prime or a composite number? Is x divisible by 2? **11**	The time is 11:05 A.M. The train left x minutes ago. What time did the train leave? **12**
Bill was born in 1939. Freddy was born the same day, but x years later. In what year was Freddy born? **13**	Which is larger: $2 * x$ or $x + 50$? **14**	There are x rows of seats. There are 9 seats in each row. How many seats are there in all? **15**	Sargon spent x cents on apples. If she paid with a $5 bill, how much change should she get? **16**

The temperature was 25°F. It dropped x degrees. What is the new temperature? **17**	Each story in a building is 10 feet high. If the building has x stories, how tall is it? **18**	Which is larger: $2 * x$ or $\frac{100}{x}$? **19**	$20 * x = ?$ **20**
Name all of the whole-number factors of x. **21**	Is x an even or an odd number? Is x divisible by 9? **22**	Shalanda was born on a Tuesday. Linda was born x days later. On what day of the week was Linda born? **23**	Will had a quarter plus x cents. How much money did he have in all? **24**
Find the perimeter and area of this square. x cm □ x cm **25**	What is the median of these weights? 5 pounds 21 pounds x pounds What is the range? **26**	$x°$?° **27**	$x^2 = ?$ 50% of $x^2 = ?$ **28**
$(3x + 4) - 8 = ?$ **29**	x out of 100 students voted for Ruby. Is this more than 25%, less than 25%, or exactly 25% of the students? **30**	There are 200 students at Wilson School. $x\%$ speak Spanish. How many students speak Spanish? **31**	People answered a survey question either Yes or No. $x\%$ answered Yes. What percent answered No? **32**

8. If the answer is correct, the player's team wins the state's electoral votes. They do the following:
  - Write the state's name and its electoral votes on a piece of scratch paper.
  - Write their first initials in pencil on the state to show that they have won it.

Once a state is won, it is out of play. The opposing team may land on the state, but they cannot get its votes.

NOTE: Alaska and Hawaii are not drawn to scale.

9. If the partners do not solve the problem(s) correctly, the state remains open. Players may still try to win its votes.

10. The next player rolls the die and moves his or her counter.

11. The first team to get at least 270 votes wins the election.

12. When all the Problem Cards have been used, shuffle the deck and use it again.

13. Each player begins a turn from the last state he or she landed on.

Notes
- "A state" means "a state or the District of Columbia (D.C.)."
- Partners may discuss the problem with one another. Each player, however, has to answer the problem on his or her own.
- If a player does not want to answer a Problem Card, the player may say "Pass," and draw another card. A player may "Pass" 3 times during a game.
- If a Problem Card contains several problems, a player must answer all the questions on a card correctly to win a state's votes.
- Suggested strategy: Look at the map to see which states have the most votes, then work with your partner to win those states.

Variations:
1. Agree on a time limit for answering problems.

2. Or give one extra point if the player can name the capital of the state landed on.

3. A shorter version of the game can be played by going through all 32 cards just once. The team with the most votes at that time is the winner.

Angle Tangle

Materials ☐ protractor
              ☐ straightedge
              ☐ blank sheets of paper

Players 2

Directions

In each round:

1. Player 1 uses a straightedge to draw an angle on a sheet of paper.

2. Player 2 estimates the degree measure of the angle.

3. Player 1 measures the angle with a protractor. Players agree on the measure.

4. Player 2's score is the difference between the estimate and the actual measure of the angle. (The difference will be a 0 or a positive number.)

5. Players trade roles and repeat Steps 1–4.

Players add their scores at the end of five rounds. The player with the lower total score wins the game.

EXAMPLE

	Player 1			Player 2		
	Estimate	Actual	Score	Estimate	Actual	Score
Round 1	120°	108°	12	50°	37°	13
Round 2	75°	86°	11	85°	87°	2
Round 3	40°	44°	4	15°	19°	4
Round 4	60°	69°	9	40°	56°	16
Round 5	135°	123°	12	150°	141°	9
Total score			48			44

Player 2 has the lower total score. Player 2 wins the game.

Baseball Multiplication (1 to 6 Facts)

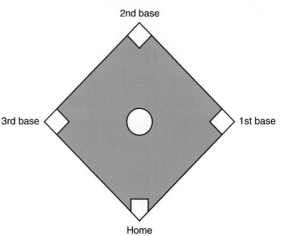

2nd base

3rd base   1st base

Home

Materials ☐ *Baseball Multiplication* Game Mat
(*Math Masters*, p. 4)
☐ 2 six-sided dice
☐ 4 pennies
☐ calculator or a
multiplication/division table

Players 2 or 2 teams

Object of the game To score the most runs in a
3-inning game.

Directions

Advance Preparation: Draw a diamond and label
Home plate, 1st base, 2nd base, and *3rd base.* Make a
Scoreboard sheet that looks like the one shown at the
right.
Take turns being the *pitcher* and the *batter*. The rules
are similar to the rules of baseball, but this
game lasts only three innings.

Inning		1	2	3	Total
Team 1	outs				
	runs				
Team 2	outs				
	runs				

1. At the start of the inning, the batter puts a penny on home
   plate. The pitcher rolls the dice. The batter multiplies the
   numbers rolled and gives the answer. The pitcher checks
   the answer and may use a calculator to do so.

2. If the answer is correct, the batter looks up the product in
   the Hitting Table at the right. If it is a hit, the batter
   moves all pennies on the field the number of bases shown
   in the table. If a product is not a hit, it is an out.

Hitting Table	
1 to 6 Facts	
1 to 9	Out
10 to 18	Single (1 base)
20 to 28	Double (2 bases)
30 to 35	Triple (3 bases)
36	Home Run (4 bases)

3. An incorrect answer is a strike and another pitch (dice roll)
   is thrown. Three strikes make an out.

4. A run is scored each time a penny crosses home plate. The
   batter tallies each run scored on the Scoreboard.

5. After each hit or out, the batter puts a penny on home plate.
   A player remains the batter for three outs. Then the players
   switch roles. The inning is over when both players have
   made three outs.

The player who has more runs at the end of three innings wins
the game. If the game is tied at the end of three innings, play
continues into extra innings until one player wins.

Baseball Multiplication (Advanced Versions)

1 to 10 Facts

Materials ☐ number cards 1–10 (4 of each)

Follow the basic rules. The pitcher draws two cards from the deck. The batter finds their product and uses the Hitting Table at the right to find out how to move the pennies.

2 to 12 Facts

Materials ☐ 4 six-sided dice

Follow the basic rules. The pitcher rolls four dice. The batter separates them into two pairs, adds the numbers in each pair, and multiplies the sums. Use the Hitting Table at the right.

How you pair the numbers can determine the kind of hit you get or whether you get an out. For example, suppose you roll a 1, 2, 3, and 5. You could add pairs in different ways and multiply as follows:

one way	a second way	a third way
1 + 2 = 3	1 + 3 = 4	1 + 5 = 6
3 + 5 = 8	2 + 5 = 7	2 + 3 = 5
3 * 8 = 24	4 * 7 = 28	6 * 5 = 30
Out	Single	Single

Three-Factors Game

Materials ☐ 3 six-sided dice

The pitcher rolls three dice. The batter multiplies the three numbers (factors) and uses the Hitting Table at the right.

10s * 10s Game

Materials ☐ 4 six-sided dice

The rules for this game are the same as for the **2 to 12 Facts** game with two exceptions:

1. A sum 2 through 9 represents 20 through 90. A sum 10 through 12 represents itself. For example,
   Roll 1, 2, 3, and 5. Get sums 6 and 5. Multiply 60 * 50.
   Roll 3, 4, 6, and 6. Get sums 12 and 7. Multiply 12 * 70.
2. Use the Hitting Table at the right.

Hitting Table
1 to 10 Facts

1 to 21	Out
24 to 45	Single (1 base)
48 to 70	Double (2 bases)
72 to 81	Triple (3 bases)
90 to 100	Home Run (4 bases)

Hitting Table
2 to 12 Facts

4 to 24	Out
25 to 49	Single (1 base)
50 to 64	Double (2 bases)
66 to 77	Triple (3 bases)
80 to 144	Home Run (4 bases)

Hitting Table
Three-Factors Game

1 to 54	Out
60 to 90	Single (1 base)
96 to 120	Double (2 bases)
125 to 150	Triple (3 bases)
180 to 216	Home Run (4 bases)

Hitting Table
10s * 10s Game

100 to 2,000	Out
2,100 to 4,000	Single (1 base)
4,200 to 5,400	Double (2 bases)
5,600 to 6,400	Triple (3 bases)
7,200 to 8,100	Home Run (4 bases)

Beat the Calculator
Multiplication Facts

Materials ☐ number cards 1–10 (4 of each)

              ☐ 1 calculator

Players 3

Directions

1. One player is the "Caller," one is the "Calculator," and one is the "Brain."

2. Shuffle the deck of cards and place it facedown.

3. The Caller draws two cards from the number deck and asks for their product.

4. The Calculator solves the problem with a calculator. The Brain solves it without a calculator. The Caller decides who got the answer first.

5. The Caller continues to draw two cards at a time from the number deck and asks for their product.

6. Players trade roles every 10 turns or so.

EXAMPLE The Caller draws a 10 and a 7 and calls out "10 times 7." The Brain and the Calculator solve the problem. The Caller decides who got the answer first.

Extended Multiplication Facts

In this version of the game, the Caller:

- Draws two cards from the number deck.
- Attaches a 0 to either one of the factors or to both factors, before asking for the product.

EXAMPLE If the Caller turns over a 4 and a 6, he or she may make up any one of the following problems:

4 * 60　　　　40 * 6　　　　40 * 60

The Brain and the Calculator solve the problem. The Caller decides who got the answer first.

Broken-Calculator Games
Broken Number Keys

Materials ☐ 1 calculator
Players 2

Directions

1. Partners pretend that one of the number keys is broken.

2. One partner says a number.

3. The other partner tries to display that number on the calculator without using the "broken" key.

> **EXAMPLE** Suppose the 8 key is "broken."
> The number 18 can be displayed by pressing 9 ⊕ 7 ⊕ 2 (Enter),
> or 9 ⊗ 2 (Enter), or 72 ÷ 4 (Enter).

Scoring: A player's score is the number of keys pressed to display the number. Scores for five rounds are totaled. The player with the lowest total wins.

Broken Operation Keys
Directions

1. Partners pretend that one of the operation keys is broken.

2. One partner says an open sentence.

3. The other tries to solve the sentence on the calculator without using the "broken" key.

> **EXAMPLE** Pretend the ⊖ is broken. What is the
> solution to the open sentence $452 + x = 735$?
>
> Replace the variable x with a number and   Try **400:** 452 ⊕ **400** (Enter) 852   400 is too big.
> see if you get a true number sentence. If it   Try **300:** 452 ⊕ **300** (Enter) 752   300 is 17 away.
> is not true, try other numbers until you get   Try **317:** 452 ⊕ **317** (Enter) 769   Wrong way!
> a true sentence. Here is one solution: Try **283:** 452 ⊕ **283** (Enter) 735   True sentence.
>
> 283 is the answer.

Scoring: A player's score is the number of guesses it took to get a true number sentence. Scores for five rounds are totaled. The player with the lowest total wins.

Build-It

Materials ☐ 1 deck of 16 *Build-It* fraction
cards (*Math Masters*, p. 101)
☐ one *Build-It* Gameboard
per player (*Math Masters*,
p. 102)

Players   2

Object of the game To be the first player to
arrange five fraction cards from smallest to
largest.

Directions

1. Each player draws and labels a game
board as shown at the right.

2. Shuffle the fraction cards. Deal one card
facedown on each of the five spaces on the
two *Build-It* game boards.

3. Put the remaining cards facedown in a
draw pile. Turn the top card over and
place it faceup in a discard pile.

4. Players turn over the five cards on their
game boards. Players may not change the
order of the cards at any time during
the game.

$\dfrac{5}{9}$	$\dfrac{1}{3}$	$\dfrac{11}{12}$	$\dfrac{1}{12}$
$\dfrac{7}{12}$	$\dfrac{3}{8}$	$\dfrac{1}{4}$	$\dfrac{1}{5}$
$\dfrac{2}{3}$	$\dfrac{3}{7}$	$\dfrac{4}{7}$	$\dfrac{3}{4}$
$\dfrac{3}{5}$	$\dfrac{4}{5}$	$\dfrac{7}{9}$	$\dfrac{5}{6}$

Closest to 0 → Closest to 1

5. Players take turns. When it is your turn:
   • Take either the top card from the facedown
     pile or the top card from the discard pile.
   • Decide whether to keep this card or put it faceup on top of
     the discard pile.
   • If you keep the card, it must replace one of the five cards
     on your *Build-It* game board. Put the replaced card faceup
     on the discard pile.

6. If all the facedown cards are used, shuffle the discard pile.
   Place them facedown in a draw pile. Turn over the top card
   to start a new discard pile.

7. The winner is the first player to have all five cards on his or
   her game board in order from the smallest fraction to the
   largest.

Buzz Games

Buzz

Materials   none
Players   5–10

Directions

1. Players sit in a circle and choose a leader. The leader names any whole number from 3 to 9. This number is the BUZZ number. The leader also chooses the STOP number. The STOP number should be at least 30.

2. The player to the left of the leader begins the game by saying "one." Play continues clockwise with each player saying either the next whole number or "BUZZ."

3. A player must say "BUZZ" instead of the next number if:
   • The number is the BUZZ number or a multiple of the BUZZ number; or
   • The number contains the BUZZ number as one of its digits.

4. If a player makes an error, the next player starts with 1.

5. Play continues until the STOP number is reached.

6. For the next round, the player to the right of the leader becomes the new leader.

> **EXAMPLE**   The BUZZ number is 4. Play should proceed as follows: 1, 2, 3, BUZZ, 5, 6, 7, BUZZ, 9, 10, 11, BUZZ, 13, BUZZ, 15, and so on.

Bizz-Buzz

Bizz-Buzz is played like *Buzz*, except the leader names two numbers: a BUZZ number and a BIZZ number.

Players say:

1. "BUZZ" if the number is a multiple of the BUZZ number.

2. "BIZZ" if the number is a multiple of the BIZZ number.

3. "BIZZ–BUZZ" if the number is a multiple of both the BUZZ number and the BIZZ number.

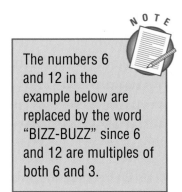

The numbers 6 and 12 in the example below are replaced by the word "BIZZ-BUZZ" since 6 and 12 are multiples of both 6 and 3.

> **EXAMPLE**   The BUZZ number is 6, and the BIZZ number is 3. Play should proceed as follows: 1, 2, BIZZ, 4, 5, BIZZ-BUZZ, 7, 8, BIZZ, 10, 11, BIZZ-BUZZ, 13, 14, BIZZ, 16, and so on.

Credits/Debits Game

Materials   ☐ 1 complete deck of number cards
☐ recording sheet

Players   2

Directions

Pretend that you are an accountant for a business. Your job is to keep track of the company's current balance. The current balance is also called the "bottom line." As credits and debits are reported, you will record them and then adjust the bottom line.

Recording Sheet			
	Start	**Change**	**End/next start**
1	+$10		
2			
3			
4			
5			
6			
7			
8			
9			
10			

1. Shuffle the deck and lay it facedown between the players.

2. The black-numbered cards are the "credits," and the blue- or red-numbered cards are the "debits."

3. Each player begins with a bottom line of +$10.

4. Players take turns. On your turn, do the following:

   • Draw a card. The card tells you the dollar amount and whether it is a credit or debit to the bottom line. Record the credit or debit in the "Change" column.

   • Use the credit or debit to adjust the bottom line.

   • Record the result in the table.

EXAMPLES   Ellen has a "Start" balance of +$20. She draws a black 9. This is a credit of $9, so she records +$9 in the "Change" column, she adds $9 to the bottom line: $20 + $9 = $29. Ellen then records +$29 in the "End" column. She also records +$29 in the "Start" column on the next line.

Larry has a "Start" balance of +$10. He draws a red 12. This is a debit of $12, so he records −$12 in the "Change" column. He subtracts $12 from the bottom line: $10 − $12 = −$2. Larry then records −$2 in the "End" column. He also records −$2 in the "Start" column on the next line.

Scoring: At the end of 10 draws each, the player with more money is the winner of the round. If both players have negative dollar amounts, the player whose amount is closer to 0 wins.

Credits/Debits Game (Advanced Version)

Materials ☐ 1 complete deck of number cards
☐ 1 penny
☐ recording sheet for each player
(*Math Masters*, p. 97)

Players 2

Directions

Pretend that you are an accountant for a business. Your job is to keep track of the company's current balance. The current balance is also called the "bottom line."

1. Shuffle the deck and lay it facedown between the players.

2. The black-numbered cards are the "credits," and the blue- or red-numbered cards are the "debits."

3. The heads side of the coin tells you to **add** a credit or debit to the bottom line. The tails side of the coin tells you to **subtract** a credit or debit from the bottom line.

4. Each player begins with a bottom line of +$10.

5. Players take turns. On your turn, do the following:
   • Flip the coin. This tells you whether to add or subtract.
   • Draw a card. The card tells you what amount in dollars (positive or negative) to add or subtract from the bottom line. Red or blue numbers are negative numbers.
   • Record the result in the table.

		Recording Sheet		
	Start	**Change**		**End, and next start**
		Addition or Subtraction	**Credit or Debit**	
1	+$10			
2				
3				
4				
5				
6				
7				
8				
9				
10				

EXAMPLES Max has a "Start" balance of $5. He draws a red 8 and records −$8 in the "Credit or Debit" column. His coin lands heads-side up and he records + in the "Addition or Subtraction" column. Max adds: $5 + (−$8) = −$3. He records −$3 in the "End" balance column and −$3 in the "Start" column on the next line.

Beth has a "Start" balance of −$20. Her coin lands tails-side up, which means subtract. She draws a black 11 (+$11). She subtracts: −$20 − (+$11) = −$31. Her "End" balance is −$31.

Scoring: After 10 turns each, the player with more money is the winner of the round. If both players have negative dollar amounts, the player whose amount is closer to 0 wins.

Division Dash

Materials ☐ calculator for each player
☐ score sheet

Players 1 or 2

Object of the game To reach 100 in as few divisions as possible.

Directions

1. On a piece of paper, prepare a score sheet as shown at the right.

Player 1		Player 2	
Quotient	Score	Quotient	Score

2. Players clear their calculator memories. Each player then chooses a number that is greater than 1,000 and enters the following key sequence on their calculator:

   Op1 ⌃ ⋅ 5 Op1 [selected number] Op1

3. Each player uses the final digit in the calculator display as a 1-digit number, and the two digits before the final digit as a 2-digit number.

4. Each player divides the 2-digit number by the 1-digit number and records the result. (This result is the quotient. Remainders are ignored.) Players calculate mentally or on paper, not on the calculator.

5. **Players do not clear their calculators.** They just press Op1 and repeat Steps 3 and 4 until the sum of one player's quotients is 100 or more. The winner is the first player to reach at least 100. If there is only one player, the object of the game is to reach 100 or more in as few turns as possible.

EXAMPLE

	Quotient	Score

First turn: Press Op1 ⌃ ⋅ 5 Op1 5678 Op1
On a 10-digit display, the result is 7 5 . 3 5 2 5 0 <u>4 9</u> <u>4</u>.
Divide 49 by 4. The quotient is 12 with a remainder of 1.   **12**   **12**

Second turn: Press Op1 . The result is 8 . 6 8 0 5 8 2 <u>0 6</u> <u>2</u>.
Divide 06, or 6, by 2. The quotient is 3.   **3**   **15**

Third turn: Press Op1 . The result is 2 . 9 4 6 2 8 2 <u>7 5</u> <u>3</u>.
Divide 75 by 3. The quotient is 25.   **25**   **40**

Continue until one player has a total score of 100 or more.

Estimation Squeeze

Materials ☐ calculator
Players 2

Object of the game To estimate the square root of a number without using the ⎡√⎤ key on the calculator.

Directions

1. Pick a number that is less than 600 and is NOT a perfect square. (See the table to the right.) This is the **target number.** Record the target number.

2. Players take turns. When it is your turn:

   • Estimate the square root of the target number and enter the estimate on the calculator.
   • Find the square of the estimate with the calculator and record it.

3. The first player who makes an estimate whose square is within 0.1 of the target number wins the game. For example, if the target number is 139, the square of the estimate must be greater than 138.9 and less than 139.1.

Perfect Squares

1	81	289
4	100	324
9	121	361
16	144	400
25	169	441
36	196	484
49	225	529
64	256	576

A perfect square is the square of a whole number.
$1 = 1 * 1, 64 = 8 * 8,$
$400 = 20^2$

EXAMPLE Use your calculator to square the number 13.5.
Press 13 ⊙ 5 ⎡∧⎤ 2 ⎡Enter⎤ , or press 13 ⊙ 5 ⊗ 13 ⊙ 5 ⎡Enter⎤ .
Answer: 182.25.

4. Do not use the ⎡√⎤ key on the calculator. This key provides the best estimate of a square root that the calculator can calculate.

EXAMPLE Target Number: 139

	Estimate	Square of Estimate	
Nick	12	144	too large
Erin	11	121	too small
Nick	11.5	132.25	too small
Erin	11.8	139.24	too large
Nick	11.75	138.0625	too small
Erin	11.79	139.0041	between 138.9 and 139.1

Erin wins.

Exponent Ball

Materials ☐ an *Exponent Ball* Gameboard (*Math Masters*, p. 90)
☐ 1 six-sided die
☐ penny or other counter
☐ calculator

Players 2

Directions

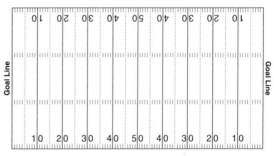

1. The game is similar to U.S. football. The player who goes first puts the ball (counter) on one of the 20-yard lines. The player's goal is to reach the goal line, 80 yards away. A turn consists of four chances to advance the counter to the goal line and score.

2. The first three chances must be runs on the ground. To run, the player rolls the die twice. The first roll names the **base,** the second roll names the **exponent.** For example, rolls of 5 and 4 name the number $5^4 = 625$.

3. The player calculates the value of the rolls. Use Table 1 on the game board page to find how far to move the ball forward (+) or backward (−).

4. If the player does not score in the first three chances, the player may choose to run or kick on the fourth chance. To kick, the player rolls the die once and multiplies the result by 10. The result is the distance the ball travels (Table 2 on the game board page).

5. If the ball reaches the goal line on a run, the player scores 7 points. If the ball reaches the goal line on a kick, the player scores 3 points.

6. If the ball does not reach the goal line in four chances, the turn ends. The second player starts where the first player stopped and moves toward the opposite goal line.

7. If the first player scores, the second player puts the ball on a 20-yard line and follows the directions above.

8. Players take turns. A round consists of four turns for each player. The player with more points wins.

Table 1: Runs		
Value of Roll	**Move Ball**	**Chances of Gaining on the Ground**
1	−15 yd	−15 yards: 1 out of 6 or about 17%
2 to 6	+10 yd	10 yards or more: 5 out of 6 or about 83%
8 to 81	+20 yd	20 yards or more: 4 out of 6 or about 67%
in the 100s	+30 yd	30 yards or more: 13 out of 36 or about 36%
in the 1,000s	+40 yd	40 yards or more: 7 out of 36 or about 19%
in the 10,000s	+50 yd	50 yards: 1 out of 18 or about 6%

Table 2: Kicks		
Value of Roll	**Move Ball**	**Chances of Kicking**
1	+10 yd	10 yards or more: 6 out of 6 or 100%
2	+20 yd	20 yards or more: 5 out of 6 or about 83%
3	+30 yd	30 yards or more: 4 out of 6 or about 67%
4	+40 yd	40 yards or more: 3 out of 6 or about 50%
5	+50 yd	50 yards or more: 2 out of 6 or about 33%
6	+60 yd	60 yards or more: 1 out of 6 or about 17%

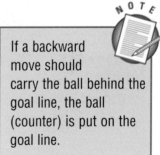

NOTE

If a backward move should carry the ball behind the goal line, the ball (counter) is put on the goal line.

Factor Bingo

Materials   ☐ number cards 2–9 (4 of each)

           ☐ *Factor Bingo* Game Mat for each player (*Math Masters,* p. 10)

           ☐ 12 pennies or counters for each player

Players   2 to 4

Directions

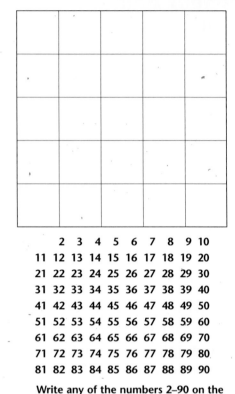

2   3   4   5   6   7   8   9 10
11 12 13 14 15 16 17 18 19 20
21 22 23 24 25 26 27 28 29 30
31 32 33 34 35 36 37 38 39 40
41 42 43 44 45 46 47 48 49 50
51 52 53 54 55 56 57 58 59 60
61 62 63 64 65 66 67 68 69 70
71 72 73 74 75 76 77 78 79 80
81 82 83 84 85 86 87 88 89 90

Write any of the numbers 2–90 on the grid above.

You may use a number only once.

Advance Preparation: Each player fills in the 25 squares on his or her game mat. Choose any 25 numbers from the numbers 2 through 90. Write one number in each square on the grid. Do not write the same number in more than one square. Every square must contain a different number. Be sure to mix the numbers up. They should not all be in order.

1. Shuffle the deck of number cards and place them facedown on the table.

2. Any player can turn over the top card. The number on this card is the **target factor.**

3. Each player places a penny or other counter on one square of their game mat. Place a counter on a square only if the target factor is a factor of the number written in the square. Do not place a counter on a square that is already covered by a counter.

> **EXAMPLE**   A 5-card is turned over. The number 5 is the target factor. A player may place a counter on any square whose number has 5 as a factor, such as 5, 10, 15, 20, 25, and so on.

4. Turn over the next card and continue in the same way.

5. The first player to get five counters in a row, column, or diagonal calls out "Bingo!" and wins the game. A player who places 12 counters anywhere on the game mat may also call "Bingo!" and win the game.

6. If all the cards are used before someone wins, shuffle the cards and continue playing.

Factor Captor

Materials
☐ calculators for each player
☐ paper and pencil
☐ a *Factor Captor* grid—either Grid 1 or Grid 2 (*Math Masters,* pp. 5 and 6)
☐ coin-size counters (48 for Grid 1, 70 for Grid 2)

Players 2

Directions

1. To start the first round, Player 1 (James) chooses a 2-digit number on the number grid. James covers it with a counter, and records the number on scratch paper. This is James's score for the round.

2. Player 2 (Emma) covers all of the factors of James's number. Emma finds the sum of the factors, and records it on scratch paper. This is Emma's score for the round.

A factor may only be covered once during a round.

3. If Emma missed any factors, James can cover them with counters and add them to his score.

4. In the next round, players switch roles. Player 2 (Emma) chooses a number that is not covered by a counter. Player 1 (James) covers all factors of that number.

5. Any number that is covered by a counter is no longer available and may not be used again.

6. The first player in a round may not cover a number less than 10, unless no other numbers are available.

7. Play continues with players trading roles in each round, until all numbers on the grid have been covered. Players then use their calculators to find their total scores. The player with the higher total score wins the game.

1	2	2	2	2	2
2	3	3	3	3	3
3	4	4	4	4	5
5	5	5	6	6	7
7	8	8	9	9	10
10	11	12	13	14	15
16	18	20	21	22	24
25	26	27	28	30	32

1	2	2	2	2	2	3
3	3	3	3	4	4	4
4	5	5	5	5	6	6
6	7	7	8	8	9	9
10	10	11	12	13	14	15
16	17	18	19	20	21	22
23	24	25	26	27	28	30
32	33	34	35	36	38	39
40	42	44	45	46	48	49
50	51	52	54	55	56	60

EXAMPLE

Round 1: James covers 27 and scores 27 points. Emma covers 1, 3, and 9, and scores 1 + 3 + 9 = 13 points.

Round 2: Emma covers 18 and scores 18 points. James covers 2, 3, and 6, and scores 2 + 3 + 6 = 11 points. Emma covers 9 with a counter, because 9 is also a factor of 18. Emma adds 9 points to her score.

Factor Top-It

Materials ☐ number cards 0–9 (4 of each)
Players ☐ 2 or more

Directions

1. Shuffle the deck and place it facedown.

2. In each round, players take turns. When it is your turn:

    - Draw two cards from the top of the deck.
    - Use the cards to make a 2-digit number.
    - Record the number and all of its factors on a piece of paper.
    - Find the sum of all the factors. This is your score for the round.

3. Play five rounds.

4. The winner is the player with the most points at the end of five rounds.

EXAMPLE Find each player's score for the round.

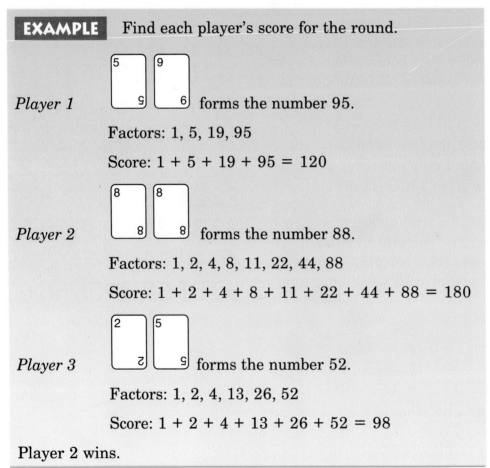

Player 1 forms the number 95.

Factors: 1, 5, 19, 95

Score: 1 + 5 + 19 + 95 = 120

Player 2 forms the number 88.

Factors: 1, 2, 4, 8, 11, 22, 44, 88

Score: 1 + 2 + 4 + 8 + 11 + 22 + 44 + 88 = 180

Player 3 forms the number 52.

Factors: 1, 2, 4, 13, 26, 52

Score: 1 + 2 + 4 + 13 + 26 + 52 = 98

Player 2 wins.

First to 100

Materials ☐ set of 32 *First to 100* Problem Cards
(*Math Masters*, pp. 46 and 47)
☐ 2 six-sided dice
☐ calculator

Players 2 to 4

Object of the game To solve problems and be the first player to collect 100 points.

Directions

1. Shuffle the Problem Cards and place them facedown in a pile.

2. Players take turns. When it is your turn:

   • Roll two dice and find the product of the numbers.

   • Turn over the top Problem Card and substitute the product for the variable x in the problem on the card.

   • Solve the problem mentally, or use paper and pencil. Then give the answer. (You have three chances to use a calculator to solve difficult problems during a game.) Other players check the answer with a calculator.

   • If the answer is correct, you win the number of points equal to the product that was substituted for the variable x. Some Problem Cards require two or more answers. In order to win any points, you must answer all parts of the problem correctly.

   • Put the used Problem Card at the bottom of the card pile.

3. The first player to get at least 100 points wins.

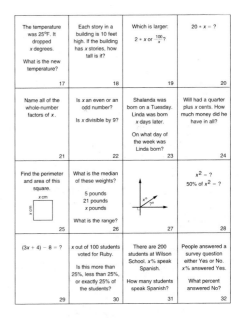

How many inches are there in x feet? How many centimeters are there in x meters? **1**	How many quarts are there in x gallons? **2**	What is the smallest number of x's you can add to get a sum greater than 100? **3**	Is 50 + x greater than 1,000? Is $\frac{x}{10}$ less than 1? **4**
$\frac{1}{2}$ of x = ? $\frac{1}{10}$ of x = ? **5**	1 − x = ? x + 998 = ? **6**	If x people share 1,000 stamps equally, how many stamps will each person get? **7**	What time will it be x minutes from now? What time was it x minutes ago? **8**
It is 102 miles to your destination. You have gone x miles. How many miles are left? **9**	What whole or mixed number equals x divided by 2? **10**	Is x a prime or a composite number? Is x divisible by 2? **11**	The time is 11:05 A.M. The train left x minutes ago. What time did the train leave? **12**
Bill was born in 1939. Freddy was born the same day, but x years later. In what year was Freddy born? **13**	Which is larger: 2 * x or x + 50? **14**	There are x rows of seats. There are 9 seats in each row. How many seats are there in all? **15**	Sargon spent x cents on apples. If she paid with a $5 bill, how much change should she get? **16**

The temperature was 25°F. It dropped x degrees. What is the new temperature? **17**	Each story in a building is 10 feet high. If the building has x stories, how tall is it? **18**	Which is larger: 2 * x or $\frac{100}{x}$? **19**	20 * x = ? **20**
Name all of the whole-number factors of x. **21**	Is x an even or an odd number? Is x divisible by 9? **22**	Shalanda was born on a Tuesday. Linda was born x days later. On what day of the week was Linda born? **23**	Will had a quarter plus x cents. How much money did he have in all? **24**
Find the perimeter and area of this square. x cm, x cm **25**	What is the median of these weights? 5 pounds, 21 pounds, x pounds. What is the range? **26**	**27**	$x^2 = ?$ 50% of $x^2 = ?$ **28**
(3x + 4) − 8 = ? **29**	x out of 100 students voted for Ruby. Is this more than 25%, less than 25%, or exactly 25% of the students? **30**	There are 200 students at Wilson School. x% speak Spanish. How many students speak Spanish? **31**	People answered a survey question either Yes or No. x% answered Yes. What percent answered No? **32**

> **EXAMPLE** Alice rolls a 5 and 6. The product is 30.
>
> She turns over a Problem Card: $20 * x = ?$
> She substitutes 30 for x and answers 600.
>
> The answer is correct. Alice wins 30 points.

Frac-Tac-Toe

2-4-5-10 Frac-Tac-Toe

Materials ☐ number cards 0–10 (4 of each)
☐ *Number Card Board: (Math Masters,* p. 62)
☐ *Game Board: (Math Masters,* p. 63)
☐ *Counters*: Counters (2 Colors) or pennies (one player using heads, the other using tails)
☐ calculator

Players 2

Advance Preparation: Separate the cards into two piles on the Number Card Board—a numerator pile and a denominator pile. For a *2-4-5-10* game, place two each of the 2, 4, 5, and 10 cards in the denominator pile. All other cards are placed on the numerator pile.

Shuffle the cards in each pile. Place the piles facedown in the left-hand spaces. When the numerator pile is completely used, reshuffle that pile, and place it facedown in the left-hand space. When the denominator pile is completely used, turn it over and place it facedown in the left-hand space without reshuffling it.

Directions

1. Players take turns. When it is your turn:
   • Turn over the top card from each pile to form a fraction (numerator card over denominator card).
   • Try to match the fraction shown with one of the grid squares on the Game Board. If a match is found, cover that grid square with your counter and your turn is over. If no match is found, your turn is over.

2. To change the fraction shown by the cards to a decimal, players may use either a calculator or the *Table of Decimal Equivalents for Fractions* on page 358.

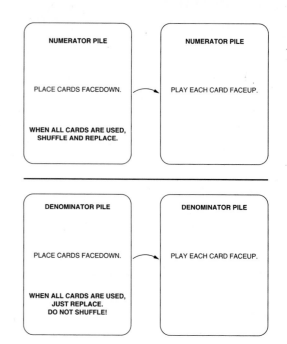

Game Board for the 2-4-5-10 Decimal Version of Frac-Tac-Toe

>1.0	0 or 1	>2.0	0 or 1	>1.0
0.1	0.2	0.25	0.3	0.4
>1.5	0.5	>1.5	0.5	>1.5
0.6	0.7	0.75	0.8	0.9
>1.0	0 or 1	>2.0	0 or 1	>1.0

EXAMPLES

The cards show the fraction $\frac{4}{5}$. The player may cover the 0.8 square, unless that square has already been covered.

The cards show the fraction $\frac{0}{5}$. The player may cover any one of the four squares labeled "0 or 1" that has not already been covered.

The cards show the fraction $\frac{4}{2}$. The player may cover any square labeled "> 1.0" or "> 1.5" that has not been previously covered. The player may not cover a square labeled "> 2.0," because $\frac{4}{2}$ is equal to, but not greater than, 2.0.

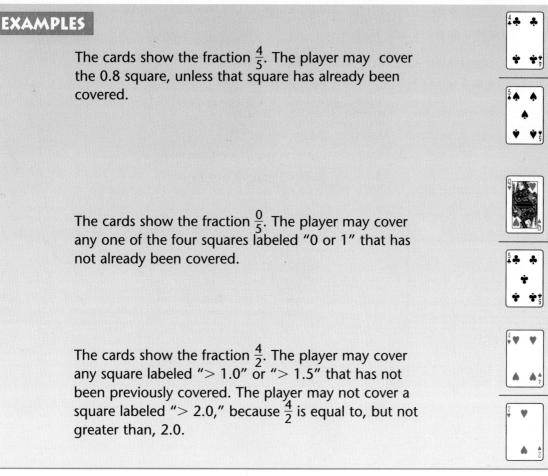

3. **Scoring** The first player covering three squares in a row in any direction (horizontal, vertical, diagonal) is the winner.

Variation: Play a version of the *2-4-5-10* game using the percent game board shown at the right. Use *Math Masters,* page 66.

>100%	0% or 100%	>200%	0% or 100%	>100%
10%	20%	25%	30%	40%
>100%	50%	>200%	50%	>100%
60%	70%	75%	80%	90%
>100%	0% or 100%	>200%	0% or 100%	>100%

Play the *2-4-8*, or the *3-6-9* version of the game. Game boards for the different versions are shown below.

- For a *2-4-8* game, place two each of the 2, 4, and 8 cards in the denominator pile. Use *Math Masters*, page 64 or 69.

- For a *3-6-9* game, place two each of the 3, 6, and 9 cards in the denominator pile. Use *Math Masters*, page 65 or 72.

2-4-8 Frac-Tac-Toe

> 2.0	0 or 1	> 1.5	0 or 1	> 2.0
1.5	0.125	0.25	0.375	1.5
> 1.0	0.5	0.25 or 0.75	0.5	> 1.0
2.0	0.625	0.75	0.875	2.0
> 2.0	0 or 1	1.125	0 or 1	> 2.0

2-4-8 Frac-Tac-Toe

>200%	0% or 100%	>150%	0% or 100%	>200%
150%	$12\frac{1}{2}$%	25%	$37\frac{1}{2}$%	150%
>100%	50%	25% or 75%	50%	>100%
200%	$62\frac{1}{2}$%	75%	$87\frac{1}{2}$%	200%
>200%	0% or 100%	$112\frac{1}{2}$%	0% or 100%	>200%

3-6-9 Frac-Tac-Toe

> 1.0	0 or 1	$0.\overline{1}$	0 or 1	> 1.0
$0.1\overline{6}$	$0.\overline{2}$	$0.\overline{3}$	$0.\overline{3}$	$0.\overline{4}$
> 2.0	$0.\overline{5}$	> 1.0	$0.\overline{6}$	> 2.0
$0.\overline{6}$	$0.\overline{7}$	$0.8\overline{3}$	$0.\overline{8}$	$1.\overline{3}$
> 1.0	0 or 1	$1.\overline{6}$	0 or 1	> 1.0

3-6-9 Frac-Tac-Toe

>100%	0% or 100%	11.1%	0% or 100%	>100%
$16\frac{2}{3}$%	22.2%	$33\frac{1}{3}$%	33.3%	44.4%
>200%	55.5%	>100%	66.6%	>200%
$66\frac{2}{3}$%	77.7%	$83\frac{1}{3}$%	88.8%	$133\frac{1}{3}$%
>100%	0% or 100%	$166\frac{2}{3}$%	0% or 100%	>100%

Fraction Action, Fraction Friction

Materials ☐ one set of 16 *Fraction Action, Fraction Friction* cards
(*Math Masters*, p. 108)

☐ one or more calculators

Players 2 or 3

$\frac{1}{2}$	$\frac{1}{3}$	$\frac{2}{3}$	$\frac{1}{4}$
$\frac{3}{4}$	$\frac{1}{6}$	$\frac{1}{6}$	$\frac{5}{6}$
$\frac{1}{12}$	$\frac{1}{12}$	$\frac{5}{12}$	$\frac{5}{12}$
$\frac{7}{12}$	$\frac{7}{12}$	$\frac{11}{12}$	$\frac{11}{12}$

Object of the game To gather a set of fraction cards
with a sum as close as possible to 2, without going over 2.

Directions

1. Shuffle the deck. Place the pile facedown between the
   players.

2. Players take turns.

   - On each player's first turn, he or she takes a card from
     the top of the pile, then places it faceup on the playing
     surface.
   - On each of the player's following turns, he or she
     announces one of the following:

     "Action" This means that the player wants an additional
     card. The player believes that the sum of the cards is not
     close enough to two to win the hand. The player thinks that
     another card will bring the sum of the cards closer to 2,
     without going over 2.

     "Friction" This means that the player does not want an
     additional card. The player believes that the sum of the
     cards is close enough to 2 to win the hand. The player
     thinks there is a good chance that taking another card will
     make the sum of the 2 cards greater than 2.

   **Once a player says "Friction," he or she cannot say
   "Action" on any turn after that.**

3. Play continues until all players have announced "Friction" or
   have a set of cards whose sum is greater than two. The player
   whose sum is closest to 2 without going over 2 is the winner
   of the hand. Players may check each other's sums on their
   calculators.

4. Reshuffle the cards and begin again. The winner of the game
   is the first player to win five hands.

Fraction/Percent Concentration

Materials ☐ 1 set of Fraction/Percent Tiles
(*Math Masters,* pp. 75 and 76)
☐ calculator

Players   2 or 3

Object of the game To match equivalent fraction tiles and percent tiles.

Directions

1. Spread out the tiles facedown on the playing surface. Create two separate piles—a fraction pile and a percent pile. Mix up the tiles in each pile. The backs of the 12 fraction tiles should have the fraction $\frac{a}{b}$ showing. The backs of the 12 percent tiles should have the percent symbol % showing.

2. Players take turns. At each turn, a player turns over a fraction tile and a percent tile. If the fraction and percent are equivalent, the player keeps the tiles. If the tiles do not match, the player turns the tiles facedown.

3. Players may use a calculator to check each other's matches.

4. The game ends when all tiles have been taken. The player with the most tiles wins.

Fraction/Percent Tiles			
10%	20%	25%	30%
40%	50%	60%	70%
75%	80%	90%	100%
$\frac{1}{2}$	$\frac{1}{4}$	$\frac{3}{4}$	$\frac{1}{5}$
$\frac{2}{5}$	$\frac{3}{5}$	$\frac{4}{5}$	$\frac{1}{10}$
$\frac{3}{10}$	$\frac{7}{10}$	$\frac{9}{10}$	$\frac{2}{2}$

Fraction Top-It

Materials ☐ 1 deck of 32 Fraction Cards
(*Math Masters*, pp. 484 and 485)

Players 2 to 4

Object of the game To collect the most cards.

Directions

Advance Preparation: Before beginning the game, write the fraction for the shaded part on the back of each card.

1. Deal the same number of cards, fraction-side up, to each player:
   - 16 cards each, if there are 2 players
   - 10 cards each, if there are 3 players
   - 8 cards each, if there are 4 players

2. Place the cards on the playing surface in front of each player, fraction-side up.

3. Starting with the dealer and going in a clockwise direction, each player plays one card.

4. Place cards on the table with the fraction-side showing.

5. The player with the largest fraction wins the round and takes the cards. Players may check who has the largest fraction by turning over the cards and comparing the amount shaded.

6. If there is a tie for the largest fraction, each player plays another card. The player with the largest fraction takes all the cards.

7. The player who takes the cards starts the next round. The game is over when all cards have been played.

The player who takes the most cards wins.

Fraction Cards 1

Fraction Cards 2

Getting to One

Materials   ☐ calculator
Players   2

Object of the game To guess a mystery number in as few tries as possible.

Directions

1. Player A chooses a mystery number that is less than 100. Suppose the mystery number is 65.

2. Player B guesses the mystery number.

3. Player A uses a calculator to divide the guessed number by the mystery number. Player A then reads the answer that appears in the calculator display. If the answer has more than two decimal places, only the first two decimal places are read.

4. Player B continues to guess until the result is 1. Player B keeps track of the number of guesses.

5. When Player B has guessed the mystery number, players trade roles and follow Steps 1–4. The player who guesses the mystery number in the fewest number of guesses wins the round. The first player to win three rounds wins the game.

> **EXAMPLE**   Player A chooses the mystery number 65.
>
> Player B guesses: 55. Player A keys in: 55 ⊡ 65 (Enter) . Answer: 0.8461538462   Too small.
>
> Player B guesses: 70. Player A keys in: 70 ⊡ 65 (Enter) . Answer: 1.076923077   Too big.
>
> Player B guesses: 65. Player A keys in: 65 ⊡ 65 (Enter) . Answer: 1   Just right!

Advanced Version Allow mystery numbers up to 1,000.

Hidden Treasure

Materials □ Each player makes two playing grids on one sheet of graph paper. (See example at right.) (*Math Masters,* p. 117)

□ pencil, red pen or crayon

Players 2

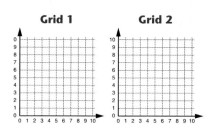

Object of the game Each player "hides" a point on a grid. Players try to "find" each other's hidden point.

Directions

1. Each player writes on his or her own pair of playing grids. Players sit so they cannot see what the other is writing.

2. Each player secretly marks a point on Grid 1. These are the "hidden" points.

3. Player 1 guesses the location of Player 2's hidden point by naming an ordered pair. To name (1,2), say "1 comma 2."

4. If Player 2's hidden point is at that location, Player 1 wins.

5. If the hidden point is not at that location, Player 2 marks the guess in pencil on Grid 1. Player 2 counts the least number of "square sides" needed to travel from the hidden point to the guessed point and tells it to Player 1. Repeat Steps 3–5 with Player 2 guessing and Player 1 answering.

Advanced Version Use a 4-quadrant grid with axes labeled from −7 to 7.

EXAMPLE

Player 1 marks a hidden point at (2,5).   Player 2 marks a hidden point at (3,7).

Player 1   Player 2

- Player 1 guesses that Player 2's hidden point is at (1,2) and marks it on Grid 2 in pencil.

- Player 2 marks the point (1,2) in pencil on Grid 1 and tells Player 1 that (1,2) is 7 units away from the hidden point.

- Player 1 writes 7 next to the point (1,2) on Grid 2.

High-Number Toss

Materials ☐ 1 six-sided die

Players 2

Object of the game To make the largest number possible.

Directions

N O T E

If you don't have a die, you can use a deck of number cards. Use the numbers 1 through 6. Instead of rolling the die, draw the top card from the facedown deck.

1. Each player draws four blank lines on a sheet of paper to record the numbers that come up on the rolls of the die.

   Player 1: ___ ___ ___ | ___

   Player 2: ___ ___ ___ | ___

2. Player 1 rolls the die and writes the number on any one of his or her four blanks. It does not have to be the first blank—it can be any of them. *Keep in mind that the larger number wins!*

3. Player 2 then rolls the die and writes the number on one of his or her blanks.

4. Players take turns rolling the die and writing the numbers three more times each.

5. Each player then uses the four numbers on his or her blanks to build a number.

   • Numbers on the first three blanks are the first three digits of the number the player builds.
   • The number on the fourth blank tells the number of zeros that come after the first three digits.

6. Each player reads his or her number. (See the place-value chart below.) The player with the larger number wins the round. The first player to win four rounds wins the game.

Hundred-Millions	Ten-Millions	Millions	,	Hundred-Thousands	Ten-Thousands	Thousands	,	Hundreds	Tens	Ones

EXAMPLE

First three digits   Number of zeros

Player 1: <u>1</u>   <u>3</u>   <u>2</u> | <u>6</u> = 132,000,000 (132 million)

Player 2: <u>3</u>   <u>5</u>   <u>6</u> | <u>4</u> =   3,560,000 (3 million, 560 thousand)

Player 1 wins.

High-Number Toss: Decimal Version

Materials ☐ number cards 0–9 (4 of each)

☐ scorecard for each player

Players 2

Object of the game To make the largest number possible.

Directions

1. Each player makes a scorecard like the one shown at the right. Players fill out their own scorecards.

2. Shuffle the cards and place the deck facedown on the playing surface.

3. In each round:

   • Player 1 draws the top card from the deck and writes that number on any one of the three blanks on the scorecard. It need not be the first blank—it can be any of them.

   • Player 2 draws the next card from the deck and writes the number on one of his or her blanks.

   • Players take turns doing this two more times. The player with the larger number wins the round.

4. **Scoring** The winner's score for a round is the difference between the two players' scores. The loser scores 0 points for the round.

Game 1	
Round 1	Score
0. __ __ __	_____
Round 2	
0. __ __ __	_____
Round 3	
0. __ __ __	_____
Round 4	
0. __ __ __	_____
Total:	_____

EXAMPLE

Player 1: <u>0</u> . <u>6</u> <u>5</u> <u>4</u>

Player 2: <u>0</u> . <u>7</u> <u>5</u> <u>3</u>

Player 2 has the larger number and wins the round.

Since $0.753 - 0.654 = 0.099$, Player 2 scores 0.099 points for the round. Player 1 scores 0 points.

5. Players take turns starting a round. At the end of four rounds, they find their total scores. The player with the larger total score wins the game.

Multiplication Bull's-eye

Materials ☐ number cards 0–9 (4 of each)
☐ 1 six-sided die
☐ calculator

Players 2

Directions

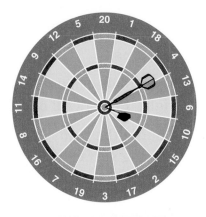

1. Shuffle the cards and place them facedown on the playing surface.

2. Players take turns. When it is your turn:

   • Roll the die. Look up the target range of the product in the table.

   • Take four cards from the top of the deck.

   • Use the cards to try to form two numbers whose product falls within the target range. **Do not use a calculator.**

   • Multiply the two numbers on your calculator to determine whether the product falls within the target range. If it does, you have hit the bull's-eye and score 1 point. If it doesn't, you score 0 points.

   • Sometimes it is impossible to form two numbers whose product falls within the target range. If this happens, you score 0 points for that turn.

3. The game ends when each player has had five turns.

4. The player scoring more points wins the game.

Number on Die	Target Range of Product
1	500 or less
2	501–1,000
3	1,001–3,000
4	3,001–5,000
5	5,001–7,000
6	more than 7,000

EXAMPLE

Tom rolls a 3, so the target range of the product is from 1,001 to 3,000.
He turns over a 5, a 7, a 2, and a 9.

Tom uses estimation to try to form two numbers whose product falls within the target range—for example, 97 and 25.

He finds the product on the calculator: 97 * 25 = 2,425.

Since the product is between 1,001 and 3,000, Tom has hit the bull's-eye and scores 1 point.

Some other possible winning products from the 5, 7, 2, and 9 cards are: 25 * 79, 27 * 59, 9 * 257, and 2 * 579.

Multiplication Wrestling

Materials ☐ number cards 0–9 (4 of each)

Players 2

Object of the game To get the largest product of two 2-digit numbers.

Directions

1. Shuffle the deck of cards and place it facedown.

2. Each player draws four cards and forms two 2-digit numbers. There are many possible ways to form 2-digit numbers using the four cards. Each player should form their two numbers so that their product is as large as possible.

3. Players create two "wrestling teams" by writing each of their numbers as a sum of tens and ones.

4. Next, each player's two teams wrestle. Each member of the first team (for example, 70 and 5) is multiplied by each member of the second team (for example, 80 and 4). Then the four products are added.

5. **Scoring:** The player with the larger product wins the round and receives 1 point.

6. To begin a new round, each player draws four new cards to form two new numbers. A game consists of three rounds.

EXAMPLE

Player 1:

Draws 4, 5, 7, 8

Forms 75 and 84

| 7 | 5 | 8 | 4 |

75 * 84

Team 1		Team 2
(70 + 5)	*	(80 + 4)

Teams: (70 + 5) * (80 + 4)

Products:	70 * 80 =	5,600
	70 * 4 =	280
	5 * 80 =	400
	5 * 4 =	20
Total		5,000
(add four products)		1,200
		+ 100
		6,300

Player 2:

Draws 1, 4, 6, 9

Forms 64 and 91

| 6 | 4 | 9 | 1 |

64 * 91

Team 1		Team 2
(60 + 4)	*	(90 + 1)

Teams: (60 + 4) * (90 + 1)

Products:	60 * 90 =	5,400
	60 * 1 =	60
	4 * 90 =	360
	4 * 1 =	4
Total		5,000
(add four products)		700
		120
		+ 4
		5,824

Name That Number

Materials ☐ 1 complete deck of number cards
Players 2 or 3

Object of the game To collect the most cards.

Directions

1. Shuffle the cards and deal five cards to each player. Place the remaining cards number-side down. Turn over the top card and place it beside the deck. This is the **target number** for the round.

2. Players try to match the target number by adding, subtracting, multiplying, or dividing the numbers on as many of their cards as possible. A card may only be used once.

3. Players write their solutions on a sheet of paper or a slate. When players have written their best solutions:

   • They set aside the cards they used to name the target number.
   • Replace them by drawing new cards from the top of the deck.
   • Put the old target number on the bottom of the deck.
   • Turn over a new target number, and play another hand.

4. Play continues until there are not enough cards left to replace all of the players' cards. The player who sets aside more cards wins the game.

EXAMPLE Target number: 16

A player's cards: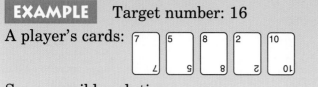

Some possible solutions:

$$10 + 8 - 2 = 16 \text{ (three cards used)}$$

$$7 * 2 + 10 - 8 = 16 \text{ (four cards used)}$$

$$8 / 2 + 10 + 7 - 5 = 16 \text{ (all five cards used)}$$

The player sets aside the cards used to make a solution and draws the same number of cards from the top of the deck.

Number Top-It (7-Digit Numbers)

Materials ☐ number cards 0–9 (4 of each)
☐ Place-Value Mat (*Math Masters,* pp. 22 and 23)

Players 2 to 5

Object of the game To make the largest 7-digit number.

Directions

1. Shuffle the cards. Place the deck number-side down on the playing surface.

2. The Place-Value Mat has rows of boxes. Each player uses one row of boxes on the game mat.

3. In each round, players take turns turning over the top card from the deck and placing it on any one of their empty boxes. Each player takes seven turns, and places seven cards on his or her row of the game mat.

4. At the end of each round, players read their numbers aloud and compare them to the other players' numbers. The player with the largest number for the round scores 1 point. The player with the next-larger number scores 2 points, and so on.

5. Players play five rounds for a game. Shuffle the deck between each round. The player with the smallest total number of points at the end of five rounds wins the game.

EXAMPLE   Roberto and Sally played 7-digit *Number Top-It.*
Here is the result for one complete round of play.

Place-Value Mat

	Millions	Hundred-Thousands	Ten-Thousands	Thousands	Hundreds	Tens	Ones
Roberto	7	6	4	5	2	0	1
Sally	4	9	7	3	5	2	4

Roberto's number is larger than Sally's number. So Roberto scores 1 point for this round. Sally scores 2 points.

Number Top-It (3-Place Decimals)

Materials ☐ number cards 0–9 (4 of each)

               ☐ Place-Value Mat for Decimals (*Math Masters,*
                  pp. 486 and 487)

Players   2 or more

Object of the game To make the largest 3-digit decimal number.

Directions

1. This game is played using the same directions as those for *Number Top-It (7-Digit Numbers)*. The only difference is that players use the Place-Value Mat for decimals.
2. In each round, players take turns turning over the top card from the deck and placing it on any one of their empty boxes. Each player takes two turns, and places two cards on his or her row of the game mat.
3. Players play five rounds for a game. Shuffle the deck between each round. The player with the smallest total number of points at the end of the five rounds wins the game.

EXAMPLE   Phil and Claire played *Number Top-It* using the Place-Value Mat for Decimals. Here is the result.

Place-Value Mat for Decimals

	Ones	.	Tenths	Hundredths	Thousandths
Phil	0	.	3	5	8
Claire	0	.	6	4	2

Claire's number is larger than Phil's number. So Claire scores 1 point for this round, and Phil scores 2 points.

Variation: Use a place-value mat that has empty boxes in the tenths, hundredths, and thousandths places. Each player takes three turns, and places three cards on his or her row of the game mat.

Polygon Capture

Materials ☐ 1 set of *Polygon Capture* pieces *(Math Journal 1,*
                  Activity Sheet 4*)*

☐ 1 set of *Polygon Capture* Property Cards
(Math Journal 2, Activity Sheet 5*)*

Players 2 or two teams of 2

Object of the game To collect the most polygons.

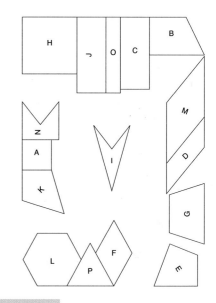

Directions

1. Spread out the polygons on the playing surface.
   Shuffle the Property Cards and sort them facedown
   into ANGLE-card and SIDE-card piles. (The cards are
   labeled on the back.)

2. Players take turns doing the following:

   • Draw the top card from each pile of Property Cards.

> **EXAMPLE** Liz has the cards "All angles are right angles"
> and "All sides are the same length." She can take all the
> squares (polygons A and H). Liz has "captured" these polygons.

   • Take all of the polygons that have both of the
     properties shown on the Property Cards.

   • If there are no polygons with both properties, draw
     one additional Property Card—either an ANGLE-
     or a SIDE-card. Look for polygons that have this
     new property and one of the properties already
     drawn. Take these polygons.

   • At the end of a turn, if a player has not captured a
     polygon he or she could have taken, the other player
     can name and capture it.

There is only one right angle.	There are one or more right angles.	All angles are right angles.	There are no right angles.
There is at least one acute angle.	At least one angle is more than 90°.	All angles are right angles.	There are no right angles.
All opposite sides are parallel.	Only one pair of sides is parallel.	There are no parallel sides.	All sides are the same length.
All opposite sides are parallel.	Some sides have the same length.	All opposite sides have the same length.	**Wild Card:** Pick your own side property.

3. When all the Property Cards have been drawn, shuffle the
   cards, and sort them again into two facedown piles. Continue
   playing.

4. The game ends when there are fewer than three polygons
   left.

5. The winner is the player with the most polygons.

Scientific Notation Toss

Materials ☐ 2 six-sided dice

Players 2

Object of the game To create the largest number, written in scientific notation.

Directions

1. Each player rolls two dice. One number is used to name a power of 10, such as 10^2 or 10^4. The other number is used to multiply that power of 10.

EXAMPLES A 5 and a 4 are rolled.	A 2 and a 3 are rolled.
Either $4 * 10^5$ or $5 * 10^4$ can be written.	Either $2 * 10^3$ or $3 * 10^2$ can be written.

2. Each player rolls the dice three times and writes each result in scientific notation.

3. Players convert their numbers from scientific notation to standard notation. Then they order the numbers from largest to smallest.

4. Players compare lists. The player who has the largest number wins. In case of a tie, they roll a fourth time.

EXAMPLE

Ann	rolls:	2 and 4	5 and 3	1 and 6
	writes:	$2 * 10^4$	$3 * 10^5$	$1 * 10^6$
		$= 2 * 10,000$	$= 3 * 100,000$	$= 1 * 1,000,000$
		$= 20,000$	$= 300,000$	$= 1,000,000$

orders: 1,000,000, 300,000, 20,000

Keith	rolls:	5 and 5	2 and 1	4 and 3
	writes:	$5 * 10^5$	$1 * 10^2$	$3 * 10^4$
		$= 5 * 100,000$	$= 1 * 100$	$= 3 * 10,000$
		$= 500,000$	$= 100$	$= 30,000$

orders: 500,000, 30,000, 100

Ann's highest number is greater than Keith's highest number. So Ann wins.

Spoon Scramble

Materials ☐ one set of 16 *Spoon Scramble* Cards
(*Math Masters,* p. 174)
☐ 3 spoons

Players 4

Object of the game To avoid getting all the letters in the word *SPOONS*.

$\frac{1}{4}$ of 24	$\frac{3}{4} * 8$	50% of 12	0.10 * 60
$\frac{1}{3}$ of 21	$3\frac{1}{2} * 2$	25% of 28	0.10 * 70
$\frac{1}{5}$ of 40	$2 * \frac{16}{4}$	1% of 800	0.10 * 80
$\frac{3}{4}$ of 12	$4\frac{1}{2} * 2$	25% of 36	0.10 * 90

Directions

1. Place the spoons in the center of the table.
2. One player is the dealer. The dealer shuffles the cards and deals four cards facedown to each player.
3. Players look at their cards. If a player has four cards of equal value, proceed to Step 5 below. Otherwise, each player chooses a card to discard and passes it, facedown, to the player on the left.
4. Each player picks up the new card and repeats Step 3. The passing of the cards should proceed as quickly as possible.
5. As soon as a player has four cards of equal value, the player places the cards faceup on the table and grabs a spoon.
6. The other players then try to grab one of the remaining spoons. The player left without a spoon in each round is assigned a letter from the word *SPOONS,* starting with the first letter. If a player incorrectly claims to have four cards of equal value, that player receives a letter instead of the player left without a spoon.
7. Players put the spoons back in the center of the table. The dealer shuffles and deals the cards. A new round begins. (Step 3 above.)
8. Play continues until three players get all the letters in the word *SPOONS.* The player who does not have all the letters is the winner.

Variations

- For three players: Eliminate one set of four equivalent *Spoon Scramble* Cards. Use only two spoons.
- Players can make their own deck of *Spoon Scramble* Cards. Each player writes four computation problems with equivalent answers on four index cards. Check to be sure the players have all chosen different values.

Subtraction Target Practice

Materials ☐ number cards 0–9 (4 of each)

☐ calculator for each player

Players 1 or more

Object of the game To get as close to 0 as possible, without going below 0.

Directions

1. Shuffle the cards and place the deck facedown on the playing surface. Each player starts at 250.

2. Players take turns doing the following:

   • Turn over the top two cards and make a 2-digit number. (You can place the cards in either order.) Subtract this number from 250 on scratch paper. Check the answer on a calculator.

   • Turn over the next two cards and make another 2-digit number. Subtract this number from the result obtained in the previous subtraction. Check the answer on a calculator.

   • Do this three more times: take two cards; make a 2-digit number; subtract it from the last result; check the answer on a calculator.

3. The player whose final result is closest to 0, without going below 0, is the winner. If the final results for all players are below 0, no one wins.

If there is only one player, the object of the game is to get as close to 0 as possible, without going below 0.

EXAMPLE

Turn 1: Draw 4 and 5. Subtract 45 or 54. $250 - 45 = 205$

Turn 2: Draw 0 and 6. Subtract 6 or 60. $205 - 60 = 145$

Turn 3: Draw 4 and 1. Subtract 41 or 14. $145 - 41 = 104$

Turn 4: Draw 3 and 2. Subtract 32 or 23. $104 - 23 = 81$

Turn 5: Draw 6 and 9. Subtract 69 or 96. $81 - 69 = 12$

Variation: Each player starts at 100 instead of 250.

3-D Shape Sort

Materials   ☐ 1 set of 12 Shape Cards
(*Math Masters,* p. 158)
☐ 1 set of 16 Property Cards
(*Math Masters,* pp. 159 and 160)

Players   2, or two teams of 2

Object of the game To collect the most Shape Cards.

Directions

1. Spread out the Shape Cards faceup on the playing surface.
Shuffle the Property Cards and sort them into VERTEX/EDGE-card and SURFACE-card piles.

2. Players take turns. When it is your turn:

   • Draw the top card from each pile of Property Cards.

   • Take all the Shape Cards that have both of the properties shown on the Property Cards.

   • If there are no Shape Cards with both properties, draw one additional Property Card—either a VERTEX/EDGE Card or a SURFACE Card. Look for Shape Cards that have the new property and one of the properties drawn before. Take those Shape Cards.

   • When all the Property Cards have been drawn, shuffle the deck, and sort them again into two facedown piles. Continue playing.

   • At the end of a turn, if you have not taken a Shape Card that you could have taken, the other player may take it.

3. The game ends when there are fewer than three Shape Cards left. The winner is the player with the most Shape Cards.

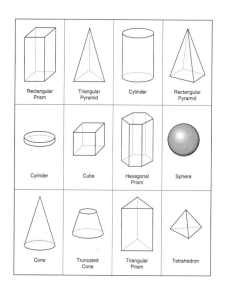

I have an even number of vertices.	I have no vertices.	I have at least 2 edges that are parallel to each other.	I have an odd number of edges.
One of my vertices is formed by an even number of edges.	I have at least one curved edge.	I have fewer than 6 vertices.	I have at least 2 edges that are perpendicular to each other.
All of my surfaces are polygons.	I have at least one face (flat surface).	I have at least one curved surface.	All of my faces are triangles.
All of my faces are regular polygons.	At least one of my faces is a circle.	I have at least one pair of faces that are parallel to each other.	**Wild Card:** Pick your own surface property.

Top-It Games

The materials, number of players, and object of the game are the
same for all *Top-It Games*.

Materials ☐ number cards 1–10 (4 of each)
            ☐ calculator (optional)

Players   2 to 4

Object of the game To collect the most cards.

Addition Top-It
Directions

1. Shuffle the cards and place the deck number-side down.

2. Each player turns over two cards and calls out the sum of the
   numbers. The player with the highest sum takes all the cards.
   In case of a tie for the highest sum, each tied player turns over
   two more cards and calls out the sum. The player with the
   highest sum takes all the cards from both plays.

3. Check answers using an Addition Table or a calculator.

4. Play ends when not enough cards are left for each player to
   have another turn.

5. The player who took the most cards wins.

Variation: Each player turns over three cards and finds their sum.

Advanced Version Use only the number cards 1–9. Each player
turns over four cards, forms two 2-digit numbers, and finds the
sum. Players should carefully consider how they form their
numbers since different arrangements have different sums. For
example, 74 + 52 has a greater sum than 25 + 47.

Subtraction Top-It
Directions

1. Each player turns over three cards, finds the sum of any two of
   the numbers, then finds the difference between the sum and
   the third number.

2. The player with the largest difference takes all the cards.

> **EXAMPLE** A 4, an 8, and a 3 are turned over. There are three ways to form the numbers. Always subtract the smaller number from the larger one.
>
> $4 + 8 = 12$ or $3 + 8 = 11$ or $3 + 4 = 7$
>
> $12 - 3 = 9$ $11 - 4 = 7$ $8 - 7 = 1$

Advanced Version Use only the number cards 1–9. Each player turns over four cards, forms two 2-digit numbers, and finds their difference. Players should carefully consider how they form their numbers. For example, $75 - 24$ has a greater difference than $57 - 42$.

Multiplication Top-It
Directions

1. The rules are the same as for *Addition Top-It*, except that players find the product of the numbers instead of the sum.

2. The player with the largest product takes all the cards. Answers can be checked with a Multiplication Table or a calculator.

Variation: Use only the number cards 1–9. Each player turns over three cards, forms a 2-digit number, then multiplies the 2-digit number by the remaining number.

Division Top-It
Directions

1. Use only the number cards 1–9. Each player turns over three cards and uses them to generate division problems as follows:
   - Choose two cards to form the dividend.
   - Use the remaining card as the divisor.
   - Divide and drop the remainder.
2. The player with the largest quotient takes all the cards.

Advanced Version Use only the number cards 1–9. Each player turns over four cards, chooses three of them to form a 3-digit number, then divides the 3-digit number by the remaining number. Players should carefully consider how they form their 3-digit numbers. For example, $462 / 5$ is greater than $256 / 4$.

Top-It Games *with Positive and Negative Numbers*

Materials ☐ 1 complete deck of number cards
☐ calculator (optional)

Players 2 to 4

Object of the game To collect the most cards.

N O T E

Black cards (spades and clubs) are *positive numbers.*

Red cards (hearts and diamonds) or blue cards (Everything Math Deck) are *negative numbers.*

Addition Top-It with Positive and Negative Numbers
Directions

1. Shuffle the cards and place the deck number-side down.

2. Each player turns over two cards and calls out their sum. The player with the highest sum takes all the cards. In case of a tie, each tied player turns over two more cards and calls out the sum. The player with the highest sum takes all the cards from both plays. If necessary, check answers with a calculator.

3. Play continues until there are too few cards left for each player to have another turn. The player who took the most cards wins.

> **EXAMPLE** Lindsey turns over a red 5 and a black 7. $-5 + 7 = 2$
>
> Fred turns over a red 3 and a red 4. $-3 + (-4) = -7$
>
> Lindsey takes all four cards because 2 is greater than -7.

Variation: Each player turns over three cards and finds the sum.

Subtraction Top-It with Positive and Negative Numbers
Directions

1. The rules are the same as above except that players find differences instead of sums.

2. Each player turns over two cards, one at a time, and subtracts the second number from the first number. The player with the highest answer takes all the cards.

> **EXAMPLE** Lindsey turns over a black 2 first, then a red 3. $+2 - (-3) = 5$
>
> Fred turns over a red 5 first, then a black 8. $-5 - (+8) = -13$
>
> Lindsey takes all four cards because 5 is greater than -13.

American Tour

Introduction

This section of the *Student Reference Book* is called the "American Tour." It uses mathematics to explore the history, people, and environment of the United States.

As you read the American Tour, you will learn how to use and interpret its maps, graphs, and tables. You will see that mathematics is a powerful tool for learning about and understanding our nation.

How to Use the American Tour

Throughout the year you will examine the American Tour with the whole class or in small groups. You should also read and analyze this section of your *Student Reference Book* on your own. As you read the American Tour, do the following:

1. Examine the information.

Ask yourself—

What am I being told? How is the information being reported? Is it a count, a measurement, a ratio, or a rate?

How exact are the numbers? Are these old or recent data?

Is this a rough estimate, an actual count, or a measure?

Are the numbers medians, averages, or ranges? Or are the numbers based on just *one* count or measurement?

2. Use the information.

Ask yourself—

What patterns and trends do I see? If I organize or display the data another way, what else will I find?

How can I use mathematics to study the data and learn something else?

3. Question the information.

Ask yourself—

Can I be sure this information is correct?

How might I check this information?

Would another count or measure show similar results?

Old Faithful Geyser at Yellowstone National Park. Yellowstone is the oldest national park in the United States.

Sears Tower in Chicago, Illinois is the tallest building in the nation.

The Grand Canyon is the largest land gorge in the world.

The First Americans

Fifty thousand years ago, much of Canada and the northern United States was covered by glaciers. These were huge sheets of ice, up to two miles thick. We call this period an Ice Age. A wide, grassy plain connected what are now Siberia and Alaska. No people lived in North or South America, but there were many animals, including mammoths, mastodons, bison, and elk.

The first humans in North America were hunters who may have crossed the land bridge from Siberia. No one knows exactly when they came. Scientists estimate it was between 15,000 and 35,000 years ago. These earliest Americans followed the animals south through a valley between glaciers. The number of humans increased. About 11,000 years ago, people reached the southernmost tip of South America.

More than 11,000 years ago, Earth's climate warmed and the glaciers began to melt. The oceans rose and covered the land bridge that the first Americans had crossed. Today, Siberia and Alaska are separated by the Bering Strait, a body of water about 50 miles wide.

Migrations of the First Americans

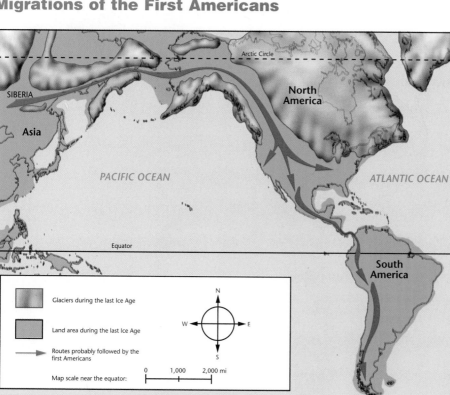

European settlers began to arrive in North America in the early 1600s. We can be fairly certain that there were at least 1 million Native Americans living in North America at that time. The map below shows that some areas contained many more Native Americans than other areas did.

Native American Population Density, 1600

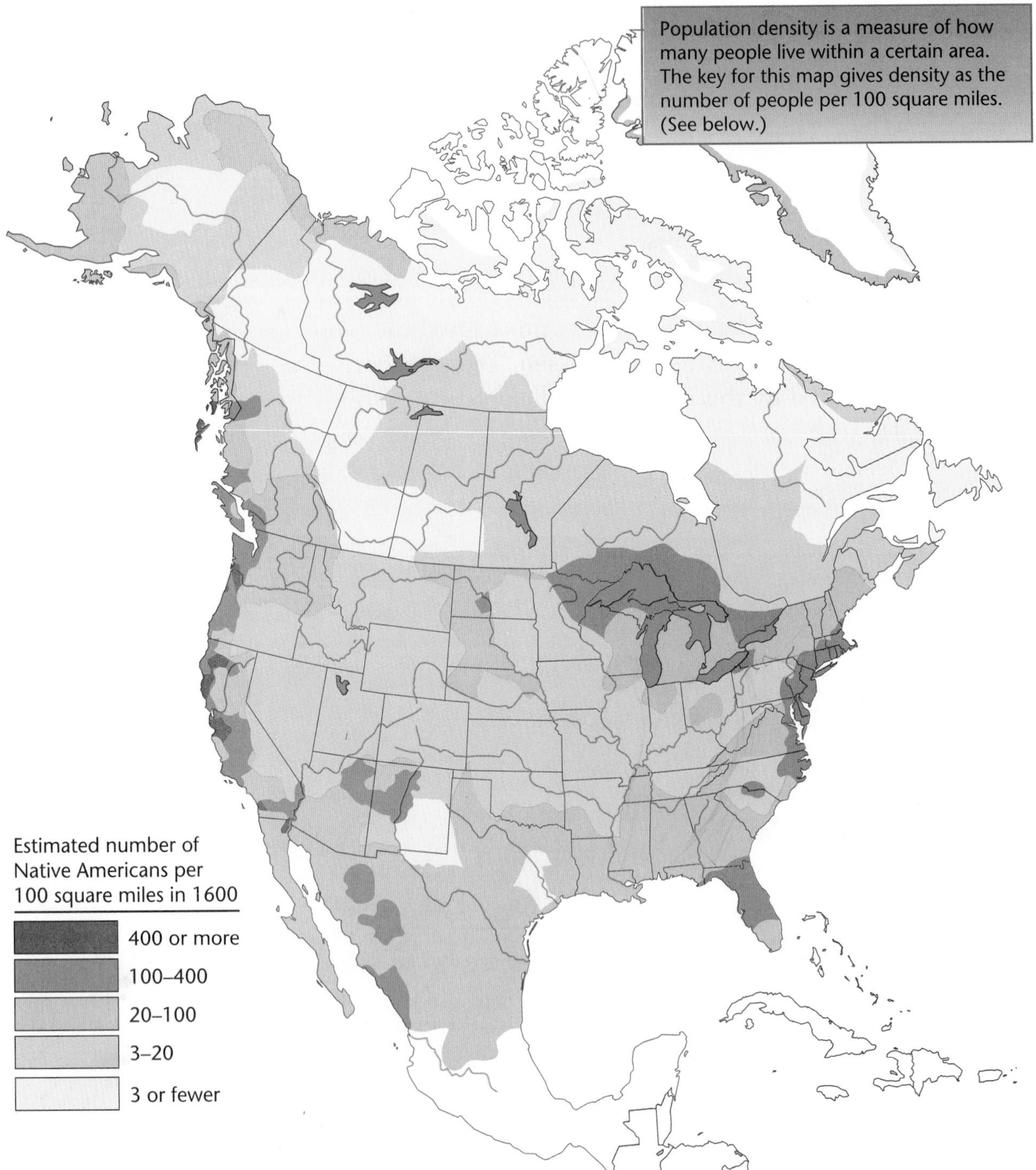

Population density is a measure of how many people live within a certain area. The key for this map gives density as the number of people per 100 square miles. (See below.)

Estimated number of
Native Americans per
100 square miles in 1600

- 400 or more
- 100–400
- 20–100
- 3–20
- 3 or fewer

From 1500 to 1900, disease and war greatly reduced the number of Native Americans. According to the 1900 census, only about 250,000 Native Americans lived inside the United States at that time. This trend has been reversed during the twentieth century. By the year 2000, about 2,400,000 citizens of the United States identified themselves as Native Americans. It is estimated that the Native American population in the United States might exceed 4 million by the year 2050.

Native Americans in the United States, 2000

The following map shows the Native American population for each state in the year 2000. Data are reported in thousands. For example, the Native American population of Michigan was about 61,000 in the year 2000.

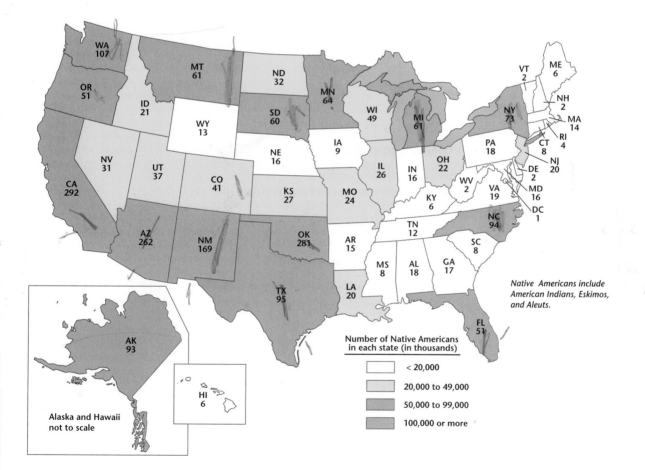

Native Americans include American Indians, Eskimos, and Aleuts.

Alaska and Hawaii not to scale

Number of Native Americans in each state (in thousands)

	< 20,000
	20,000 to 49,000
	50,000 to 99,000
	100,000 or more

A Diverse Nation

The year 1788 is often considered to be when the United States of America became a nation. In that year, eleven of the thirteen original states agreed to accept the new Constitution.

Almost 70 percent of the new nation's people had English or West African ancestors. A smaller percent had roots in Scotland, Ireland, Wales, Germany, France, or the Netherlands. Native Americans are not counted in these estimates nor shown on the graph at the right.

At least nine out of every ten Africans in the United States in 1790 were slaves. They endured terrible cruelty and hardship. They also played a major role in building the new nation. They cleared land, made roads, raised crops, and built houses. Some were skilled craftspeople. During the Revolutionary War, more than 5,000 African Americans fought alongside the colonists against the British.

The number of free African Americans increased during the first half of the nineteenth century. But most African Americans did not gain their freedom until after the Civil War. In 1865, the Thirteenth Amendment to the Constitution was adopted. It states that "neither slavery nor involuntary servitude...shall exist within the United States."

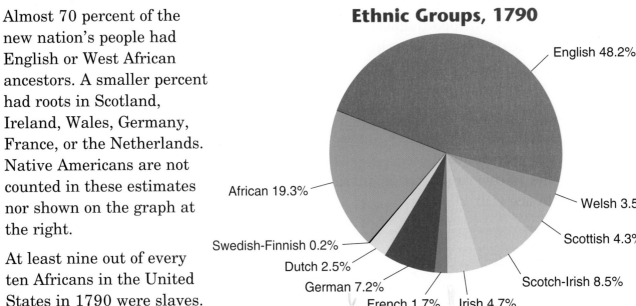

Ethnic Groups, 1790

- English 48.2%
- Welsh 3.5%
- Scottish 4.3%
- Scotch-Irish 8.5%
- Irish 4.7%
- French 1.7%
- German 7.2%
- Dutch 2.5%
- Swedish-Finnish 0.2%
- African 19.3%

African American Population

Year	Number	Percent of U.S. Total Population
1790	757,000	19%
1850	3,639,000	16%
1900	8,834,000	12%
1950	15,042,000	10%
2000	35,454,000	13%

Number of Immigrants

An **immigrant** is a person who moves permanently from one country to another country. Millions of immigrants have come to the United States in search of a better life.

The graph below shows the number of immigrants who entered the United States each year, beginning in 1820. The total number of immigrants entering between 1820 and 2000 was approximately 65 million.

Immigration Rate in Peak Years

Year	Immigrants per 1,000 residents
1854	16.0
1882	15.2
1907	14.8
1921	7.4
1991	7.2

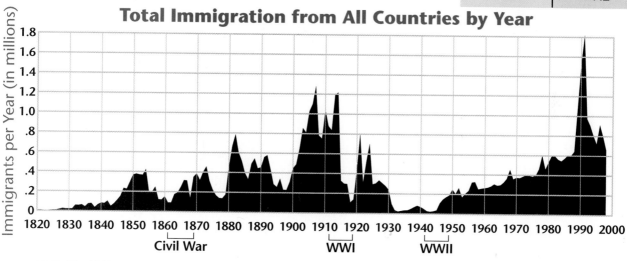

Total Immigration from All Countries by Year

NOTE: The 1989–1991 figures include people already residing in the U.S. who were granted permanent resident status.

Foreign-Born Population

About 10 percent (1 in 10) of the current U.S. population was not born in the United States. Mexico is the most common country of birth among those who were born in other countries.

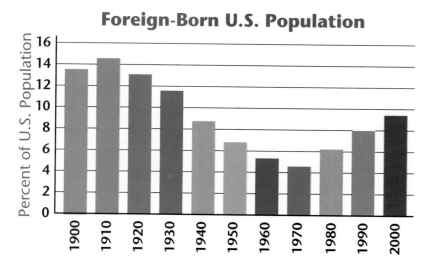

Foreign-Born U.S. Population

Leading Countries of Birth

Country of Birth	Number Living in the United States in 2000
Mexico	More than 7 million
Philippines Cuba Vietnam China	More than 1 million from each country
El Salvador India Dominican Republic Great Britain Korea	More than 500,000, but fewer than 1 million, from each country

Non-English Speaking Population

About 15 percent of the U.S. population speaks a language
other than English at home. More than half this number speak
Spanish.

**People at Least 5 Years Old Who Speak a Language
Other Than English at Home** (subdivisions within states are counties)

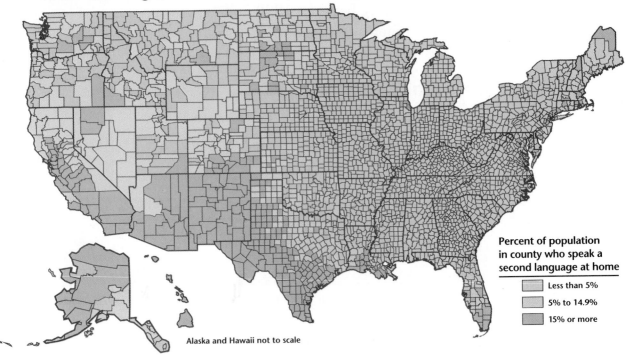

Percent of population
in county who speak a
second language at home

	Less than 5%
	5% to 14.9%
	15% or more

Alaska and Hawaii not to scale

In the United States, each state is divided into smaller areas
called *counties*. There are slightly more than 3,000 counties in
the United States. On the map above, the heavy black lines are
state boundaries; and the thin black lines are county boundaries.

Each county is colored orange, green, or purple. The color
indicates the percent of population in that county who speak a
language other than English at home. For example, the map
key shows that in the orange-colored counties, less than 5% of
the people speak a second language at home.

EXAMPLE   There are 15 counties in the state of Arizona,
and 13 of them are colored purple. At least 15% of the people in
each of these 13 counties speak a language other than English
at home. The other two counties in Arizona are colored green.
In both of those counties, between 5% and 14.9% of the people
speak a language other than English at home.

Westward Expansion

In 1790, almost all of the people of the United States lived within 200 miles of the Atlantic Ocean. In the 1800s, the nation grew westward. Native Americans lived in the new areas that were added. Settlers from France, Spain, and Mexico also lived in these areas. By 1900, the land area of the United States had quadrupled (become four times as large). The population had begun a migration to the West that still continues.

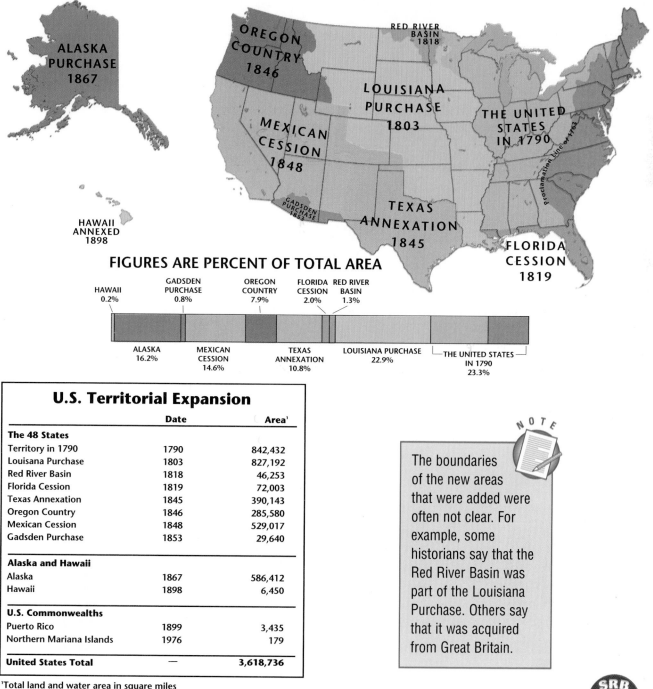

FIGURES ARE PERCENT OF TOTAL AREA

| HAWAII 0.2% | GADSDEN PURCHASE 0.8% | OREGON COUNTRY 7.9% | FLORIDA CESSION 2.0% | RED RIVER BASIN 1.3% |

| ALASKA 16.2% | MEXICAN CESSION 14.6% | TEXAS ANNEXATION 10.8% | LOUISIANA PURCHASE 22.9% | THE UNITED STATES IN 1790 23.3% |

U.S. Territorial Expansion

	Date	Area¹
The 48 States		
Territory in 1790	1790	842,432
Louisana Purchase	1803	827,192
Red River Basin	1818	46,253
Florida Cession	1819	72,003
Texas Annexation	1845	390,143
Oregon Country	1846	285,580
Mexican Cession	1848	529,017
Gadsden Purchase	1853	29,640
Alaska and Hawaii		
Alaska	1867	586,412
Hawaii	1898	6,450
U.S. Commonwealths		
Puerto Rico	1899	3,435
Northern Mariana Islands	1976	179
United States Total	—	3,618,736

¹Total land and water area in square miles

NOTE

The boundaries of the new areas that were added were often not clear. For example, some historians say that the Red River Basin was part of the Louisiana Purchase. Others say that it was acquired from Great Britain.

19th Century Settlement Patterns

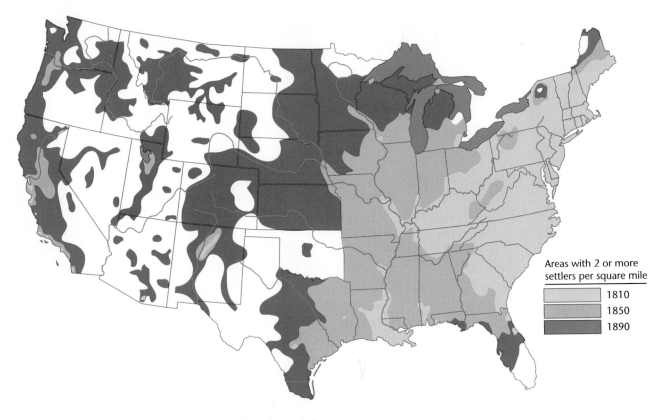

Areas with 2 or more settlers per square mile

	1810
	1850
	1890

The Center of Population Moving West

Imagine a map of the United States that is thin, flat, and rigid (can't bend). Suppose that a 1-ounce weight is set on the map for each person in the United States at the place where that person lives. The **center of population** is the point on the map where the map would balance.

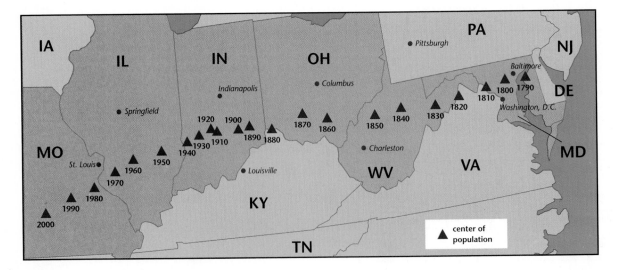

European Exploration, Settlement, and Statehood

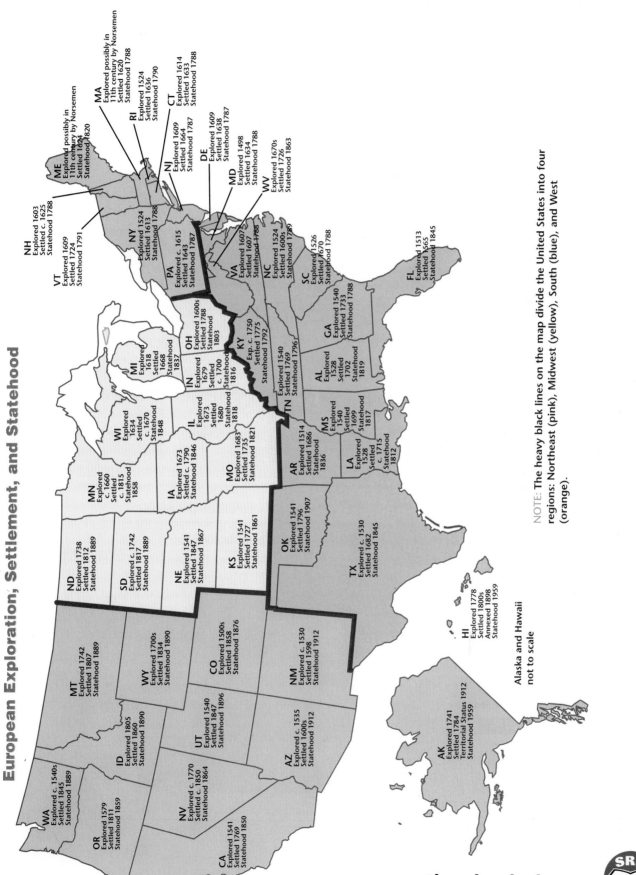

NH
Explored 1603
Settled c. 1625
Statehood 1788

VT
Explored 1609
Settled 1724
Statehood 1791

ME
Explored possibly in
11th century by Norsemen
Settled 1624
Statehood 1820

MA
Explored possibly in
11th century by Norsemen
Settled 1620
Statehood 1788

RI
Explored 1524
Settled 1636
Statehood 1790

CT
Explored 1614
Settled 1633
Statehood 1788

NY
Explored 1524
Settled 1613
Statehood 1788

NJ
Explored 1609
Settled 1664
Statehood 1787

DE
Explored 1609
Settled 1638
Statehood 1787

MD
Explored 1498
Settled 1634
Statehood 1788

WV
Explored 1670s
Settled 1726
Statehood 1863

PA
Explored c. 1615
Settled 1643
Statehood 1787

VA
Explored 1607
Settled 1607
Statehood 1788

NC
Explored 1524
Settled 1600s
Statehood 1789

SC
Explored 1526
Settled 1670
Statehood 1788

FL
Explored 1513
Settled 1565
Statehood 1845

OH
Explored 1600s
Settled 1788
Statehood 1803

KY
Exp. c. 1750
Settled 1775
Statehood 1792

GA
Explored 1540
Settled 1733
Statehood 1788

MI
Explored 1618
Settled 1668
Statehood 1837

IN
Explored 1679
Settled c. 1700
Statehood 1816

TN
Explored 1540
Settled 1769
Statehood 1796

AL
Explored 1528
Settled 1702
Statehood 1819

WI
Explored 1634
Settled c. 1670
Statehood 1848

IL
Explored 1673
Settled 1680
Statehood 1818

MS
Explored 1540
Settled 1699
Statehood 1817

MN
Explored c. 1660
Settled c. 1815
Statehood 1858

IA
Explored 1673
Settled c. 1790
Statehood 1846

MO
Explored 1683
Settled 1735
Statehood 1821

AR
Explored 1514
Settled 1686
Statehood 1836

LA
Explored 1528
Settled c. 1715
Statehood 1812

ND
Explored 1738
Settled 1812
Statehood 1889

SD
Explored c. 1742
Settled 1817
Statehood 1889

NE
Explored 1541
Settled 1847
Statehood 1867

KS
Explored 1541
Settled 1727
Statehood 1861

OK
Explored 1541
Settled 1796
Statehood 1907

TX
Explored c. 1530
Settled 1682
Statehood 1845

MT
Explored 1742
Settled 1807
Statehood 1889

WY
Explored 1700s
Settled 1834
Statehood 1890

CO
Explored 1500s
Settled 1858
Statehood 1876

NM
Explored c. 1530
Settled 1598
Statehood 1912

ID
Explored 1805
Settled 1860
Statehood 1890

UT
Explored 1540
Settled 1847
Statehood 1896

AZ
Explored c. 1535
Settled 1600s
Statehood 1912

WA
Explored c. 1540s
Settled 1845
Statehood 1889

OR
Explored 1579
Settled 1811
Statehood 1859

NV
Explored c. 1770
Settled c. 1850
Statehood 1864

CA
Explored 1541
Settled 1769
Statehood 1850

HI
Explored 1778
Settled 1800s
Annexed 1898
Statehood 1959

AK
Explored 1741
Settled 1784
Territorial Status 1912
Statehood 1959

Alaska and Hawaii
not to scale

NOTE: The heavy black lines on the map divide the United States into four
regions: Northeast (pink), Midwest (yellow), South (blue), and West
(orange).

The United States in 1790

Area Map

Area: 842,000 square miles

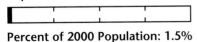

Percent of 2000 Area: 23%

Population: 3,929,000

Percent of 2000 Population: 1.5%

The white region on the map above and below is
included in the area total but not in the population total.

Population Distribution

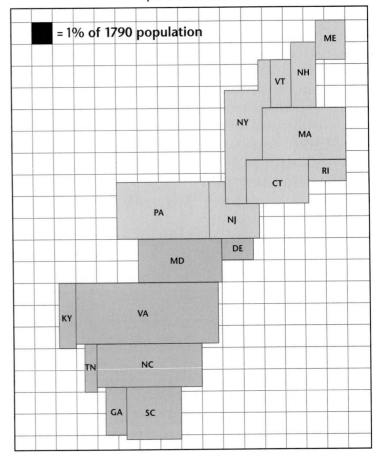

= 1% of 1790 population

The United States in 1850

Area Map

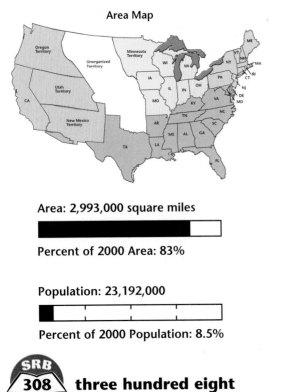

Area: 2,993,000 square miles

Percent of 2000 Area: 83%

Population: 23,192,000

Percent of 2000 Population: 8.5%

Population Distribution

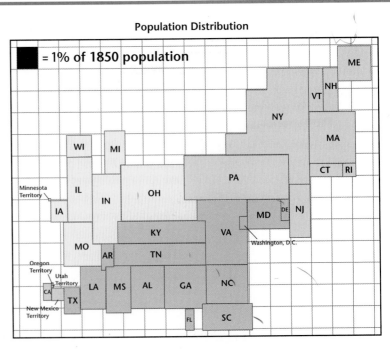

= 1% of 1850 population

The United States in 1900

Area Map

Area: 3,619,000 square miles

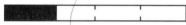

Percent of 2000 Area: 100%

Population: 76,212,000

Percent of 2000 Population: 28%

The white region on the map is included in the area total but not in the population total.

Population Distribution

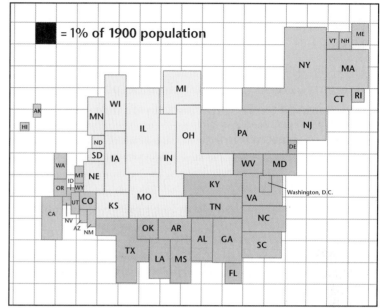

= 1% of 1900 population

The United States in 2000

Area Map

Area: 3,619,000 square miles

Percent of 2000 Area: 100%

Population: 274,634,000

Percent of 2000 Population: 100%

Population Distribution

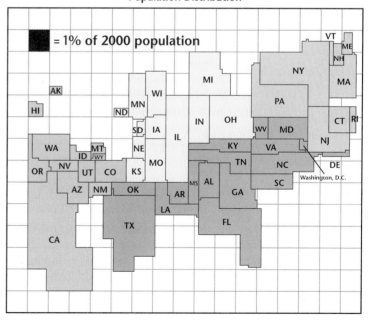

= 1% of 2000 population

Travel

Travel in the 1700s

During the colonial period, travel was difficult and often dangerous. Even under good conditions, it could take a week or longer to travel 200 miles. In 1787, the Constitutional Convention was delayed for eleven days because many delegates could not reach Philadelphia. Spring rains had turned the roads to mud and washed out many bridges.

Much of what we know about travel back then comes from diaries and letters. In the late 1700s, a traveler named Samuel Beck described a trip from New York to Boston. He wrote—

> One way was by clumsy stage that travels about 40 miles a day...Rising at 3 or 4 o'clock and prolonging the day's ride into the night, one made to reach Boston in six days.

Another source of information is the speed of mail delivery. The table below shows how fast mail could be delivered when travel conditions were good. Using a system created by Benjamin Franklin, a series of riders took turns carrying the mail. When one rider got tired, another took over. So the times reported below are much faster than the time it would take one person to travel between the cities.

Travel Times for 24-Hour Express Postal Riders, 1775

From New York City to ...

Boston, Massachusetts	2 to 4 days
Philadelphia, Pennsylvania	2 to 4 days
Baltimore, Maryland	4 to 8 days
Williamsburg, Virginia	8 to 12 days
Wilmington, North Carolina	12 to 16 days
Charleston, South Carolina	More than 16 days

Travel in the 1800s

During the 19th century, ordinary Americans traveled farther and more often than people in any other country. On foot and on horseback, by stagecoach, wagon, steamboat, and railroad, Americans were on the move.

In 1828, a Boston newspaper reported: "There is more traveling in the United States than in any part of the world. Here, the whole population is in motion, whereas, in old countries, there are millions [of people] who have never been beyond the sound of the parish [church] bell."

Between 1775 and the mid-1800s, the speed and comfort of travel increased. Roads and stagecoaches were improved. The steamboat and railroad were invented. Travel was typically faster in the more developed eastern United States. Travel was slower in the West, which had more trails than roads. In addition, the Rocky and Sierra Nevada Mountains made travel difficult.

Top Travel Speeds	
East of the Mississippi River, 1800–1840	
Foot	25 to 35 miles per day
Horseback	60 to 70 miles per day
Stagecoach	8 to 9 miles per hour
Railroad	15 to 25 miles per hour [1]
Transcontinental Travel, 1840–1860	
Wagon Train	2,000 miles in 5 to 6 months
Stagecoach	3,000 miles in 130 to 150 days
Clipper Ship	New York to San Francisco via Cape Horn (about 17,000 miles) in 90 to 120 days
Train Travel, 1860–1900	
1860 New York to Chicago	Less than 2 days
1880 New York to San Francisco	8 days
1900 New York to San Francisco	Less than 5 days

[1]Railroads first appeared in the 1830s. Until the 1850s, service was limited.

Elevation along the 39th Parallel

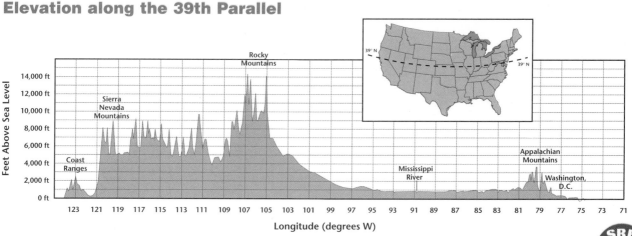

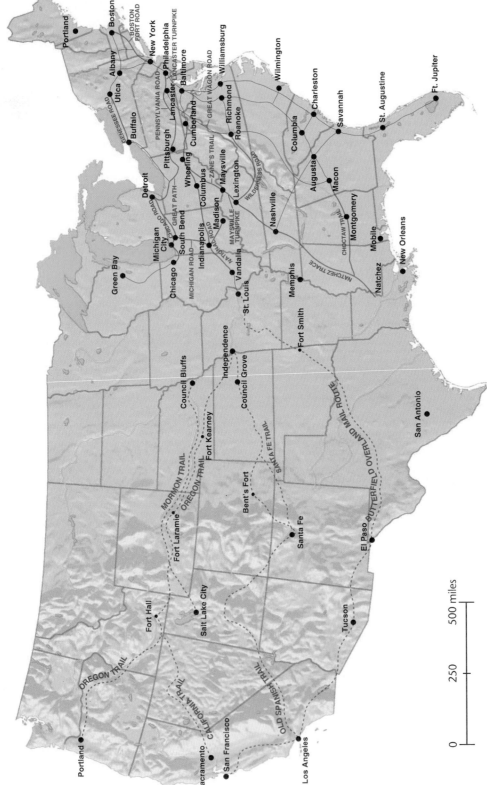

Main Roads and Trails, 1840–1860

Portland
Boston
BOSTON POST ROAD
New York
Albany
Philadelphia
LANCASTER TURNPIKE
Utica
Baltimore
Lancaster
PENNSYLVANIA ROAD
Williamsburg
Buffalo
GENESSEE ROAD
GREAT WAGON ROAD
Wilmington
Richmond
Charleston
Cumberland
Roanoke
Savannah
Pittsburgh
St. Augustine
Ft. Jupiter
Wheeling
Columbia
Detroit
ZANE'S TRAIL
Columbus
Augusta
Macon
CHICAGO ROAD
GREAT PATH
Maysville
Lexington
WILDERNESS ROAD
Montgomery
Michigan City
South Bend
Madison
MAYSVILLE TURNPIKE
Nashville
CHOCTAW TRAIL
Mobile
Indianapolis
NATIONAL ROAD
Green Bay
Chicago
MICHIGAN ROAD
Vandalia
New Orleans
Natchez
NATCHEZ TRACE
St. Louis
Memphis
Fort Smith
Council Bluffs
Independence
Council Grove
San Antonio
Fort Kearney
BUTTERFIELD OVERLAND MAIL ROUTE
MORMON TRAIL
OREGON TRAIL
Bent's Fort
SANTA FE TRAIL
Santa Fe
El Paso
OREGON TRAIL
Fort Laramie
Fort Hall
Salt Lake City
CALIFORNIA TRAIL
Tucson
OLD SPANISH TRAIL
Portland
Sacramento
San Francisco
Los Angeles

0   250   500 miles

Travel from 1870 to the Present

The first railroad connecting the east and west coasts of the United States was completed on May 10, 1869. Twenty-six years later, in 1895, the first practical American automobile was manufactured. In 1903, the Wright brothers flew the first successful airplane. The flight lasted just 12 seconds and covered only 120 feet, but it was the start of modern aviation.

These three events—these three "firsts"—marked the beginning of the modern era of travel and transportation. Trains, automobiles, trucks, and airplanes have made it easy for people and goods to move from one corner of the nation to another. As a result, everyday life has changed dramatically.

Train Schedule between New York and Chicago, 2000

Three Rivers
New York . . .
Pittsburgh . . . Chicago

41			◄ Train Number ►			40
Daily			◄ Days of Operation ►			Daily
Read Down	Mile	▼			▲	Read Up
12 45P	0	Dp	New York, NY–Penn Sta.	(ET)	Ar	7 25P
1 03P	10		Newark, NJ–Penn Sta.			6 53P
1 48P	58		Trenton, NJ			6 00P
2 20P	91	Ar	Philadelphia, PA–30th St. Sta.		Dp	5 25P
3 00P		Dp			Ar	4 52P
3 29P	110		Paoli, PA			4 13P
4 20P	159		Lancaster, PA			3 24P
5 05P	195	Ar	Harrisburg, PA (Scranton,		Dp	2 31P
5 25P		Dp	Reading)		Ar	2 16P
6 37P	256		Lewistown, PA			12 47P
7 17P	293		Huntingdon, PA			12 06P
8 03P	327		Altoona, PA			11 20A
9 07P	366		Johnstown, PA			10 14A
9 59P	413		Greensburg, PA			9 22A
10 55P	444	Ar	Pittsburgh, PA		Dp	8 38A
11 25P		Dp			Ar	8 23A
1 15A	518		Youngstown, OH			5 58A
2 14A	571		Akron, OH (Canton)			4 50A
4 10A	682		Fostoria, OH (Lima)			3 05A
5 42A	817		Nappanee, IN (Warsaw)	(ET)		11 38P
7 00A	900		Hammond-Whiting, IN	(CT)		10 14P
8 25A	915	Ar	Chicago, IL–Union Sta.	(CT)	Dp	9 20P

(ET)	Eastern Time
(CT)	Central Time

Airline Schedule, Chicago to New York, 2000

Departure	Arrival
6:00 A.M.	8:59 A.M.
6:20 A.M.	1:12 P.M.[1]
7:00 A.M.	9:56 A.M.
7:00 A.M.	10:04 A.M.
8:00 A.M.	11:00 A.M.
8:45 A.M.	2:00 P.M.[1]
9:00 A.M.	12:00 P.M.
10:00 A.M.	12:58 P.M.
10:20 A.M.	3:19 P.M.[1]
11:00 A.M.	1:55 P.M.
12:00 P.M.	3:00 P.M.
1:00 P.M.	3:55 P.M.
1:20 P.M.	4:21 P.M.
1:20 P.M.	6:45 P.M.[1]
1:30 P.M.	4:39 P.M.
2:00 P.M.	5:09 P.M.
3:00 P.M.	6:04 P.M.
4:00 P.M.	7:00 P.M.
4:14 P.M.	9:19 P.M.[1]
4:40 P.M.	7:30 P.M.
5:00 P.M.	8:01 P.M.
6:00 P.M.	9:02 P.M.
7:00 P.M.	10:00 P.M.

[1]Flight makes other stops

Note: Times on schedules are local. New York (Eastern Time) is 1 hour ahead of Chicago (Central Time).

Work

During the last 100 years, the fraction of the population doing certain kinds of work has greatly decreased. In other cases, it has greatly increased.

Working People Who Were ...

	Farm Workers	Engineers
1900	1 in 3	1 in 764
1930	1 in 4	1 in 224
1960	1 in 16	1 in 78
2000	1 in 40	1 in 64

There is a third pattern. In some occupations, the number of people has grown at about the same rate as the total population. Why might this be?

Working People Who Were ...

	Clergy	Photographers
1900	1 in 316	1 in 1,161
1930	1 in 327	1 in 1,475
1960	1 in 337	1 in 1,283
2000	1 in 405	1 in 854

Total Number of Working People

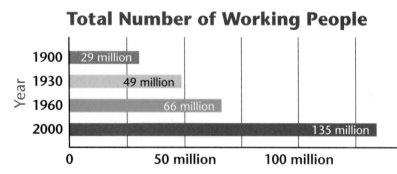

Year	
1900	29 million
1930	49 million
1960	66 million
2000	135 million

NOTE: Figures for 1900 and 1930 are based on workers 14 years and older. Figures for 1960 and 2000 are based on workers 16 years and older. All figures are for the civilian population only. Members of the Armed Forces are excluded.

For many kinds of jobs, more work is being done by fewer people. This is because technology keeps improving and workers are better educated. As a result, fewer workers are needed in some occupations (such as farming).

In 1900

There were about 10 million farm workers.

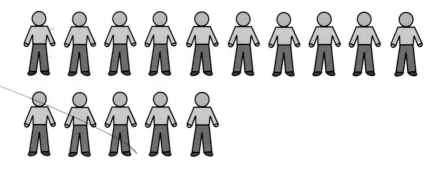

The farms fed a population of about 75 million people.

In 2000

There were about 3 million farm workers.

Key

 Farm worker population of 5 million people

 Population of 5 million people

The farms fed a population of about 275 million people.

Entertainment

During the first half of the twentieth century, going to movies was the most popular form of entertainment.

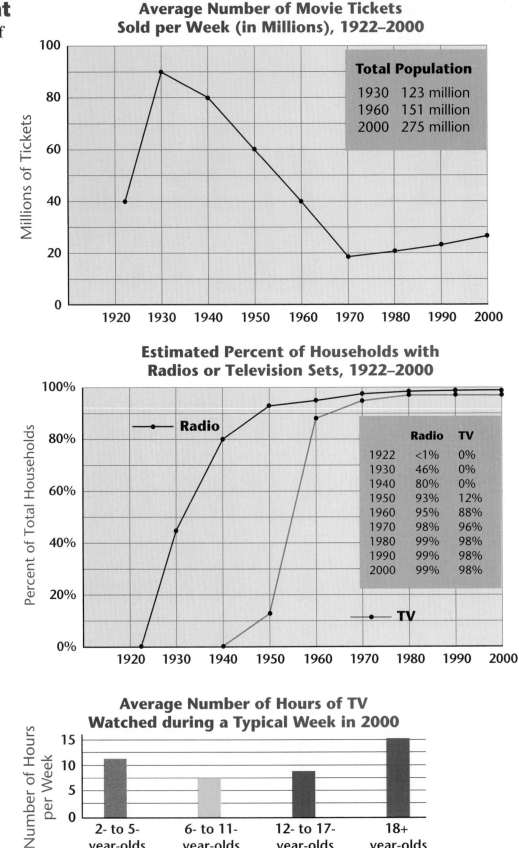

Average Number of Movie Tickets Sold per Week (in Millions), 1922–2000

Total Population	
1930	123 million
1960	151 million
2000	275 million

In the second half of the twentieth century, movies had to compete with other forms of entertainment.

Estimated Percent of Households with Radios or Television Sets, 1922–2000

	Radio	TV
1922	<1%	0%
1930	46%	0%
1940	80%	0%
1950	93%	12%
1960	95%	88%
1970	98%	96%
1980	99%	98%
1990	99%	98%
2000	99%	98%

Today, watching television is the most popular form of entertainment.

Average Number of Hours of TV Watched during a Typical Week in 2000

Play

What kinds of sports and outdoor activities do 11-year-olds participate in? The table below shows how popular different activities are among 11-year-olds, other age groups, all people, males, and females.

The data are from a sample of 15,000 households. Unless otherwise noted, the data estimate the percent of people who engaged in these activities more than once during the year.

Participation in Selected Activities during a Year

Activity	11 Years	35–44 Years	65+ Years	Male	Female	All People	Rank (for all people)
Aerobic Exercising[1]	7 %	12 %	5 %	5 %	16 %	11 %	10 %
Backpacking	7	6	0.3	6	4	5	19
Baseball	20	4	0.2	9	3	6	16
Basketball	35	9	0.9	18	8	13	8
Bicycle Riding[1]	47	17	5	21	16	19	4
Bowling	30	19	5	20	17	19	5
Calisthenics[1]	8	4	2	5	5	5	20
Camping	29	23	6	22	17	19	6
Exercise Walking[1]	17	36	32	24	39	32	1
Exercising with Equipment[1]	10	25	12	19	21	20	3
Fishing, Freshwater	23	18	6	23	10	16	7
Fishing, Saltwater	5	6	3	7	3	5	21
Football, Touch	15	2	0.1	8	2	5	22
Golf	8	14	7	18	5	11	11
Hiking	15	14	3	13	10	12	9
Hunting with Firearms	6	9	2	13	1	7	13
Racquetball	1	2	0.1	3	1	2	25
Running/Jogging[1]	14	9	1	11	7	9	12
Skiing, Alpine/Downhill	5	4	0.3	4	3	4	24
Skiing, Cross-Country	1	1	0.3	1	1	1	26
Soccer	23	2	0.3	7	4	6	17
Softball	14	6	0.4	8	6	7	14
Swimming[1]	51	24	8	24	25	25	2
Target Shooting	6	7	0.9	9	2	6	18
Tennis	6	5	0.9	5	4	5	23
Volleyball	15	7	0.4	7	7	7	15

[1] Participant engaged in this activity at least six times in a year.

What Do Adults Do?

In the year 2000, there were approximately 200 million adults living in the United States. During the year, the following numbers of adults did these things at least once:

- 132 million (66%) went to a movie.
- 126 million (63%) read a book for pleasure.
- 114 million (57%) visited an amusement park.
- 94 million (47%) visited a historical park.
- 82 million (41%) went to a sports event.
- 70 million (35%) visited an art museum.

- 32 million (16%) attended a classical music performance.
- 24 million (12%) attended a jazz music performance.
- 12 million (6%) attended a ballet performance.

School

Throughout the history of the United States, schooling has been important.

The Northwest Ordinance of 1787 created the rules for forming new states. It also showed the nation's belief in the importance of schooling. It stated—

> Being necessary to good government and the happiness of mankind, schools and the means of education shall forever be preserved.

Who Went to School in 1790?

In the northern states, most children between the ages of 4 and 14 went to school for part of the year. In the southern states, many, but not all, white children of these ages went to school. African Americans who were slaves did not receive formal schooling. Often they were not allowed to learn how to read. Some, however, found ways to learn secretly.

Most schools were in rural areas. Many children had to walk long distances to reach them. Schools were often in session for only two to three months in winter and then again in the summer. After age 10, many children attended school only in the winter, when farm work was light.

Who Went to School in 1900?

In 1900, parents reported to census takers that 80% of 10- to 14-year-olds had attended school at some point during the previous six months.

Almost all children who went to school in 1900 attended elementary school, which usually had eight grades. Approximately 15 million students attended public school in 1900. Only about 500,000, or roughly 3%, were in high school.

In rural schools, students were usually not separated by age. Five- and 6-year-olds were often in the same elementary classroom with 15- and 16-year-olds. The older students were not slow learners. They had to do farm work and could only attend school part time.

Three examples of early American schoolhouses.

How Much Schooling Did Students Receive in 1900?

In 1900, the number of days students attended school was different from state to state. Students in North Carolina were in school only about 36 days per year, while students in Massachusetts were in school about 145 days per year.

The following tables and graph show three different ways to examine these data. In the first table, state averages are ranked from high to low for each region.

Average Number of Days in School per Student, 1900

Northeast	Days	South	Days	Midwest	Days	West	Days
Massachusetts	145	Delaware	116	Illinois	123	California	121
Rhode Island	136	Maryland	110	Ohio	122	Nevada	108
Connecticut	135	Louisiana	89	Indiana	115	Utah	101
New York	131	Kentucky	72	Michigan	115	Colorado	93
Pennsylvania	123	Texas	71	Wisconsin	111	Oregon	84
New Jersey	119	Virginia	70	South Dakota	111	Washington	82
Vermont	111	West Virginia	69	Iowa	105	Arizonia	77
New Hampshire	106	Georgia	69	Nebraska	102	Wyoming	73
Maine	105	Florida	69	Missouri	92	Montana	71
		Tennessee	67	Minnesota	91	Idaho	63
		South Carolina	63	North Dakota	87	New Mexico	59
		Oklahoma	61	Kansas	84		
		Alabama	61				
		Mississippi	59				
		Arkansas	48				
		North Carolina	36				

NOTE: No data is available for Alaska and Hawaii.

The stem-and-leaf display[1] shows all the state averages in the table above.

Days in School, 1900: State Averages

Stems (10s)	Leaves (1s)
3	6
4	8
5	9 9
6	1 1 3 3 7 9 9 9
7	0 1 1 2 3 7
8	2 4 4 7 9
9	1 2 3
10	1 2 5 5 6 8
11	0 1 1 5 5 6 9
12	1 2 3 3
13	1 5 6
14	5

[1]**How to read this stem-and-leaf display:** It shows that there was only one state where the number of days was in the 30s. That number was 36. Eight states had numbers in the 60s. Those numbers were 61, 61, 63, 63, 67, 69, 69, and 69. Other numbers are shown in a similar way.

The bar graph shows the median number of days in school for each region.

Days in School, 1900: Regional Medians

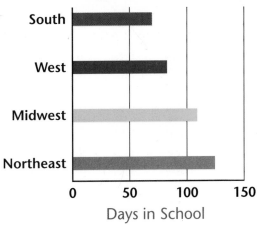

Elementary Schooling in the Twentieth Century

During the first half of the twentieth century, elementary schooling became a requirement for all children. The official school year was made longer. The number of student absences decreased. The time students spent in school rose. In 1900, students averaged 99 days per year in school. By 1960, they were in school an average of 160 days per year. After 1960, the average number of school days per year increased very little.

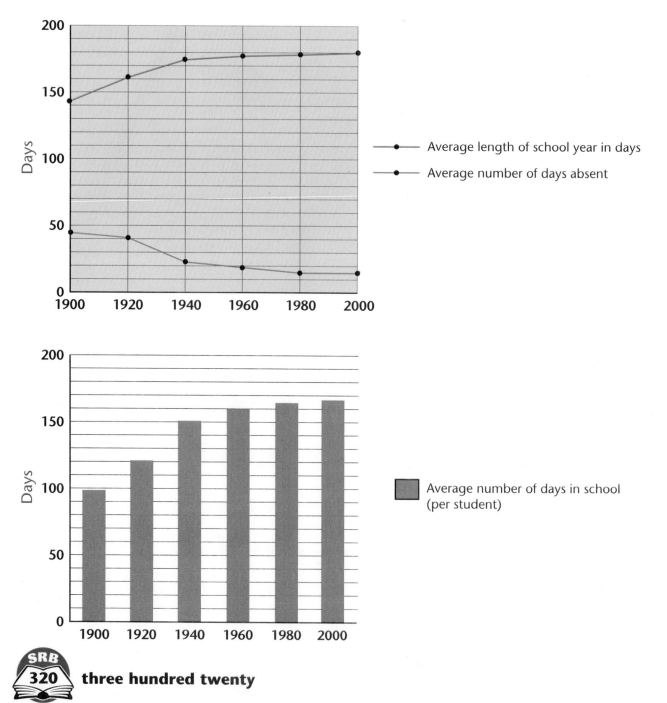

Average length of school year in days

Average number of days absent

Average number of days in school (per student)

Food

The American diet has changed over the last 30 years. The table below shows patterns of increased use and decreased use for many basic foods.

From 1970 to 2000, there has been a 31% increase in the amount of bananas, apples, oranges, and grapes consumed. There has been a 51% increase in the amount of lettuce, carrots, tomatoes, and broccoli consumed.

A current food guide pyramid (a guide to daily food choices) recommends that a person should eat 3–5 servings from the vegetable group and 2–4 servings from the fruit group each day. An example of a food guide pyramid is shown at the right.

As you study the table, remember that *per capita* means "for each person."

Per Capita[1] Food Consumption, 1970–2000
(pounds per person per year)

Foods	1970	1980	1990	2000
Red Meat	132	126	112	111
Poultry	34	41	56	65
Fish	12	12	15	15
Cheese	11	18	25	28
Ice Cream	18	18	16	16
Butter and Margarine	16	16	15	13
Wheat Flour	111	117	136	150
Sugar	102	84	64	67
Bananas	17	21	24	28
Apples	17	19	20	19
Oranges	16	14	12	14
Grapes	2.5	3.5	8	8
Lettuce	22	26	28	24
Carrots	6	6	8	13
Tomatoes	12	13	16	19
Broccoli	0.5	1.5	3.5	5

[1] *Per capita* means "by or for each individual person."

Age

The two graphs shown below are called **age-pyramid graphs.**
They show how the sizes of different age groups have changed
during the past 100 years.

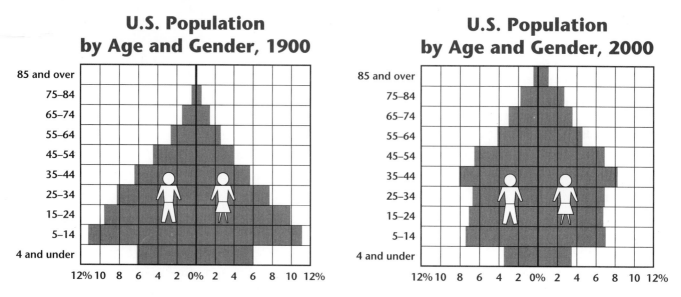

**U.S. Population
by Age and Gender, 1900**

**U.S. Population
by Age and Gender, 2000**

Each age-pyramid graph shows information for both males and
females. Data for males are shown to the left of the center line.
Data for females are shown to the right of the center line.

EXAMPLE   The bottom bar on each graph shows information
for children ages 4 and under.

- In 1900, 6.1% of the total U.S. population was male, ages 4
  and under; and 6.0% was female, ages 4 and under.
- In 2000, 3.5% of the population was male, ages 4 and under;
  and 3.4% was female, ages 4 and under.

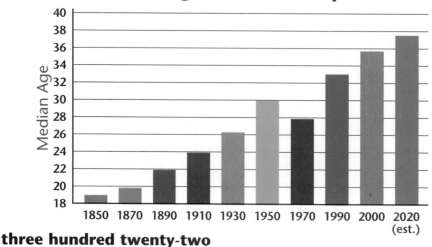

Median Age of the U.S. Population

Life Expectancy

The average lifetime for a person born in the United States in 1900 was about 47 years. By 2000, the average lifetime had increased to about 76 years.

Better health care is one of the major reasons for this increase. During the last 100 years, doctors have developed new and more efficient ways to treat illness. We have been able to control many infectious diseases. The development and use of vaccines has become commonplace.

Improved highway safety, safer workplaces, and better nutrition have also helped people live longer.

Years of Life Expected at Birth, 1900–2010
(males and females combined)

	1900	1910	1920	1930	1940	1950	1960	1970	1980	1990	2000	2010 (estimated)
Years of Life Expected at Birth	47.3	50.0	54.1	59.7	62.9	68.2	69.7	70.8	73.7	75.4	76.4	77.4

Average lifetimes are different for males and females. The table above gives expected years of life for males and females combined. The graph below shows the data for males and females as separate lines.

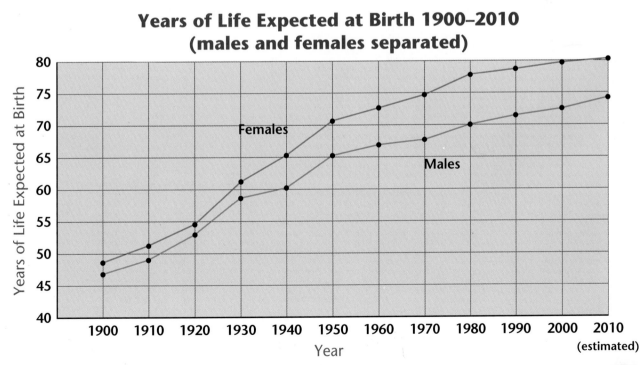

Years of Life Expected at Birth 1900–2010
(males and females separated)

Government

The laws that govern the United States are passed by Congress and signed by the president. The Congress is divided into two bodies.

House of Representatives	Senate
There are 435 representatives.	There are 100 senators.
Representatives are elected for two-year terms.	Senators are elected for six-year terms.
The entire House of Representatives is elected in each even-numbered year.	One-third of the Senate is elected in each even-numbered year.
A representative must be at least 25 years old and must have been a U.S. citizen for at least seven years.	A senator must be at least 30 years old and must have been a U.S. citizen for at least nine years.
The number of representatives from each state is based on population. Population is counted in the Census every ten years. The total population of the 50 states is divided by 435. In 2000, this resulted in each state receiving one representative for approximately every 630,000 people in the state. If a state's population was less than 630,000, it was allowed one representative.	The number of senators from each state is not based on population. Each state elects two senators.

Number of Representatives in the 2000s

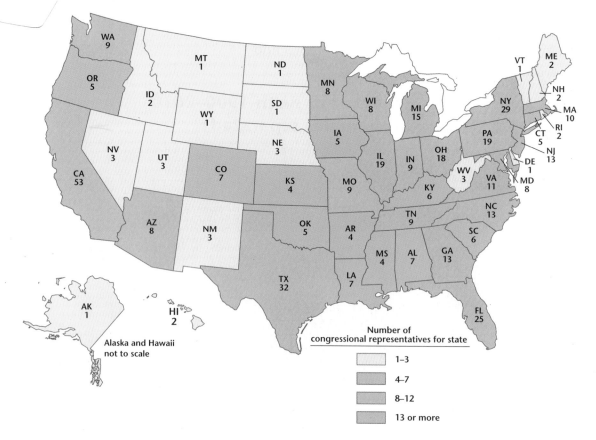

Number of congressional representatives for state

- 1–3
- 4–7
- 8–12
- 13 or more

Alaska and Hawaii not to scale

Electing a President

The president of the United States is elected every four years. The president must be at least 35 years old. He or she must have been born in the United States.

When people vote for president, they are really voting to tell someone called an **elector** how to vote. Each state has as many electors as it has representatives and senators. In addition, Washington, D.C., has 3 electors. The electors in a state vote for the candidate who receives the greatest number of votes (called **popular votes**) in the state. So the candidate who receives the most popular votes in a state wins all of that state's **electoral votes.**

To become president, a candidate must win more than half of all the electoral votes. In 1824, 1876, 1888, and 2000 the candidates with the most popular votes did not become president because they did not win more than half of the electoral votes.

	Electoral Vote	Popular Vote
1824[1]		
John Quincy Adams	84	108,740
Andrew Jackson	99	152,544
Henry Clay	37	47,136
W.H. Crawford	41	46,618
1876		
Rutherford B. Hayes	185	4,036,572
Samuel Tilden	184	4,284,020
1888		
Benjamin Harrison	233	5,447,129
Grover Cleveland	168	5,537,857
2000		
George W. Bush	271	49,820,518
Albert Gore	266	50,158,094

[1]No candidate received more than half of the electoral votes. The election was decided in the House of Representatives. It voted to elect John Quincy Adams.

Electoral Votes in the 2000s

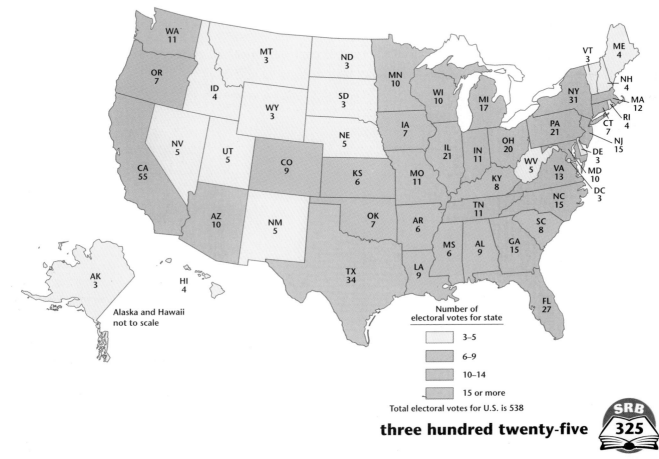

Number of electoral votes for state

- 3–5
- 6–9
- 10–14
- 15 or more

Total electoral votes for U.S. is 538

Percent of Eligible Voters Who Voted in Presidential Elections, 1824–2000

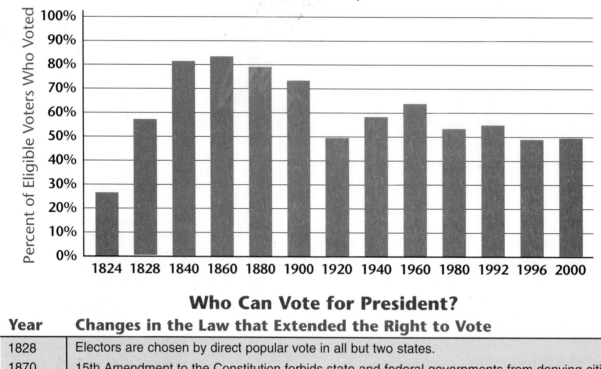

Who Can Vote for President?

Year	Changes in the Law that Extended the Right to Vote
1828	Electors are chosen by direct popular vote in all but two states.
1870	15th Amendment to the Constitution forbids state and federal governments from denying citizens the right to vote due to "race, color, or previous condition of servitude."
1920	19th Amendment to the Constitution gives women the same voting rights as men.
1964	24th Amendment to the Constitution prohibits charging a poll tax[1] in federal elections.
1965	Civil Rights Act of 1965 prohibits use of literacy tests for voters.
1971	26th Amendment to the Constitution lowers the voting age from 21 to 18.

[1]A tax that must be paid before a person is permitted to vote.

The U.S. Decennial Census

What Is It?

A census is a count of a nation's population. Other information is also usually collected as the people are counted.

The word *census* comes from the Latin word *censere,* meaning "to tax," or "to appraise." The U.S. Census is called decennial because it is taken every ten years.

How Do We Take It?

Since 1970, most census forms have been sent out and returned by mail. Some people are hard to reach by mail or do not respond. Personal visits and phone calls are used to collect information from these people.

Why Do We Take It?

It's the law. Although many countries throughout history have taken censuses, the United States was the first nation in history to require a regular census in its Constitution. The following passages are taken from Article I Section 2 of the U.S. Constitution:

> Representatives ... shall be apportioned [divided up] among the several states which may be included within this union according to their respective numbers....

> The actual enumeration shall be made within three years after the first meeting of the Congress of the United States, and within every subsequent term of ten years...

How Do We Use It?
The population information collected by the census has always been used to determine how many representatives each state will have in the House of Representatives. Population totals are also used to determine boundaries for congressional districts within each state. Many government offices and private businesses use the census information to plan and provide services.

1790 Census	2000 Census
Information collected in person.	Most information collected by mail.
Asked 5 questions.	Asked 53 questions.
Every household was asked the same set of questions	Some questions were asked only of a sample group of 1 in 6 households.
Took 18 months to collect information.	Most information was collected in the first 3 months.
Tabulated by hand.	Processed by computer.
Most people lived in isolated rural areas; roads were scarce and of poor quality.	Many people were difficult to find or reach because they were traveling, homeless, or lived in remote locations. People living in the country illegally were also difficult to find and count.
Many people did not understand reasons for the census. People would hide from enumerators—and sometimes attack them!	

The table below is a reproduction of the official report of the 1790 Census. This was the first official counting of Americans.

The last two areas in the "DISTRICTS" column are not state names.

- "S.Weft Territory" means Southwest Territory. This area included what is now the state of Tennessee.
- "N.Do." means Northwest Territory. This area included what is now the states of Ohio, Indiana, Michigan, Illinois, Wisconsin, and part of Minnesota. The first census did not count people in the Northwest Territory.

SCHEDULE of the whole number of PERSONS within the several Districts of the United States, taken according to " An Act providing for the Enumeration of the Inhabitants of the United States ;" passed March the 1st, 1790.

DISTRICTS.	Free white Males of sixteen years & upwards including heads of families.	Free white Males under sixteen years.	Free white Females including heads of families.	All other free perfons.	Slaves.	Total.
* Vermont	22,435	22,328	40,505	255	16	85,539
New Hampfhire	36,086	34,851	70,160	630	158	141,885
Maine	24,384	24,748	46,870	538	-	96,540
Massachusetts	95,453	87,289	190,582	5,463	-	378,787
Rhode Island	16,019	15,799	32,652	3,407	948	68,825
Connecticut	60,523	54,403	117,448	2,808	2,764	237,946
New York	83,700	78,122	152,320	4,654	21,324	340,120
New Jerfey	45,251	41,416	83,287	2,762	11,423	184,139
Pennfylvania	110,788	106,948	206,363	6,537	3,737	434,373
Delaware	11,783	12,143	22,384	3,899	8,887	59,096
Maryland	55,915	51,339	101,395	8,043	103,036	319,728
Virginia	110,936	116,135	215,046	12,866	292,627	747,610
Kentucky	15,154	17,057	28,922	114	12,430	73,677
North Carolina	69,988	77,506	140,710	4,975	100,572	393,751
South Carolina	35,576	37,722	66,880	1,801	107,094	249,073
Georgia	13,103	14,044	25,739	398	29,264	82,548
					Total,	3,893,635

	Free white males of twenty-one years and upwards, including heads of families.	Free males under twenty-one years of age.	Free white females, including heads of families.	All other perfons.	Slaves.	Total.
S. Weft. Territory	6,271	10,277	15,365	361	3,417	35,691
N. Do.	-	-	-	-	-	-

Truly stated from the original returns deposited in the office of the Secretary of State.

TH: JEFFERSON.

October 24th, 1791.

* This return was not figned by the marfhal, but was enclofed and referred to in a letter written and figned by him.

Population Estimates for Colonial and Continental Periods, 1610–1790

Year	Vermont	New Hampshire[1]	Maine	Massachusetts[1]	Rhode Island[1]	Connecticut[1]	New York[1]	New Jersey[1]	Pennsylvania[1]	Delaware[1]	Maryland[1]	Virginia[1]	Kentucky	North Carolina[1]	South Carolina[1]	Georgia[1]	Tennessee	TOTAL
1610	—	—	—	—	—	—	—	—	—	—	—	210	—	—	—	—	—	210
1620	—	—	—	100	—	—	—	—	—	—	—	2,400	—	—	—	—	—	2,500
1630	—	500	400	1,300	—	—	500	—	—	—	—	3,000	—	—	—	—	—	5,700
1640	—	800	700	14,000	300	2,000	1,000	—	—	—	1,500	7,600	—	—	—	—	—	28,000
1650	—	1,400	1,000	18,000	800	6,000	3,000	—	—	—	4,500	17,000	—	—	—	—	—	52,000
1660	—	2,300	—[3]	25,000[3]	1,500	8,000	6,000	—	—	—	8,000	33,000	—	1,000	—	—	—	85,000
1670	—	3,000	—[3]	30,000[3]	2,500	10,000	9,000	2,500	—	—	15,000	40,000	—	2,500	—	—	—	115,000
1680	—	4,000	—[3]	40,000[3]	4,000	13,000	14,000	6,000	—	500[4]	20,000	49,000	—	4,000	1,100	—	—	156,000
1690	—	5,000	—[3]	54,000[3]	5,000	18,000	20,000	9,000	12,000[4]	—[4]	25,000	58,000	—	3,000	4,500	—	—	214,000
1700	—	6,000	—[3]	70,000[3]	6,000	24,000	19,000	14,000	20,000[4]	—[4]	31,000	72,000	—	5,000	8,000	—	—	275,000
1710	—	7,500	—[3]	80,000[3]	8,000	31,000	26,000	20,000	35,000[4]	—[4]	43,000	87,000	—	7,000	13,000	—	—	358,000
1720	—	9,500	—[3]	92,000[3]	11,000	40,000	36,000	26,000	48,000[4]	—[4]	62,000	116,000	—	13,000	21,000	—	—	474,000
1730	—[2]	12,000	—[3]	125,000[3]	17,000	55,000	49,000[2]	37,000	65,000[4]	—[4]	82,000	153,000	—	30,000	30,000	—	—	655,000
1740	—[2]	22,000	—[3]	158,000[3]	24,000	70,000	63,000[2]	52,000	100,000[4]	—[4]	105,000	200,000	—	50,000	45,000	—	—	889,000
1750	—[2]	31,000	—[3]	180,000[3]	35,000	100,000	80,000[2]	66,000	150,000[4]	—[4]	137,000	275,000	—	80,000	68,000	5,000	—	1,207,000
1760	—[2]	38,000	—[3]	235,000	44,000	142,000	113,000[2]	91,000	220,000[4]	—[4]	162,000	346,000	—	115,000	95,000	9,000	—	1,610,000
1770	25,000	60,000	34,000	265,000	55,000	175,000	160,000	110,000	250,000	25,000	200,000	450,000[5]	—[5]	230,000	140,000	26,000	—	2,205,000
1780	40,000	85,000	56,000	307,000	52,000	203,000	200,000	137,000	335,000	37,000	250,000	520,000	45,000[5]	300,000	160,000	55,000	—	2,781,000
1790	86,000	142,000	97,000	379,000	69,000	238,000	340,000	184,000	434,000	59,000	320,000	748,000	74,000	394,000	249,000	83,000	36,000	3,929,000

[1] Original colony

[2] Vermont was included with New York, 1730–1760. Vermont was admitted to statehood in 1791.

[3] Maine was included with Massachusetts, 1660–1760. Maine was admitted to statehood in 1820.

[4] Delaware was included with Pennsylvania, 1690–1760.

[5] Kentucky was included with Virginia in 1770. Kentucky became a state in 1792.

Most estimates in the table have been rounded to the nearest thousand.

The bottom line of the table shows the state totals given in the 1790 Census report. The census counts have been rounded to the nearest thousand.

2000 United States Census Questionnaire

In March of 2000, a census questionnaire was sent to all households in the United States. Every household was required to answer a small number of population and housing questions. A longer form was sent to a sample of 17% of all households.

The Bureau of the Census included this letter with each census questionnaire:

U.S. Department of Commerce
Bureau of the Census
Washington, D.C. 20233-2000

United States Census 2000

Office of the Director

March 13, 2000

To all households:

This is your official form for the United States Census 2000. It is used to count every person living in this house or apartment—people of all ages, citizens and non-citizens.

Your answers are important. First, the number of representatives each state has in Congress depends on the number of people living in the state.

The second reason may be more important to you and your community. The amount of government money your neighborhood receives depends on your answers. That money gets used for schools, employment services, housing assistance, roads, services for children and the elderly, and many other local needs.

Your privacy is protected by law (Title 13 of the United States Code), which also requires that you answer these questions. That law ensures that your information is only used for statistical purposes and that no unauthorized person can see your form or find out what you tell us—no other government agency, no court of law, NO ONE.

Please be as accurate and complete as you can in filling out your census form, and return it in the enclosed postage-paid envelope. Thank you.

Sincerely,

Kenneth Prewitt
Director, Bureau of the Census

Every household was required to answer a short list of questions. Some of these questions are shown below.

One out of six households was asked to answer a longer list of questions. Some of these questions are shown below.

3. What is Person 1's name? *Print name below.*

Last Name

| | | | | | | | | | | | | | | | |

First Name   MI

| | | | | | | | | | | | | | | | |

4. What is Person 1's telephone number? *We may call this person if we don't understand an answer.*

Area Code + Number

| | | | | | | | | | | | | | | | |

5. What is Person 1's sex? Mark ☒ ONE box.

☐ Male   ☐ Female

6. What is Person 1's age and date of birth?

Age on April 1, 2000

| | | | |

Print numbers in boxes.

Month   Day   Year of Birth

| | | | | | | | | | |

→ **NOTE: Please answer BOTH Questions 7 and 8.**

7. Is Person 1 Spanish/Hispanic/Latino? *Mark ☒ the "No" box if **not** Spanish/Hispanic/Latino.*

☐ **No,** not Spanish/Hispanic/Latino   ☐ Yes, Puerto Rican

☐ Yes, Mexican, Mexican Am., Chicano   ☐ Yes, Cuban

☐ Yes, other Spanish/Hispanic/Latino—*Print group.*

| | | | | | | | | | | | | | | | |

8. What is Person 1's race? *Mark ☒ **one or more races** to indicate what this person considers himself/herself to be.*

☐ White

☐ Black, African Am. or Negro

☐ American Indian or Alaska Native—*Print name of enrolled or principal tribe.*

| | | | | | | | | | | | | | | | |

☐ Asian Indian   ☐ Japanese   ☐ Native Hawaiian

☐ Chinese   ☐ Korean   ☐ Guamanian or Chamorro

☐ Filipino   ☐ Vietnamese   ☐ Samoan

☐ Other Asian—*Print race.*   ☐ Other Pacific Islander—*Print race.*

| | | | | | | | | | | | | | | | |

☐ Some other race—*Print race.*

| | | | | | | | | | | | | | | | |

→ **If more people live here, continue with Person 2.**

8. b. What grade or level of school was this person attending? *Mark ☒ ONE box.*

☐ Nursery school, preschool

☐ Kindergarten

☐ Grade 1 to grade 4

☐ Grade 5 to grade 8

☐ Grade 9 to grade 12

☐ College undergraduate (freshman to senior)

☐ Graduate or professional school *(for example: medical, dental, or law school)*

10. What is this person's ancestry or ethnic origin?

| | | | | | | | | | | | | | | | |

(For example: African Am., Mexican, Polish)

11. a. Does this person speak a language other than English at home?

☐ Yes   ☐ No → *Skip to 12*

b. What is this language?

| | | | | | | | | | | | | | | | |

c. How well does this person speak English?

☐ Very well   ☐ Well

☐ Not well   ☐ Not at all

12. Where was this person born?

☐ In the United States—*Print name of state.*

| | | | | | | | | | | | | | | | |

☐ Outside the United States—*Print name of foreign country, or Puerto Rico, Guam, etc.*

| | | | | | | | | | | | | | | | |

21. LAST WEEK, did this person do ANY work for either pay or profit? *Mark ☒ the "Yes" box even if the person only worked 1 hour, or helped without pay in a family business or farm for 15 hours or more, or was on active duty in the Armed Forces.*

☐ Yes   ☐ No → *Skip to 25a*

41. Is there telephone service available in this house, apartment, or mobile home from which you can both make and receive calls?

☐ Yes   ☐ No

State Populations, 1790–2010

State	1790	1850	1900	1950	2000	2010 (estimated)
NORTHEAST REGION	**1,968,000**	**8,627,000**	**21,047,000**	**39,478,000**	**52,107,000**	**53,692,000**
Maine	97,000	583,000	694,000	914,000	1,259,000	1,323,000
New Hampshire	142,000	318,000	412,000	533,000	1,224,000	1,329,000
Vermont	86,000	314,000	344,000	378,000	617,000	651,000
Massachusetts	379,000	995,000	2,805,000	4,691,000	6,199,000	6,431,000
Rhode Island	69,000	148,000	429,000	792,000	998,000	1,038,000
Connecticut	238,000	371,000	908,000	2,007,000	3,284,000	3,400,000
New York	340,000	3,097,000	7,269,000	14,830,000	18,146,000	18,530,000
New Jersey	184,000	490,000	1,884,000	4,835,000	8,178,000	8,638,000
Pennsylvania	434,000	2,312,000	6,302,000	10,498,000	12,202,000	12,352,000
SOUTH REGION	**1,961,000**	**8,983,000**	**24,524,000**	**47,197,000**	**97,614,000**	**107,597,000**
Delaware	59,000	92,000	185,000	318,000	768,000	817,000
Maryland	320,000	583,000	1,188,000	2,343,000	5,275,000	5,657,000
District of Columbia	—	52,000	279,000	802,000	523,000	560,000
Virginia	748,000	1,119,000	1,854,000	3,319,000	6,997,000	7,627,000
West Virginia	—	302,000	959,000	2,006,000	1,841,000	1,851,000
North Carolina	394,000	869,000	1,894,000	4,062,000	7,777,000	8,552,000
South Carolina	249,000	669,000	1,340,000	2,117,000	3,858,000	4,205,000
Georgia	83,000	906,000	2,216,000	3,445,000	7,875,000	8,824,000
Florida	—	87,000	529,000	2,771,000	15,233,000	17,363,000
Kentucky	74,000	982,000	2,147,000	2,945,000	3,995,000	4,170,000
Tennessee	36,000	1,003,000	2,021,000	3,292,000	5,657,000	6,180,000
Alabama	—	772,000	1,829,000	3,062,000	4,451,000	4,798,000
Mississippi	—	607,000	1,551,000	2,179,000	2,816,000	2,974,000
Arkansas	—	210,000	1,312,000	1,910,000	2,631,000	2,840,000
Louisiana	—	518,000	1,382,000	2,684,000	4,425,000	4,683,000
Oklahoma	—	—	790,000	2,233,000	3,373,000	3,639,000
Texas	—	213,000	3,049,000	7,711,000	20,119,000	22,857,000

NOTE: The state and region totals are taken from final census reports for 1790, 1850, 1900, and 1950. Totals for 2000 are U.S. Census Bureau estimates prior to the publication of a final census report for 2000. Totals for 2010 are U.S. Census Bureau projections. All totals have been rounded to the nearest thousand.

State Populations, 1790–2010 (continued)

State	1790	1850	1900	1950	2000	2010 (estimated)
MIDWEST REGION	—	5,404,000	26,333,000	44,461,000	63,502,000	65,914,000
Ohio	—	1,980,000	4,158,000	7,947,000	11,319,000	11,505,000
Indiana	—	988,000	2,516,000	3,934,000	6,045,000	6,318,000
Illinois	—	851,000	4,822,000	8,712,000	12,051,000	12,515,000
Michigan	—	398,000	2,421,000	6,372,000	9,679,000	9,836,000
Wisconsin	—	305,000	2,069,000	3,435,000	5,326,000	5,590,000
Minnesota	—	6,000	1,751,000	2,982,000	4,830,000	5,147,000
Iowa	—	192,000	2,232,000	2,621,000	2,900,000	2,968,000
Missouri	—	682,000	3,107,000	3,955,000	5,540,000	5,864,000
North Dakota	—	—	319,000	620,000	662,000	690,000
South Dakota	—	—	402,000	653,000	777,000	826,000
Nebraska	—	—	1,066,000	1,326,000	1,705,000	1,806,000
Kansas	—	—	1,470,000	1,905,000	2,668,000	2,849,000
WEST REGION	—	179,000	4,309,000	20,190,000	61,412,000	70,511,000
Montana	—	—	243,000	591,000	950,000	1,040,000
Idaho	—	—	162,000	589,000	1,347,000	1,557,000
Wyoming	—	—	93,000	291,000	525,000	607,000
Colorado	—	—	540,000	1,325,000	4,168,000	4,658,000
New Mexico	—	62,000	195,000	681,000	1,860,000	2,155,000
Arizona	—	—	123,000	750,000	4,798,000	5,522,000
Utah	—	11,000	277,000	689,000	2,207,000	2,551,000
Nevada	—	—	42,000	160,000	1,871,000	2,131,000
Washington	—	1,000	518,000	2,379,000	5,858,000	6,658,000
Oregon	—	12,000	414,000	1,521,000	3,397,000	3,803,000
California	—	93,000	1,485,000	10,586,000	32,521,000	37,644,000
Alaska	—	—	64,000	129,000	653,000	745,000
Hawaii	—	—	154,000	500,000	1,257,000	1,440,000
UNITED STATES TOTAL	3,929,000	23,192,000	76,212,000	151,326,000	274,634,000	297,714,000

NOTE: The state and region totals are taken from final Census reports for 1790, 1850, 1900, and 1950. Totals for 2000 are U.S. Census Bureau estimates prior to the publication of a final Census report for 2000. Totals for 2010 are U.S. Census Bureau projections. All totals have been rounded to the nearest thousand.

The United States in 1790

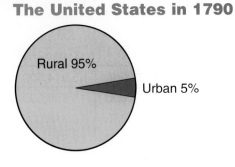

Rural 95%

Urban 5%

Travel Time, New York to Chicago:
about 4–6 weeks by horse, foot, and canoe

Household Size

12%	39%	49%
1 or 2 people	3–5 people	6 or more people

The United States in 1850

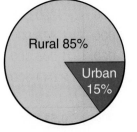

Rural 85%

Urban 15%

Travel Time, New York to Chicago:
about 2–3 weeks by stagecoach

Household Size

14%	42%	44%
1 or 2 people	3–5 people	6 or more people

The United States in 1900

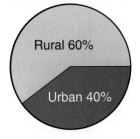

Rural 60%

Urban 40%

Travel Time, New York to Chicago:
about 18 hours by train

Household Size

20%	49%	31%
1 or 2 people	3–5 people	6 or more people

The United States in 2000

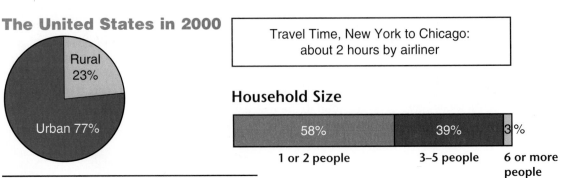

Rural 23%

Urban 77%

Travel Time, New York to Chicago:
about 2 hours by airliner

Household Size

58%	39%	3%
1 or 2 people	3–5 people	6 or more people

Urban means communities with 2,500 or more people.
Rural means communities with fewer than 2,500 people.

Population Density in 2000, by State

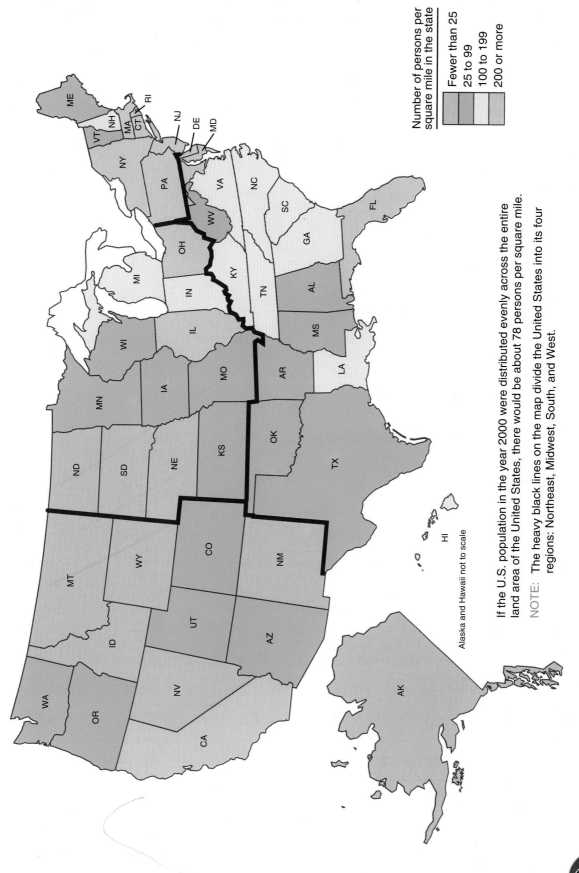

Number of persons per square mile in the state

- Fewer than 25
- 25 to 99
- 100 to 199
- 200 or more

Alaska and Hawaii not to scale

If the U.S. population in the year 2000 were distributed evenly across the entire land area of the United States, there would be about 78 persons per square mile.

NOTE: The heavy black lines on the map divide the United States into its four regions: Northeast, Midwest, South, and West.

Climate
Average Temperature in...
January

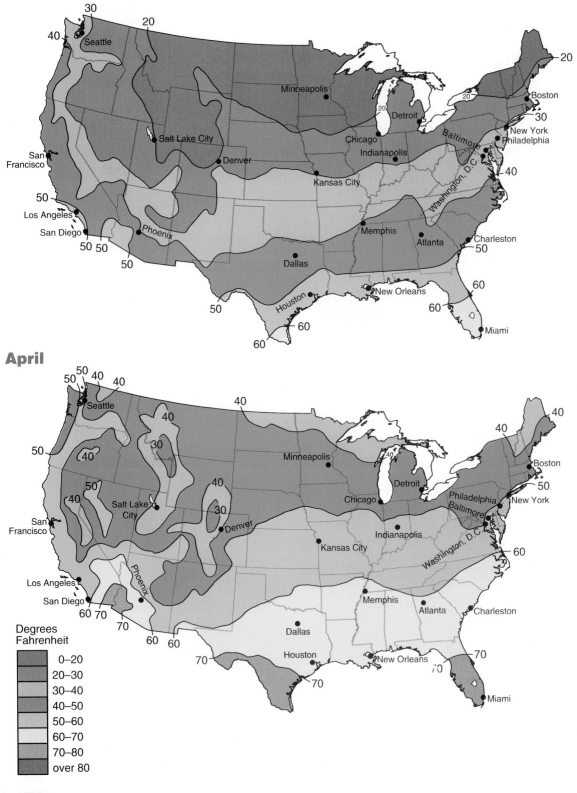

Degrees Fahrenheit

- 0–20
- 20–30
- 30–40
- 40–50
- 50–60
- 60–70
- 70–80
- over 80

April

Average Temperature in...
July

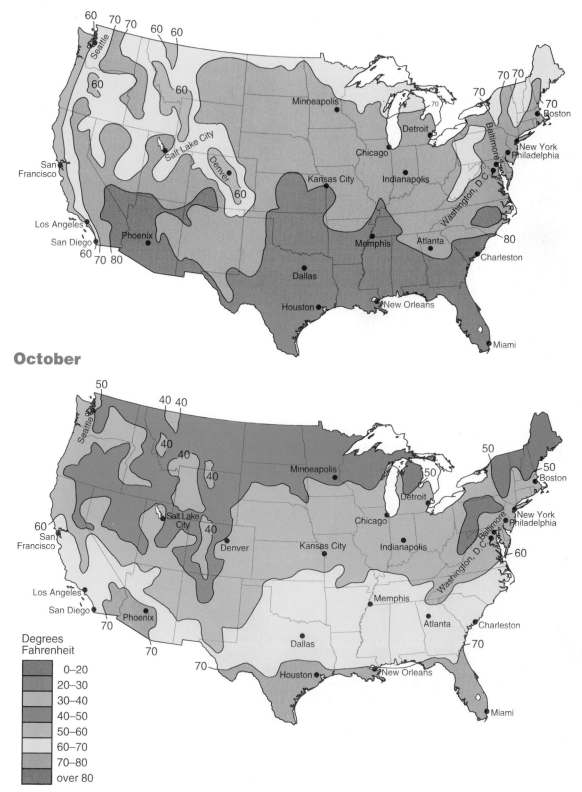

October

Degrees
Fahrenheit

	0–20
	20–30
	30–40
	40–50
	50–60
	60–70
	70–80
	over 80

Growing Seasons in the United States

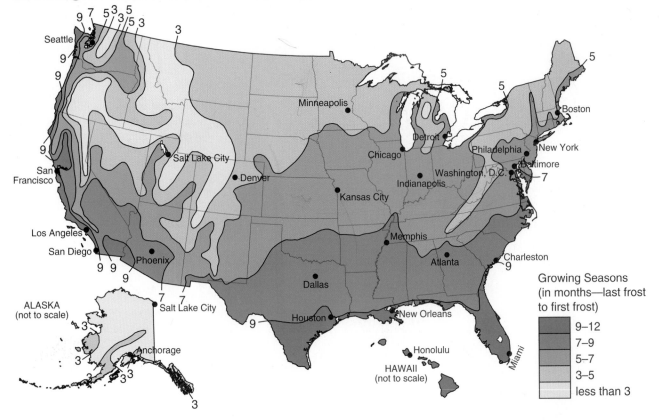

Seattle

9 7 5 3 3 5
9 7 5 3 5 5 3 3

3

5

Minneapolis

Detroit

5

5

Chicago

Philadelphia

New York

9

Salt Lake City

Washington, D.C.

Baltimore

San Francisco

Denver

Indianapolis

7

Kansas City

9

Los Angeles

Memphis

San Diego

9

Charleston

9 9

Phoenix

Atlanta

9

ALASKA
(not to scale)

7 7

Salt Lake City

Dallas

3

9

Houston

New Orleans

Anchorage

3

3 3

Honolulu

HAWAII
(not to scale)

3

**Growing Seasons
(in months—last frost
to first frost)**

9–12
7–9
5–7
3–5
less than 3

Average Yearly Precipitation in the United States

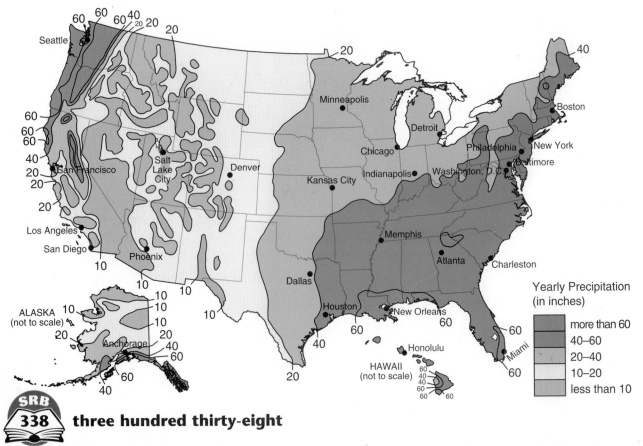

60 60 60 40 20 20 20

Seattle

20

40

60
60
60

40
20
20

20

Minneapolis

Detroit

Boston

60

Chicago

Philadelphia

New York

Salt Lake City

Denver

Indianapolis

Washington, D.C.

Baltimore

San Francisco

Kansas City

20

Los Angeles

Memphis

San Diego

Phoenix

Atlanta

Charleston

10

10

10 10

Dallas

ALASKA
(not to scale)

10

10
10

Houston

New Orleans

10

60

10

20

20

Anchorage

40

60

20

40

60

Honolulu

HAWAII
(not to scale)

60

Miami

60

40
40
60
60 60

**Yearly Precipitation
(in inches)**

more than 60
40–60
20–40
10–20
less than 10

Geography
Landform Map of the United States

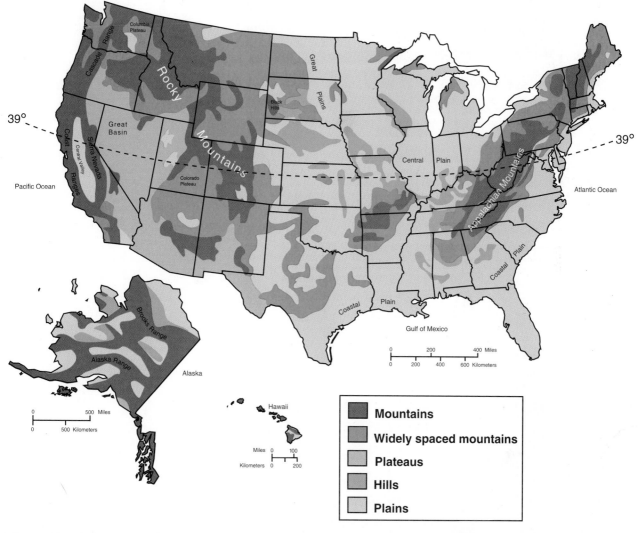

39°

39°

Columbia
Plateau

Cascade
Range

Rocky

Great
Plains

Great
Basin

Black
Hills

Coast
Ranges

Sierra Nevada

Central Valley

Colorado
Plateau

Mountains

Central   Plain

Appalachian Mountains

Pacific Ocean

Atlantic Ocean

Brooks Range

Alaska Range

Alaska

Coastal   Plain

Coastal
Plain

Coastal
Plain

Gulf of Mexico

Hawaii

| 0 | 200 | 400 Miles |
| 0 | 200 | 400 | 600 Kilometers |

| 0 | 500 Miles |
| 0 | 500 Kilometers |

| Miles | 0 | 100 |
| Kilometers | 0 | 200 |

| ■ Mountains |
| ■ Widely spaced mountains |
| ■ Plateaus |
| ■ Hills |
| ■ Plains |

Elevation along the 39th Parallel

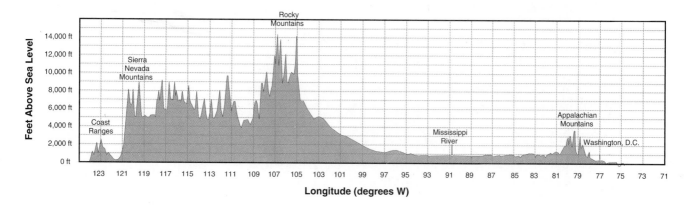

Rocky
Mountains

14,000 ft

12,000 ft

10,000 ft

Sierra
Nevada
Mountains

8,000 ft

6,000 ft

4,000 ft

Coast
Ranges

Mississippi
River

Appalachian
Mountains

2,000 ft

Washington, D.C.

0 ft

Feet Above Sea Level

123 121 119 117 115 113 111 109 107 105 103 101 99 97 95 93 91 89 87 85 83 81 79 77 75 73 71

Longitude (degrees W)

Estimated Percent of Land that is Farmland and Forest

■ Forest ■ Farmland ■ Other

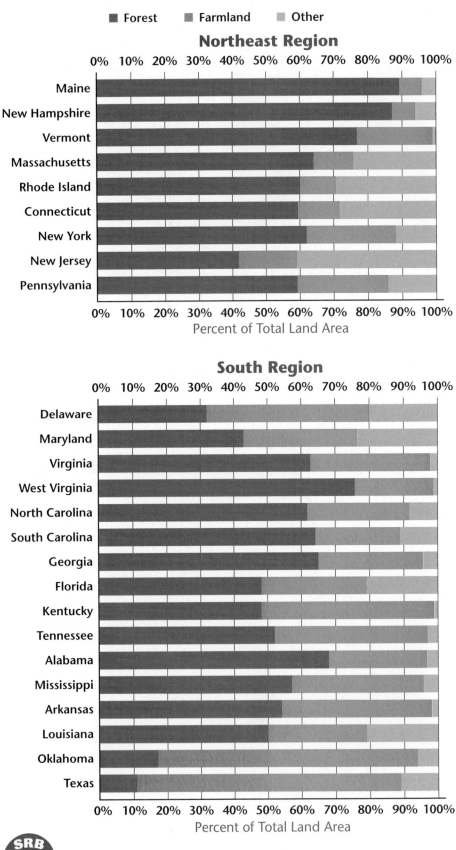

Northeast Region

Percent of Total Land Area

Farmland includes cropland, rangeland, and pastureland.

South Region

Percent of Total Land Area

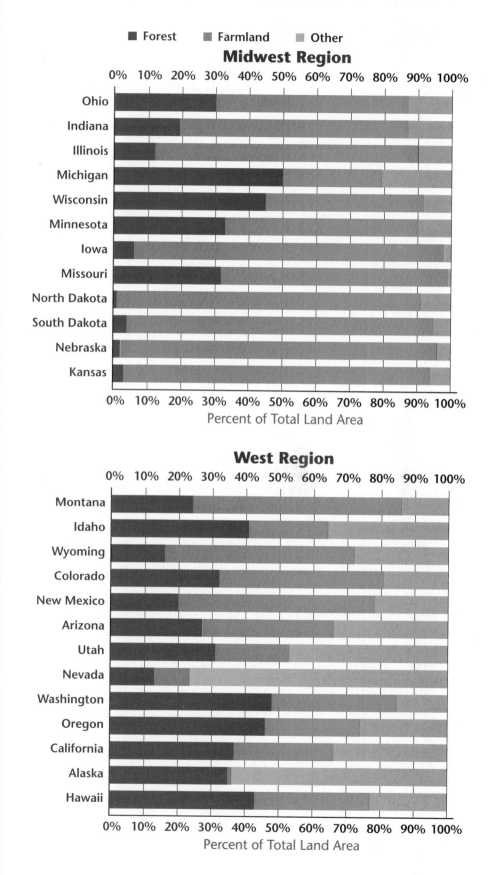

■ Forest   ■ Farmland   ■ Other

Midwest Region

0% 10% 20% 30% 40% 50% 60% 70% 80% 90% 100%

Ohio
Indiana
Illinois
Michigan
Wisconsin
Minnesota
Iowa
Missouri
North Dakota
South Dakota
Nebraska
Kansas

0% 10% 20% 30% 40% 50% 60% 70% 80% 90% 100%
Percent of Total Land Area

West Region

0% 10% 20% 30% 40% 50% 60% 70% 80% 90% 100%

Montana
Idaho
Wyoming
Colorado
New Mexico
Arizona
Utah
Nevada
Washington
Oregon
California
Alaska
Hawaii

0% 10% 20% 30% 40% 50% 60% 70% 80% 90% 100%
Percent of Total Land Area

Highest and Lowest Elevations in the United States

State	Highest Point	Altitude (ft)	Lowest Point	Elevation (ft)
Alabama	Cheaha Mountain	2,405	Gulf of Mexico	Sea level
Alaska	Mount McKinley	20,320	Pacific Ocean	Sea level
Arizona	Humphreys Peak	12,633	Colorado River	70
Arkansas	Magazine Mountain	2,753	Ouachita River	55
California	Mount Whitney	14,494	Death Valley	−282
Colorado	Mount Elbert	14,433	Arkansas River	3,350
Connecticut	Mount Frissell	2,380	Long Island Sound	Sea level
Delaware	Ebright Road (New Castle Co)	448	Atlantic Ocean	Sea level
Florida	Sec. 30, T6N, R20W (Walton Co)[1]	345	Atlantic Ocean	Sea level
Georgia	Brasstown Bald	4,784	Atlantic Ocean	Sea level
Hawaii	Mauna Kea	13,796	Pacific Ocean	Sea level
Idaho	Borah Peak	12,662	Snake River	710
Illinois	Charles Mound	1,235	Mississippi River	279
Indiana	Franklin Township (Wayne Co)	1,257	Ohio River	320
Iowa	Sec. 29, T100N, R41W (Osceola Co)[1]	1,670	Mississippi River	480
Kansas	Mount Sunflower	4,039	Verdigris River	679
Kentucky	Black Mountain	4,139	Mississippi River	257
Louisiana	Driskill Mountain	535	New Orleans	−8
Maine	Mount Katahdin	5,267	Atlantic Ocean	Sea level
Maryland	Backbone Mountain	3,360	Atlantic Ocean	Sea level
Massachusetts	Mount Greylock	3,487	Atlantic Ocean	Sea level
Michigan	Mount Arvon	1,979	Lake Erie	571
Minnesota	Eagle Mountain	2,301	Lake Superior	600
Mississippi	Woodall Mountain	806	Gulf of Mexico	Sea level
Missouri	Taum Sauk Mountain	1,772	St. Francis River	230
Montana	Granite Peak	12,799	Kootenai River	1,800
Nebraska	Johnson Township (Kimball Co)	5,424	Missouri River	840
Nevada	Boundary Peak	13,140	Colorado River	479
New Hampshire	Mount Washington	6,288	Atlantic Ocean	Sea level
New Jersey	High Point	1,803	Atlantic Ocean	Sea level
New Mexico	Wheeler Peak	13,161	Red Bluff Reservoir	2,842
New York	Mount Marcy	5,344	Atlantic Ocean	Sea level
North Carolina	Mount Mitchell	6,684	Atlantic Ocean	Sea level
North Dakota	White Butte	3,506	Red River	750
Ohio	Campbell Hill	1,549	Ohio River	455
Oklahoma	Black Mesa	4,973	Little River	289
Oregon	Mount Hood	11,239	Pacific Ocean	Sea level
Pennsylvania	Mount Davis	3,213	Delaware River	Sea level
Rhode Island	Jerimoth Hill	812	Atlantic Ocean	Sea level
South Carolina	Sassafras Mountain	3,560	Atlantic Ocean	Sea level
South Dakota	Harney Peak	7,242	Big Stone Lake	966
Tennessee	Clingmans Dome	6,643	Mississippi River	178
Texas	Guadalupe Peak	8,749	Gulf of Mexico	Sea level
Utah	Kings Peak	13,528	Beaverdam Wash	2,000
Vermont	Mount Mansfield	4,393	Lake Champlain	95
Virginia	Mount Rogers	5,729	Atlantic Ocean	Sea level
Washington	Mount Rainier	14,410	Pacific Ocean	Sea level
West Virginia	Spruce Knob	4,861	Potomac River	240
Wisconsin	Timms Hill	1,951	Lake Michigan	579
Wyoming	Gannett Peak	13,804	Belle Fourche River	3,099

[1] "Sec." means Section; "T" means Township; "R" means Range; "N" means North; and "W" means West.

Latitude and Longitude of State Capitals

Postal Abbreviation	State	Capital	Latitude	Longitude
AL	Alabama	Montgomery	32° 23' N	86° 19' W
AK	Alaska	Juneau	58° 18' N	134° 25' W
AZ	Arizona	Phoenix	33° 27' N	112° 04' W
AR	Arkansas	Little Rock	34° 45' N	92° 17' W
CA	California	Sacramento	38° 35' N	121° 30' W
CO	Colorado	Denver	39° 45' N	104° 59' W
CT	Connecticut	Hartford	41° 46' N	72° 41' W
DE	Delaware	Dover	39° 10' N	75° 31' W
FL	Florida	Tallahassee	30° 27' N	84° 17' W
GA	Georgia	Atlanta	33° 45' N	84° 24' W
HI	Hawaii	Honolulu	21° 18' N	157° 52' W
ID	Idaho	Boise	43° 37' N	116° 12' W
IL	Illinois	Springfield	39° 48' N	89° 39' W
IN	Indiana	Indianapolis	39° 46' N	86° 10' W
IA	Iowa	Des Moines	41° 35' N	93° 37' W
KS	Kansas	Topeka	39° 03' N	95° 40' W
KY	Kentucky	Frankfort	38° 11' N	84° 52' W
LA	Louisiana	Baton Rouge	30° 27' N	91° 11' W
ME	Maine	Augusta	44° 19' N	69° 46' W
MD	Maryland	Annapolis	38° 58' N	76° 30' W
MA	Massachusetts	Boston	42° 21' N	71° 03' W
MI	Michigan	Lansing	42° 44' N	84° 33' W
MN	Minnesota	St. Paul	44° 57' N	93° 06' W
MS	Mississippi	Jackson	32° 18' N	90° 11' W
MO	Missouri	Jefferson City	38° 34' N	92° 11' W
MT	Montana	Helena	46° 36' N	112° 02' W
NE	Nebraska	Lincoln	40° 49' N	96° 42' W
NV	Nevada	Carson City	39° 10' N	119° 46' W
NH	New Hampshire	Concord	43° 12' N	71° 32' W
NJ	New Jersey	Trenton	40° 13' N	74° 46' W
NM	New Mexico	Santa Fe	35° 41' N	105° 56' W
NY	New York	Albany	42° 39' N	73° 45' W
NC	North Carolina	Raleigh	35° 47' N	78° 38' W
ND	North Dakota	Bismarck	46° 48' N	100° 47' W
OH	Ohio	Columbus	39° 58' N	83° 00' W
OK	Oklahoma	Oklahoma City	35° 28' N	97° 31' W
OR	Oregon	Salem	44° 56' N	123° 02' W
PA	Pennsylvania	Harrisburg	40° 16' N	76° 53' W
RI	Rhode Island	Providence	41° 50' N	71° 25' W
SC	South Carolina	Columbia	34° 00' N	81° 02' W
SD	South Dakota	Pierre	44° 22' N	100° 21' W
TN	Tennessee	Nashville	36° 10' N	86° 47' W
TX	Texas	Austin	30° 16' N	97° 45' W
UT	Utah	Salt Lake City	40° 45' N	111° 53' W
VT	Vermont	Montpelier	44° 16' N	72° 35' W
VA	Virginia	Richmond	37° 32' N	77° 26' W
WA	Washington	Olympia	47° 03' N	122° 54' W
WV	West Virginia	Charleston	38° 21' N	81° 38' W
WI	Wisconsin	Madison	43° 04' N	89° 23' W
WY	Wyoming	Cheyenne	41° 08' N	104° 49' W

125°W   120°W   115°W   110°W   105°W   100°W

50°N

WASHINGTON
Seattle
Olympia
Spokane

Columbia River

45°N
Portland
Salem

Helena

MONTANA

Missouri River

NORTH
DAKOTA
Bismarck

OREGON

Boise
IDAHO

SOUTH
DAKOTA
Pierre

Snake River

Sioux Fal

40°N

Sacramento River

Great Salt Lake

WYOMING

NEBRASKA

Sacramento

Cheyenne

Platte River

San Francisco

Carson City

Salt Lake City

Oakland
San Jose

NEVADA

UTAH

Denver
Colorado
Springs

Lincol

35°N

Fresno

Colorado River

COLORADO

Arkansas River

KANSAS
Wichita

CALIFORNIA
Las Vegas

Los Angeles
Long Beach

Santa Fe
Albuquerque

OKLAHOMA
Oklahoma
City

Amarillo

San Diego

ARIZONA
Phoenix
Mesa

NEW
MEXICO

Red Rive

30°N

PACIFIC
OCEAN

Tucson

Dallas
Fort Worth Arling

El Paso

Brazos River

TEXAS

Rio Grande

M E X I C O

Austin

San Antonio

70°N
170°W 160°W 150°W 140°W 130°W 120°W
Arctic Circle
CANADA
Yukon River
ALASKA
Anchorage
60°N
Bering
Sea
Juneau

50°N
PACIFIC OCEAN

0   350   700
1 inch represents
700 miles.

160°W 155°W
H A W A I I
Honolulu
20°N

0   125   250
1 inch represents
250 miles.
PACIFIC OCEAN

115°W   110°W   105°W   100°W

95°W 90°W 85°W 80°W 75°W 70°W 65°W

50°N

45°N

CANADA

MAINE

MINNESOTA

Lake Superior

Augusta

Montpelier

WISCONSIN

St. Paul

MICHIGAN

VERMONT

NEW HAMPSHIRE

Concord

Minneapolis

Milwaukee

Madison

Lake Michigan

Lake Huron

Lansing

Grand Rapids

Detroit

Lake Ontario

Buffalo

NEW YORK

Albany

Boston

MASSACHUSETTS

Hartford

Providence

RHODE ISLAND

CONNECTICUT

40°N

IOWA

Chicago

Toledo

Lake Erie

Cleveland

PENNSYLVANIA

Harrisburg

Pittsburgh

Philadelphia

Newark

New York

Trenton

NEW JERSEY

Dover

DELAWARE

Des Moines

ILLINOIS

INDIANA

OHIO

Columbus

Cincinnati

WEST VIRGINIA

Baltimore

Annapolis

Washington, D.C.

MARYLAND

Omaha

Kansas City

Springfield

Indianapolis

Frankfort

Charleston

Richmond

Virginia Beach

35°N

Jefferson City

St. Louis

Ohio River

Louisville

Lexington

VIRGINIA

MISSOURI

KENTUCKY

NORTH CAROLINA

Nashville

Raleigh

Tulsa

ARKANSAS

TENNESSEE

Tennessee River

Charlotte

Columbia

ATLANTIC OCEAN

Little Rock

Memphis

SOUTH CAROLINA

MISSISSIPPI

Birmingham

Atlanta

Charleston

LOUISIANA

Jackson

ALABAMA

Montgomery

GEORGIA

Chattahoochee River

Savannah

30°N

Mobile

Jacksonville

Baton Rouge

Tallahassee

Houston

New Orleans

FLORIDA

Orlando

★ National Capital

★ State Capital

● City

Tampa

Gulf of Mexico

25°N

0   100   200

1 inch represents 200 miles.

Miami

95°W   90°W   85°W   80°W

U.S. Highway Distances (Miles)

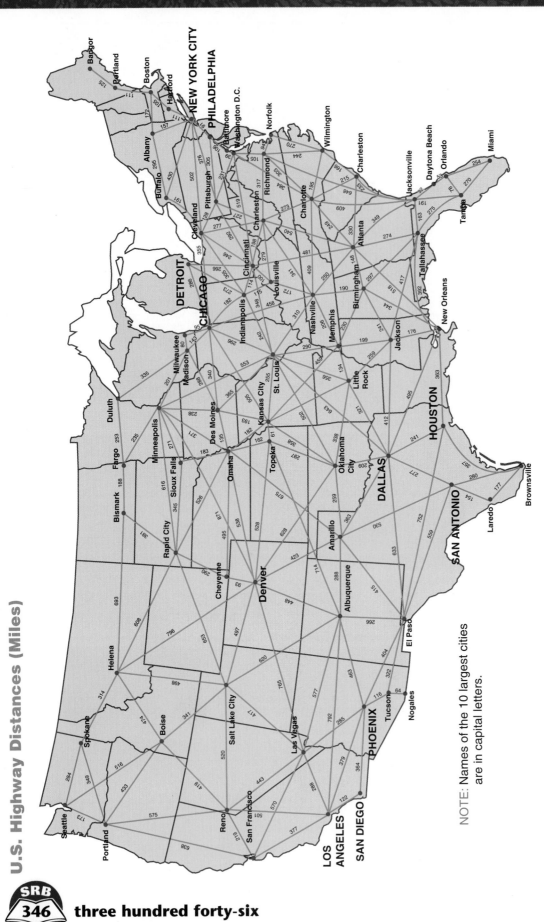

NOTE: Names of the 10 largest cities are in capital letters.

U.S. Air Distances (miles)

	Atlanta	Boston	Chicago	Dallas	Denver	Detroit	Houston	Kansas City	Los Angeles	Miami	Minneapolis	New Orleans	New York	Omaha	Philadelphia	Phoenix	Pittsburgh	Portland	St. Louis	Salt Lake City	San Francisco	Seattle
Boston	940																					
Chicago	600	860																				
Dallas	720	1550	790																			
Denver	1200	1760	900	650																		
Detroit	590	630	230	980	1130																	
Houston	680	1600	920	210	860	1090																
Kansas City	680	1250	400	450	540	630	640															
Los Angeles	1940	2610	1740	1240	840	1970	1370	1360														
Miami	590	1250	1190	1110	1710	1140	960	1230	2340													
Minneapolis	900	1120	330	850	690	520	1040	390	1530	1500												
New Orleans	420	1360	830	430	1060	930	300	690	1670	670	1040											
New York	760	180	740	1380	1630	500	1410	1110	2470	1090	1020	1180										
Omaha	820	1280	410	580	480	650	790	150	1330	1390	280	840	1150									
Philadelphia	660	280	670	1290	1560	450	1320	1030	2400	1010	980	1090	90	1090								
Phoenix	1580	2300	1440	870	580	1680	1010	1040	370	1970	1270	1300	2140	1030	2080							
Pittsburgh	520	490	410	1060	1300	200	1120	760	2130	1010	720	910	340	820	260	1810						
Portland	2170	2530	1730	1630	980	1950	1830	1490	830	2700	1420	2050	2450	1360	2410	1000	2140					
St. Louis	480	1040	250	540	780	440	660	220	1590	1060	440	600	890	340	810	1260	550	1700				
Salt Lake City	1580	2100	1240	1010	380	1480	1200	910	590	2080	990	1420	1980	830	1930	500	1650	630	1150			
San Francisco	2130	2700	1840	1470	950	2070	1630	1490	330	2580	1580	1910	2580	1430	2520	650	2250	550	1730	590		
Seattle	2180	2490	1720	1670	1010	1930	1870	1480	950	2720	1390	2080	2420	1360	2380	1100	2120	130	1700	680	670	
Washington, D.C.	530	410	590	1160	1460	380	1180	920	2280	910	900	960	220	1000	130	1950	180	2330	690	1830	2410	2300

Area, Length, and Width of States

State	Land Area (sq mi)	Inland Water Area (sq mi)	Total Area (sq mi)	Length[1] (mi)	Width[1] (mi)
Alabama	50,750	968	51,718	330	190
Alaska	570,374	17,501	587,875	1,480	810
Arizona	113,642	364	114,006	400	310
Arkansas	52,075	1,107	53,182	260	240
California	155,973	2,674	158,647	770	250
Colorado	103,729	371	104,100	380	280
Connecticut	4,845	161	5,006	110	70
Delaware	1,955	71	2,026	100	30
Florida	53,937	4,683	58,620	500	160
Georgia	57,919	1,011	58,930	300	230
Hawaii	6,423	36	6,459	—	—
Idaho	82,751	823	83,574	570	300
Illinois	55,593	750	56,343	390	210
Indiana	35,870	315	36,185	270	140
Iowa	55,875	401	56,276	310	200
Kansas	81,823	459	82,282	400	210
Kentucky	39,732	679	40,411	380	140
Louisiana	43,566	4,153	47,719	380	130
Maine	30,865	2,263	33,128	320	190
Maryland	9,775	680	10,455	250	90
Massachusetts	7,838	424	8,262	190	50
Michigan	56,809	1,704	58,513	490	240
Minnesota	79,617	4,780	84,397	400	250
Mississippi	46,914	781	47,695	340	170
Missouri	68,898	811	69,709	300	240
Montana	145,556	1,490	147,046	630	280
Nebraska	76,878	481	77,359	430	210
Nevada	109,806	761	110,567	490	320
New Hampshire	8,969	314	9,283	190	70
New Jersey	7,419	371	7,790	150	70
New Mexico	121,364	234	121,598	370	343
New York	47,224	1,888	49,112	330	283
North Carolina	48,718	3,954	52,672	500	150
North Dakota	68,994	1,710	70,704	340	211
Ohio	40,953	376	41,329	220	220
Oklahoma	68,679	1,224	69,903	400	220
Oregon	96,002	1,050	97,052	360	261
Pennsylvania	44,820	490	45,310	283	160
Rhode Island	1,045	168	1,213	40	30
South Carolina	30,111	1,006	31,117	260	200
South Dakota	75,896	1,225	77,121	380	210
Tennessee	41,219	926	42,145	440	120
Texas	261,914	4,959	266,873	790	660
Utah	82,168	2,736	84,904	350	270
Vermont	9,249	366	9,615	160	80
Virginia	39,598	1,000	40,598	430	200
Washington	66,581	1,545	68,126	360	240
West Virginia	24,087	145	24,232	240	130
Wisconsin	54,314	1,831	56,145	310	260
Wyoming	97,105	714	97,819	360	280

[1]Length and Width are approximate averages for each state.
Land area equals dry land and land temporarily or partially covered by water, such as marshland and swamps.

Facts and Questions

National Facts

Fact or Feature	Location	Data Recorded as of 2000
Largest State	Alaska	615,230 sq mi
Smallest State	Rhode Island	1,231 sq mi
Northernmost Point	Point Barrow, Alaska	71° 23' N
Southernmost Point	Ka Lae (South Cape), Hawaii	18° 55' N
Easternmost Point	Semisopochnoi Island, Alaska[1]	179° 46' E
Westernmost Point	Amatignak Island, Alaska	179° 06' W
Highest Settlement	Climax, Colorado	11,360 ft above sea level
Lowest Settlement	Calipatria, California	184 ft below sea level
Oldest National Park	Yellowstone National Park Wyoming, Montana, Idaho	Established 1872
Largest National Park	Wrangell–St. Elias, Alaska	13,006 sq mi
Smallest National Park	Hot Springs, Arkansas	9 sq mi
Highest Waterfall	Yosemite Falls:	
	Total of three sections	2,425 ft
	Upper Yosemite Fall	1,430 ft
	Cascades in middle section	675 ft
	Lower Yosemite Fall	320 ft
Longest River	Mississippi–Missouri	3,710 mi
Highest Mountain	Mount McKinley, Alaska	20,320 ft above sea level
Lowest Point	Death Valley, California	282 ft below sea level
Deepest Lake	Crater Lake, Oregon	1,932 ft
Rainiest Spot	Mt. Waialeale, Hawaii	Annual average rainfall: 460 inches
Largest Gorge	Grand Canyon, Colorado River, Arizona	277 mi long, 600 ft to 18 mi wide, 1 mi deep
Deepest Gorge	Hell's Canyon, Snake River, Idaho–Oregon	7,900 ft deep
Strongest Surface Wind	Mount Washington, New Hampshire, recorded 1934	231 mph
Biggest Dam	New Cornelia Tailings, Tenmile Wash, Arizona	274,026,000 cu yds of material used
Tallest Building	Sears Tower, Chicago, Illinois	1,454 ft
Largest Building	Boeing 747 Manufacturing Plant, Everett, Washington	205,600,000 cu ft; covers 47 acres
Tallest Structure	TV Tower, Blanchard, North Dakota	2,063 ft
Longest Bridge Span	Verrazano–Narrows, New York	4,260 ft
Highest Bridge	Royal Gorge, Colorado	1,053 ft above water
Deepest Well	Gas Well, Washita County, Oklahoma	31,441 ft

[1] Alaska's Aleutian Islands extend into the Eastern Hemisphere. The Aleutian Islands technically contain the easternmost point in the United States. If Alaska is excluded, the easternmost point in the United States is West Quoddy Head, Maine (66° 57' W).

Abbreviations: ft = foot   mi = mile   mph = miles per hour
sq mi = square mile   cu ft = cubic foot
cu yd = cubic yard

Explore More

Here are some questions that can be answered with information in the American Tour. Think of more questions of your own.

- How does your state compare with other states? Use data displays to compare your state to the average or median state, or to show where your state falls in the distribution of all states. Place your results in the American Tour corner of your classroom.

- What are some interesting features and facts about your state or another state? Use the information in the American Tour to create a State Almanac. For example, in what year did your state become a state? What are the highest and lowest points in your state? How does your state's population in 2000 compare with its population in 1900? In 1850? In 1790?

Here are some questions that can be answered by looking in other almanacs, atlases, and reference books.

- What are the highest and lowest recorded temperatures in different states? Make a display that shows which states had their highest and lowest temperatures in each decade of the twentieth century. Look for patterns.

- How has technology spread? How many cars, telephones, computers, and other devices were there in each decade of the twentieth century? How many of each were there per person? Make a line graph or bar graph that shows this information.

- In the last U.S. presidential election, how many electoral and popular votes did each candidate receive? What percent of the total electoral or popular vote did each receive? What percent of the total popular vote did each candidate receive in your state? Make circle graphs that display this information.

- When did important historical events occur? When were things such as the telephone, polio vaccine, or the computer invented, discovered, or first used? When did famous people, such as artists, actors, scientists, or sports figures, live? Make timelines to show your findings.

References

Bibliography

The American Almanac. Austin, Texas: The Reference Press, 1993, 1994.

The Cambridge Factfinder. David Crystal, editor. New York: Cambridge University Press, 1997.

A Century of Population Growth 1790–1900. Reprint of 1909 publication by the Government Printing Office. Baltimore: Genealogical Publishing Company, 1989.

Hakim, Joy. *Colonies to Country* (Book 3 in A *History of US*). *Liberty for All* (Book 5 in *A History of US*). New York: Oxford University Press, 1994.

Hammond United States Atlas. Gemini Edition. Maplewood, New Jersey: Hammond Inc., 1993.

Historical Atlas of the United States. Vols. 1 and 2. William Graves, editor. Washington, D.C.: National Geographic Society, 1993.

Historical Statistics of the United States: Colonial Times to 1970. U.S. Department of Commerce, Bureau of the Census. Washington, D.C.: Government Printing Office. 1975.

Kaestle, Carl. *Pillars of the Republic: Common Schools and American Society 1780–1860.* New York: Hill and Wang, 1983.

Larkin, Jack. *The Reshaping of Everyday Life 1790–1840.* New York: HarperCollins, 1989.

National Center for Education Statistics. U.S. Department of Education. Washington, D.C.: http://nces.ed.gov/

The New York Public Library Book of Chronologies. Bruce Wetterau, editor. New York: Prentice Hall, 1990.

Prisoners of Time. National Education Commission on Time and Learning. Washington, D.C.: Government Printing Office, 1994.

Snipp, C. Matthew. *American Indians: The First of This Land.* New York: Russell Sage Foundation, 1989.

Statistical Abstract of the United States. U.S. Department of Commerce, Bureau of the Census. Washington, D.C.: Government Printing Office, 1999, 2000.

Statistical Atlas of the United States. Washington, D.C.: Government Printing Office, 1914.

Statistics of State School Systems. U.S. Bureau of Education. Washington, D.C.: Government Printing Office, 1901.

The Universal Almanac. Kansas City, Missouri: Andrews & McMeel. 1995.

The World Almanac® and Book of Facts 2000. Mahwah, New Jersey: World Almanac Books, 1999.

The United States Bureau of the Census, Washington, D.C.
http://www.census.gov/

Sources

299 Information and migration map: Derived from UCSMP research.

300 Map: *Historical Atlas of the United States.*

301 Map: based on information from U.S. Census Bureau projections and *Statistical Abstract of the United States.*

302 Graph: *Historical Atlas of the United States;* Table: data from *Statistical Abstract of the United States.*

303 Immigration Graph and Table: *Historical Statistics of the United States* and *Statistical Abstract of the United States;* Foreign-Born Population Graph and Table: *The World Almanac 2000.*

304 Map: based on 1990 U.S. Census data.

305 Map: *Historical Atlas of the United States;* Percent bar and table: information from *Historical Statistics of the United States.*

306 "19th Century Settlement Patterns" Map: based on information from *Statistical Atlas of the United States;* "The Center of Population Moving West" Map: based on *The American Almanac* and UCSMP research.

307 Map: information from *The New York Public Library Book of Chronologies.*

308–309 Data for Area taken from *Historical Statistics of the United States;* Data for Population taken from *Statistical Abstract of the United States,* and *The World Almanac 2000,* and U.S. Census Bureau projections.

310 Table: data based on *A Century of Population Growth 1790–1900.*

311 Table: information from *Historical Atlas of the United States;* Larkin; and Hakim, *Liberty for All;* Graph: based on *Historical Atlas of the United States.*

312 Map: information from *Historical Atlas of the United States.*

313 Information from *The New York Public Library Book of Chronologies;* Train schedule information from Amtrak; Airline schedule information from American Airlines.

314–315 Data from *Historical Statistics of the United States, Statistical Abstract of the United States,* and *The World Almanac 2000.*

316 Data from *Historical Statistics of the United States, The World Almanac 2000, Statistical Abstract of the United States,* and Nielsen Research.

317 Data from *Statistical Abstract of the United States.*

318 "Who Went to School in 1790?" information from Kaestle; "Who Went to School in 1900?" information from 1900 U.S. Census and *Statistics of State School Systems.*

319 Data from *Statistics of State School Systems.*

320 Graphs: data from National Center for Education Statistics.

321 Data from *Statistical Abstract of the United States.*

322 Graph "U.S. Population by Age and Gender, 1900": data from *Twelfth Census of the United States,1900;* Graph "U.S. Population by Age and Gender, 2000": data from U.S. Census Bureau projections; Graph "Median Age of the U.S. Population: data from *Statistical Abstract of the United States* and *The World Almanac 2000.*

323 Table and Graph: data from *The World Almanac 2000* and *Statistical Abstract of the United States.*

324–325 Information from the U.S. Constitution, *Historical Statistics of the United States,* and the 2000 Census.

326 Information from *Historical Statistics of the United States*; Graph: data from *Historical Statistics of the United States, The American Almanac,* and UCSMP research.

327–328 Information from U.S. Bureau of the Census.

329 Data from *A Century of Population Growth 1790–1900.*

330–331 Derived from 2000 U.S. Census Forms D-61A and D-61B.

332–333 Data from *The Universal Almanac* and *Statistical Abstract of the United States* and U.S. Census Bureau projections.

334 Urban/Rural Population data from *Historical Statistics of the United States* and United Nations Statistics Division; Household Size data from *Statistical Abstract of the United States.*

335 Map: information from *The World Almanac 2000.*

336–337 Temperature Maps: based on data from National Oceanic and Atmospheric Administration.

338 Growing Seasons Map: based on data from National Weather Service; Precipitation Map: based on data from National Oceanic and Atmospheric Administration.

339 Landform Map: based on data from U.S. Geological Survey; Graph: based on *Historical Atlas of the United States.*

340–341 Based on data from *The World Almanac 2000.*

342 Data from *The World Almanac 2000.*

343 Data from *The World Almanac 2000.*

344–345 Map: based on data from ArcWorld 1:3m and World 25m by ESRI Data & Maps.

346 Highway distances: based on Rand McNally *Road Atlas 2000.*

347 Air distances: based on *The Cambridge Factfinder.*

348 Land and Inland Water Area: data from *Statistical Abstract of the United States*; Length and Width: data from *World Almanac 2000.*

349 Information from *The World Almanac 2000.*

Place-Value Chart

	billions	100 millions	10 millions	millions	100 thousands	10 thousands	thousands	hundreds	tens	ones	.	tenths	hundredths	thousandths
	1,000 millions	100,000,000s	10,000,000s	1,000,000s	100,000s	10,000s	1,000s	100s	10s	1s	.	0.1s	0.01s	0.001s
	10^9	10^8	10^7	10^6	10^5	10^4	10^3	10^2	10^1	10^0	.	10^{-1}	10^{-2}	10^{-3}

Prefixes

uni- . . . . .one	tera- . . . .trillion (10^{12})
bi- . . . . .two	giga- . . . .billion (10^9)
tri- . . . . .three	mega- . . .million (10^6)
quad- . . . . . . .four	kilo- . . . . .thousand (10^3)
penta- . . . . . . .five	hecto- . . .hundred (10^2)
hexa- . . . . . . .six	deca- . . .ten (10^1)
hepta- . . . . . . .seven	uni- . . . . .one (10^0)
octa- . . . . .eight	deci- . . . .tenth (10^{-1})
nona- . . . . . . .nine	centi- . . . .hundredth (10^{-2})
deca- . . . . . . .ten	milli- . . . .thousandth (10^{-3})
dodeca- . . . . .twelve	micro- . . .millionth (10^{-6})
icosa- . . . . . . .twenty	nano- . . .billionth (10^{-9})

Multiplication and Division Table

*,/	1	2	3	4	5	6	7	8	9	10	11	12
1	1	2	3	4	5	6	7	8	9	10	11	12
2	2	4	6	8	10	12	14	16	18	20	22	24
3	3	6	9	12	15	18	21	24	27	30	33	36
4	4	8	12	16	20	24	28	32	36	40	44	48
5	5	10	15	20	25	30	35	40	45	50	55	60
6	6	12	18	24	30	36	42	48	54	60	66	72
7	7	14	21	28	35	42	49	56	63	70	77	84
8	8	16	24	32	40	48	56	64	72	80	88	96
9	9	18	27	36	45	54	63	72	81	90	99	108
10	10	20	30	40	50	60	70	80	90	100	110	120
11	11	22	33	44	55	66	77	88	99	110	121	132
12	12	24	36	48	60	72	84	96	108	120	132	144

Rules for Order of Operations

1. Do operations within parentheses or other grouping symbols before doing anything else.
2. Calculate all powers.
3. Do multiplications or divisions in order, from left to right.
4. Then do additions or subtractions in order, from left to right.

Metric System
Units of Length

1 kilometer (km)	= 1,000 meters (m)
1 meter	= 10 decimeters (dm)
	= 100 centimeters (cm)
	= 1,000 millimeters (mm)
1 decimeter	= 10 centimeters
1 centimeter	= 10 millimeters

Units of Area

1 square meter (m^2)	= 100 square decimeters (dm^2)
	= 10,000 square centimeters (cm^2)
1 square decimeter	= 100 square centimeters
1 square kilometer	= 1,000,000 square meters

Units of Volume

1 cubic meter (m^3)	= 1,000 cubic decimeters (dm^3)
	= 1,000,000 cubic centimeters (cm^3)
1 cubic decimeter	= 1,000 cubic centimeters

Units of Capacity

1 kiloliter (kL)	= 1,000 liters (L)
1 liter	= 1,000 milliliters (mL)
1 cubic centimeter	= 1 milliliter

Units of Mass

1 metric ton (t)	= 1,000 kilograms (kg)
1 kilogram	= 1,000 grams (g)
1 gram	= 1,000 milligrams (mg)

System Equivalents

1 inch is about 2.5 cm (2.54)
1 kilometer is about 0.6 mile (0.621)
1 mile is about 1.6 kilometers (1.609)
1 meter is about 39 inches (39.37)
1 liter is about 1.1 quarts (1.057)
1 ounce is about 28 grams (28.350)
1 kilogram is about 2.2 pounds (2.205)

U.S. Customary System
Units of Length

1 mile (mi)	= 1,760 yards (yd)
	= 5,280 feet (ft)
1 yard	= 3 feet
	= 36 inches (in.)
1 foot	= 12 inches

Units of Area

1 square yard (yd^2)	= 9 square feet (ft^2)
	= 1,296 square inches ($in.^2$)
1 square foot	= 144 square inches
1 acre	= 43,560 square feet
1 square mile (mi^2)	= 640 acres

Units of Volume

1 cubic yard (yd^3)	= 27 cubic feet (ft^3)
1 cubic foot	= 1,728 cubic inches ($in.^3$)

Units of Capacity

1 gallon (gal)	= 4 quarts (qt)
1 quart	= 2 pints (pt)
1 pint	= 2 cups (c)
1 cup	= 8 fluid ounces (fl oz)
1 fluid ounce	= 2 tablespoons (tbs)
1 tablespoon	= 3 teaspoons (tsp)

Units of Weight

1 ton (T)	= 2,000 pounds (lb)
1 pound	= 16 ounces (oz)

Units of Time

1 century	= 100 years
1 decade	= 10 years
1 year (yr)	= 12 months
	= 52 weeks (plus one or two days)
	= 365 days (366 days in a leap year)
1 month (mo)	= 28, 29, 30, or 31 days
1 week (wk)	= 7 days
1 day (d)	= 24 hours
1 hour (hr)	= 60 minutes
1 minute (min)	= 60 seconds (sec)

Decimal and Percent Equivalents for "Easy" Fractions

"Easy" Fractions	Decimals	Percents
$\frac{1}{2}$	0.50	50%
$\frac{1}{3}$	$0.\overline{3}$	$33\frac{1}{3}\%$
$\frac{2}{3}$	$0.\overline{6}$	$66\frac{2}{3}\%$
$\frac{1}{4}$	0.25	25%
$\frac{3}{4}$	0.75	75%
$\frac{1}{5}$	0.20	20%
$\frac{2}{5}$	0.40	40%
$\frac{3}{5}$	0.60	60%
$\frac{4}{5}$	0.80	80%
$\frac{1}{6}$	$0.1\overline{6}$	$16\frac{2}{3}\%$
$\frac{1}{8}$	0.125	$12\frac{1}{2}\%$
$\frac{3}{8}$	0.375	$37\frac{1}{2}\%$
$\frac{5}{8}$	0.625	$62\frac{1}{2}\%$
$\frac{7}{8}$	0.875	$87\frac{1}{2}\%$
$\frac{1}{10}$	0.10	10%
$\frac{3}{10}$	0.30	30%
$\frac{7}{10}$	0.70	70%
$\frac{9}{10}$	0.90	90%

The Global Grid

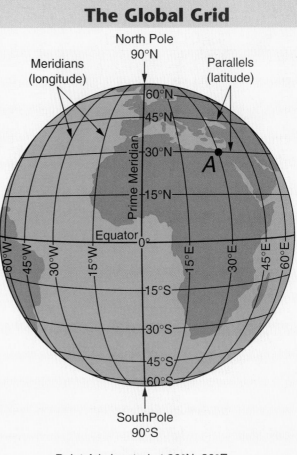

Point A is located at 30°N, 30°E.

Fraction-Decimal Number Line

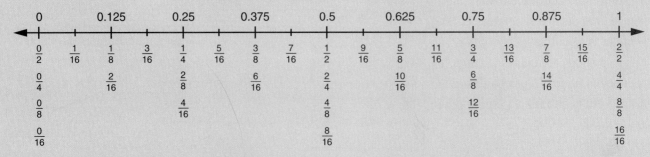

Fraction-Stick and Decimal Number-Line Chart

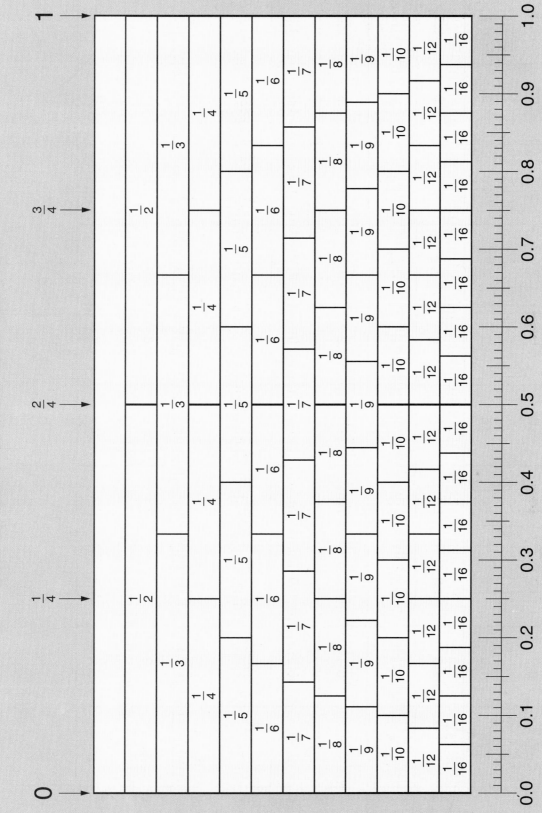

Table of Decimal Equivalents for Fractions

Denominator \ Numerator	1	2	3	4	5	6	7	8	9	10
1	1.0	2.0	3.0	4.0	5.0	6.0	7.0	8.0	9.0	10.0
2	0.5	1.0	1.5	2.0	2.5	3.0	3.5	4.0	4.5	5.0
3	$0.\overline{3}$	$0.\overline{6}$	1.0	$1.\overline{3}$	$1.\overline{6}$	2.0	$2.\overline{3}$	$2.\overline{6}$	3.0	$3.\overline{3}$
4	0.25	0.5	0.75	1.0	1.25	1.5	1.75	2.0	2.25	2.5
5	0.2	0.4	0.6	0.8	1.0	1.2	1.4	1.6	1.8	2.0
6	$0.1\overline{6}$	$0.\overline{3}$	0.5	$0.\overline{6}$	$0.8\overline{3}$	1.0	$1.1\overline{6}$	$1.\overline{3}$	1.5	$1.\overline{6}$
7	$0.\overline{142857}$	$0.\overline{285714}$	$0.\overline{428571}$	$0.\overline{571428}$	$0.\overline{714285}$	$0.\overline{857142}$	1.0	$1.\overline{142857}$	$1.\overline{285714}$	$1.\overline{428571}$
8	0.125	0.25	.375	0.5	0.625	0.75	0.875	1.0	1.125	1.25
9	$0.\overline{1}$	$0.\overline{2}$	$0.\overline{3}$	$0.\overline{4}$	$0.\overline{5}$	$0.\overline{6}$	$0.\overline{7}$	$0.\overline{8}$	1.0	$1.\overline{1}$
10	0.1	0.2	0.3	0.4	0.5	0.6	0.7	0.8	0.9	1.0

Equivalent Fractions, Decimals, and Percents

															Decimal	Percent
1/2	2/4	3/6	4/8	5/10	6/12	7/14	8/16	9/18	10/20	11/22	12/24	13/26	14/28	15/30	0.5	50%
1/3	2/6	3/9	4/12	5/15	6/18	7/21	8/24	9/27	10/30	11/33	12/36	13/39	14/42	15/45	$0.\overline{3}$	$33\frac{1}{3}\%$
2/3	4/6	6/9	8/12	10/15	12/18	14/21	16/24	18/27	20/30	22/33	24/36	26/39	28/42	30/45	$0.\overline{6}$	$66\frac{2}{3}\%$
1/4	2/8	3/12	4/16	5/20	6/24	7/28	8/32	9/36	10/40	11/44	12/48	13/52	14/56	15/60	0.25	25%
3/4	6/8	9/12	12/16	15/20	18/24	21/28	24/32	27/36	30/40	33/44	36/48	39/52	42/56	45/60	0.75	75%
1/5	2/10	3/15	4/20	5/25	6/30	7/35	8/40	9/45	10/50	11/55	12/60	13/65	14/70	15/75	0.2	20%
2/5	4/10	6/15	8/20	10/25	12/30	14/35	16/40	18/45	20/50	22/55	24/60	26/65	28/70	30/75	0.4	40%
3/5	6/10	9/15	12/20	15/25	18/30	21/35	24/40	27/45	30/50	33/55	36/60	39/65	42/70	45/75	0.6	60%
4/5	8/10	12/15	16/20	20/25	24/30	28/35	32/40	36/45	40/50	44/55	48/60	52/65	56/70	60/75	0.8	80%
1/6	2/12	3/18	4/24	5/30	6/36	7/42	8/48	9/54	10/60	11/66	12/72	13/78	14/84	15/90	$0.1\overline{6}$	$16\frac{2}{3}\%$
5/6	10/12	15/18	20/24	25/30	30/36	35/42	40/48	45/54	50/60	55/66	60/72	65/78	70/84	75/90	$0.8\overline{3}$	$83\frac{1}{3}\%$
1/7	2/14	3/21	4/28	5/35	6/42	7/49	8/56	9/63	10/70	11/77	12/84	13/91	14/98	15/105	0.143	14.3%
2/7	4/14	6/21	8/28	10/35	12/42	14/49	16/56	18/63	20/70	22/77	24/84	26/91	28/98	30/105	0.286	28.6%
3/7	6/14	9/21	12/28	15/35	18/42	21/49	24/56	27/63	30/70	33/77	36/84	39/91	42/98	45/105	0.429	42.9%
4/7	8/14	12/21	16/28	20/35	24/42	28/49	32/56	36/63	40/70	44/77	48/84	52/91	56/98	60/105	0.571	57.1%
5/7	10/14	15/21	20/28	25/35	30/42	35/49	40/56	45/63	50/70	55/77	60/84	65/91	70/98	75/105	0.714	71.4%
6/7	12/14	18/21	24/28	30/35	36/42	42/49	48/56	54/63	60/70	66/77	72/84	78/91	84/98	90/105	0.857	85.7%
1/8	2/16	3/24	4/32	5/40	6/48	7/56	8/64	9/72	10/80	11/88	12/96	13/104	14/112	15/120	0.125	$12\frac{1}{2}\%$
3/8	6/16	9/24	12/32	15/40	18/48	21/56	24/64	27/72	30/80	33/88	36/96	39/104	42/112	45/120	0.375	$37\frac{1}{2}\%$
5/8	10/16	15/24	20/32	25/40	30/48	35/56	40/64	45/72	50/80	55/88	60/96	65/104	70/112	75/120	0.625	$62\frac{1}{2}\%$
7/8	14/16	21/24	28/32	35/40	42/48	49/56	56/64	63/72	70/80	77/88	84/96	91/104	98/112	105/120	0.875	$87\frac{1}{2}\%$
1/9	2/18	3/27	4/36	5/45	6/54	7/63	8/72	9/81	10/90	11/99	12/108	13/117	14/126	15/135	$0.\overline{1}$	$11\frac{1}{9}\%$
2/9	4/18	6/27	8/36	10/45	12/54	14/63	16/72	18/81	20/90	22/99	24/108	26/117	28/126	30/135	$0.\overline{2}$	$22\frac{2}{9}\%$
4/9	8/18	12/27	16/36	20/45	24/54	28/63	32/72	36/81	40/90	44/99	48/108	52/117	56/126	60/135	$0.\overline{4}$	$44\frac{4}{9}\%$
5/9	10/18	15/27	20/36	25/45	30/54	35/63	40/72	45/81	50/90	55/99	60/108	65/117	70/126	75/135	$0.\overline{5}$	$55\frac{5}{9}\%$
7/9	14/18	21/27	28/36	35/45	42/54	49/63	56/72	63/81	70/90	77/99	84/108	91/117	98/126	105/135	$0.\overline{7}$	$77\frac{7}{9}\%$
8/9	16/18	24/27	32/36	40/45	48/54	56/63	64/72	72/81	80/90	88/99	96/108	104/117	112/126	120/135	$0.\overline{8}$	$88\frac{8}{9}\%$

Note: The decimals for sevenths have been rounded to the nearest thousandth.

Probability Meter

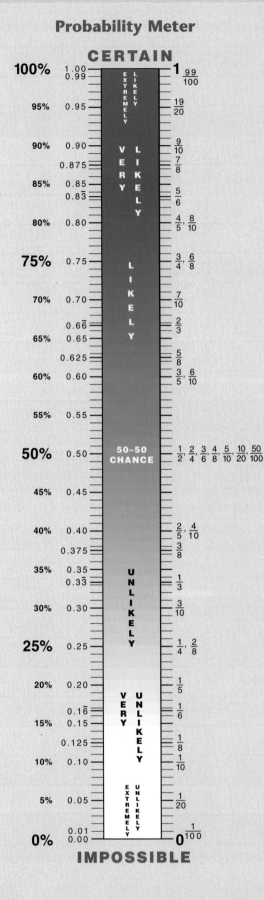

Formulas	**Meaning of Variables**
Rectangles • Perimeter: $p = (2 * l) + (2 * w)$ • Area: $A = (b * h)$	p = perimeter; l = length; w = width A = area; b = length of base; h = height
Squares • Perimeter: $p = 4 * s$ • Area: $A = s^2$	p = perimeter; s = length of side A = area
Parallelograms • Area: $A = b * h$	A = area; b = length of base; h = height
Triangles • Area: $A = \frac{1}{2} * b * h$	A = area; b = length of base; h = height
Regular Polygons • Perimeter: $p = n * s$	p = perimeter; n = number of sides; s = length of side
Circles • Circumference: $c = \pi * d$, or $c = 2 * \pi * r$ • Area: $A = \pi * r^2$	c = circumference; d = diameter; r = radius A = area
Rectangular Prisms • Volume: $V = B * h$, or $V = l * w * h$ • Surface area: $S = 2 * ((l * w) + (l * h) + (w * h))$	V = volume; B = area of base; l = length; w = width; h = height S = surface area
Cubes • Volume: $V = e^3$ • Surface area: $S = 6 * e^2$	V = volume; e = length of edge S = surface area
Cylinders • Volume: $V = B * h$, or $V = \pi * r^2 * h$ • Surface area: $S = (2 * \pi * r^2) + ((2 * \pi * r) * h)$	V = volume; B = area of base; h = height; r = radius of base S = surface area
Pyramids • Volume: $V = \frac{1}{3} * B * h$	V = volume; B = area of base; h = height
Cones • Volume: $V = \frac{1}{3} * B * h$, or $V = \frac{1}{3} * \pi * r^2 * h$	V = volume; B = area of base; h = height; r = radius of base
Distances • $d = r * t$	d = distance traveled; r = rate of speed; t = time of travel

Abundant number A number whose *proper factors* add up to more than the number itself. For example, 12 is an abundant number because the sum of its proper factors is $1 + 2 + 3 + 4 + 6 = 16$, and 16 is greater than 12. See also *proper factor, deficient number,* and *perfect number.*

Acre In the U.S. customary system of measurement, a unit of *area* equal to 43,560 square feet. An acre is roughly the size of a football field. A square mile is 640 acres.

Addend One of two or more numbers that are added. For example, in $5 + 3 + 1$, the addends are 5, 3, and 1.

Adjacent angles Angles that are next to each other; adjacent angles have a common side, but no other overlap. In the diagram, Angles 1 and 2 are adjacent angles. So are Angles 2 and 3, Angles 3 and 4, and Angles 4 and 1.

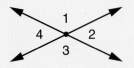

Algebraic expression An expression that contains a variable. For example, if Maria is 2 inches taller than Joe, and if the variable M represents Maria's height, then the algebraic expression

$M - 2$ represents Joe's height. See also *expression.*

Algorithm A set of step-by-step instructions for doing something, such as carrying out a computation or solving a problem.

Angle A figure that is formed by two rays or two line segments with a common endpoint. The common endpoint is called the *vertex* of the angle. An *acute angle* has a measure greater than 0° and less than 90°. An *obtuse angle* has a measure greater than 90° and less than 180°. A *reflex angle* has a measure greater than 180° and less than 360°. A *right angle* measures 90°. A *straight angle* measures 180°. See also *endpoint, ray,* and *vertex.*

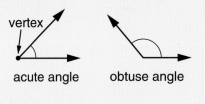

acute angle   obtuse angle

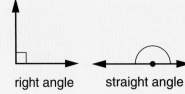

right angle   straight angle

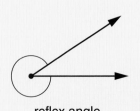

reflex angle

Apex In a pyramid or a cone, the vertex opposite the base. See also *base of a pyramid or a cone.*

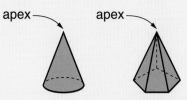

apex   apex

Area The amount of surface inside a closed boundary. Area is measured in square units, such as square inches or square centimeters.

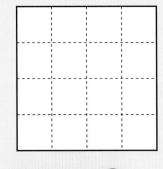

Two ways to model area

Area model A model for multiplication problems in which the length and width of a rectangle represent the factors, and the area of the rectangle represents the product. Also, a model for showing fractions as parts of circles, rectangles, or other geometric figures.

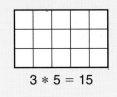

$3 * 5 = 15$

Array An arrangement of objects in a regular pattern, usually rows and columns. Arrays can be used to model multiplication. For example, the array below is a model for $3 * 5 = 15$. See also *rectangular array*.

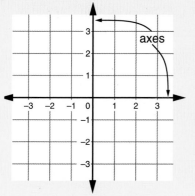

Associative property A property of addition and multiplication (but not of subtraction or division) that says that when you add or multiply three numbers, it doesn't matter which two are added or multiplied first. For example: $(4 + 3) + 7 = 4 + (3 + 7)$ and $(5 * 8) * 9 = 5 * (8 * 9)$.

Average A typical value for a set of numbers. The word *average* usually refers to the *mean* of a set of numbers, but there are other averages. See also *mean, median,* and *mode*.

Axis plural: *axes* (1) Either of the two number lines that intersect to form a *coordinate grid*.

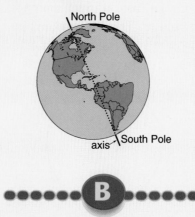

(2) A line about which a solid figure rotates.

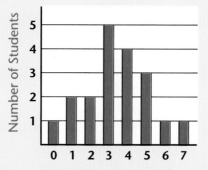

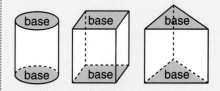

Bar graph A graph that uses horizontal or vertical bars to represent data.

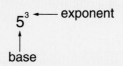

Base (in exponential notation) The number that is raised to some power. For example, in 5^3, the base is 5. See also *exponential notation*.

$$5^3 \leftarrow \text{exponent}$$
$$\uparrow$$
$$\text{base}$$

Base of a polygon A side on which a polygon "sits." The height of a polygon may depend on which side is called the base. See also *height of a parallelogram and height of a triangle*.

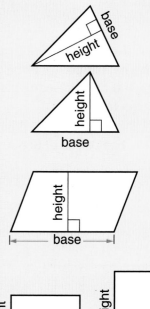

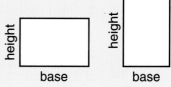

Base of a prism or a cylinder Either of the two parallel and congruent faces that define the shape of a prism or a cylinder.

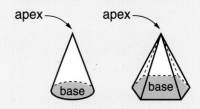

Base of a pyramid or a cone The face of a pyramid or a cone that is opposite its apex.

Base-10 The feature of our number system that results in each place having a value 10 times the place to its right. See also *place value*.

Broken-line graph A graph in which data points are connected by line segments. Same as *line graph*.

Attendance for the First Week of School

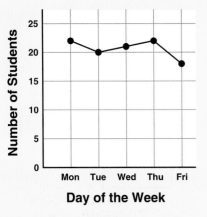

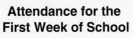

Capacity The amount a container can hold. Also, the heaviest weight a scale can measure.

Census An official count of a country's population. The census is taken every 10 years in the United States.

Change diagram A diagram used in *Everyday Mathematics* to represent situations in which quantities are increased or decreased.

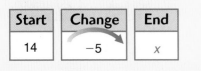

Start	Change	End
14	−5	x

Circle The set of all points in a plane that are a given distance from a given point in the plane. The given point is the *center* of the circle and the given distance is the *radius*.

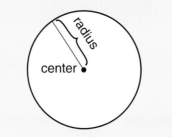

Circle graph A graph in which a circle and its interior are divided into parts to show the parts of a set of data. The whole circle represents the whole set of data. Same as *pie graph*.

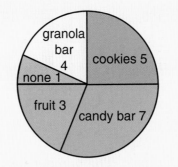

Circumference The distance around a circle or a sphere; the perimeter of a circle.

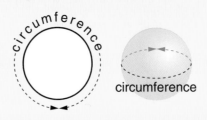

Column-addition method A method for adding numbers in which the addends' digits are first added in each place-value column seperately and then 10-for-1 trades are made until each column has only one digit. Lines are drawn to separate the place-value columns.

100s	10s	1s
2	4	8
+ 1	8	7
3	12	15
3	13	5
4	3	5

Column-division method A division procedure in which vertical lines are drawn between the digits of the dividend. The lines make the procedure easier to carry out.

$$
\begin{array}{c|c|c|c}
 & 1 & 7 & 2 \\
\hline
5\overline{)} & 8 & \cancel{6} & \cancel{3} \\
 & -5 & 36 & 13 \\
\hline
 & \cancel{3} & -35 & -10 \\
\hline
 & & \cancel{1} & 3 \\
\end{array}
$$

863 / 5 → 172 R3

Common denominator Any number, except zero, that is a multiple of the denominators of two or more fractions. For example, the fractions $\frac{1}{2}$ and $\frac{2}{3}$ have the common denominators 6, 12, 18, and so on. See also *denominator*.

Common factor A number that is a factor of two or more numbers. For example, 4 is a common factor of 8 and 12 because 8 = 4 * 2 and 12 = 4 * 3.

Commutative property A property of addition and multiplication (but not of subtraction or division) that says that changing the order of the numbers being added or multiplied doesn't change the answer. For example: 5 + 10 = 10 + 5 and 3 * 8 = 8 * 3.

Comparison diagram A diagram used in *Everyday Mathematics* to represent situations in which two quantities are compared.

Quantity
12

Quantity	Difference
9	?

Complementary angles Two angles whose measures total 90°.

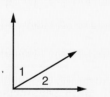

∠1 and ∠2 are complementary

Composite number A whole number that has more than two factors. For example, 4 is a composite number because it has three factors: 1, 2, and 4.

Concave polygon A polygon in which at least one vertex is "pushed in." Not every line segment with endpoints on a concave polygon is entirely inside the polygon. Same as *nonconvex polygon*.

concave polygons

Concentric circles Circles that have the same center but radii of different lengths.

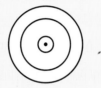

Cone A 3-dimensional shape that has a circular *base*, a curved surface, and one vertex which is called the *apex*. The points on the curved surface of a cone are on straight lines connecting the apex and the circumference of the base.

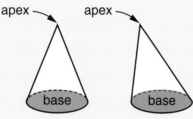

Congruent Having exactly the same shape and size.

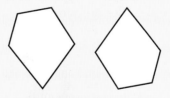

congruent pentagons

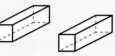

congruent prisms

Contour line A curve on a map through places where a certain measurement (such as temperature or elevation) is the same. Often, contour lines separate regions that have been colored differently to show a range of conditions. See also *contour map*.

Contour map A map that uses *contour lines* to show a particular feature, such as elevation or climate. See also *contour line*.

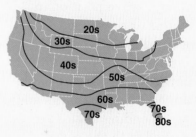

Convex polygon A polygon in which all vertices are "pushed outward." Any line segment with endpoints on a convex polygon lies entirely inside the polygon.

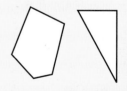

Coordinate A number used to locate a point on a number line, or one of two numbers used to locate a point on a coordinate grid. See also *coordinate grid*.

Coordinate grid A device for locating points in a plane using *ordered number pairs,* or *coordinates.* A *rectangular coordinate grid* is formed by two number lines that intersect at right angles at their zero points. See also *coordinate* and *ordered number pair.*

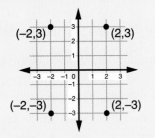

Corresponding Having the same relative position in *similar* or *congruent figures.* In the diagram, pairs of corresponding sides are marked with the same number of slash marks and corresponding angles are marked with the same symbols.

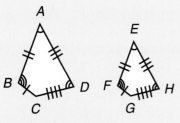

corresponding sides and angles

Counting numbers The numbers used to count things. The set of counting numbers is {1, 2, 3, 4, ...}. Sometimes 0 is considered to be a counting number.

Cube A polyhedron with 6 square faces. A cube has 8 vertices and 12 edges.

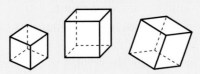

Cubic centimeter A metric unit of volume equal to the volume of a cube that is 1 cm on each side. 1 cubic centimeter is equal to 1 milliliter.

Cubic unit A unit used in measuring volume, such as cubic centimeters or cubic feet.

Cubit An ancient unit of length, measured from the point of the elbow to the end of the middle finger. A cubit is about 18 inches. The Latin word *cubitum* means "elbow."

Curved surface A surface that is rounded rather than flat.

Cylinder A 3-dimensional shape that has two circular or elliptical bases that are parallel and congruent and are connected by a curved surface. The points on the curved surface of a cylinder are on straight lines connecting corresponding points on the bases. A can is shaped like a cylinder.

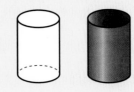

Data Information that is gathered by counting, measuring, questioning, or observing.

Decimal A number that contains a decimal point, such as 2.54. See also *standard notation.*

Decimal point A dot used to separate the ones and the tenths places in decimal numbers.

Deficient number A number whose proper factors add up to less than the number itself. For example, 10 is a deficient number because the sum of its proper factors is $1 + 2 + 5 = 8$, and 8 is less than 10. See also *proper factor, abundant number,* and *perfect number.*

Degree (°) A unit of measure for angles based on dividing a circle into 360 equal parts. Also a unit of measure for temperature. A small raised circle (°) is used to show degrees.

An angle measuring 1°.

Denominator The number below the line in a fraction. In a fraction where a whole is divided into equal parts, the denominator represents the number of equal parts into which the whole (the ONE or unit) is divided. In the fraction $\frac{a}{b}$, b is the denominator.

Density A *rate* that compares the *mass* of an object with its *volume*. For example, suppose a ball has a mass of 20 grams and a volume of 10 cubic centimeters. To find its density, divide its mass by its volume: 20 g / 10 cm³ = 2 g / cm³, or 2 grams per cubic centimeter.

Diameter A line segment that passes through the center of a circle or a sphere and has endpoints on the circle or the sphere; also, the length of this line segment. The diameter of a circle or a sphere is twice the length of its radius.

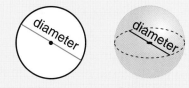

Difference The result of subtracting one number from another.

Digit One of the number symbols 0, 1, 2, 3, 4, 5, 6, 7, 8, 9.

Discount The amount by which the regular price of an item is reduced.

Distributive property A property that relates multiplication and addition or subtraction. This property gets its name because it "distributes" a factor over terms inside parentheses.

Distributive property of multiplication over addition:

$a * (b + c) = (a * b) + (a * c)$, so
$2 * (5 + 3) = (2 * 5) + (2 * 3)$
$= 10 + 6 = 16$

Distributive property of multiplication over subtraction:

$a * (b - c) = (a * b) - (a * c)$
$2 * (5 - 3) = (2 * 5) - (2 * 3)$
$= 10 - 6 = 4$

Dividend The number that is being divided in division. For example, in $35 \div 5 = 7$, the dividend is 35.

Divisibility test A test to find out whether a whole number is *divisible by* another whole number without actually doing the division. A divisibility test for 5, for example, is to check the last digit: if the last digit is 0 or 5, then the number is divisible by 5.

Divisible by One whole number is divisible by another whole number if there is no remainder when you divide. For example, 28 is divisible by 7 because 28 divided by 7 is 4 with a remainder of 0.

Divisor In division, the number that divides another number. For example, in $35 \div 5 = 7$, the divisor is 5.

Dodecahedron A polyhedron with 12 faces.

Edge A line segment where two faces of a polyhedron meet.

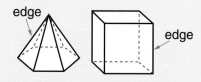

Endpoint A point at the end of a line segment or ray. A line segment is normally named using the letter labels of its endpoints. See also *line segment* and *ray*.

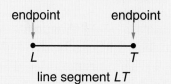

line segment *LT*

Enlarge To increase the size of an object or figure. See also *size-change factor*.

Equation A number sentence that contains an equal sign. For example, 15 = 10 + 5 is an equation.

Equilateral triangle A triangle with all three sides equal in length. In an equilateral triangle, all three angles have the same measure.

Glossary

Equivalent fractions
Fractions that have different denominators but name the same amount. For example, $\frac{1}{2}$ and $\frac{4}{8}$ are equivalent fractions.

Estimate An answer that is close to an exact answer. Also, to calculate an answer that is close to the exact answer.

Evaluate To find a value for. To evaluate a mathematical expression, you replace the variables (if there are any) with numbers, then carry out the operations. See also *expression*.

Even number A whole number that can be divided by 2 with no remainder. The even numbers are 2, 4, 6, 8, and so on. 0 may be considered even.

Exponent A small, raised number in *exponential notation* that tells how many times the base is to be multiplied by itself. For example, in 5^3, the exponent is 3. See also *base* and *exponential notation*.

Exponential notation A way to show repeated multiplication by the same factor. For example, 2^3 is exponential notation for $2 * 2 * 2$. The small, raised 3 is the exponent. It tells how many times the number 2, called the base, is used as a factor.

$2^3 \longleftarrow$ exponent
$\uparrow$
base

Expression A group of mathematical symbols that represents a number—or can represent a number if values are assigned to any variables in the expression.

Extended multiplication fact A multiplication fact involving multiples of 10, 100, and so on. In an extended multiplication fact, each factor has only one digit that is not 0. For example, $6 * 70$, $60 * 7$, and $60 * 70$ are extended multiplication facts.

Face A flat surface on a 3-dimensional shape.

Fact family A set of related addition and subtraction facts or related multiplication and division facts. For example, $5 + 6 = 11$, $6 + 5 = 11$, $11 - 5 = 6$, and $11 - 6 = 5$ are a fact family. $5 * 7 = 35$, $7 * 5 = 35$, $35 \div 5 = 7$, and $35 \div 7 = 5$ are another fact family.

Factor One of two or more numbers that are multiplied to give a product. The numbers that are multiplied are called *factors* of the product. For example, 4 and 3 are factors of 12, because $4 * 3 = 12$. As a verb, to factor means to find two (or more) smaller numbers whose product equals a given number. 15, for example, can be factored as $5 * 3$.

$4 * 3 = 12$
$\uparrow \quad \uparrow \qquad \uparrow$
factors   product

Factor pair Two whole-number factors of a number whose product is the number. A number may have more than one factor pair. For example, the factor pairs for 18 are 1 and 18, 2 and 9, and 3 and 6.

Factor rainbow A way to show factor pairs in a list of all the factors of a number. A factor rainbow can be used to check whether a list of factors is correct.

factor rainbow for 24

Factor string A number written as a product of at least two whole-number factors. For example, a factor string for the number 24 is $2 * 3 * 4$. This factor string has three factors, so its length is 3. The number 1 is never part of a factor string.

Factor tree A way to get the *prime factorization* of a number. The original number is written as a product of factors, then each of these factors is written as a product of factors, and so on, until the factors are all prime numbers. A factor tree looks like an upside down tree, with the root (the original number) at the top and the leaves (the factors) beneath it. See also *prime factorization.*

Fair Free from bias. Each side of a fair die or coin will come up about equally often. In a fair game, every player has the same chance of winning.

False number sentence A number sentence in which the relation symbol does not accurately relate the two sides. For example, $8 = 5 + 5$ is a false number sentence.

Fathom A unit used by people who work with boats and ships to measure depths under water and lengths of cables. A fathom is now defined as 6 feet.

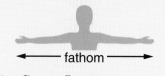

← fathom →

Flip See *reflection.*

Formula A general rule for finding the value of something. A formula is often written using letters, called variables, that stand for the quantities involved. For example, the formula for the area of a rectangle may be written as $A = l * w$, where A represents the area of the rectangle, l represents its length, and w represents its width.

Fraction A number in the form $\frac{a}{b}$ or a/b. Fractions can be used to name parts of a whole, to compare quantities, or to represent division. For example, $\frac{2}{3}$ can be thought of as 2 divided by 3. See *numerator* and *denominator.*

Fraction stick A diagram used in *Everyday Mathematics* to represent simple fractions.

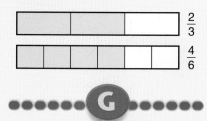

●●●●●● **G** ●●●●●●

Geometric solid A 3-dimensional shape, such as a prism, pyramid, cylinder, cone, or sphere. Despite its name, a geometric solid is hollow; it does not contain the points in its interior.

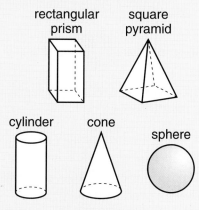

rectangular prism   square pyramid

cylinder   cone   sphere

geometric solids

Geometry Template An *Everyday Mathematics* tool that includes a millimeter ruler, a ruler with sixteenth-inch intervals, half-circle and full-circle protractors, a

percent circle, pattern-block shapes, and other geometric figures. The Template can also be used as a compass.

Great span The distance from the tip of the thumb to the tip of the little finger (pinkie) when the hand is stretched as far as possible. Also called *hand span.*

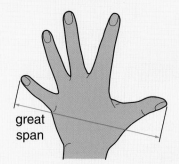

great span

Greatest common factor (GCF) The largest factor that two or more numbers have in common. For example, the common factors of 24 and 36 are 1, 2, 3, 4, 6, and 12; the greatest common factor of 24 and 36 is 12.

●●●●●● **H** ●●●●●●

Height of a parallelogram The shortest length between the base of a parallelogram and the line containing the side opposite its base. The height is perpendicular to the base. See also *base of a polygon.*

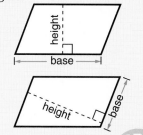

height

base

height

base

Height of a prism or a cylinder The shortest length from a base of a prism or a cylinder to the plane containing the opposite base. See also *base of a prism or a cylinder*.

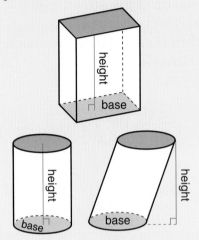

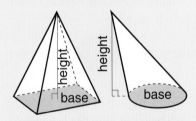

Height of a pyramid or a cone The shortest length from the vertex of a pyramid or a cone to the plane containing its base. See also *base of a pyramid or a cone*.

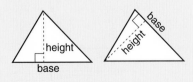

Height of a triangle The shortest length between the line containing a base of a triangle and the vertex opposite that base. See also *base of a polygon*.

Hemisphere Half of the Earth's surface. Also, half of a sphere.

Heptagon A polygon with seven sides.

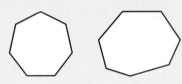

Hexagon A polygon with six sides.

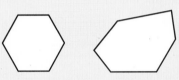

Hexagram A 6-pointed star formed by extending the sides of a regular hexagon.

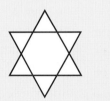

Horizontal In a left-right orientation, parallel to the horizon.

Icosahedron A polyhedron with 20 faces.

Image The reflection of an object that you see when you look in a mirror. Also, a figure that is produced by a transformation (a reflection, translation, or rotation, for

example) of another figure. See also *preimage*.

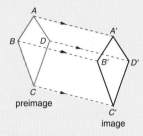

Improper fraction A fraction whose numerator is greater than or equal to its denominator. For example, $\frac{4}{3}$, $\frac{5}{2}$, $\frac{4}{4}$, and $\frac{24}{12}$ are improper fractions. In *Everyday Mathematics,* improper fractions are sometimes called "top-heavy" fractions.

Inequality A number sentence with $>$, $<$, $\geq$, $\leq$, or $\neq$. For example, the sentence $8 < 15$ is an inequality.

Inscribed polygon A polygon whose vertices are all on the same circle.

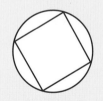

inscribed square

Integer A number in the set $\{..., -4, -3, -2, -1, 0, 1, 2, 3, 4, ...\}$; a *whole number* or the *opposite* of a whole number.

Interior The inside of a closed 2-dimensional or 3-dimensional figure. The interior is usually not considered to be part of the figure.

Intersect To meet or cross.

Intersecting Meeting or crossing one another. Lines, segments, rays, and other figures can intersect.

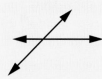

intersecting lines   intersecting planes

Irrational number A number that cannot be written as a fraction where both the numerator and denominator are *integers* and the denominator is not zero. For example, π is an irrational number.

Isosceles triangle A triangle with at least two sides that are the same length. In an isosceles triangle, at least two angles have the same measure.

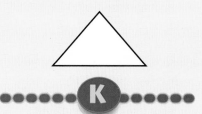

●●●●●● **K** ●●●●●●

Kite A quadrilateral with two pairs of adjacent equal sides. The four sides cannot all have the same length, so a rhombus is not a kite.

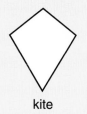

kite

●●●●●● **L** ●●●●●●

Landmark A notable feature of a data set. Landmarks include the *mean, median, mode, maximum, minimum,* and *range.*

Latitude A measure, in degrees, of the distance of a place north or south of the equator.

Lattice method A very old way to multiply multidigit numbers.

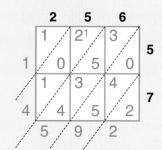

256 * 57 = 14,592
lattice multiplication

Least common denominator (LCD) The *least common multiple* of the denominators of every fraction in a given collection. For example, the least common denominator of $\frac{1}{2}$, $\frac{4}{5}$, and $\frac{3}{8}$ is 40. See also *least common multiple.*

Least common multiple The smallest number that is a multiple of two or more numbers. For example, while some common multiples of 6 and 8 are 24, 48, and 72, the least common multiple of 6 and 8 is 24.

Like denominators Denominators that are the same, as in $\frac{3}{5}$ and $\frac{1}{5}$.

Line A straight path that extends infinitely in opposite directions.

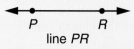

P   *R*
line *PR*

Line graph See *broken-line graph.*

Line of reflection (mirror line) A line halfway between a figure (preimage) and its reflected image. In a reflection, a figure is "flipped over" the line of reflection. See also *reflection.*

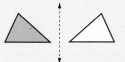

Line of symmetry A line drawn through a figure that divides it into two parts that look exactly alike but are facing in opposite directions.

Line plot A sketch of data in which check marks, Xs, or other marks above a labeled line show the frequency of each value.

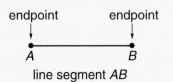

Number of Children	x x		
	x x		
	x x x		
	x x x	x

0 1 2 3 4
Number of Siblings

Line segment A straight path joining two points. The two points are called the *endpoints* of the segment.

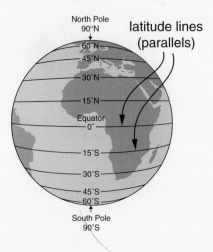

endpoint   endpoint

A   B

line segment *AB*

Lines of latitude Lines that run east-west on a map or globe and indicate the location of a place with reference to the equator, which is also a line of latitude. Lines of latitude are called parallels because each one is parallel to the equator

North Pole
90°N
latitude lines (parallels)
60°N
45°N
30°N
15°N
Equator
0°
15°S
30°S
45°S
60°S
South Pole
90°S

Lines of longitude Lines that run north-south on a map or globe and indicate the location of a place with reference to the prime meridian, which is also a line of longitude. Lines of longitude are semicircles that meet at the North and South Poles. They are also called meridians.

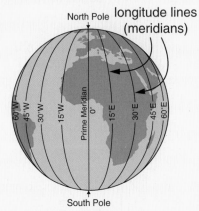

North Pole   longitude lines (meridians)

60°W 45°W 30°W 15°W Prime Meridian 0° 15°E 30°E 45°E 60°E

South Pole

Longitude A measure, in degrees, of how far east or west of the prime meridian a place is.

Lowest terms See *simplest form*.

Magnitude estimate A very rough estimate. A magnitude estimate tells whether an answer should be in the tens, hundreds, thousands, ten thousands, and so on.

Map legend (map key) A diagram that explains the symbols, markings, and colors on a map.

Map scale A tool that helps you estimate distances between places shown on a map by relating distances on the map to distances in the real world. For example, a map scale may show that one inch on a map represents 100 miles in the real world. See also *scale*.

Maximum The largest amount; the greatest number in a set of data.

Mean The sum of a set of numbers divided by the number of numbers in the set. The mean is often referred to simply as the *average*.

Median The middle value in a set of data when the data are listed in order from smallest to largest. If there is an even number of data points, the median is the *mean* of the two middle values.

Metric system of measurement A measurement system based on the base-ten numeration system. It is used in most countries around the world.

Minimum The smallest amount; the smallest number in a set of data.

Minuend The number that is reduced in subtraction. For example, in $19 - 5 = 14$, the minuend is 19.

Mixed number A number that is written using both a whole number and a fraction. For example, $2\frac{1}{4}$ is a mixed number equal to $2 + \frac{1}{4}$.

Mode The value or values that occur most often in a set of data.

Multiple of a number n (1) A product of n and a counting number. The multiples of 7, for example, are 7, 14, 21, 28, ... (2) A product of n and an integer. The multiples of 7, for example, are ..., -21, -14, -7, 0, 7, 14, 21, ...

Multiplication diagram A diagram used for problems in which there are several equal groups. The diagram has three parts: a number of groups, a number in each group, and a total number. Also called *multiplication / division diagram*. See also *rate diagram*.

rows	chairs per row	total chairs
15	25	?

Name-collection box A diagram that is used for writing equivalent names for a number.

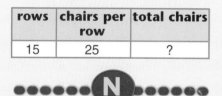

25		
37 − 12		20 + 5
ҋ ҋ ҋ ҋ ҋ		
twenty-five		*veinticinco*

Negative number A number that is less than zero; a number to the left of zero on a horizontal number line or below zero on a vertical number line.

n**-gon** A polygon with n sides. For example, a 5-gon is a pentagon and an 8-gon is an octagon.

Nonagon A polygon with nine sides.

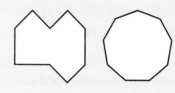

Nonconvex polygon See *concave polygon*.

Normal span The distance from the tip of the thumb to the tip of the first (index) finger of an outstretched hand. Also called *span*.

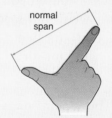

normal span

Number-and-word notation A way of writing a large number using a combination of numbers and words. For example, *27 billion* is number-and-word notation for 27,000,000,000.

Number model A number sentence that models or fits a number story or situation. For example, the story *Sally*

had $5.00, and then she earned $8.00 can be modeled as $5 + 8 = 13$.

Number sentence A sequence at least two numbers or expressions separated by a relation symbol ($=, >, <, \geq, \leq, \neq$). Most number sentences also contain at least one operation symbol ($+, -, \times, *, \bullet, \div, /$). Number sentences may also have grouping symbols, such as parentheses.

Number story A story with a problem that can be solved using arithmetic.

Numerator The number above the line in a fraction. In a fraction where the whole is divided into a number of equal parts, the numerator represents the number of equal parts that are being considered. In the fraction $\frac{a}{b}$, a is the numerator.

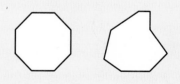

Octagon A polygon with eight sides.

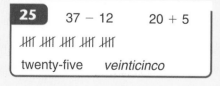

Octahedron A polygon with 8 faces.

Odd number A whole number such as 1, 3, 5, and so on, that cannot be evenly divided by 2. When an odd number is divided by 2, there is a remainder of 1. The odd numbers are 1, 3, 5, 7, and so on.

ONE See *whole*.

Open sentence A *number sentence* which has *variables* in place of one or more missing numbers and which is neither true or false. For example, $5 + x = 13$ is an open sentence. See also *number sentence* and *variable*.

Operation symbol A symbol used to stand for a particular mathematical operation. The most widely used operation symbols are $+$, $-$, $\times$, $*$, $\bullet$, $\div$, and $/$.

Opposite of a number A number that is the same distance from 0 on the number line as a given number, but on the opposite side of 0. For example, the opposite of $+3$ is -3, and the opposite of -5 is $+5$.

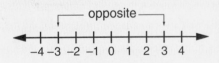

Order of operations Rules that tell in what order to perform operations in arithmetic and algebra.

1. Do the operations in parentheses first. (Use rules 2–4 inside the parentheses.)

2. Calculate all the expressions with exponents.

3. Multiply and divide in order from left to right.

4. Add and subtract in order from left to right.

Ordered number pair Two numbers that are used to locate a point on a *coordinate grid*. The first number gives the position along the horizontal axis, and the second number gives the position along the vertical axis. The numbers in an ordered pair are called *coordinates*. Ordered pairs are usually written inside parentheses: (5,3). See *coordinate grid* for an illustration.

Origin The 0 point on a number line or in a coordinate grid.

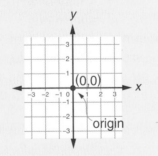

Pan balance A tool used to weigh objects or compare their weights.

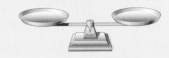

Parallel Never meeting and always the same distance apart. Lines, line segments, and rays in a plane are parallel if they never meet, no matter how far they are extended. The symbol $\parallel$ means "is parallel to."

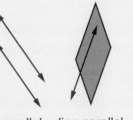

parallel lines   line parallel to a plane   parallel planes

Parallelogram A quadrilateral with two pairs of parallel sides. Opposite sides of a parallelogram are congruent.

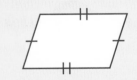

Parentheses Grouping symbols, ( ), used to tell which parts of an expression should be calculated first.

Partial-differences method
A way to subtract in which differences are computed for each place (ones, tens, hundreds, and so on) separately. The partial differences are then added to give the final answer.

```
        9 3 2
      - 3 5 6
900 - 300   →     6 0 0
30 - 50     → -     2 0
2 - 6       → -       4
600 - 20 - 4 →    5 7 6
```

Partial-products method A way to multiply in which the value of each digit in one factor is multiplied by the value of each digit in the other factor. The final product is the sum of the several partial products.

```
          6 7
        × 5 3
50 × 60 → 3 0 0 0
50 × 7  →   3 5 0
3 × 60  →   1 8 0
3 × 7   → +   2 1
          3 5 5 1
```

Partial-quotients method A way to divide in which the dividend is divided in a series of steps, and the quotients for each step (called partial quotients) are added to give the final answer.

```
6)1010
 - 600  | 100
   410
 - 300  | 50
   110
 -  60  | 10
    50
 -  48  | 8
     2  | 168
     ↑     ↑
Remainder  Quotient
```

1,010 / 6 → 168 R2

Partial-sums method A way to add in which sums are computed for each place (ones, tens, hundreds, and so on) separately and are then added to give the final answer.

```
                    2 6 8
                  + 4 8 3
Add the 100s.  →    6 0 0
Add the 10s.   →    1 4 0
Add the 1s.    →  +   1 1
Add partial sums. →  7 5 1
```

Parts-and-total diagram A diagram used in *Everyday Mathematics* to represent situations in which two or more quantities are combined.

Total	
13	
Part	**Part**
8	?

Pentagon A polygon with five sides.

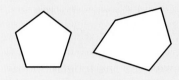

Per-unit rate A *rate* with 1 in the denominator.

Percent (%) Per hundred, or out of a hundred. For example, "48% of the students in the school are boys" means that 48 out of every 100 students in the school are boys.

Percent Circle A tool on the *Geometry Template* that is used to measure or draw figures that involve percents (such as circle graphs). See also *Geometry Template*.

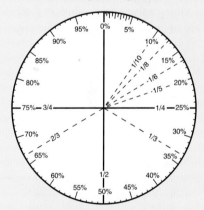

Perfect number A number whose proper factors add up to the number itself. For example, 6 is a perfect number because the sum of its proper factors is $1 + 2 + 3 = 6$. See also *proper factor, abundant number,* and *deficient number.*

Perimeter The distance around a closed 2-dimensional shape. A formula for the perimeter of a rectangle is $P = 2 * (l + w)$, where l represents the length and w represents the width of the rectangle.

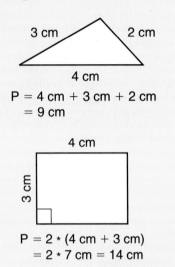

$P = 4\text{ cm} + 3\text{ cm} + 2\text{ cm}$
$= 9\text{ cm}$

$P = 2 * (4\text{ cm} + 3\text{ cm})$
$= 2 * 7\text{ cm} = 14\text{ cm}$

Perpendicular Meeting at right angles. Lines, rays, line segments, and planes that meet at right angles are perpendicular. The symbol $\perp$ means "is perpendicular to."

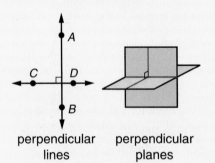

perpendicular lines   perpendicular planes

Pi (π) The ratio of the *circumference* of a circle to its *diameter*. Pi is the same for every circle and is approximately 3.14. Pi is the sixteenth letter of the Greek alphabet and is written **π**.

Pictograph A graph constructed with pictures or icons. A pictograph allows you to compare at a glance the relative amounts of two or more counts or measures.

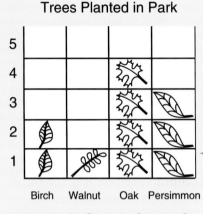

Trees Planted in Park

Birch   Walnut   Oak   Persimmon

Pie graph See *circle graph*.

Place value A system that values a digit according to its position in a number. In standard notation, each place has a value that is ten times that of the place to its right and one-tenth the value of the place to its left. For example, in the number 456, the 4 is in the hundreds place and has a value of 400.

Plane A flat surface that extends forever.

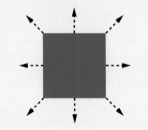

Point An exact location in space. The center of a circle is a point.

Polygon A closed, 2-dimensional figure that is made up of line segments joined end to end. The line segments of a polygon may not cross.

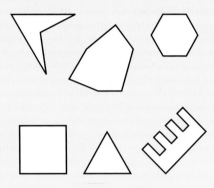

Polyhedron A closed 3-dimensional figure whose surfaces, or faces, are all formed by polygons and their interiors.

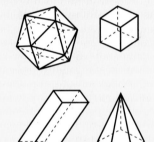

Population In data collection, the collection of people or objects that is the focus of study.

Power of a number Usually, a product of factors that are all the same. For example, 5 * 5 * 5 (or 125) is called "5 to the third power" or "the third power of 5," because 5 is a factor three times. 5 * 5 * 5 can also be written as 5^3.

Power of 10 A whole number that can be written using only 10s as factors. For example, 100 is equal to $10 * 10$, or 10^2. 100 can be called the second power of 10 or 10 to the second power. A number that can be written using only $\frac{1}{10}$ as a factor is known as a negative power of 10.

Preimage A geometric figure that is somehow changed (by a *reflection*, a *rotation*, or a *translation*, for example) to produce another figure. See also *image*.

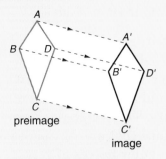

preimage

image

Prime factorization A whole number expressed as a product of prime factors. Every whole number greater than 1 has a unique prime fractorization. For example, the prime factorization of 24 is $2 * 2 * 2 * 3$.

Prime meridian An imaginary semicircle that connects the North and South Poles and passes through Greenwich, England.

Prime number A whole number that has exactly two *factors*: itself and 1. For example, 5 is a prime number because its only factors are 5 and 1.

Prism A solid with two parallel *faces*, called *bases*, that are congruent polygons, and other *faces* that are all parallelograms. The points on the lateral faces of a prism are all on lines connecting corresponding points on the bases. Prisms are named for the shape of their bases.

triangular prism

rectangular prism

hexagonal prism

Probability A number from 0 to 1 that tells the chance that an event will happen. The closer a probability is to 1, the more likely the event is to happen.

Product The result of multiplying two numbers called *factors*. For example, in $4 * 3 = 12$, the product is 12.

Proper factor Any whole-number *factor* of a number except the number itself. For example, the *factors* of 10 are 1, 2, 5, and 10, but the *proper factors* of 10 are 1, 2, and 5.

Proper fraction A fraction in which the numerator is less than the denominator; a proper fraction names a number that is less than 1. For example, $\frac{3}{4}$, $\frac{2}{5}$, and $\frac{12}{24}$ are proper fractions.

Proportion A number model that states that two fractions are equal. Often the fractions in a proportion represent rates or ratios. For example, the problem "Alan's speed is 12 miles per hour. At the same speed, how far can he travel in 3 hours?" can be modeled by the porportion:

$$\frac{12 \text{ miles}}{1 \text{ hour}} = \frac{n \text{ miles}}{3 \text{ hours}}$$

Protractor A tool for measuring and drawing angles. A half-circle protractor can be used to measure and draw angles up to 180°; a full-circle protractor, to measure and draw angles up to 360°.

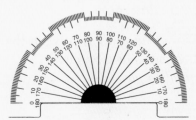

half-circle protractor

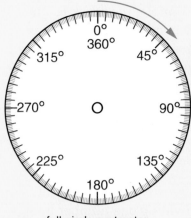

full-circle protractor

Pyramid A solid in which one face, the *base,* is any polygon and all the other *faces* are triangles that come together at a point called the *vertex* or *apex*. Pyramids are named for the shape of their bases.

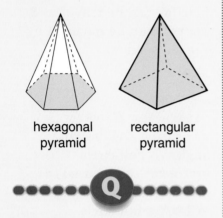

hexagonal pyramid   rectangular pyramid

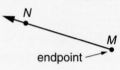

Quadrangle A polygon that has four angles. Same as *quadrilateral*.

Quadrilateral A polygon that has four sides. Same as *quadrangle*.

Quick common denominator (QCD) The product of the denominators of two or more fractions. For example, the quick common denominator of $\frac{1}{4}$ and $\frac{3}{6}$ is $4 * 6$, or 24. As the name suggests, this is a quick way to get a *common denominator* for a collection of fractions, but it does not necessarily give the *least common denominator*.

Quotient The result of dividing one number by another number. For example, in $35 \div 5 = 7$, the quotient is 7.

Radius A line segment from the center of a circle (or sphere) to any point on the circle (or sphere); also, the length of such a line segment.

Random number A number that has the same chance of appearing as any other number. Rolling a *fair* die will produce random numbers.

Range The difference between the *maximum* and the *minimum* in a set of data.

Rate A comparison by division of two quantities with unlike, or different, units. For example, a speed such as 55 miles per hour is a rate that compares distance with time. See also *ratio*.

Rate diagram A diagram used to model rate situations. See also *multiplication diagram*.

number of pounds	cost per pound	total cost
3	79¢	$2.37

Ratio A comparison by division of two quantities with like, or the same, units. Ratios can be expressed with fractions, decimals, percents, or words. Sometimes they are written with a colon between the two numbers that are being compared. For example, if a team wins 3 games out of 5 games played, the ratio of wins to total games can be

written as $\frac{3}{5}$, 0.6, 60%, 3 to 5, or 3:5. See also *rate*.

Rational number A number that can be written as a fraction using only whole numbers and their opposites.

Ray A straight path that extends infinitely from a point called its *endpoint*.

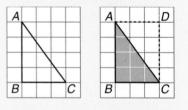

endpoint

Real number Any *rational* or *irrational number*.

Rectangle A parallelogram with four right angles.

Rectangle method A method for finding area in which rectangles are drawn around a figure or parts of a figure. The rectangles form regions that are rectangles or triangular halves of rectangles. The area of the original figure can be found by adding or subtracting the areas of these regions.

Rectangular array An arrangement of objects in rows and columns such that each row has the same number of objects and each column has the same number of objects.

Similar Exactly the same shape but not necessarily the same size.

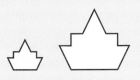

similar figures

Simpler form A fraction can be put in simpler form by dividing its numerator and denominator by a whole number that is greater than 1. For example, $\frac{18}{24}$ can be put in simpler form by dividing the numerator and the denominator by 2. The result, $\frac{9}{12}$, is in simpler form than $\frac{18}{24}$.

Simplest form A fraction less than 1 is in simplest form if there is no number other than 1 that divides its numerator and denominator evenly. A *mixed number* is in simplest form if its fractional part is in simplest form.

Size-change factor A number that tells the amount of enlargement or reduction. See also *enlarge* and *reduce*.

Slide See *translation*.

Slide rule A tool used to perform calculations.

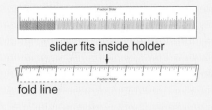

slider fits inside holder

fold line

Solution of an open sentence A value for the variable in an *open sentence* that makes the sentence true. For example, 7 is the solution of $5 + n = 12$.

Span See *normal span*.

Speed A rate that compares a distance traveled with the time taken to travel that distance. For example, if you went 100 miles in 2 hours, your speed was 100 mi / 2 hr or 50 miles per hour.

Sphere The set of all points in space that are a given distance from a given point. The given point is the center of the sphere and the given distance is the radius.

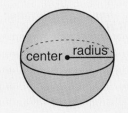

Square A rectangle with all sides equal.

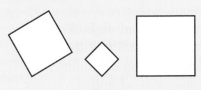

Square number A number that is the product of a counting number multiplied by itself. For example, 25 is a square number because $25 = 5 * 5$. The square numbers are 1, 4, 9, 16, 25, and so on.

Square of a number The product of a number multiplied by itself. For example, 81 is the square of 9 because $81 = 9 * 9$.

Square root of a number The square root of a number n is a number which, when multiplied by itself, gives the number n. For example, 4 is the square root of 16 because $4 * 4 = 16$.

Square unit A unit used in measuring area, such as square centimeters or square feet.

Standard notation The most familiar way of representing whole numbers, integers, and decimals. In standard notation, the value of each digit depends on where the digit is. For example, standard notation for three hundred fifty-six is 356. See also *place value*.

Stem-and-leaf plot A display of data in which digits with larger *place values* are "stems" and digits with smaller *place values* are "leaves."

Data List: 24, 24, 25, 26, 27, 27, 31, 31, 32, 32, 36, 36, 41, 41, 43, 45, 48, 50, 52

Stems (10s)	Leaves (1s)
2	4 4 5 6 7 7
3	1 1 2 2 6 6
4	1 1 3 5 8
5	0 2

Straightedge A tool used to draw line segments. A straightedge does not have measure marks on it, so if you use a ruler as a straightedge, you should ignore the marks on it.

Subtrahend In subtraction, the number that is being taken away from another number. For example, in $19 - 5 = 14$, the subtrahend is 5.

Sum The result of adding two or more numbers. For example, in $5 + 3 = 8$, the sum is 8.

Supplementary angles Two angles whose measures total $180°$.

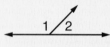

∠1 and ∠2 are supplementary angles

Surface (1) the outside boundary of an object; the part of an object that is next to the air. Common surfaces include the top of a body of water, the outermost part of a ball, and the topmost layer of ground that covers the Earth. (2) Any 2-dimensional layer, such as a plane or the faces of a polyhedron.

Survey A study that collects data.

Symmetric Having the same size and shape on either side of a line, or looking the same when turned by some amount less than $360°$. See also *line symmetry* and *rotation symmetry*.

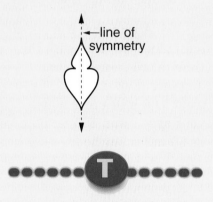

line of symmetry

Tally chart A table that uses marks, called tallies, to show how many times each value appears in a set of data.

Number of Pull-Ups	Number of Children
0	‖‖ /
1	‖‖
2	////
3	//

tally chart

Terminating decimal A decimal that ends. For example, 0.5 and 0.125 are terminating decimals. See also *decimal* and *repeating decimal*.

Tessellate To make a *tessellation;* to *tile*. See also *tessellation*.

Tessellation An arrangement of shapes that covers a surface completely without overlaps or gaps. Also called a *tiling*.

Tetrahedron A polyhedron with 4 faces.

3-dimensional (3-D) Solid objects that take up volume. 3-dimensional objects have length, width, and thickness.

Trade-first subtraction A subtraction method in which all trades are done before any subtractions are carried out.

Transformation Something done to a geometric figure (the *preimage*) that produces a new figure (the *image*). The most common transformations are *translations* (slides), *reflections* (flips), and *rotations* (turns).

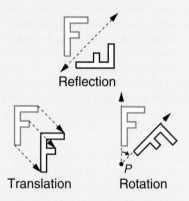

Reflection

Translation

Rotation

Translation A movement of a figure along a straight line; a "slide."

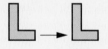

Trapezoid A quadrilateral that has exactly one pair of parallel sides.

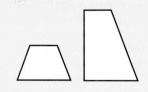

Triangle A polygon with three sides and three angles.

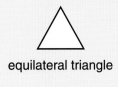

equilateral triangle

isosceles triangle

scalene triangle

Triangular numbers Numbers that can be shown by triangular arrangements of dots. The triangular numbers are 1, 3, 6, 10, 15, 21, 28, 36, 45, ...

1   3   6   10

True number sentence A number sentence in which the relation symbol accurately relates the two sides. For example, $15 = 5 + 10$ and $25 > 20 + 3$ are both true number sentences.

Turn See *rotation*.

Turn-around facts A pair of multiplication (or addition) facts in which the order of the factors (or addends) is reversed. For example, $3 * 9 = 27$ and $9 * 3 = 27$ are turn-around multiplication facts and $4 + 5 = 9$ and $5 + 4 = 9$ are turn-around addition facts. There are no turn-around facts for subtraction or division.

Turn-around rule A rule for solving addition and multiplication problems based on the *commutative property*. For example, if you know that $6 * 8 = 48$, then, by the turn-around rule, you also know that $8 * 6 = 48$. See also *commutative property*.

Twin primes Two *prime numbers* that are separated by just one *composite number*. For example, 3 and 5 are twin primes; 11 and 13 are also twin primes.

2-dimensional (2-D) Having length and width, but not thickness. 2-dimensional shapes have area but not volume. Circles and polygons are 2-dimensional.

U.S. customary system of measurement The measuring system most frequently used in the United States.

Unit A label used to put a number in context. In measuring length, for example, inches and centimeters are units. In "5 apples," the word *apples* is the unit. See also *whole*.

Unit fraction A fraction whose numerator is 1. For example, $\frac{1}{2}$, $\frac{1}{3}$, $\frac{1}{8}$, and $\frac{1}{20}$ are unit fractions.

Unit percent One percent (1%).

Unit price The cost for one item or for one unit of measure.

Unit rate A *rate* with 1 in the numerator.

Unlike denominators Denominators that are different, as in $\frac{1}{2}$ and $\frac{1}{3}$.

"Unsquaring" a number Finding the *square root* of a number.

Variable A letter or other symbol that represents a number. A variable can represent one specific number or it can stand for many different numbers.

Vertex The point where the rays of an angle, the sides of a polygon, or the edges of a polyhedron meet.

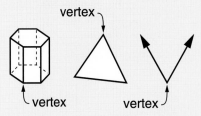

vertex

vertex   vertex

Vertex point A point where corners of shapes in a *tessellation* meet.

Vertical Upright; perpendicular to the horizon.

Vertical (or opposite) angles When two lines intersect, the angles that do not share a common side. Vertical angles have equal measures.

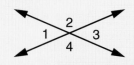

∠ 1 and ∠ 3 are vertical angles.
∠ 2 and ∠ 4 are also vertical angles.

Volume The amount of space inside a 3-dimensional object. Volume is usually measured in cubic units, such as cubic centimeters or cubic inches. Sometimes volume is measured in units of capacity, such as gallons or liters.

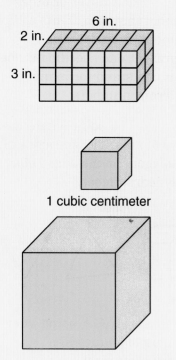

1 cubic centimeter

1 cubic inch

What's My Rule? A type of problem in which you try to figure out a rule for relating two sets of numbers. Also, a type of problem in which you try to figure out one of the sets of numbers, given a rule and the other set of numbers.

Whole (or ONE or unit) The entire object, collection of objects, or quantity being considered—the ONE, the unit, 100%.

Whole number Any of the numbers 0, 1, 2, 3, 4, and so on.

Page 4
1. 9,000   **2.** 900,000
3. 90   **4.** 90,000

Page 6
1. 36   **2.** 64   **3.** 1,000,000
4. 9   **5.** 207,936   **6.** 38,416

Page 7
1. $\frac{1}{16}$ **2.** $\frac{1}{1000}$ **3.** 1
4. $\frac{1}{3}$ **5.** 32   **6.** 1

Page 8
1. 25   **2.** 27   **3.** 8
4. 5,000,000   **5.** 840,000   **6.** $6 * 10^2$
7. $5.5 * 10^4$ **8.** $8 * 10^8$

Page 9
1. false   **2.** false   **3.** true   **4.** true

Page 10
1. 1, 2, 4, and 8   **2.** 1,3, 9, and 27
3. 1, 7, and 49   **4.** 1, 2, 3, 4, 6, 9 12, 18, and 36
5. 1 and 13   **6.** 1, 2, 4, 5, 10, 20, 25, 50, and 100

Page 11
1. 3, 5   **2.** 2, 3, 5, 6, and 10   **3.** 2
4. 3, 9   **5.** 2, 3, 5, 6, 9, and 10

Page 12
1. $2 * 2 * 3$ **2.** $2 * 2 * 7$ **3.** $2 * 5 * 5$
4. $2 * 2 * 3 * 3$ **5.** $2 * 2 * 2 * 2 * 2$
6. $2 * 2 * 3 * 5$

Page 14
1. 688   **2.** 113   **3.** 221
4. 1,117   **5.** 965   **6.** 1,030

Page 15
1. 36   **2.** 481   **3.** 349
4. 272   **5.** 3,346

Page 16
1. 243   **2.** 246   **3.** 126   **4.** 223

Page 17
1. 376   **2.** 464   **3.** 162   **4.** 1,807

Page 18
1. 800   **2.** 49,000   **3.** 4,900
4. 45,000   **5.** 3,600   **6.** 48,000

Page 19
1. $3 * 200 = 600$
$3 * 80 = 240$
$3 * 4 = 12$
$284 * 3 = 852$
2. $30 * 70 = 2,100$
$30 * 5 = 150$
$7 * 70 = 490$
$7 * 5 = 35$
$37 * 75 = 2,775$
3. $60 * 60 = 3,600$
$60 * 7 = 420$
$0 * 60 = 0$
$0 * 7 = 0$
$60 * 67 = 4,020$
4. $70 * 40 = 2,800$
$70 * 3 = 210$
$8 * 40 = 320$
$8 * 3 = 24$
$78 * 43 = 3,354$
5. $50 * 200 = 10,000$
$50 * 30 = 1,500$
$50 * 7 = 350$
$237 * 50 = 11,850$

Page 20
1.

$7 * 89 = 623$

2.

$44 * 25 = 1,100$

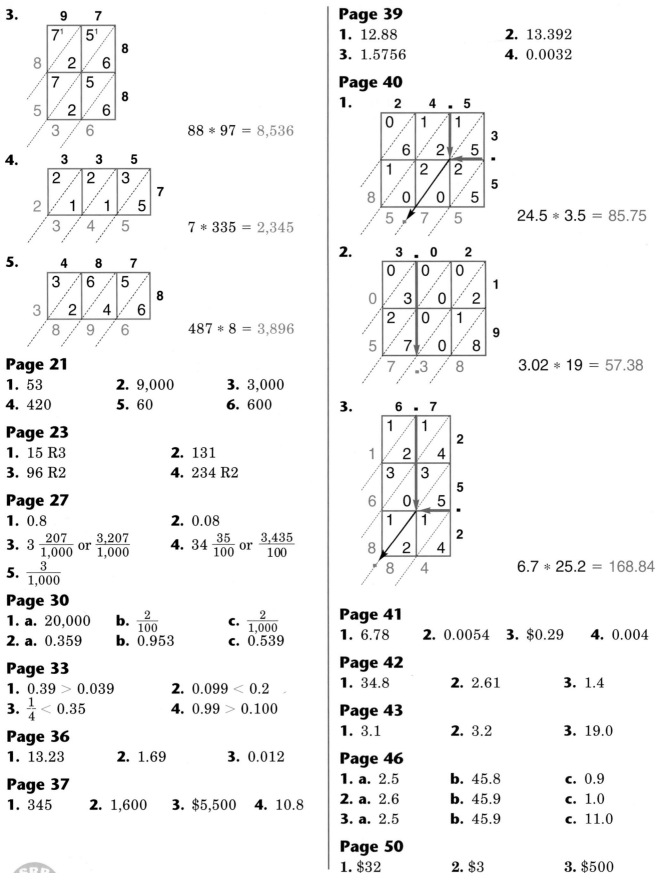

3.

88 * 97 = 8,536

4.

7 * 335 = 2,345

5.

487 * 8 = 3,896

Page 21

1. 53 **2.** 9,000 **3.** 3,000
4. 420 **5.** 60 **6.** 600

Page 23

1. 15 R3 **2.** 131
3. 96 R2 **4.** 234 R2

Page 27

1. 0.8 **2.** 0.08
3. $3\frac{207}{1,000}$ or $\frac{3,207}{1,000}$ **4.** $34\frac{35}{100}$ or $\frac{3,435}{100}$
5. $\frac{3}{1,000}$

Page 30

1. a. 20,000 **b.** $\frac{2}{100}$ **c.** $\frac{2}{1,000}$
2. a. 0.359 **b.** 0.953 **c.** 0.539

Page 33

1. 0.39 > 0.039 **2.** 0.099 < 0.2
3. $\frac{1}{4}$ < 0.35 **4.** 0.99 > 0.100

Page 36

1. 13.23 **2.** 1.69 **3.** 0.012

Page 37

1. 345 **2.** 1,600 **3.** $5,500 **4.** 10.8

Page 39

1. 12.88 **2.** 13.392
3. 1.5756 **4.** 0.0032

Page 40

1.

24.5 * 3.5 = 85.75

2.

3.02 * 19 = 57.38

3.

6.7 * 25.2 = 168.84

Page 41

1. 6.78 **2.** 0.0054 **3.** $0.29 **4.** 0.004

Page 42

1. 34.8 **2.** 2.61 **3.** 1.4

Page 43

1. 3.1 **2.** 3.2 **3.** 19.0

Page 46

1. a. 2.5 **b.** 45.8 **c.** 0.9
2. a. 2.6 **b.** 45.9 **c.** 1.0
3. a. 2.5 **b.** 45.9 **c.** 11.0

Page 50

1. $32 **2.** $3 **3.** $500

Page 51
1. $2   **2.** $2

Page 53
1. $160   **2.** $150   **3.** 31.6 million

Page 59
Sample answers:
1. $\frac{3}{6}$ **2.** $\frac{3}{9}$ **3.** $\frac{10}{12}$

Page 60
Sample answers:
1. a. $\frac{9}{12}$ **b.** $\frac{25}{40}$ **c.** $\frac{16}{20}$ **d.** $\frac{4}{14}$
2. a. $\frac{3}{4}$ **b.** $\frac{3}{5}$ **c.** $\frac{4}{6}$ **d.** $\frac{15}{20}$

Page 61
1. a. true   **b.** true   **c.** true
2. Sample answers:
$\frac{4}{6}, \frac{6}{9}, \frac{8}{12}, \frac{10}{15}$

Page 63
1. $\frac{15}{4}$ **2.** $\frac{16}{3}$ **3.** $\frac{23}{5}$
4. $8\frac{2}{3}$ **5.** $7\frac{4}{5}$ **6.** $18\frac{1}{4}$

Page 64
1. 12   **2.** 20   **3.** 45

Page 65
Sample answers:
1. $\frac{4}{6}$ and $\frac{1}{6}$ **2.** $\frac{5}{10}$ and $\frac{4}{10}$ **3.** $\frac{12}{40}$ and $\frac{30}{40}$

Page 67
1. >   **2.** <   **3.** =
4. <   **5.** <

Page 69
1. $\frac{7}{24}$ **2.** $\frac{3}{8}$ **3.** $\frac{2}{12}$
4. $\frac{8}{12}$ **5.** $\frac{23}{24}$

Page 70
1. $4\frac{1}{4}$ **2.** $8\frac{11}{12}$ **3.** $10\frac{2}{6}$

Page 72
1. $3\frac{1}{4}$ **2.** $2\frac{3}{5}$ **3.** $2\frac{4}{6}$

Page 73
1. $2\frac{1}{2}$ **2.** $4\frac{2}{4}$ **3.** $2\frac{2}{5}$

Page 74
1. 9   **2.** 27   **3.** 16
4. Rita gets $10. Hunter gets $5.

Page 75
1. 48   **2.** 6   **3.** 24

Page 76
1. $\frac{1}{6}$ **2.** $\frac{3}{20}$ **3.** $\frac{15}{60}$

Page 78
1. $\frac{6}{4}$ **2.** 24   **3.** $16\frac{2}{10}$

Page 80
1. 12   **2.** 16   **3.** 10
  $6 \div \frac{1}{2} =$ $8 \div \frac{1}{2} =$ $5 \div \frac{1}{2} =$

Page 84
1. 0.25   **2.** 0.80   **3.** 2.50   **4.** 0.65

Page 85
1. 0.30   **2.** 0.875   **3.** 4.33   **4.** 0.75

Page 87
1. 0.375   **2.** 0.167   **3.** 0.56

Page 88
1. 0.375   **2.** 0.62   **3.** 0.625
4. 0.86   **5.** 0.58   **6.** 0.13

Page 90

Fraction	Decimal	Percent
$\frac{1}{4}$	0.25	25%
$\frac{1}{3}$	0.33	33%
$\frac{1}{2}$	0.50	50%
$\frac{2}{3}$	0.67	67%
$\frac{1}{10}$	0.10	10%
$\frac{4}{5}$	0.80	80%

Page 92
1. -2 **2.** -6 **3.** 3   **4.** -8

Page 94
1. -8 **2.** 11   **3.** -4 **4.** -13

Answer Key

Page 97

1. $\dfrac{5\ \text{dollars}}{1\ \text{hour}}$

dollars	5	10	15	20
hour	1	2	3	4

2. $\dfrac{8\ \text{pounds}}{1\ \text{gallon}}$

pounds	8	16	24	32
gallon	1	2	3	4

Page 99

1. 15 ft   **2.** $5   **3.** $25   **4.** 48¢

Page 101

1. $16   **2.** 16

Page 102

1. $\dfrac{3}{5}$ **2.** $\dfrac{2}{3}$ **3.** 40%

Page 104

1. 6 cm   **2.** 750 miles

Page 106

1. 9.42 inches   **2.** 1.91 inches

Page 111

1.

Number of Hits	Number of Players
0				
1		
2						
3			
4		

2.

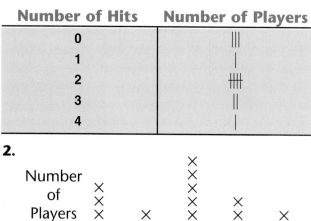

Page 112

1.

Number of Points	Number of Games
10–19		
20–29	||||
30–39	|||
40–49	|||

2.

Number of Points Scored

Stems (10s)	Leaves (1s)
1	7
2	9 6 8 7 1
3	5 5 5
4	4 6 5

Page 113

1. 0   **2.** 4   **3.** 4   **4.** 2   **5.** 2

Page 114

1. min. = 0; max. = 4; range = 4; mode = 2, 3 and 4; median = 2.5

2. 14

Page 115

Jason's mean (average) is 80.91.

Page 116

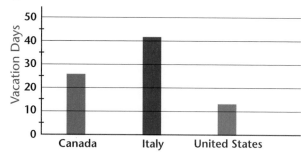

Page 118

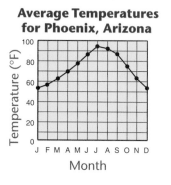

Average Temperatures for Phoenix, Arizona

Page 119

3rd grade represents 62% – 45%, or 17%;
4th grade represents 85% – 62%, or 23%;
5th grade represents 100% – 85%, or 15%

Page 120

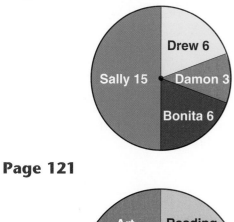

Page 121

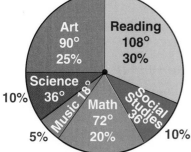

Measurements in Degrees:
Reading 108°; Social Studies 36°; Math 72°;
Music 18°; Science 36°; Art 90°

Page 123

1. 6/8 = 3/4 = 75%   **2.** 4/8 = 1/2 = 50%

Page 124

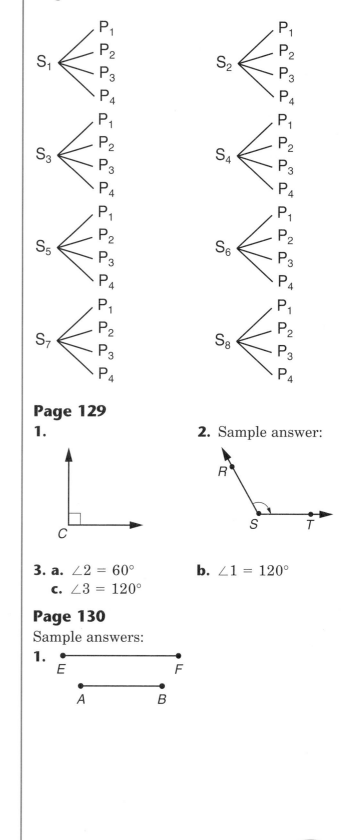

Page 129

1.

2. Sample answer:

3. a. ∠2 = 60°   **b.** ∠1 = 120°
c. ∠3 = 120°

Page 130

Sample answers:

1.

2.

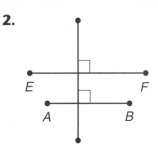

Page 131
Sample answers:

1.

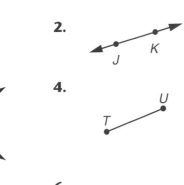

2.

3.

4.

5.

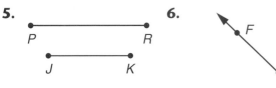

6.

Page 133
1. a. hexagon
  b. quadrangle or quadrilateral
  c. octagon
2. Sample answers:

  a.   **b.**

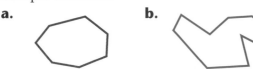

3. The sides of the cover of the journal are not all the same length.

Page 134
Sample answers:
1.

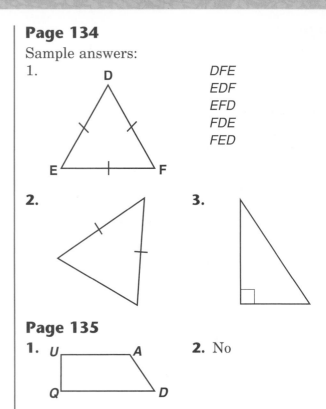

DFE
EDF
EFD
FDE
FED

2.   **3.**

Page 135
1.   **2.** No

3. *UADQ, ADQU, DQUA, QDAU, DAUQ, AUQD, UQDA*

Page 136
Sample answers:
1. All four sides of a square are equal. A rectangle has two pairs of equal sides that are different lengths.
2. All four sides of a rhombus are equal. Two adjacent sides of a kite are one length and the other two sides are a different length.
3. A trapezoid has exactly one pair of parallel sides. A parallelogram has two pairs of parallel sides.

Page 138
Sample answers:
1. **a.** They each have at least one circular face. They each have a curved surface.
   b. A cylinder has three surfaces; a cone has two. A cylinder has a flat top and a flat bottom. A cone has a flat bottom and comes to a point at the top.
2. **a.** They each have at least one vertex. They each have a flat base.
   b. A cone has a curved surface; a pyramid has flat surfaces. A cone has only one vertex. A pyramid has at least four vertices.

Page 139
1. **a.** 5   **b.** 1
2. **a.** 6   **b.** 6
3. triangular prism

Page 140
1. **a.** 8   **b.** 18   **c.** 12
2. decagonal prism

Page 141
1. **a.** 4   **b.** 6   **c.** 4
2. pentagonal pyramid
3. Sample answers:
   a. They each have flat surfaces. Their base shape is used to name them.
   b. They differ in the number of edges and the number of faces.

Page 142
1. tetrahedron, octahedron, icosahedron
2. **a.** 12   **b.** 6
3. Sample answers:
   a. Their faces are equilateral triangles.
   b. A tetrahedron has four faces; an octahedron has eight faces. A tetrahedron has four vertices; an octahedron has six vertices.

Page 145
a, b, c, d, or, all of these

Page 148
1.
2. C

Page 149
1.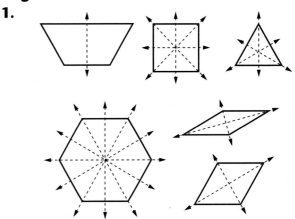
2. infinite; any line drawn directly through its center is a line of symmetry.

Pages 154–164
Answers vary.

Page 167
1. millimeter, gram, meter, centimeter
2. $\frac{1}{1,000}$ **3.** 2,000 mg

Page 170
1. 21 feet 10 inches   **2.** 39 inches

Page 171
1. 24 mm   **2.** 75.4 mm   **3.** 44.0 in.

Page 173
1. 6 square units   **2.** 38 in.^{2}
3. 36 m^2

Page 175
1. 8 square units   **2.** 15 square units
3. 20 square units

Page 176
1. 192 ft^2 **2.** 80 in.^{2} **3.** 2.2 cm^2

Page 177
1. 24 in.^{2} **2.** 27 cm^2 **3.** 10.8 yd^2

Page 178
1. 18 mm   **2.** 9 mm
3. 254.5 mm^2

Page 181
1. 42 yd^3 **2.** 1,000 cm^3 **3.** 288 ft^3

Page 183
1. 64 yd^3 **2.** 80 cm^3 **3.** 100 ft^3

Page 184
1. 340 cm^2 **2.** 48 in.^{2} **3.** 150 in.^{2}

Page 185
1. 94.2 cm^2

Page 186
1. 180 grams; 170.1 grams   **2.** 555 ounces

Page 190
1. 45°   **2.** 210°   **3.** 62°
Sample answers:
4.   **5.**
70°   280°

6.
55°

Page 191
1. a. 2   **b.** 3   **c.** 6   **d.** 10
2. 540°   **3.** 135°
4. number of triangles = number of sides − 2

Page 192
1–4.

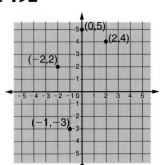

Page 201
1. $\frac{1}{2}x = 32$ or $\frac{x}{2} = 32$
2. $n = 16 * 3$
3. $C = \pi * d = \pi * 2$ cm $= 6.28$ cm
4. $C = \pi * d = \pi * 3$ in. $= 9.42$ in.

Page 202
1. a. $B = A - 4$ **2.** $M = 3 * D$
3. 5   **4.** 4   **5.** 1

Page 203
1. $y = 45$ **2.** $x = 600$ **3.** $w = 24$
4. $v = 56$ **5.** $25 - (15 + 10) = 0$
6. $60 = 5 * (9 + 3) = 0$
7. $5 = 3 + (6 * 3)/(3 * 3)$
8. $24 = (8 + 4) * 2$

Page 204
1. 13   **2.** 13   **3.** 1

Page 206
1. $7 * (13 + 11) = (7 * 13) + (7 * 11)$
2. $(6 * 21) + (6 * 31) = 6 * (21 + 31)$
3. $12 * (19 - 17) = (12 * 19) - (12 * 17)$

Page 207
1. true   **2.** false   **3.** true
4. true   **5.** false   **6.** true

Page 208
1. false   **2.** true   **3.** false
4. $-50 < 10$ **5.** $\frac{1}{8} = 0.125$ **6.** $-3 > -10$

Page 209
1. $y = 27$ **2.** $z = 6$ **3.** $m = 13$

Page 211
1. $\$11.95 - \$8.50 = x$, $x = \$3.45$
2. $28 * \$4.25 = \$119$

Page 213
1. One cube weighs the same as 2 marbles.
2. One cube weighs the same as 3 marbles.

Page 214
1. 14: even

●●●●●●●
●●●●●●●

2. 25: square odd

●●●●●
●●●●●　●
●●●●●　●●●●●●●●●●
●●●●●　●●●●●●●●●●
●●●●●

3. 20: rectangular even

●●●●●
●●●●●　●●●●●●●●●●
●●●●●　●●●●●●●●●●
●●●●●

4. 15: triangular odd

●
●●　●
●●●　●●●●●●●
●●●●　●●●●●●●
●●●●●

Page 216
1.

in	out
v	2 * v + 1
0	1
1	3
2	5

2.

in	out
z	5z
5	25
9	45
20	100

3.

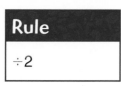

Rule
÷2

Page 218
1. $10.00
2. 300 miles

Page 221
1. The 15-ounce box is a better buy. It costs $0.24 per ounce; the 10-ounce box costs $0.25 per ounce.
2. a. 150 miles　　**b.** 25 miles
　c. 125 miles　　**d.** 600 miles

Page 223
1. 100 squares (Think: $1+3+5+7+9+11+13+15+17+19$)
2. 2,500 squares (Notice the pattern: 5 steps tall $= 5^2 = 25$ squares; 10 steps tall $= 10^2 = 100$ squares; 50 steps tall $= 50^2 = 2,500$ squares)

Page 226
1. Emily is not correct. Using leading-digit estimation gives $900+300+600=1,800$. She should check her work.
2. Luis is not correct. Using leading-digit estimation gives $800/40 = 20$. He should check his work.

Page 227
1. 75,700　　**2.** 80,000　　**3.** 75,700

Page 228
1. thousands　　**2.** hundreds　　**3.** thousands

Page 233
1. 21　　**2.** 39　　**3.** 65　　**4.** 169

Page 239
1. 0.417　**2.** $\frac{235}{1000}$　**3.** 72%　**4.** 3.65
5. 87.5%　**6.** $\frac{95}{100}$　**7.** 0.538　**8.** $\frac{587}{1000}$
9. 98%　**10.** 4.75　**11.** 75%　**12.** $\frac{25}{100}$

Page 243
1. 22,350　　**2.** 22,400　　**3.** 22,000

Page 245
1. 0.0065　　　**2.** 9,800,000
3. 76,000,000　　**4.** 0.00034

Page 246

1. $8.966 * 10^{15}$ **2.** $2.117 * 10^{11}$

3. $9.329 * 10^{16}$ **4.** $2.657 * 10^{15}$

5. 6,022,000,000   **6.** 9,800,000

Page 248

1. $1,017.88 \text{ ft}^2$

Page 249

1. Tip: $6.83

2. Tip: $13.05

Page 252

1. 12, 17, 22, 27, 32.   **2.** 15, 27, 39, 51, 63.

A